Advocacy

putyourknowledgeintopractice

- Written specifically for students on the Bar Professional Training Course

- Expert author teams include barristers and BPTC tutors

- Clear, authoritative guides to legal practice and procedure

Advocacy

Company Law in Practice

Conference Skills

Criminal Litigation & Sentencing

Drafting

Employment Law in Practice

Evidence

Family Law in Practice

Opinion Writing & Case Preparation

Professional Ethics

Remedies

 Online Resource Centre

www.oxfordtextbooks.co.uk/orc/barmanuals

The Bar Manuals are also supported by an Online Resource Centre with further materials and updates to selected manuals.

The Bar Manuals are published by Oxford University Press in conjunction with The City Law School

Advocacy — Edited by Robert McPeake — 17th Edition

Conference Skills — Edited by Marcus Soanes — 17th Edition

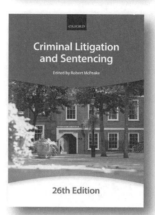
Criminal Litigation and Sentencing — Edited by Robert McPeake — 26th Edition

Drafting — Edited by David Emmet — 17th Edition

Evidence — Edited by Paul McKeown — 17th Edition

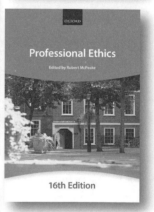
Professional Ethics — Edited by Robert McPeake — 16th Edition

Remedies — Edited by David Emmet — 17th Edition

Advocacy

The City Law School
CITY UNIVERSITY LONDON

Authors

The late Evan Ashfield, Barrister, Lincoln's Inn
Susan Blake, Barrister, Associate Dean, The City Law School
Debbie Chatting, Voice and Accents Coach
Paul Corben, Barrister, Gray's Inn
David Emmet, Barrister, former Reader, The City Law School
Stuart Lindsay, Barrister, Senior Lecturer, The City Law School
Robert McPeake, Barrister, Principal Lecturer, The City Law School
Nikki Matthews, Barrister, Senior Lecturer, The City Law School
Snigdha Nag, Barrister, Senior Lecturer, The City Law School
Conor Quigley, Queen's Counsel, Gray's Inn
Suzanne Reece, Solicitor, Lecturer, The City Law School
Charles Scott, Barrister, Middle Temple
Stuart Sime, Barrister, Professor of Law, The City Law School
Margot Taylor, Solicitor, former Principal Lecturer, The City Law School
Andrew Worthley, Barrister, Senior Lecturer, The City Law School

Editor

Robert McPeake, Barrister, Principal Lecturer, The City Law School

Series Editor

Julie Browne, Barrister, Senior Lecturer, The City Law School

OXFORD
UNIVERSITY PRESS

OXFORD

UNIVERSITY PRESS

Great Clarendon Street, Oxford, OX2 6DP,
United Kingdom

Oxford University Press is a department of the University of Oxford.
It furthers the University's objective of excellence in research, scholarship,
and education by publishing worldwide. Oxford is a registered trade mark of
Oxford University Press in the UK and in certain other countries

Published in the United States of America by Oxford University Press
198 Madison Avenue, New York, NY 10016, United States of America

British Library Cataloguing in Publication Data
Data available

ISBN 978–0–19–871446–0

Printed in Great Britain by
Ashford Colour Press Ltd, Gosport, Hampshire

Links to third party websites are provided by Oxford in good faith and
for information only. Oxford disclaims any responsibility for the materials
contained in any third party website referenced in this work.

FOREWORD

These manuals have been written by a combination of practitioners and members of staff of the City Law School (formerly the Inns of Court School of Law), and are designed primarily to support training on the Bar Professional Training Course (BPTC), wherever it is taught. They provide an extremely useful resource to assist in acquiring the skills and knowledge that practising barristers need. They are updated regularly and are supported by an Online Resource Centre, which can be used by readers to keep up to date throughout the academic year.

This series of manuals exemplifies the practical and professional approach that is central to the BPTC. I congratulate the authors on the excellent standard of the manuals and I am grateful to Oxford University Press for their ongoing and enthusiastic support.

Peter Hungerford-Welch
Barrister
Assistant Dean (Professional Programmes)
The City Law School
City University London
2014

GUIDE TO USING THIS BOOK

The Bar Manuals series includes a range of tools and features to aid your learning. This guide will outline the approach to using this book, and help you to make the most out of each of the features within.

Practical based approach

The authors have taken a practical based approach to teaching advocacy. This will help you enhance the skills that you will need, not only for exams but in practice when it is necessary to apply the law to real life scenarios.

Case studies

You are supplied with documents that outline the criminal case of *R v Heath,* a scenario which allows you to run through the techniques outlined within the book. This will help you to appreciate the planning involved in preparing for a case in practice.

Exercises

This title uses a variety of exercises to aid preparation for advocacy, notably posture, breathing, articulation, and resonance exercises, as well as memory and recall exercises.

Examples

This title provides lists of abbreviations, examples for questioning and cross-examination and skeleton arguments to enable you to apply the law and procedures that have been outlined within the book.

Pedagogical features

Tables, flowcharts and diagrams offer visual representations to enable you to fully grasp more complex areas.

Online Resource Centre updates

For further material and updates to selected manuals in this series please visit the Online Resource Centre at www.oxfordtextbooks.co.uk/orc/barmanuals/.

OUTLINE CONTENTS

DETAILED CONTENTS

Part I

Introduction

Introduction

1.1 Why should you read a manual on advocacy?

Advocacy is one of the skills that form the core of the Bar Professional Training Course (BPTC). It is actually composed of several disparate skills that, when merged, produce the person recognisable as 'the competent barrister'. When you begin reading this manual, and especially this chapter, you may have little idea what constitutes this 'competent barrister'. You will have seen actor/barristers in films, in plays, on television and heard them on the radio. Do not confuse dramatic effect with reality. These players are addressing themselves to audiences measured in hundreds, thousands or even in millions. As a real barrister, you will address your words to an audience often as small as one and rarely larger than a dozen. Furthermore, these films and plays can never show the constant consideration, and rejection, of alternating courses of action and even of words that precede the final performance of the barrister. You should spend some time in a barristers' chambers and the courts on a mini or a full pupillage. Then, you will start to experience for yourself the effort and planning that goes into producing what the public sees in court. Until you do this, you may find it difficult to judge whether a barrister is competent or not.

The early parts of the manual are designed to introduce you to those skills that are necessary in order to perform competently as a barrister. Many of them are really 'everyday' skills, but thinking about them in that context should help to get you started on this course. The manual takes you first to the preparatory skills that any good advocate depends upon. Following on from those, we consider how to open and close a case. These important aspects should always play a significant part in your planning and preparation for advocacy. Then we move onto working with witnesses, another fundamental part of the advocate's armoury. Finally, you will find a toolbox of how-to-do-it guides, covering a broad range of applications and submissions that you might make to a court or tribunal. These guides meld the advocacy skills and the practical know-how to give you a thorough insight into what will be expected of you in each of these hearings. When you have grasped the skills successfully, you will be better equipped to 'think on your feet', to maintain your composure and fluency when a witness gives a 'difficult' answer to one of your questions, or to recall at the end of a trial exactly what a witness said three days earlier. These are skills that the competent barrister has and that, if you do not possess them already, can be acquired through hard work and practice.

1.2 What this manual cannot do

It is not expected that this manual alone can render you competent to represent someone in court (it would be nice if things were that easy!). Armed with the manual and having completed the BPTC, you will have some experience and understanding of the practices and procedures that constitute the professional life of the barrister. You will then be going into pupillage, and that offers something that no classes or manual can—daily access to a practising barrister, with the chance to read all the case briefs that your pupil supervisor receives, perhaps to do some 'devilling' work on them and go into court and observe what goes on, fully informed about the issues in each case and its background. It is likely, though, that if you have worked through this manual diligently, your experience of pupillage may be enhanced by the awareness you have already of certain techniques or practices; equally, pupillage should improve and sharpen your understanding of what is demanded of an advocate. The sooner you start to visit courts and see how the rules are used and what the advocates do, the sooner you will accelerate your own development.

1.3 How to use the manual

As stated earlier, a competent performance by a barrister draws on a variety of skills and abilities. It would be possible to write a manual that simply told you about those skills but that would not be particularly helpful. Experience has shown us that you will understand and acquire these skills more easily if you can do two things. First, obtain some criteria by which to assess your own performances and those of others that you see (whether fellow beginners or practitioners in court). It is not enough to watch someone who is an acknowledged leader—you must have the ability to evaluate what you see. To say that a speech was 'compelling' or 'obviously persuasive' does not really help you to see what made it so. We have developed a set of advocacy training criteria, which we use as the basis for feedback in all of our advocacy classes (see **Chapters 4** and **19**). If you read them carefully now, and always try to apply them later, you will be able to learn a lot more when you observe others or review your own performances. It should be noted that, while these training criteria are written with advocacy skills in mind, they largely represent transferable skills that are extremely useful in many areas of an advocate's practice (and beyond).

Second, it should help comprehension if you see the skills presented in the practical situations where they are likely to occur in reality. This manual has several chapters that deal with the typical transactions in a courtroom—making speeches and questioning witnesses—see **Parts 4** and **5**. **Part 4** looks at opening *and* closing speeches. This has been done because, although in the courtroom they would be separated by all of the evidence in the trial, you would start to plan both how to start and how you intended to end the trial within a short time of receiving the papers in the case. As planning for the two should not be viewed as two separate processes but as a single coherent approach to the case, we have put them in the same section. **Part 5** looks at witnesses and the evidence they give. The chapters there explain, with practical examples, the techniques and objectives of questioning witnesses. Also, in **Part 6**, **Chapters 38** and **39** deal with the more 'mechanical' aspects of two applications or submissions that are often made to courts and are directly relevant to the evidence (either actual or potential) in the trial—namely, the *voir dire* and the submission of no case to answer.

After the Parts that mix skills and tasks to show you the skills in commonplace or recognisable situations, comes **Part 6**. This has several short chapters that are more like guides to specific transactions, telling you how to do it. They reinforce and repeat the skills that are involved in the earlier chapters but the emphasis has shifted so that you are learning as much about the transaction as about the skill. These chapters look at particular applications or submissions that you could make in court, or particular procedures that you might use. The objective when selecting topics for inclusion here is to show those matters that the junior advocate (or pupil) will encounter most often in practice. Many of these applications will require a skeleton argument, so **Part 6** begins with a guide to these.

Please remember to refer to this manual **throughout** the course. It is always useful to refresh your memory or even rework a topic in the light of experience. Soon, practice should ensure that many of the techniques and skills become more familiar and almost habitual. In particular, **Part 3** deals with some ancillary skills without which we will never succeed in gaining competence as advocates. Whenever you want a case to practise with, turn to the **Appendix** and use *R v Heath*.

1.4 The importance of thorough preparation

You should note now that preparation is as important as the 'performance' in court. Your objectives and how you may achieve them will differ from case to case and even within a single case. You need to identify what you are being asked to do at the outset—only then will you be able to plan the means of fulfilling those objectives. In particular, your lay client's needs and wishes are paramount. You must be able to discover what they are as efficiently and effectively as possible, then agree on an appropriate solution and the means of achieving it. To do all of this competently, you should become as familiar with other essential skills as you are with those in advocacy. Important examples are those of legal research, fact management and conference skills. Without a fluency in these sorts of skills to assist you in preparing for an appearance in court, you will always be working in court 'flying by the seat of your pants'. For any barrister this is an uncomfortable position to be in—anything that you can do to avoid it should be done. You must appreciate that when you make your first few appearances in court for real clients, you are bound to find these moments both nerve-wracking and intimidating, as well as very exciting. There are some simple steps that you can take in order to minimise the worst effects of your nerves. Arrive early at court, go into the courtroom in which you will be appearing. Stand where you will be standing when acting as an advocate. Make yourself as comfortable as you can. Try your voice out. Arrange your papers as if you are beginning the case. When the court is sitting and you are due to begin, take two or three deep breaths to counteract the breathlessness you will feel. If you can, arm yourself with a glass of water to deal with the dryness in the mouth you will experience. The pounding in the chest, the roaring in the ears, the loss of your stomach to an area adjacent to your shoe laces you can do nothing about. You are not odd. You are not alone in experiencing all this. Everyone does.

But do not add to your problems by a sudden realisation that you have not mastered your brief thoroughly. If you do, then you will be adding to the problems of your client, the very person you are in court to assist. You ought to use this manual (and its companions) as a guide during the BPTC and to help you make a more comfortable transition from student to practitioner.

1.5 A cautionary note

Please remember that certain practices and procedures used by barristers are governed by rules. Sometimes these are legal rules, sometimes they are customary in origin (eg wearing a wig and gown in open court). Whatever their basis, the rules mean that these procedures always occur in the same manner (until the law is changed or someone thinks up a better method, which then becomes the custom).

It is not the function of either this manual or the advocacy course to challenge accepted practices at the Bar but you should note that, sometimes, there is more than one way of doing something. The aim may be the same but two barristers may differ, quite properly, on how best to achieve that aim. So long as you abide by the legal rules and the rules of professional conduct, you are able to develop your own style and preferences as an advocate. If the method that you choose suits you and the particular situation, then that is acceptable. Do not do something in a particular way simply because someone else has told you to. They may know better than you—if so, you should follow their advice. Never do so unquestioningly.

Oxford University Press has a website for this manual—the current address is shown on the back cover. We would welcome your thoughts, comments and suggestions as to the content of this manual and your own ideas about advocacy, especially advocacy training. Our aim is to build up this website into something really useful for everyone involved in advocacy—whether as a trainer or someone undergoing training or from practitioners reflecting upon their own practices.

1.6   Objectives and teaching theory for the advocacy course

It may be helpful for you, when reading this manual, to understand what The City Law School is doing on its advocacy course because this manual exists primarily to support that course. What we aim to do, for everyone on the advocacy course, is as follows.

1.6.1   Training objectives

(a) to demonstrate that competence in advocacy can be understood by reference to skills-based criteria;

(b) to familiarise students with the essential criteria by which competence in advocacy should be judged;

(c) to enable students to observe performances of advocacy and judge what is and is not competent;

(d) to allow students as much practice of advocacy skills in the classroom as can practically be arranged;

(e) to encourage students to practise their advocacy skills as much as is reasonably practicable;

(f) to offer students criteria-referenced feedback on their performances of advocacy skills, whether in the classroom or on DVD;

(g) to demonstrate to students various practices and procedures encountered by an advocate, either on video or through live performance;

(h) to familiarise students with basic techniques for advocacy, including questioning techniques and preparation for court;

(i) through all of the foregoing, to enable students to perform one or more advocacy tasks with a degree of competence that shows they are ready for pupillage and are likely to benefit from pupillage through their continued practice and observation of advocacy.

1.6.2 Teaching theory

Our teaching theory for advocacy, although it also applies to the other legal skills, is:

> People learn skills best through practice. Such practice is most useful if it is preceded by thorough preparation and followed by specific and informed feedback.

This theory leads us to abide by the following guidance, for the purpose of course design:

(a) Preparation should be as thorough as circumstances allow. Particularly, one should know the facts or allegations in the case and understand the relevant laws, substantive and adjectival, in order to determine which facts, allegations and evidence are material to the present task. By the end of the course, a student should be able to analyse factual material and have such existing knowledge of substantive and procedural law that an informed decision can be taken as to any appropriate advocacy tasks that may be undertaken.

(b) Preparation may be general and, in the early stages of learning advocacy skills, may need to be repeated often. Examples might be control over breathing and nerves, the ability to speak clearly and fluently and the ability to construct a logical argument. At a less general level, examples are the ability to use different questioning techniques in appropriate situations, to empathise with witnesses or judges and to listen with eyes as well as ears. Preparation may also be specific (that is related to a particular case or task) and this type of preparation should complement general preparation during the early stages of learning. By the end of the course, the competent student should have mastered the basic skills needed for general preparation and be able to demonstrate them, whenever called upon to do so.

(c) Unless very basic skills are to be practised or demonstrated, it is best to practise or demonstrate in the context of a specific advocacy task, using a particular set of case papers. This should assist in showing the relevance of the exercise and may encourage an insight into the application of an individual basic skill in many varied situations, that is transferability.

(d) Learning may occur through a variety of ways. It may be through performance, or observation of oneself on video or of one's peers or of experienced demonstrators. Such observation may take place in class or through video but will always be of maximum benefit when the performance is accompanied by feedback and explanation. Learning may also occur through reading a book or working through a computer-led lesson, but neither format is likely to be as effective as observing others or performing a skill personally, with explanation and feedback.

(e) A student will learn best how to improve their skills, as well as identifying strengths and weaknesses, if he or she performs a skill (usually in the context of an advocacy task) and that performance is reviewed (either instantly or later) by an observer who is able to apply skills-related criteria to the performance and articulate the degree to which that performance satisfied each of those criteria.

(f) Any skill **may** be learned through sheer repetition alone and untutored. It may not be learned well, though. Many of the greatest advocates were effectively self-taught but it may now be agreed that early learning is done best with supervision. The student should be guided by an instructor who can demonstrate and observe, provide explanation and feedback. Self-tuition should be left until later, when the advocate's own professional experience, and familiarity with the criteria that should be used to judge competence, can replace the instructor.

(g) Students learn best in small groups with one or more instructors. While they learn most about their own abilities by performing in groups of one or two plus an instructor, they should experience larger groups as these will expose them to a variety of methods and thinking, as well as examples of good and bad practice. The student sometimes needs to see bad practice since it may be that only by being told it is bad, and why, will the student know and understand that some aspect of the performance was faulty. The group has become too large when one or more students are denied the opportunity to perform and to discuss a particular skill or task in the class, for whatever reason.

(h) Feedback should be based on clear and objective criteria that are relevant to the skill and/or task, and are made known to the student in advance. Giving useful feedback is itself a skill that can be learned and should be practised often. An infrequent instructor may not have great familiarity with the relevant criteria and may not refer to them at all when giving feedback. New instructors (or occasional instructors) should be trained to give feedback and, if resources permit, be accompanied in classes by experienced instructors.

(i) In the course of offering feedback, an instructor should have an opportunity to illustrate certain points by a brief demonstration. It should be possible to check that the feedback has been understood by observing an improvement when the student next performs.

(j) Feedback may be limited to a single issue, for reasons of time or because the student is at a very early stage on the course. Single-issue feedback will work best when the student has many further opportunities to perform and those will occur in a short space of time. If future performances will be separated by a considerable period (say, a week), it may be better to offer 'multi-issue' feedback to the student, indicating a variety of strengths and weaknesses as the student will have ample time to reflect on each issue.

1.7 General bibliography

You may find helpful information and techniques in the following books:

Bergman, P. *Trial Advocacy in a Nutshell*, 5th edn, West Academic Publishing, 2013 (USA).

Du Cann, R.L.D., Q.C. *The Art of the Advocate*, Penguin, 1999, revised.

Evans, K. *Advocacy in Court*, 2nd edn, OUP, 1995.

Evans, K. *Common Sense Rules of Advocacy for Lawyers: A Practical Guide for Anyone who Wants to be a Better Advocate*, TheCapitol.Net, Inc., 2010 (USA).

Foster, C., Gilliatt, J., Bourne, C., and Popat, P. *Civil Advocacy: A Practical Guide,* 2nd edn, Routledge-Cavendish, 2001.

Fridd, N. and Weddle, S. *Basic Practice in Courts, Tribunals and Inquiries,* 3rd edn, Sweet & Maxwell, 2000.

Goodman, A. *Effective Written Advocacy*, 2nd edn, Wildy, Simmons and Hill, 2012.

Hyam, His Honour Judge Michael. *Advocacy Skills*, 4th edn, OUP, 2001.

Lubet, S. Modern *Trial Advocacy: Analysis and Practice*, NITA, 2004 (USA).

Morley, I. *The Devil's Advocate*, 2nd edn, Sweet & Maxwell, 2009.

Nathanson, S. *Non-trial Advocacy: A Case Study Approach,* Routledge-Cavendish, 2001.

Pannick, D. *Advocates,* OUP, 1993.

Scamardella, R., and Craghill, K. *On Your Feet—Magistrates Court*, <http://www.lulu.com>, 2012.

Stone, M. *Cross-Examination in Criminal Trials*, 3rd rev. edn, Tottel Publishing, 2009.

Welsh, J., Bevitt, A., and Stanton, L. *Advocacy in the Magistrates' Courts,* Routledge-Cavendish, 2003.

(Other books and articles may also be referred to within the following chapters.)

2

The qualities of the advocate

2.1 Introduction

The barrister is known as a person of integrity, someone whom judges can trust. The best barristers are also known for the qualities they display in the courtroom. They have mastered their briefs—they know the evidence and the contentious issues in each case, how to handle a 'difficult' witness and, perhaps above all, how to get the triers of fact to see the case from the standpoint of their client.

These practitioners have accumulated several of the disparate qualities that make up the able barrister. Some of these qualities are to do with personality and this course is unlikely to change that. Either you are the sort of person who will stand up to an unpleasant judge to safeguard your client or you are not—all that can now be attempted is to encourage you to use your latent strength of character. Similarly, no one can make you behave in an honest fashion; they can only stress the vital importance of doing so. Honesty is important—to you professionally; to your client in a case where your dishonesty might harm his or her interests; and to ensuring public confidence in the judicial system.

Other qualities can be acquired or improved, for example eloquence and detachment. There are others. Although opinions may differ as to the entire spectrum of such qualities or as to their relative importance, those qualities or skills set out in the rest of this chapter are particularly important. Considerable reliance has been placed on Richard Du Cann, QC's excellent book *The Art of the Advocate*.

2.2 The essentials of advocacy

2.2.1 Practice and hard work

You may not currently have much experience in public speaking. The idea of being the only voice heard in a courtroom may fill you with a sense of dread as well as great anticipation. Two things are certain though. First, you should get better with practice, so never miss a chance to gain experience—debates, moots or mock trials, for example. These opportunities may occur infrequently. All your fellow students will, at least should, read this manual, so you may encounter some competition. So practise with your friends, better still with your relatives for they will be more long-suffering. Force yourself to listen to what you are saying. Force yourself to criticise yourself as you are speaking. Ask yourself all day and every day: 'Was that the best word, was that the best way of expressing myself?' Never be content with the answer: 'Well, that's how I always do it.' In due course, your performance is going to be judged by the audiences you are to face and address. Their opinion will be based on their assessment, not yours.

Second, you must be prepared thoroughly for every case you take. The need for solid preparation and planning is emphasised in every skills manual for this course, but it is important to stress that the conduct of an application or trial, the handling of an examination-in-chief or a cross-examination in a competent fashion will not happen by some magical process. It is the product of hours of hard work or, as Richard Du Cann puts it, industry.

The advocate, as Lord Hewart said, must 'claw the facts'. If he or she does not, all the virtues and brilliant improvisations will not help him or her. The facts must all be retained in his or her memory, so long as the case lasts: dates, names, times, exhibit numbers. Then as fast as they were mastered they must be forgotten so that others in the next case he or she does can take their place. Memorising facts of this kind is sheer drudgery. To do it properly the advocate must be prepared to forgo the pleasures of private life at the most inconvenient moments and for indefinite periods.

2.2.2 Tenacity, courage and self-control

Tenacity and self-control are two distinct but related qualities—both depend upon you having the strength of character necessary to do a good job in adverse circumstances. Tenacity is needed when you encounter a difficult witness—perhaps one who is out to show the court he or she is smarter than you or is just wilfully contrary. As Richard Du Cann says:

> Counsel must expect to cross-examine many witnesses whose evidence he will fail to destroy. He must also expect to come across a number who believe that attack is the best method of defence and who will do all they can to embarrass him . . . Two qualities are required on these occasions more than any others: tenacity and a form of question which allows no opportunity to the witness to score.

You also need self-control in such circumstances—the advocate who is readily embarrassed or angered into an obvious flush will show signs of losing control of himself or herself and the case. The position is worse if your reaction is more than a mere blush; one of the most unpleasant sights in a courtroom is to see a barrister and a witness engaged in a row (unless, of course, to do so is part of a deliberate plan on your part). To quote Du Cann again:

> Control of his feelings there must be, in particular of his temper. If he cannot, he will not keep control of his tongue and he will not keep control of the case. Forensically simulated emotion should be one of the armaments of the advocate. Personal sensitivity is not.

Finally, you will require courage. You will sometimes find that those in a position of authority seek to test you, occasionally to dominate or bully you. On such occasions make sure of your position. If it is untenable, abandon it. As stated in Du Cann:

> It is always right to be seen to admit wrong. To fail to do so can do immense harm.

But if, on checking, you are satisfied that you are right, press on and stick to your point even if it means confronting a judge. You should be fearless in promoting or defending your client's interests. Remember, though, that judgement is also a quality possessed by the competent advocate. As Du Cann says:

> There is a time to stand and a time to sit for every advocate, and unless he can solemnise some form of marriage between courage and judgment he will never reach the first rank of the profession.

Your point may have been made the first time. To persist in pressing a matter may do more harm than good. Such judgement cannot be taught, it must be acquired through experience and reflection. Never be afraid to ask your colleagues, especially senior ones, for advice on such matters.

2.2.3   Honesty

The rules of professional conduct require the barrister to maintain a sense of etiquette in court but the quality of honesty is one that is essential. If you have made a mistake, for example referred inaccurately to some evidence in your closing speech or forgotten to put a point in cross-examination, never be too egotistic to admit your error. Also, never mislead the court. If you have said anything that may have done so, always retrieve the matter before anything irremediable occurs. This must be adhered to no matter what the cost to one's reputation or self-esteem and, sometimes, regardless of the cost to your client. Richard Du Cann gives a memorable example from the libel action brought by Harold Laski. (Note that Slade is the QC appearing for the [claimant], Laski; Hastings and Wentworth Day are leading and junior counsel for the defence.)

In the Laski case Slade contended that the plea of justification (the claim that the words printed in the newspaper were true) included the claim that Laski had been guilty of cowardice by remaining in America during the First World War since this was the suggestion made by Wentworth Day's question to Laski. If this was right it meant that Hastings also had to prove that Laski was a coward. If he did not, Laski was bound to succeed. During Slade's final speech to the jury Lord Goddard interrupted to raise a matter of law, then Hastings intervened:

> HASTINGS: . . . I distinctly recollect hearing Mr Slade say that he was not making a substantive claim in respect of that [ie that Laski was a coward] and therefore I have not even addressed my mind to it.

> After further legal argument Slade left the point saying:

> SLADE: . . . I shall be very astonished to find that . . . I have allowed this case to proceed on a footing that the jury could find the whole of these words to be true, which would mean that Mr Laski had been guilty of cowardice.

Half an hour later Hastings intervened again. He had found a passage in the transcript when Sir Valentine Holmes, Slade's junior in the case, had said during an exchange with the judge: 'We are not asking the jury as regards the part relating to cowardice to give Mr Laski damages. . . .' In that possibly ill-considered sentence, which was not vital to the argument then taking place, the whole of Slade's point, one upon which he believed he could win the whole case, was swept away in the middle of his final speech. Whatever the obligations to his client and whatever the personal feelings he had himself, Slade recognised the most important single fact of the situation: Hastings had already addressed the jury on the basis that the point was abandoned. So he told Goddard:

> SLADE: . . . I am not going back on anything Sir Valentine Holmes said, any more than I should go back on anything I said myself; and I therefore prefer to err on the side of fairness, and I shall not ask the jury to deal with that part of the libel at all.

2.2.4   Language and humanity

Given the possession of the qualities of tenacity, courage, self-control, judgement and honesty, the advocate requires an understanding and a love of language, and the trial advocate requires also an understanding of and love for humanity. These latter qualities cannot be taught. You have either got them or you have not. But you can be alerted to the need to value both. You can be taught the need to demonstrate that you value both. Take language first.

Throughout your future professional life, words will assume a dominant position. Some, boringly, will be inflexible because the practice of law and human affairs has made them so: *'mens rea'*, 'bills of exchange', 'charterparty', 'Scott schedules', 'maliciously', the list is endless. From these you will be unable to escape. It is not so with the rest of the natural English vocabulary. But you will find when you are on your feet that you use one word and can then become a prisoner of it. Words like 'situation' and 'relationship', once used, become traps. This can only be avoided if you train your mind concisely to be a movable *Roget's Thesaurus,* alert to the use of alternative words apt both for the occasion and the different clients, witnesses and audiences that you will face. Your language, as Lord Chesterfield said in 1750, must be 'the language for them all'. Take the simple example used by Du Cann from *R v Gardiner.* Ernest Wild, QC is cross-examining a labourer who claims to have seen the accused entering a building with the victim.

> WILD: Where did you see him [the defendant] first?
> WRIGHT: Against Church Lane.
> WILD: So he saw you?
> WRIGHT: Yes.
> WILD: You were loitering about.
> WRIGHT: No, I was going down the road.

But the youth was leaning against the edge of the witness-box, his hands in his pockets. 'Loitering' was what the jury were going to remember. Wild continued:

> WILD: When did you see him the second time?
> WRIGHT: He came down the road.
> WILD: He saw you then?
> WRIGHT: Yes.
> WILD: And the third time too?
> WRIGHT: Yes, he spoke to me.
> WILD: He must have seen you all the time?
> WRIGHT: Yes.
> WILD: And he must have known you were about?
> WRIGHT: Yes, he spoke to me.
> WILD: Do you represent that, knowing you were about, he went into the chapel and behaved in the way you state?
> WRIGHT: Well, he did.

When striving to hit your target in this fashion, it is essential to keep one eye on the judge/jury/magistrates to see if they have taken your point. Also, try to observe the witness as much as possible—something in their demeanour may be very useful. In short, be alert and be observant.

Finally, always remember to whom you are talking. In the first instance, this may be the witness but, through him or her, you are talking to the triers of fact. Try to see whatever you do in terms of how they will see it and understand it. Almost the last word goes to Richard Du Cann—this time referring to Marshall Hall.

> He had an understanding of human frailty which enabled him to catch the throats of all who heard him speak. When he was quite young he defended a prostitute charged with murdering one of her clients. She was forty-seven, her former attraction devoured by the life she had been forced to lead. At the end of his speech as he was about to sit down, he caught sight of her sitting hunched in the dock. On the spur of the moment he added these words:
>
> Look at her, gentlemen of the jury. Look at her. God never gave her a chance—won't you?

You might note that this style of advocacy seems a little dated now—indeed that has sometimes been said to the writer. A more recent example of a celebrated advocate is

George Carman, QC. He was criticised by opposing counsel in a libel trial (*Mona Bauwens v The People Newspaper*) for:

> . . . painting a rather crude picture of Mr Mellor [then the Government's Heritage Secretary] behaving like an ostrich and putting his head in the sand 'thereby exposing his thinking parts'.

Maybe rather than consider whether styles of advocacy have 'dated', one should simply ask at the end of each case, 'did it work?'.

Ethics, etiquette and cross-cultural communication in the courtroom

3.1 Introduction

There are various rules of professional conduct that must be observed by any advocate, breach of which will lead to serious consequences. There are also certain conventions of etiquette to be observed in the courtroom and guidelines relating to cross-cultural communication of which you should be aware. The following sections cover the main points but are not exhaustive.

3.2 Rules of professional conduct

3.2.1 Duties to the court

You must:

- bring to the attention of the court all relevant decisions and legislative provisions of which you are aware, whether or not their effect is favourable to your case;
- assist the court in the fair administration of justice;
- bring any procedural irregularity to the court's attention during the trial itself and not reserve such matter to be raised on appeal;
- take all reasonable and practical steps to avoid unnecessary expense or waste the court's time;
- observe the rules relating to disclosure of documents/information.

You must not:

- deceive or knowingly or recklessly mislead the court. For example, if your client tells you that he or she has committed a similar offence in the past for which he or she was never caught, you cannot tell the court in mitigation that this was the 'only time' your client has done such a thing. Equally, if your client tells you he or she is guilty but insists on pleading not guilty, you may continue to represent him or her and make the prosecution prove their case against him—but the ways in which you can test the prosecution case against him or her will be limited. You can test and probe the view that the witness had of the alleged perpetrator, exposing the fact that the lighting conditions were poor or the witness was quite far away from the scene, but you cannot assert that which you know to be false, for example you cannot suggest to a witness that your client was elsewhere at the time;

- misquote the evidence;
- make assertions of fraud without clear instructions to do so and without reasonably credible material that establishes a prima facie case of fraud;
- manufacture or assist your client to manufacture a defence or other explanation for his or her conduct;
- devise facts that will assist in advancing your lay client's case;
- make statements or ask questions that are merely scandalous or intended or calculated only to vilify, insult or annoy either a witness or some other person;
- express your personal opinions, view or belief to the court unless invited by the court to do so;
- by assertion in a speech impugn a witness whom you have had the opportunity to cross-examine unless in cross-examination you have given the witness the opportunity to answer the allegation.

3.3   Conventions of etiquette

These derive from custom, and can be divided into dos and don'ts.
Do:

- dress and robe appropriately;
- use the correct mode of address for the judge or tribunal;
- stand when the judge enters and leaves the courtroom. He or she will normally bow before being seated and you should return the bow. You should also bow to the judge when leaving court and, if the judge is already in the courtroom, as you sit down;
- sit down if your opponent rises to object. Only one advocate should be on their feet at the same time unless the judge is addressing you both;
- show courtesy and respect to your opponent and the other personnel in the courtroom;
- accept blame when you are at fault and apologise.

Don't:

- leave the judge 'unattended', ie if there is no other advocate present in the courtroom, wait for a signal from the judge before leaving;
- speak or shuffle papers while a witness is taking the oath;
- comment on the evidence as it is being given;
- make faces/sigh to show a jury your incredulity of an opponent's witness;
- show your emotions at a verdict or a judge's ruling;
- continue to argue a point after the judge has heard the arguments and ruled upon it: the proper place for this is an appeal.

3.4   Cross-cultural communication in the courtroom

It is not suggested that any advocate will intentionally cause offence to any party in the courtroom. However, working in a multi-cultural society often requires sensitivity to the ways in which norms and customs may differ from one community to another.

It is important to recognise the influence of your own cultural background on your unconscious perceptions and behaviours and to bear in mind that:

- no matter how well intentioned, use of racial and ethnic terms (such as coloured or oriental) are liable to give offence;
- cultural differences in body language can contribute to misunderstandings and conflicts between members of ethnic minorities and, for example, police officers;
- on the other hand, stereotyped notions about the body language of particular cultures should be avoided;
- there may be differences in language—jargon, slang, and metaphors—which may not be familiar to all witnesses/jury members, and so on;
- words may not have the same meaning in all cultures, for example descriptions of family relationships (eg uncle, cousin) and times of the day (afternoon and evening);
- just because someone responds to questions in English in court, that does not mean that person necessarily understands fully what has been said;
- in some cultures, looking away rather than maintaining eye contact is not necessarily a sign of dishonesty or disrespect—it may be the opposite! Equally, raised voices do not necessarily equate with loss of control or aggression.

3.5 Preconceptions

A preconception is an opinion or idea that is conceived or framed prior to *actual* knowledge. It is important to recognise your own preconceptions and how these may affect your judgement in your work as a barrister.

- Is a client more likely to be guilty because he or she is unemployed?
- Do you believe what a client tells you more easily if he or she is well dressed, articulate, educated?
- Do you listen less easily to what a client has to say because he or she is inarticulate or poorly educated?
- Does the fact that a client has a previous conviction for dishonesty mean that he or she is more likely to have committed a crime of violence?
- Do you believe your opponent is trustworthy because she is attractive and initially friendly?
- Do you assume your opponent is less competent than you because she looks younger than you? Or because she confides that she has not done a lot of this type of work before?
- Do you believe your opponent is more competent than you because he looks older than you?
- Do you let your opponent's bragging of her experience undermine your confidence so that you advise your client to compromise on less favourable terms?

Of course, the answer to all these questions is 'no'; yet, in practice, many barristers forget this. They fail to recognise their own preconceptions and the manner in which they may affect their conduct of the case.

As a barrister you cannot pick and choose your clients so that you only represent those whom you like to believe in. You are bound to observe the 'cab-rank principle'.

Unless you recognise your preconceptions about the client, they are likely to affect your judgement; the way in which you approach, prepare and present the case; the way you communicate with the client, your opponent, the court; the way in which you advise, negotiate or argue the case. By relying on premature assumptions or beliefs, you will be less able to communicate effectively with the client; you may lose the confidence of the client and your solicitor; you are likely to convey to your opponent and the court, by gestures or body language, your apathy towards the client. With the growth of conditional fees, the art of assessing the possible success of a case is growing. Make sure all your judgements are objective.

The most important factor in dealing with preconceptions is to recognise them, either in ourselves or in others. You must learn to differentiate between assumptions and actual knowledge, so that you can identify where you have anticipated without justification. You must be careful not to prejudge a client, an opponent or a tribunal.

Once you learn to recognise preconceptions you can then determine their possible effects and uses. Ask yourself:

- Have they affected my judgement or approach to the case in any way?
- To what extent?
- Are they more/less/equally likely to affect my opponent/the court's approach/ judgement?
- Is my opponent proceeding on the basis of an assumption I haven't made?
- Is it likely to undermine or support his or her case?
- Is the court likely to proceed on the basis of any preconception?
- Is it likely to influence the jury?
- Can I use it to my advantage?
- Do I need to dispel it?

It is only by being alert to these possibilities that you can ensure that you recognise the existence of preconceptions, their dangers, uses, advantages and disadvantages.

Part II

The basic components for applications and submissions

4

Recognising competence— advocacy skills criteria

4.1 Introduction

Isn't this a rather strange chapter to put in a book of this sort? After all, any time that you go into a court or tribunal, you should see people acting as advocates and (usually) being paid to do so. Aren't they all competent advocates? And isn't it safe simply to mimic their techniques and style? Well, 'No' is the answer. When you see an advocate in court, it may be their first time in such a court, or it may be that they have good points and bad points (regardless of how much experience they have). The latter is more likely to be the case.

The point is that you cannot afford simply to adopt wholesale and uncritically whatever you hear being said and see being done by advocates in court. It would be fantastic if you could do so but that is not the case. As a novice advocate, you will be tempted to regard all other advocates as more experienced than you (probably true) and therefore better advocates (not necessarily true) and highly competent in everything they do (almost always not true). All of us have strengths and weaknesses, things we do well and things we do badly. It is a fact that when advocates appear in court, they very seldom receive any feedback on the quality of their performance. You might say that they learn whether they are potential silks or should start looking for another job by the amount of work they are sent to do. Unfortunately, that may depend on a number of factors, only some of which are connected to the advocate's ability. Even then, there may be things that the (soon-to-be-ex-) advocate does well. Until very recently, there has been no formal system for helping advocates to monitor the standards of their advocacy, more is the pity. Indeed, most practitioners would look aghast if you (or anyone else) offered them some constructive criticism after seeing them in court. In partnership with the Solicitors Regulation Authority and the Institute for Legal Executives, the Bar Standards Board has recently launched QASA, the Quality Assurance Scheme for Advocates. For barristers, this currently applies only to the Criminal Bar and it has met with considerable resistance for various reasons, too complicated to explore here.

For the time being then, the best that can be done is to look out for yourself the best way you can. How can you do this? One of the best methods is to have a set of criteria that you can take into any court or tribunal. Then, when you watch other advocates in action, you can judge for yourself how well (or otherwise) they are performing all of their functions and be confident that you have identified those functions and the proper standards to be attained.

4.2   How should we define competence?

4.2.1   Different things to different people?

It is plain nonsense to suggest that the degree of expertise that we should expect from an experienced advocate is the same as that which we are likely to find in a beginner. Nevertheless, it is a fact that professional advocates must be capable of achieving a certain minimum level of competence, no matter what their experience. This is an essential requirement; one need only point to the public interest in litigation being conducted by competent advocates (for the avoidance of miscarriage of justice and achieving an efficient and effective system for litigation, for example) to see that there must be a basic level of competence that must be achieved before it is safe to employ someone to be an advocate in court.

4.2.2   A basic level of competence

What should we expect of any advocate, regardless of expertise or experience? This could be defined in terms of knowledge, perhaps.

4.2.3   Knowledge

We might say that any advocate should know and be able to make effective use of the rules of procedure (ie those rules that govern the way that the relevant court functions). We should not expect an encyclopaedic familiarity with all such rules but the advocate should know all those rules of general, common relevance—on costs, for example. The competent advocate should also know when he or she is confronted by a more unusual rule, where to find it and how to apply it. The same goes for the rules that govern the evidence that can be put forward in court. So we can say that a competent advocate should have a good accurate knowledge of the rules of evidence and procedure, those matters that are adjectival to the subject matter of the litigation.

In a similar fashion, we can say that any competent advocate should have a good working knowledge of various, commonly met, bodies of substantive law. Examples might be the criminal law, the laws governing contracts and the laws governing liability for negligence. In addition, the advocate should have a thorough knowledge of the laws that are relevant to the particular matter that is before the court (ie the subject of the present litigation). That knowledge may have been acquired through previous experience of such litigation, it may have been acquired through post-qualification study or it may have been acquired specifically for the purposes of this litigation. Any competent advocate should know (and have the ability to research, if necessary) the substantive legal rules that are or may be relevant to the current litigation.

It is a fact that professional advocates in this country (that is barristers and solicitors) will have spent a considerable amount of time in learning a large body of law, before they ever obtained their professional qualification. The vast majority of advocates will have law degrees and the rest will have a non-law degree and have gone through a shorter, intensive law course. There are certain core law subjects in which all would-be professional advocates must have passed examinations (there is no need to rehearse them here). Furthermore, during their training period for their professional qualification, they must have passed examinations on the rules of procedure and evidence (see the BPTC and Legal Practice Course (LPC) requirements). We might be safe in assuming a basic level of competence as far as legal knowledge is concerned. How about the application of that knowledge? And what about factual knowledge? Advocates must be familiar with the allegations in the litigation, the available evidence and, combining legal and factual knowledge, the advocate must know in every case what facts need to be proved in order to achieve the outcome that their client seeks.

These intellectual qualities must be gained **in advance** of the hearing where the advocate is to perform. How the knowledge was gained is irrelevant although we can learn effective techniques for both the law and the facts. What we need, as an observer in court, is a criterion that relates to **preparation.** Often, we will not know exactly what the advocate has had to do in order to be prepared for this piece of litigation (although a trainee or pupil connected with the advocate should have observed the advocate's preparation). What we can do is observe what the advocate says and does in court, and judge whether those words and deeds are appropriate and relevant to the laws and allegations in this particular piece of litigation. That relates to the **content** of the advocate's performance and we should have a criterion to judge that, too. Since we are beginning to look at this in terms of what the competent advocate should be able to say and do, we can see it as the definition of a skill—or, rather, as the definition of a collection of skills that might be summed up as advocacy skills.

4.3 Advocacy skills

This part of the chapter follows the standard City Law School philosophy of separating out the bundle of related but disparate skills that typically are used together to produce a competent performance in the courtroom. We have spent a great deal of time looking into what makes for a competent piece of advocacy. We have looked at those skills that are required for a submission or application to a court, as these are the tasks on which most advocates cut their teeth. We have also analysed the skills that advocates use when questioning witnesses; we think that slightly different skills are used or objectives set, depending upon whether one is engaged in examining one's own witness or one called for the opponent. We have produced sets of criteria that can be used to produce an objective critique of an advocate's work, whatever the context.

We should note here that we regularly review our advocacy criteria and make any changes that we consider to be necessary. There are of course many other providers of advocacy training, both in the UK and further afield, who may set out their own criteria in a different way or who perhaps use additional or different criteria. No criticism of these other criteria is intended by the focus on our own here. Indeed, if you think that we should amend any of our criteria, we would be glad to hear from you with the reasons for the suggested change. You can contact us via the web address shown on the back cover of this manual.

The training criteria for making (or opposing) an application to a court are set out in **4.3.1**; those for submissions in the course of a hearing are in **4.3.2**. The criteria for handling a witness are set out in **Chapter 19**. Some criteria are always relevant—such as the ability to speak clearly and fluently—others are relevant either to making a submission or to questioning a witness but not to both (eg the use of appropriate questioning techniques). In the main, we are looking at *transferable skills*, that is, at skills that can be used in more than one context.

4.3.1   Advocacy training criteria for applications

In order to be regarded as competent, the advocate should show his or her ability to do the following:

SKELETON ARGUMENT

1   *English language*

(i)   Draft a skeleton argument that is written in clear grammatical English, correctly spelt, properly punctuated and that uses appropriate abbreviations.

2   *Style and structure*

(i)   Draft a skeleton argument in an appropriate style, and which is precise and concise.

(ii)   Draft a skeleton argument with a clear and logical structure, and appropriate formatting.

3   *Written arguments*

(i)   Draft these so that they identify the relevant issues.

(ii)   They must accurately summarise the relevant principles of law and procedure.

(iii) They set out a sustainable argument on each of the issues.

ORAL PERFORMANCE

4   *Structure*

(i)   Structure the application in a clear and logical way, making efficient use of the time available.

5   *Content of oral arguments*

(i)   Present coherent submissions on the main issues to be resolved.

(ii)   Refer to law, sources, your skeleton argument as appropriate.

(iii) Respond appropriately to the interventions of the judge.

(iv) Deal appropriately with points raised by the other side.

6   *Delivery*

(i)   Deliver the application clearly and fluently, and with appropriate pacing.

(ii)   Deliver the application using appropriate language and manner.

(iii) Seek to persuade the judge to decide the application in favour of your client.

Remember that the rules of professional conduct should always be observed.

4.3.2   Advocacy training criteria for submissions

After the court has heard oral evidence, counsel will make a submission (akin to a closing speech at the end of a trial). Because it is impossible to predict with certainty what evidence will be before the court following testimony, it is difficult to submit a skeleton argument that can deal comprehensively with the issues and arguments before the court. Frequently, for this reason, such closing submissions will be made without a skeleton argument. It is also likely that the judge will not intervene while counsel is addressing the court. The training criteria that would otherwise apply (for applications to the court) need to be recast as follows, to meet this situation.

In order to perform this task satisfactorily, you must show your ability to:

(a) prepare the case effectively, by understanding the relevant law, facts and procedure, and planning your submission;

(b) make a submission that is appropriate, relevant and legally and factually sound, and in which you respond appropriately to points made by the other side;

(c) structure your submission in a clear and logical way;

(d) deliver your submission clearly and fluently, using appropriate language and manner, referring to notes when necessary or desirable;

(e) make a submission that is effective and persuasive.

Remember that the rules of professional conduct should always be observed.

4.3.3 The training criteria in more detail

Those criteria are explored in more detail in the following five chapters, with one exception. Professional conduct and ethical behaviour is the subject of the separate *Professional Ethics* manual and it is better to look at that manual for expert coverage of the topic. For present purposes, we might say that the advocate is bound by a code of conduct established by the legal profession. A simple understanding of (and adherence to) the standards that the courts, clients and the public are entitled to expect from an advocate should enable you to do the right thing in most situations. Further guidance and the current (9th) edition of the Bar's Code of Conduct can be found in the BSB Handbook, on the website of the Bar Standards Board at <http://www.barstandardsboard.org.uk>.

5

Preparing for court

5.1 Introduction

This is a job that has to be done sometime and by someone; you can only hope that it is you doing it in plenty of time before you are due in court. Of course, life doesn't always work out like that and you may be heavily reliant on someone else's notes of interviews with the client, background research on the law and the evidence, etc. That does not mean that you can simply breeze into court with little preparation. A classic example of how things can suddenly go wrong is when you are asked to go to court on some simple matter and ask the court to make 'the usual order'. Somehow, courts have a knack of discerning those advocates who are working to someone else's script and when you stand up and ask for 'the usual order', you may be asked, 'And what is that then?' or 'Why do you say you should have it?'. The competent advocate has considered these points in advance and has a reply ready; the incompetent advocate will become flustered and begin searching among their papers in the vain hope that the answer will magically appear there.

Of course, there is a third category of advocate, too. Neither wholly competent nor wholly incompetent, this category is perhaps best described by the label 'beginner'. Anyone just starting out on their career as an advocate will be only too well aware of the high-profile nature of the job. It matters not that there may be only three people in the room to witness your performance—you, your opponent and the district judge, perhaps—in your eyes, that's two too many! You will prepare the case to the best of your ability, devoting far more time to it than your more experienced colleagues seem to spend on their preparation. When someone passes you a file or brief and says, 'Just ask him for the usual order, and don't worry, he's a pussy cat', you won't accept that. You will read books, ask people to explain, try to be prepared. Then you go to court and everything falls apart; that great point you discovered at 2 am last night is never argued in court because:

- you were too nervous about it; or
- you were too intimidated by the judge or your opponent or the situation to raise it; or
- you couldn't find it in your notes; or
- you forgot it.

This has happened to every advocate at one time or another but it happens to some more than most and it happens to beginners more than to experienced advocates. What can you do to stop it from happening to you?

There are three basic lessons to learn. First, prepare thoroughly for your appearance in court. Second, deliver the performance that you have prepared. Third, be prepared to adapt in court to a fluid situation. Let's consider these in a little more depth.

5.2 **Thorough preparation**

When you go into any court or tribunal, in fact whenever you want to speak on someone else's behalf, you should be prepared. You should be familiar with the relevant procedure and rules that apply in that court; you should be familiar with the law that is relevant to the case; you should be familiar with the evidential material that is (or might be) available for this hearing.

For example, you are sent to argue for summary judgment in a hearing before a Master in the Queen's Bench Division in the High Court. Before entering the room, you should know the procedural rules set out in Part 24 of the Civil Procedure Rules, together with any related rules, for example those dealing with the possible costs orders that may be made. You should be familiar with any rules governing the evidence that you (or your opponent) wish to use, for example has your client's affidavit been served on your opponent in good time? If not, are there any rules that you can use to seek extraordinary permission to use that evidence? You should also know the relevant substantive law, that is the law that deals with the claim. Since your claim is for summary judgment, more likely than not your client alleges that the defendant has no defence to the claim. In order to substantiate that allegation, if required to do so, you should be familiar with the relevant legal principles, first, as to why the claim should succeed and, second, why there is no viable defence to it.

It follows that you must be familiar with the factual allegations made in the case (for which you will need to know the statements of case and your client's affidavit in support), because it is the synthesis of the legal framework with the specific factual allegations in this case that produce the argument that your client's claim must succeed and there is no reason why the case should go to a full trial.

Once you have gone through all of this preparation, you will need to write a skeleton argument to submit to the court in advance. These are increasingly used, both in civil trials and interim applications. What you put into a skeleton argument will depend partly on your style and preferences and partly what you learn suits the court. However, it should cover the following matters:

- the nature of the application or submission;
- what the case is about (where necessary);
- the issues between the parties (if necessary);
- the argument in the form of a series of legal propositions and submissions supported by authority and evidence (with references to pages and paragraphs as necessary).

The skeleton argument should also:

- assist the court to assimilate your argument easily;
- persuade the court to grant the order that you seek;
- identify precisely what you are asking the court to do.

It may also be appropriate to hand in a separate chronology to the court. More detailed guidance on skeleton arguments can be found in **Chapter 25**.

Is that all you need to do in order to be fully prepared for this application? I'm afraid it is not that easy. Let's go back to the first two of our three basic lessons. First was thorough preparation and second was deliver the performance that you had prepared; in sporting parlance, don't leave your performance in the dressing room! It makes little difference to the outcome whether you prepared the case poorly or prepared yourself poorly for court. What you have done with your preparation so far is to work on the content of your advocacy performance; the necessity to do that will never change from one case to another. What you must do now is to prepare the delivery of your performance.

5.3   Prepare your delivery

Delivery will be the subject of an in-depth exploration in **Chapter 8**, so what you have here is a summary of the points that you will need to work on.

For many people, the ubiquity of the video camera, the camcorder and even mobile phone camera has meant that many of us now know what we look like to others, much more realistically than we would by simply looking into a mirror. Video footage shows us what we look like when we move, stand or sit, it reveals our gestures to us and it tells us how we sound to others. You may have already seen the picture that you present to others, the value of which was once described by Robert Burns, in 'To a Louse', as follows:

> O wad some Pow'r the giftie gie us
> To see oursels as others see us!
> It wad frae mony a blunder free us,
> An' foolish notion.

If you have seen yourself, you may have been minded to make some changes but that is unlikely to have been done if the video was shot on a social occasion. What you need to do now is record yourself delivering a piece of advocacy. Try to create the sort of conditions that will be present in court. For example, dress in formal court clothes, and deliver a straightforward speech or submission to the camera. Five minutes' worth should be enough to start with! Then review it. How do you look? Are you standing up straight or slouching? Are your hands in your pockets or fiddling with a pen? Can you hear yourself? Are you speaking too fast? Are you looking at the camera or away from it?

All of these points, and others, will be addressed in **Chapter 8**. For now, it is enough that you appreciate that, for many lawyers, preparing the law and the evidence for each case is relatively straightforward. After all, you have a law degree, are used to working on researching legal points in a law library, have a fund of basic legal knowledge; you have read the statements of case in this case (and maybe many others during your training), you have seen the evidence (in witness statements, affidavits and the like) and can remember it. If you can't remember it, now is the time to read **Chapter 11** of the manual. What is not straightforward is the transition from **lawyer** to **advocate**.

5.4   From lawyer to advocate

On the face of it, this transition should be simple. After all, don't we all advocate almost every day of our lives? When you are at the supermarket and debating with your partner which brand of breakfast cereal to buy, if you want the cornflakes you will argue in favour of buying them and your objective will be to persuade your partner of the merit of your choice. What is so different about 'advocating' something in a courtroom?

Perhaps it is the fact that you are now arguing for someone else, so there is a sense of responsibility. Perhaps it is because you are now being judged on the quality of your argument by someone who has power, over both you and your client. Perhaps it is the public nature of the advocacy; whereas you may be happy and relaxed to debate points on a private level and at a private volume, when called on to do so with an audience and at much greater volume, the situation becomes less familiar and more uncomfortable. It should be clear that the more appearances that you make as an advocate, the more familiar and less uncomfortable it should all become. How do you survive until then?

Practice is the answer. You will find things becoming easier as you get more and more appearances under your belt. What you need to do is to increase your number of performances artificially, by using the video camera and working with others in a similar situation, as well as with more experienced advocates who can point out things that you may have overlooked. In the same way that pilots train on a flight simulator, so you can clock up more hours by working on advocacy simulations and getting more experience that way.

In the **Appendix** at the end of the manual, you will find an entire case to use as a vehicle for some advocacy work.

5.5 Being adaptable

The third basic lesson that has to be grasped is that you must retain the ability to adapt and respond to a changing situation. It is sometimes said that advocates are quick-witted and have the ability to 'think on their feet' in court. What that really means is that the advocate is sufficiently well versed in the relevant law and evidence that, even if something unexpected happens, the advocate can cope with it. The unexpected may be just being asked a question by a judge in the middle of your submission to the court; the judge wants to know about a particular point and wants to hear your answer now. For all the judge knows, you were just about to deal with that point. If so, it should be no problem for you to tackle it now. If you were going to deal with it later on in your submissions, you should know the answer even if you have to think about it a little more carefully. When that happens, you then have to make a judgement on whether to go back to the topic you were dealing with before the question or carry on from the point that your answer has now taken you to. The choice you make depends on what points you had to skip past to get the answer: were any of them important to your case, or contentious? If so, it's probably better to go back and deal with them. If not, carry on from the point that interested the judge.

It is a little different when you are questioning a witness. Here, the witness is meant to be under your control in as much as they are in the witness-box to answer your questions. There is more chance that something unexpected will emerge from a witness than there was with the judge (at least we can expect the judge to appreciate concepts like legal relevance, admissibility and know the relevant legal framework for the case). So when the unexpected, and possibly inadmissible, answer is given, you should be prepared with your response. First, don't let your mouth open wide with surprise, don't flush with embarrassment and don't start stumbling over your words. If the answer was irrelevant to the issues in the case, you might ignore it or perhaps admonish the witness to listen carefully to your questions and simply answer them (this is likely to draw more attention to the unexpected answer). If the answer was relevant to the issues in the case, you may want some time to consider your response, in which case say something like:

Perhaps we will return to that later, Mr Jones. For now, perhaps you could tell the court . . .

Having bought some time, you may want to leave the subject well alone but, if the answer came from a witness you were cross-examining, you might decide it has to be squashed. You could do that by attacking the credibility of the answer, for example why is this the first we've heard of that? Is it something the witness has just made up? If they have made written statements some months (or even years) ago and the subject is not raised in the statement, why not? An alternative is to challenge the witness's memory of events that may have happened a long time ago; another might be to suggest that the witness, however innocently, is enhancing their account in a bid to help the court.

The central point is that you should be ready with an array of possible responses to the unexpected, like a collection of arrows in your quiver, so that you can calmly select the appropriate one to use in any given situation. Problems start when you don't expect the unexpected; you approach the trial or hearing with the mental equivalent of blinkers on and you are so focused on your own case and how to present it that anything that upsets your planned strategy pushes you completely off course. If you can remember that things seldom turn out exactly the way you anticipated before going into court, then you won't be so shocked when that prediction comes true.

5.6   Planning a route to your destination

We have looked at the need to understand (and perhaps research) the relevant law, to acquire a thorough grasp of the allegations, the evidence and the areas of dispute between the parties. We have also looked at the need to present yourself clearly in court and to be adaptable. The last hint is that before you finally start out on your journey through this case, you must have a clear idea of where you want to be at the end of it. You have to identify your client's objectives: what does he or she want out of this litigation? A judgment that they are not liable to the claimant? An award of damages? A verdict of not guilty? Then, what might you need to do in order to achieve those objectives? To answer these questions you will need to predict the arguments that you want to present to the court at the end of the case. Only then can you start to work backwards to consider how you can best guarantee that those arguments are in fact available to you at the end of the case.

It is often said that the advocate needs to start planning the closing speech for a trial before setting foot in the court. Really, you need to have a very clear picture in your mind of how the hearing will work—who will be there, what they are likely to say—so that you can start to see the time spent in court as a whole, rather than a series of isolated events. In a trial, what counsel says in opening the case may present a certain version of the case; the opponent needs to know whether that version might be challenged. As each witness appears in the witness box, the advocate cannot ignore what preceding witnesses have said, their answers will help to determine the questions that **this** witness is asked. At the start of a trial, a judge's notebook is blank, apart from the names of the parties perhaps. By the end of the evidence and speeches, it will have been filled up; the advocates cannot change its contents but they had a large role in determining what was written in it. During the course of the hearing, the thorough advocate has to keep in mind what he or she wants to have in the notebook, what is **actually** going into it, and what **might** still be put in.

5.7 A work plan for a criminal trial and conference

5.7.1 Introduction

The remaining paragraphs of this chapter contain a short, simple plan to use when preparing for a trial in the Crown Court, either as the prosecutor or for the defence. It is intended to act partly as a checklist of the things you should cover in your preparation and also as a guide to organising your materials.

There is also a plan for a conference with the defendant in a criminal case and some points to consider when questioning witnesses in court and making speeches. Some of these will be covered in greater detail in other chapters.

You could try to create your own checklists after studying a particular situation; perhaps add your points to the one given here for the defence conference. Remember, what you find here is always open to improvement or adaptation. This section of the chapter provides a start for you—build on it!

5.7.2 Work plan

On receiving the brief:
Read the instructions: What are you being asked to achieve?

5.7.2.1 Defence brief

(a) Look at the *indictment*. **Never** prepare a case without the indictment. Compare the counts with the charges on which the case was sent for trial. Are they the same? If they differ, ask yourself why. Always consider what alternative convictions could be recorded.

(b) Read prosecution statements and exhibits: do the papers disclose a prima facie case?

(c) Are your instructions a plea of guilty or not guilty?

Not guilty

(a) Is that supportable on your instructions? If not, conference/advice.

(b) Is a conference required in any event? (Desirable in all but the simplest of cases.)

(c) Are your instructions adequate? If not, request further and better particulars.

(d) Points of law: PACE 1984; CJA 2003. What additional evidence may be needed, for example, custody record and relevant police officers; medical reports of any examination of victim/defendant?

(e) Additional evidence required generally: for example, proofs to be taken from potential witnesses; plans; photos.

(f) What is in the defence statement? Has proper disclosure been made?

(g) Expert evidence: must be served on prosecution if intended to be relied upon at trial.

(h) Alibi:

    (i)   is it an alibi case?

    (ii) if so, has anything been done about it—defence statement?

(i) Notices of additional evidence: do we require the witnesses to attend?

(j) Unused material. Has this been served? Is an application necessary?

(k) As a result of your instructions/conference, can you offer any sensible pleas to the prosecution? If so, solicitors should write at once.

Note: most of the above points are far better covered in a written advice than in a chat over the telephone.

Guilty

(a) On your instructions is that a proper plea or is it equivocal?

(b) On your instructions is a *Newton* hearing likely on issue(s) of fact? If so, consider a discussion in advance with prosecution to try to agree a 'basis of plea' and put it into writing. Failing that, witnesses can be warned to attend, thus avoiding need for adjournment.

(c) Any evidence required in support of mitigation, for example, proof of job?

(d) Any character witnesses, references, service records, etc?

(e) Request extension to public funding for psychiatric/medical report (if appropriate).

(f) Research authorities on sentence for type of offence and assess likely range, or talk directly to the prosecuting advocate to find out what, if any, pleas of guilty might be acceptable to the prosecution, or possibly if the prosecution would be willing to allow the court simply to bind the defendant over to keep the peace.

(g) Advise solicitors to inform court of fact of guilty plea. Always prepare for a best and a worst result. If best, an acquittal, be ready to argue costs. If worst, be ready to make a speech in mitigation of sentence **and** to advise on appeal.

5.7.2.2 Prosecution brief (not guilty)

(a) *Indictment:*

    (i)   draft it if requested;

    (ii) if already drafted, check it is correctly drafted and that there is evidence to support it.

(b) *Advice:*

    (i)   additional evidence if needed and photos;

    (ii) disclosure/non-disclosure in accordance with the Criminal Procedure and Investigations Act 1996 and relevant case law and Protocol; disclose any previous convictions of any prosecution witness.

(c) *Opening note:*

    (i)   contents must be borne out by reference to admissible evidence;

    (ii) plan structure: enough law/fact to help the jury, not confuse them;

    (iii) visual aids: OHP, video, graphics, schedules—will they help?

(d) *Preparation of jury bundle:*

    (i)   only what's really necessary;

    (ii) make sure it's legible;

(iii) include plans, agreed schedules, glossaries, etc;

(iv) folders/binders, etc.

(e) *Order of witnesses:*

(i) defence (and judge) always want to know this.

Tight preparation = Strong presentation.

5.7.2.3 Defence conference

(a) Keep requisite degree of formality: avoid use of first names with client and (during conference) with solicitor (often difficult to do!).

(b) Put client at ease: explain what you are going to discuss: be prepared to **listen** and not just **talk**.

(c) Explain what the charge means.

(d) Explain strengths/weaknesses in the defence ⎤ be frank: this avoids the 'why

(e) Explain possible sentence upon conviction ⎦ didn't you tell me?' afterwards.

(f) If this is the defendant's first Crown Court trial: explain what will actually happen at court.

The idea of points (a)–(f) is that they remove uncertainty in the client's mind and help to make the client confident that:

(i) you understand the case; and

(ii) you are in charge and capable of running it.

5.7.2.4 Examination-in-chief

(Much harder than cross-examination in many ways because you are not allowed to lead the answers from the witness.)

In advance

(a) Be clear in your own mind what it is that you want to adduce from the witness.

(b) A statement is often badly put together and you may well not want to follow its sequence. As a result a plan/checklist of sequence and content may be helpful. (Note: if you are going to ask questions on matters not covered at all, then a further statement should be taken and served on the defence.)

(c) Try to put the witness at ease—courtrooms can be very intimidating. A relaxed witness is far more likely to come up to proof.

(d) 'Difficult' witness: **Don't** rush to make him or her **hostile** in law: try 'going round again'; if it's a memory problem, seek a short adjournment so that he or she can refresh his or her memory—a trial is not a memory test. (Note: there will almost always be an argument over this in the absence of the jury.)

5.7.2.5 Cross-examination

(a) You have a duty to put your main challenges to the witness during cross-examination, for example, 'it never happened'; 'you've made it up'; 'you're mistaken', etc.

(b) From the statement and your instructions, **plan** what you're going to ask in order to try to **assist** your case: ie are there obvious areas where the witness is vulnerable and you can make a good point? Are there obvious areas where the witness is strong and will simply be 'firmed up' if pressed by the defence?

(c) Don't try to get the witness to make comments: he or she is unlikely to want to help you and you can make the comment in your closing speech without fear of getting the wrong answer.

(d) When you have got a favourable answer: **stop**. Many cases have been lost by pushing a question too far.

(e) Don't be frightened **not** to ask questions: if a witness has been favourable to you or failed to identify/mention your client, **leave well alone**, however tempting to try to score a few points.

Both in examination-in-chief and cross-examination:

(a) make sure that the witness is keeping his or her voice up;

(b) don't go too fast: follow the judge's pen;

(c) let the witness answer before asking your next question;

(d) try to keep questions short: nothing is worse than when your clever but convoluted question is met by blankness and 'Sorry, I don't understand what you're getting at'.

5.7.2.6   Speeches

(a) Speeches should be as short as possible: juries do not need 20 minutes on the burden and standard of proof, for example.

(b) Make your good points and sit down: don't spoil them by waffle and numerous bad points.

(c) If you are concerned that your client won't feel you have 'had a good go' if you make a very short speech, explain to him or her beforehand why you're doing so—they normally understand.

(d) Prosecution:

(i)   fair presentation and comment on evidence;

(ii) no duty to secure conviction at all costs;

(iii) no duty to 'sum up' case to them by rehearsing all the law and facts (again).

The content of your application

6.1 Introduction

To a certain extent, the answer to the question implied in the title of this chapter must be found in **Chapter 5**. It is unlikely that you will be able to say the right things at the right times unless you have prepared for your appearance very thoroughly. So, hasn't the job been done? Well, the proof of the pudding comes when it is eaten and even the best preparation in the world is just wasted effort if you cannot say the right things and take the right decisions once you get into the courtroom. Every advocate has to make use of their knowledge of the law and put it together with their analysis of the evidence and issues in dispute to produce what the court requires, namely a performance that is (i) appropriate, (ii) relevant, (iii) legally sound, and (iv) factually sound. It is worth looking in more detail at these requirements, in particular to see how they might apply to the range of tasks that the advocate may be asked to perform.

6.2 The content of submissions

In a sense, the four essentials for content are set out in **6.1** the wrong way round: if the advocate does not put forward arguments on a submission that are 'legally sound and factually sound', there is little chance that the arguments will be 'appropriate and relevant'. Although the twin requirements of appropriateness and relevance are more important than simply being sound on the law and facts, the advocate must first know the 'facts' and the necessary law in order to construct the legal and factual framework within which it becomes possible to gauge whether an argument is appropriate or relevant.

6.2.1 Appropriate and relevant

6.2.1.1 Your submission

Whenever you are called on to make an application or submission to a court, one of your earliest steps in preparing will be to digest exactly what appears in the statements of case. Of course, it is a little different in criminal cases but there will still be a charge sheet, summons, or indictment to consider. Looking at these will help you to discover the issues between the parties, who alleges what, when, and who bears the burden of proof. It will also be the start of your legal analysis, when the causes of action are disclosed or the elements of the offence revealed.

'Relevance' denotes some sort of relationship between things; what you say in court must be directed to identifying the issues in the case and how they should be resolved.

When you dissect a set of papers prior to going into court with them, you have to learn a lot of things that you did not know before. Someone else may have been through a sorting process already, so that if you are instructed on behalf of Mr Smith in his careless driving prosecution, you don't suddenly find a lot of documents to do with his pending divorce. Similarly, when you open your mouth in court, you should not just say anything that appeared in the case papers (or your instructions). You must regularly gauge whether what you are about to do, whether it be drawing the court's attention to some factual allegation or addressing an argument to the court, is connected to the issues that are of concern to the court.

If 'relevant' means that you should talk only about matters that are likely to be (and should properly be) considered by the court when adjudicating in the case, what does that leave for 'appropriate' to do? Appropriate means that you are sensitive to your surroundings, the context in which you are operating. For example, in a prosecution for grievous bodily harm it may be clear that the victim has suffered nasty injuries. A defence advocate who has to allege that in fact the 'victim' was the protagonist and the accused was simply acting in self-defence must appreciate that the court is likely to feel a considerable sympathy for the injured person. That may make it necessary to (a) adopt certain tactics or arguments that acknowledge that sympathy and (b) appreciate that, when putting forward the defence case, there may be a lot of resistance. Again, it may be 'appropriate' in a hearing seeking an interim payment of damages for personal injury to tell the court what the claimant requires the money for, even though the legal test for making the interim payment doesn't require you to do so. A piece of factual information or an argument may be 'appropriate' without strictly being 'relevant' in a legal sense.

6.2.1.2   Opposing a submission

When a court hears a submission or application, it is generally the case that the advocates and the judge all have the same documentary information (affidavits and statements of case have been served on the opposing party in advance). No one is usually taken by surprise at the hearing. However, just because the advocates have access to the same information it does not follow that they will make the same use of it. Different people see different arguments, disagree over what is a strength and what is a weakness in the case. When you are opposing a submission or application, your task is twofold.

First, you must prepare to respond as best you can, so you should try to anticipate your opponent's arguments. What will the other side be emphasising? Which of the weaknesses in your case will they seek to exploit? When preparing to respond, it is tempting to plan for every eventuality and that has some sense to it. But you must be ready to adapt your strategy or your arguments to meet the situation on the day; you must not present your case like an automaton, blithely assuming that everything is going just the way you thought it would. Suppose that you spotted a weak point in your evidence while preparing the case, then you should work out a tactic to deal with it, but you must still listen in court. If your opponent does not raise that topic, for whatever reason, you should consider very carefully whether you now need to say anything about it when you respond. If you do, you may just remind your opponent of a forgotten argument or alert your learned friend to the existence of a weakness (they may not have seen the point in those terms until now). Thus, what is relevant and appropriate can change quite rapidly in the course of competing arguments on a submission. The second part of your task, then, is to monitor constantly what the other side is saying and the response of the court, and to tailor your arguments to suit the circumstances as they are at the moment.

6.2.1.3 Skeleton arguments

In a civil case, your application or submission may be supported by a skeleton argument. This document will be prepared by you in advance of the hearing and supplied to both the court and your opponent. Assume that both have read it before the application starts. Clearly, the content of your skeleton argument should fulfil the same criteria as your oral argument—it should be appropriate, relevant and sound in fact and law. It may be that there is adequate coverage of a point in your skeleton and you can therefore either take it very shortly in addressing the court orally, or perhaps simply refer the court to the passage in the skeleton. For further guidance on skeleton arguments, see **Chapter 25**.

6.2.2   Legally and factually sound

Whatever you say in court as an advocate, it must be a fair and accurate representation of the facts in the case and the law relating to the case (or the particular hearing at least). You should never knowingly mislead the court on the law or the evidence (whether going to a disputed fact or not). If you do so innocently and in good faith, then as soon as you realise your error you should draw the court's attention to it and correct yourself.

Let's look at how your submission might be legally and factually sound. In an application for summary judgment, the test is to be found in the Civil Procedure Rules (CPR), r 24. No judge will need you to tell him or her that but they will expect you to base your arguments, for or against summary judgment, on an accurate understanding of what the criteria are for summary judgment. For that, you need the current text of CPR, r 24, to hand. As this rule is interpreted and applied by the courts over time, some elements may assume greater or lesser significance. You will need to be as up to date as you can be on how the courts are using CPR, r 24, and be able to use that knowledge as the basis of your arguments to the court.

As for being factually sound, you should know the number of affidavits or statements in the case, who swore them, when they were sworn and, most importantly, what they say (and don't say). Anything you say to the court of a factual nature must be accurate: don't say the unpaid debt is £12,500 if it is £15,200, for example. On a more mundane level, if one of the witnesses is named John Tyler, don't refer to him as Jack Taylor. We all make little slips like that from time to time but the important thing is to listen to yourself. Even if you know the witness is called John Tyler, it may not always come out like that. As stated, that slip is probably quite inconsequential but for one thing—it may plant a seed of doubt in the court's mind whether you know what you are talking about. If you can make an error over something as simple as a name, especially when it is on a document in front of you, what else might you be mistaken about?

6.2.3   Reference to legal sources

On most applications or submissions, your court will probably be legally qualified (a judge, a district judge, a Master) and the last thing such people want is a lecture on the law. After all, they are likely to know it as well as you, if not better, and use it more frequently too. What the court wants, then, is not copious references to the legal sources for your arguments, it wants you to have extracted the legal principle from the case of *Smith v Jones,* say, and apply it to the allegations and evidence in the present case. On an application by the defence advocate in a Crown Court trial to exclude an interview between the police and the accused from being heard by the jury, the judge will not want to hear from counsel about the legal history of the Police and Criminal Evidence Act 1984, s 76. The judge will want the advocate to have identified the relevant part(s) of s 76—maybe 'oppression'—and then present the arguments, based on a synthesis of the relevant law and evidence.

Structuring your application

7.1 Introduction

The subject of structure needs to be seen in two distinct ways. First, you can deal with structure in the context of applications or submissions made to a court or tribunal. These may be applications at an ad hoc hearing (eg application for summary judgment) or in the course of a trial (eg *voir dire*). The second context is in the examination of witnesses, whether called by your client or by other parties in the litigation. This chapter looks at structure within these two contexts but it is important to note, at the outset, that there are three basic requirements that are relevant to structure, whatever the context.

7.1.1 Three basic requirements

The three basic requirements for structure are:

- be clear;
- be logical; and
- be responsive.

Remember, **clarity** is everything, obscurity is nothing. Your ultimate aim is to persuade and, to do that, you must communicate accurately with the tribunal. You are most likely to do that if everything you say and do is clear in its meaning. A clear structure is a good guarantee for that. Coupled with clarity is the need to be **logical**. Despite the critiques of the human reasoning process that have been made (see, for example, the works of Edward de Bono), it is a fact that the most common process for reaching conclusions relies heavily (although not solely) on logic.

When devising a structure for your work, you should choose one that 'makes sense'. To achieve that, it should make sense to others too. That is not to say that there can only be one logical structure, although there may be a 'normal' or common structure to particular applications. One might present information on the basis of a chronological order, or a geographical order, or even 'best point first'. Perhaps the best general description is that individual points should flow clearly from one to another, rather than appear as a motley collection of unrelated data.

Finally, **respond** to the other players in the drama. Even when there is only you and the judge (maybe on an application when no one appears for the opponent), you may still face questions from the court. Deal with them as they arise if at all possible. If you really cannot provide an immediate response, indicate that you will be doing so shortly. Whether making an application or questioning a witness, you cannot afford to stick to preconceived notions or a particular structure *regardless* of what others are saying or thinking. A script is almost useless in court for many reasons but here it hampers good advocacy by imposing a straitjacket on the advocate. You must have a clear and logical structure certainly, but you must never adhere to it just for its own sake. If there is no need to amend or adapt it while you are in court, so much the better, but your planning should have enabled you to be flexible in your work. You should be alert to what the tribunal or your opponent or the witness are saying, doing or thinking. They are communicating with you and each other either directly or indirectly and you cannot afford to ignore what they are saying.

7.2 Applications to a court

7.2.1 Clear and logical: your application

Your first consideration is, what stage of the proceedings are we at? Has the hearing been arranged primarily for the purpose of the application you are to make, or is the application merely incidental to a more wide-ranging hearing? For example, is this an application for summary judgment or is it an application, during a trial, to exclude evidence?

In an ad hoc hearing, introductions are required. The court needs to know who the advocates are and courtesy dictates that you tell the court, even if it clearly knows their identities already. The court also needs to know who the parties are to the litigation and which advocate represents which party. The court may require you to tell it something about the case itself, before you launch into the application. Where the application is made during the trial, on the other hand, such introductions would be unnecessary at best and bizarre at worst.

7.2.1.1 The ad hoc hearing

A general structure for such a hearing could look like this:

(a) Introduce advocates, parties, the case, the application, all very briefly.

(b) Check that the court has all the relevant documents. Be specific, don't just say, 'Have you got the papers in this case?'

(c) Briefly state the order in which you propose to present the rest of your application.

(d) Explain the background to the application, if appropriate.

(e) Present the substance of the application:

    (i) Set out the arguments in support of your application, combining the specific evidence in this case with the relevant legal rules. Don't lecture the court on the law, or spend time stating what you understand the law to be in some abstract way. Always apply the law to the evidence and remember that the court has probably heard a great many of these applications; it does not need to receive the benefit of your legal research!

    (ii) If necessary, anticipate and deal with the arguments of your opponent. If these counter-arguments will be on points that you need to establish to succeed in the application, deal with the point as you interpret it first and then indicate why the counter-argument has no merit.

    (iii) For any application, there may be several legal requirements on which the court needs to be satisfied before your application can succeed. You should have an argument designed to deal with each such point.

(f) Summarise your strongest arguments, by way of a conclusion, and offer to assist the court with any questions that it may have.

(g) Allow your opponent to make his or her arguments to the court.

(h) Ask to be allowed to reply to those arguments, if necessary.

(i) The court announces its decision.

(j) Raise any supplementary points that are relevant now that the main decision has been reached.

That is fine as a framework but it may not turn out that way in practice. For example, suppose your opponent keeps interrupting your arguments? Or the judge keeps asking questions, none of which seem relevant to the point you are dealing with? The answer is to be flexible and responsive. You might suggest that it would be simpler for all concerned if you could present all your arguments first and then give the floor to your opponent. That is responsive as it does not require you to carry on as if your opponent was saying nothing. If the judge asks a question, you should deal with it. You might then return to your previous point, or you could skip to that part of your plan that follows on from the judge's question. If in doubt, ask the judge.

7.2.1.2   The application within a trial

Typically, this type of application will arise after the beginning of the trial, perhaps concerned with an issue of evidence. Here, one can afford to be much more specific as the court should be fully aware of the context of your application. So, a general plan might work like this:

(a) State that an application now needs to be made. In circumstances where questions of law are decided by different people from those who decide questions of fact, this is all you should say at present, then wait for the triers of fact to leave the court.

(b) State what the application is (eg an application to exclude evidence of a confession, pursuant to the Police and Criminal Evidence Act 1984, s 76).

(c) If the application places the burden of proof on you (not always the case; see, for example, s 76 of the 1984 Act), set out the allegations of fact that you rely on, relating each of them to the legal requirements on which you must satisfy the court. Do not deal with the relevant law unless you are applying it to the alleged facts.

(d) Allow your opponent to present any counter-arguments.

(e) Ask for an opportunity to reply, if you need one.

(f) The court announces its decision on the application.

(g) Carry on with the trial, at a point and in a manner consistent with the court's decision.

7.2.2   Clear and logical: opposing an application

Much of what concerns the advocate who is making an application is inapplicable to an advocate who must respond to that application. Typically, it will be unnecessary to introduce yourself when you first speak to the court as that should have been done by your opponent. Any relevant documentation should also be before the court by now and you can simply make use of it, without needing to introduce it.

Clarity here simply requires that each of your arguments is clearly differentiated. Do not conflate two separate points; keep your arguments as simple as they can be. Logic will often dictate that the order in which you raise issues and present your arguments on them is the same as the order adopted by your opponent. That may be unfortunate for two reasons. First, their order may differ from your preferred order for tactical reasons and, secondly, you may have to rearrange your running order at the last possible moment. Even so, that is probably the best course of action rather than sticking to your own intended order unless the order chosen by your opponent was, in your opinion, defective for some reason. In this situation you may want to indicate that you will not be following the order of points used by your opponent, and perhaps explain why. Then you should go on to explain what your order will be, to minimise any confusion for the court.

It is not of great assistance to work on a framework when you are opposing an application, for reasons just stated. But you should have an order for the arguments, in case you want to substitute your order for that used by your opponent. Thinking about the appropriate order for your arguments also requires you to think about which arguments are your strengths and which are your weaknesses. This is an extremely useful process when preparing for court and should never be overlooked. The judge may have already asked your opponent some questions. These questions could indicate matters that the judge is concerned about. You might then concentrate on those matters in your submission.

Delivering your application

8.1 Introduction

Once again, as with several of these chapters, you will wonder why on earth we need a chapter on such an ordinary topic—isn't speaking something that you do every day? Yes, like most of the skills that are used by a competent advocate, we all use our speaking skills every day. But now the circumstances are different; we are not speaking privately or personally, as we are used to doing; we are to speak in public, on behalf of someone else and, in a sense, on the record. Our client is depending on our ability to speak well for him or her, and other people are judging us on our speaking ability, among other things. In short, we are now in the public eye and what we are engaged in is public speaking. You may have had a taste of this already, in a variety of situations as diverse as a debating society, a mooting competition or a wedding. If so, you will be familiar with the nerves that accompany your first efforts at speaking to an audience, with the strain you feel in trying to project your voice into a large room and with the problems you seem to be having with your breathing.

Speaking as an advocate imposes stress on the speaker and that stress manifests itself in several symptoms. These are most common in the novice and become more bearable (and thus less noticeable) with experience. However, it is much better to work on such matters before your first appearance as an advocate, so that your personal discomfort may be reduced and there is less danger of your client's interests suffering because of your inexperience.

Chapter 10 gives you some guidance on techniques to use for working on relaxation and breathing, as well as articulation and projection. If you have ever done any public speaking, pause now and consider if there are any nervous mannerisms that you are aware of: do you include lots of ums, ers and ehs? Do you pause in the right places to give the appropriate emphasis to your words? Do you speak too fast? Or too slow? Are you happy that you get the volume right so that others can hear you clearly? Now imagine that you are doing the same thing again, but this time in a courtroom with other people present. Do you think your performance will be better, or any more comfortable, now?

It is time to realise that, although not all advocates are frustrated actors, the competent advocate requires many of the techniques that are commonly used in drama. Actors on a stage do not get themselves heard at the back of the auditorium if they use the same voice that they use when talking to a friend on the telephone. If you want to be heard in court, you need to be able to utilise the same techniques that actors use to ensure that their voices are heard and their words are clear.

8.2   Speak clearly and fluently

Communication is the name of this game. If you don't speak clearly, then your words might just as well have never been uttered. Worse still, they may be misunderstood and convey a wrong impression to your listeners. For the advocate must be both the creator and the performer: you have to think of the words and you have to say them. The first part calls for good language skills, a broad vocabulary and a basic understanding of grammar. The second part requires you to articulate those words so that your listeners can:

- hear your words;
- comprehend your words; and
- attach the correct interpretation to them.

So do not mutter, do not use a 'small' voice, do not look at the floor, do not speak at a pace so fast that your listeners cannot keep up nor so slow that they lose interest or concentration. Do look at your listeners, take care over your pronunciation, speak at a reasonable pace, use appropriate variations in tone and use pauses, too.

Writing as someone who has spent several years listening to people taking their first steps in training as advocates, I have found the common faults of speaking to be concerned with the following.

8.2.1   The pace of speaking

This can be too fast or too slow but typically it is too fast. Why? It seems that the appearance in court is an ordeal that the speaker wants to get over as quickly as possible. It also seems to be believed that, by speaking fast and maintaining a steady stream of 'noise', there may be less opportunity for anyone else to intervene and do anything unsettling such as asking a question, or changing the subject.

The more competent performer will speak at a more normal pace, will pause for breath whenever necessary and, indeed, will make positive use of **pauses**. What do I mean by that? A pause may be used for various purposes: to get your breath; to mark a transition between one point and the next; to give emphasis to the previous point; and finally to allow the listener to make a note if that is what they are doing. A competent advocate should feel able to use pauses in all of these ways and not be frightened that someone may intervene or 'take the floor' from them. If that happens, you should be prepared for it and respond, for example by answering a question. When that happens, you impress the questioner that you are in control, of both yourself and this case; that is a persuasive plus for you.

8.2.2   The volume of your voice

It is important to remember that you will often be addressing your listener over a distance of several feet. You may be across a table from, say, a district judge in his or her room or you may be 20 feet away from a judge in a courtroom. Both must be able to hear you, and neither should think that you are speaking too loudly or too quietly. It is likely that you will find less of a problem in speaking at the right volume to someone across a table, than across a room. Generally, we are unaccustomed to speaking over such distances, other than in a classroom during our schooldays. You must be able to turn up the volume, whenever the situation demands it. That does not mean that you should start shouting, though!

8.2.3   Fluency

When required to speak in public, it is often the case that one's mind goes blank and ideas have almost to be forced out. Your voice becomes more staccato, less natural and the number of ums, ers and ehs increases dramatically. Try to eliminate these 'fillers' if you can; they can become very distracting to the listener. All they really are is a subconscious way of trying to disguise the fact that you have nothing better to say at present. Worse, they may have become a habit that is present whenever you speak, on a par with 'like' or 'you know'. These phrases are meaningless and should always be avoided. Although to eradicate them from your speech may require some attention, and the initial attempts to do so will simply result in your becoming more aware of them and self-conscious, the longer that you consciously try to do without them when you speak, the easier it will be for your listener to follow the words that really matter.

8.3   Use appropriate language and manner

What is meant by the phrase 'appropriate language and manner'? Our aim, when talking, is to communicate with our listeners and we will do so most effectively when our vocabulary is a shared one and our listeners have no distractions.

When I say 'appropriate language', this does not include nor require anyone to use what critics sometime call 'legalese'. The competent advocate should always use a vocabulary that is suited to both the listener and the situation. So you should ask yourself, who am I talking to, who is listening to me? In many situations, the answers will be the same, but that is not so when dealing with a witness, for example.

8.3.1   Obscene language

As an advocate, you must show respect for the court; there should be no place for obscene language or swearwords of any kind from you certainly and, if they come from a witness, you should stop them immediately. There is one exception to this, though, and that is where the evidence relevant to the litigation contains swearwords itself. An example might be found in *R v M*, The Times, 23 April 1996, where evidence was produced in a murder trial that the appellant had described 'cutting' her victim because he was 'acting like a fucking hero'. Here, the obscenity is an integral part of the appellant's words and it would be appropriate to present the court with the unexpurgated version, both as part of the evidence and within a closing speech in the trial.

8.3.2   Vernacular language or slang

Again, this has to do with respect for the court; it also has to do with clarity. A single word may have a variety of different meanings and the way that words most quickly acquire new meanings is through the language of the streets. If we use (or allow others to use) words that have a slang sense and are being used thus, our listeners who do not share this vocabulary may lose the message that we are trying to convey.

Don't use vernacular words or phrases yourself unless, as before, they are a relevant piece of the evidence before the court. Even then, some explanation or clarification may be called for so that the correct interpretation can be put on the words by your listeners. Occasionally, you may find that your listeners needed no such explanation but it is better to err on the side of caution.

8.3.3   Jargon

Try to avoid this if you can. Perhaps, if you are appearing before a professional judge and another qualified advocate, you may use common spoken 'shorthand', as long as you are certain that there can be no misunderstanding by your listeners. Otherwise, there will be lay people present, your client, perhaps, or a witness, or even people in the public gallery in court and all these people are entitled to understand and follow what you are saying. In those circumstances, while it may be tempting to abbreviate words or use Latin tags, for example, you would do much better to use plain English. Often, it is tempting to use jargon because you may think that it shows that you are on the inside, in the know, an experienced advocate. In fact, there are many other ways by which those who are experienced will judge whether you know what you are talking about; jargon alone will not convince them that you are experienced in your work if all of the other signs do not.

One particular situation that cries out for you to use jargon is when dealing with an expert witness. Now the temptation is to prove to others not that you are an experienced lawyer but that you are an expert in another field altogether. This is a tactic fraught with danger as the likelihood is that either you are not an expert and do not fully understand the expert's jargon, or the person deciding the facts in the case does not understand the jargon. In this latter situation, the fact-finder will feel, rightly, that he or she is being excluded from the dialogue between you and the witness. That may eventually result in some information not being communicated to the fact-finder successfully, at best, and in a feeling of hostility towards you (and maybe your client, too), at worst. The North Americans have a saying, 'Keep it simple, stupid' and this sums up (albeit rather brutally) what should be your guiding principle, both here and in other areas.

8.3.4   Labels for people

How should you refer to the other people in court? They fall into five basic categories:

- (a) the tribunal itself;
- (b) your fellow advocates;
- (c) parties to the litigation;
- (d) witnesses;
- (e) everyone else.

8.3.4.1   The tribunal

Novice advocates are told how to address judges in various courts. A High Court judge is always 'My Lord/Lady' or 'Your Lordship/Ladyship'; these are not interchangeable. 'My Lord' is the equivalent of the judge's name (it represents the vocative case), while 'Your Lordship' is simply the equivalent of 'you' (the accusative case). While wishing to adhere to the earlier injunction against using jargon, one must bow to what is standard practice in every court.

Don't use 'you' when speaking to a High Court judge, although I don't think anything adverse would happen if you did say, 'Have you got the Particulars of Claim in front of you?' This sort of innocuous question, incidentally, can cause problems for even the most conscientious novice. The question coalesces in their mind as it appears above. It strikes them as a reasonable question to ask, little danger of it backfiring, so they engage first gear and start to ask it. As they do so, they remember that a High Court judge should be addressed as 'Your Lordship' and not 'you'. The question emerges as 'Has Your Lordship [well done!] got the Particulars of Claim in front of . . .' and then their voice fades as they begin to see where this is leading them. Avoid a surfeit of 'My Lords' and 'Your Lordships'; they are not necessary and can become extremely repetitive. The question would have been perfectly acceptable as 'Has Your Lordship got the Particulars of Claim?' (For further help with addressing judges, see **Chapter 13**.)

Two other possible problem areas are juries and magistrates. Juries can usually be addressed as simply 'members of the jury'. Statements to justices of the peace are usually addressed to the chairperson, who is referred to as 'Sir' or 'Madam'. For a reason obscure to me, it is quite common for police officers and solicitors to address magistrates as 'Your Worships', while barristers rarely if ever use the expression.

8.3.4.2 Fellow advocates

It is usual to refer to a barrister as 'my learned friend' and a solicitor as 'my friend' (in the vocative case), and to use 'him' or 'her', 'his' or 'hers' and 'you' wherever you would normally do so.

8.3.4.3 Parties to the litigation

The parties to the litigation are given titles, separate from their names. So the person who is suing in a civil claim becomes 'the claimant' while the person being sued becomes 'the defendant'. If many people are suing, they are 'the first claimant', 'the second claimant', etc. Typically, they are referred to by these titles, rather than as (say) 'Mrs Freda Barrett', when the advocate is addressing the court, but they are addressed as (say) 'Mrs Barrett' when appearing as a witness.

8.3.4.4 Witnesses

When talking to, or referring to, a witness, you should give them their full and correct title when first addressing them and usually do so thereafter. For example, a witness who, when asked to tell the court his name, replies, 'Eric Barrett', should be referred to subsequently as either 'Eric Barrett' or 'Mr Barrett'. To abbreviate this to 'Barrett' would imply a lack of respect for the witness; that in turn requires an exercise of judgement by you and that is never the function of an advocate.

8.3.4.5 Everyone else

What about everyone else? There aren't too many people left whom you might need to address but people associated with the court will usually be referred to by their job description, as in, for example, 'Usher, could you give this to the witness?'; 'I wonder if the stenographer could read the witness's previous answer to the jury?'; or 'I will hand this letter up to the clerk'.

8.3.5 Appropriate manner

It is sensible to remember that, as an advocate, you are appearing in a court of law and important issues are being decided in the litigation (at least as far as the parties to the matter are concerned). This is not the appropriate place to look in detail at non-verbal language but do note that you need to give the appearance of taking things seriously, and of giving due respect to the court. Furthermore, your ultimate aim as an advocate is to persuade the tribunal to decide in your client's favour; you must appear to have confidence in the merits of your arguments or evidence and you must do nothing that may interfere with your communications with the tribunal.

It follows that:

(a) you will stand up when saying anything in open court, unless it is the practice in that court not to do so;

(b) you will stand up when being spoken to;

(c) you will not put your hands behind your head and lean back in your seat as if to convey an air of innate superiority;

(d) you will not speak to anyone in court with your hands in your pockets;

(e) you will not do anything discourteous at all (such as pick your nose, clean out your fingernails);

(f) when not speaking in court, you should be taking a note of what is being said or done (that should help to occupy your hands);

(g) when speaking in court, you should try not to distract your listeners from your words with any gesture or movement of the hands, unless it has some relevance to your words (so, no fiddling with pens, scratching your nose/ears/neck, stroking your chin, playing with keys, pocket snooker, etc).

8.4   Refer to notes when necessary or desirable

It is a fact that there are some very experienced advocates around who use very detailed plans for their work in court. One example is Brian Leveson, LJ, who as QC was noted by reporters to have used almost a script when appearing for the prosecution in the trial of Rosemary West for murder (in 1995). That is perhaps a good illustration of the truism that what works for one does not necessarily work for all. If you or I tried to work to a script, the effectiveness of our advocacy might well fall sharply. Let us consider the pros and cons.

8.4.1   Pros and cons of a script

First, the pros:

- you have all of your preparation to hand;
- there is little danger of you missing something out if you stick to your script;
- you will deal with topics in the order you intended;
- your delivery is quite likely to be clear and fluent.

What about the cons?

- you will be reading from your script so your delivery may be flat or monotonous;
- because you are reading, you are looking at your notes, not at the judge or jury or magistrates or witness;
- you cannot respond easily or swiftly to questions or other unexpected deviations from your plan because:
  (a) although you may have the answer in your plan, you don't have it in your mind;
  (b) your plan is so full, it is time-consuming to find specific pieces of information within it; and
  (c) you may lose your place in your plan and lose your concentration;

- although you will deal with all of the points that you planned to, others may have arisen in the course of the trial or hearing that you hadn't planned for and those may now be overlooked.

On balance, I think that the evidence is strongly in favour of **not** using a script.

8.4.2   Why you should not use a script

It is quite understandable that, when you are first on your feet as an advocate, one of your main fears is 'drying up', when your mind goes blank and all your careful preparation evaporates into thin air. That has happened to all advocates at one time or another. Another big worry is that you will overlook something important; although you had planned to deal with *argument x,* in all of the cut and thrust somehow you forgot to say it. So people often use plans to guarantee fluency and ensure a thorough coverage of the issues. That is understandable but the disadvantages are so great that very few advocates can overcome them.

Imagine what it is like to be spoken to by someone who never looks at you, indeed who never looks at anything except the pages clutched in his or her hands? Does that person inspire confidence? Do they look as if they have a good understanding of the case, or even their own arguments? Do you believe them? It is true in some cultures that it is considered rude to maintain eye contact and that it is more polite to look down when addressing someone in a position of authority. Plainly, in a multi-cultural society you should be aware of that **but** that will not help you if you do not come from such a culture or, if you do, the people that you are addressing are not aware of your cultural background. As a general rule, in this country many people rely, at least in part, on assessing credibility by measuring eye contact. Expressions such as 'looking shifty' and 'he couldn't even look me in the eye' are indications of the importance that is often attached to eye contact. There is at least a danger that by using a script you will begin to lose some of your credibility.

Imagine someone talking to you about something of interest to both of you. You ask them a question but they don't answer it. You might be puzzled. If it happened again, you might be annoyed. If it keeps happening, and you are a judge, you just might stop listening to what that person has to say—they are not talking to you but at you. The advocate has to be someone who responds to those around him or her. If you have a very short note or plan, that will force you to concentrate on holding all of your arguments in your head. If you know what you want to say but only decide exactly how to say it seconds before you do so, then your words will have a more natural ring to them. If you are watching your judge and see that a certain argument (or even a phrase or word) has the judge nodding in agreement, then you might want to make more use of that argument (or phrase or word) than you had intended originally.

The final nail in the coffin for scripts, I hope, is this. Suppose that you are due to question a witness. It is almost impossible to predict how a witness is going to behave in the witness-box—whether they will be garrulous or monosyllabic, nervous or relaxed, helpful or not—until you actually see them in that box. That is one reason why examination-in-chief is so much harder than cross-examination: you haven't had time to gauge the witness's demeanour and ability to answer questions. In those circumstances, it is really very difficult to plan an exact sequence of questions and stick to them. The planning is easy of course, but witnesses seldom turn out quite the way you planned they would. To use a detailed script here (a bit like the notes of a police interview but with the answers still to be filled in) would almost certainly result in a total loss of flexibility: you would be unable to respond to the witness's last answer by adapting the next question to suit. That must suggest that you are not listening to the witness's answers and, if you appear not to be, why should anyone else?

8.4.3   Why you don't need a script

Remember what I said your two big worries were as a novice advocate? (See **8.4.2**.) The first was drying up and the second was overlooking some topic or argument. It might not seem like it when you are starting out but these are both easily overcome. As for drying up, this is simply a product of your nerves and what you need to do is relax. Your first move is to pause; this is quite natural and no one will suddenly think that you are incompetent and don't deserve to be an advocate. Then take a deep breath or two and try not to think of anything for a second or two, if you can. If that doesn't work and you need longer, ask for it. 'If I might have a minute, Your Honour' is a phrase not unknown to Her Majesty's judiciary. The judge is unlikely to be unsympathetic; after all, it has probably happened to him or her more times than they care to remember.

Once you have relaxed a little, your mind is more likely to recollect what you wanted to say. Suppose that does not happen? Why not say, 'I should like to return to that point a little later, if I might' and move onto your next point? Your next point should not be hard to find, as it is in your plan. Now we come to the second big worry, overlooking something. You should not have a script but you should have some sort of plan; its function is really that of a prompt. It is not there as a substitute for your memory, nor as a comfort blanket whose thickness clearly shows the number of hours' preparation you have put into this case. Your plan needs to be short and the points expressed concisely. A bullet-point format is ideal. If you look down at your plan and see 'Negligence' or 'No serious issue to be tried', for example, that should act as a trigger for your memory and the relevant arguments (or questions) should come to mind. The bonus for you is that, as you carry on with the case, the point that you have dried up on, or forgotten, will often come back and you can deal with it a little later than planned. This is not usually fatal to your chances of success in the action. So be relaxed, have faith in your memory, use bullet points in your plan and you should have few hiccups; those that do afflict you will be less painful.

8.4.4   Using a skeleton argument

If you find that you are to make an application before a court and you are expected to prepare a skeleton argument, the points above may need some modification. First, the skeleton argument is written to support the application and the judge will normally receive and read it in advance of the application hearing. Typically, a copy will also have been supplied to your opponent. In this situation, it makes sense to acknowledge the existence of the skeleton in planning and making your application (or opposing one). A skeleton is not a script and the last thing the judge will want is you simply reading out large excerpts from it (let alone all of it!). Use it sparingly, make occasional references to it and regard it as a resource that allows you to take points more shortly where appropriate to do so. For example:

> Your Honour, clearly I must persuade the court that there is a serious question to be tried. I have addressed that matter in my skeleton at paragraph 4 and, unless Your Honour has any questions, I do not propose to add anything to that.

Persuasion

9.1 Introduction

When we look at persuasion, we begin to explore what lies at the heart of 'advocacy'. Is it a skill, or a knack? Are great advocates born, not made, as some would assert? The *Concise Oxford English Dictionary* defines *persuade* as:

to cause another to believe

to convince

to induce

to lure, attract, entice, etc.

These may (or may not) have been put in descending order but, as advocates, we might try to identify with the first couple of definitions, while hoping to avoid accusations of the latter pair.

When we watch advocates in practice, we often come to a conclusion about an individual's persuasiveness. Perhaps we should try to define in more detail exactly what we mean, in order that we may try to emulate it.

9.2 How do we persuade?

It is beyond the scope of this manual to devote the amount of space to this topic that it deserves. There are other books that concentrate wholly on this topic and you are recommended to go and seek them out. There are a couple of points to use as starters, though.

First, the more that your message is one that the trier(s) of fact can identify with and the more your proposition strikes the listener as just 'common sense', the more likely you are to persuade your audience that what you say is correct (we don't need to start exploring notions of 'truth' or what 'really happened' as we don't really look for these in court).

Second, your message must be memorable. If your judge (or jury or magistrates) cannot recollect your message at the important time, ie when coming to a decision, then you have lost the case. So your presentation of your case must be designed to give the maximum help to your audience to remember your points.

These basic points both refer to your 'message'. What we need to look at are your communication skills, a basic grasp of psychology (or understanding human nature, if you prefer) and a brilliant grasp of the facts of your case. The *Penguin Dictionary of Psychology* defines **persuasion** as 'a process of inducing a person to adopt a particular set of values, beliefs or attitudes'.

It goes on to say that a number of factors are likely to be used in this process, both rational and non-rational, for example, credibility and persuasive communication. Persuasive communication, the dictionary says, consists of both external aspects:

- the message itself;
- the arguments presented;
- the credibility of the source;
- the medium used;

and internal aspects:

- the person's original beliefs;
- the person's credulity.

As to communication skills, the ability to speak clearly and fluently is dealt with elsewhere (in **Chapter 8**) but it is understood that you must possess the ability to articulate at an appropriate pace, with suitable volume. If you are not heard (because you are too loud, too quiet or too fast), the message will not get through. But you need more than the ability to talk; you need a facility for language. Very often, what decides a case is the ability to choose the right phrase, or the best word, for the situation. There may be many ways to describe something or someone—an incident, a document, a witness—and part of being persuasive is the ability to select the description that 'fits' best. That means 'fits' for your listener, not for you. What is important here is getting your message across, communicating with the court. The choice of words or phrases is of great importance to your success as an advocate.

What about understanding human nature? Well, that arises in various ways. For example, judges generally don't like to be lectured about the law. From time to time, you will have a case that requires argument on a point of law, but even then judges don't want a lecture on the history of the legal topic, what they want is help; whatever you say must be of direct and clear relevance to the dispute that the judge has to settle. Similarly, where someone has suffered some type of loss or damage (especially physical injury), any court is likely to have some sympathy for that person and the advocate representing the 'other side' must be sensitive to that. This doesn't mean that if, say, your case is that the 'victim' was in fact 100% contributorily negligent, you shouldn't say so; it does mean that you should appreciate that it may be a difficult message for the court to accept.

Last point, for now—having a brilliant grasp of the facts of your case. It does not matter if by 'facts' we mean the undisputed facts in the case, or a combination of what's not in dispute and your client's version of what is in dispute, you should have a clear understanding of both. Further, as far as it is possible to, you should have a clear understanding of your opponent's case, too. Lord Hewart CJ once said that the advocate must 'claw the facts' and indeed you should work very hard to have the fullest possible understanding of the detail in each case, from the microscopic (eg what the likely answer will be to **this** question) through to the macroscopic (eg which of the possible case theories is the best 'fit' here).

We should not leave this section without observing that you must have a good understanding of the law that is relevant to the case, too. Without it, all the other skills are useless. But gaining that understanding should be relatively straightforward for you; in many cases, you will already possess all the legal knowledge that you need before you receive the case papers. Legal knowledge is something that you can improve every day, with no reference to anything other than statutes, law reports and textbooks. You should of course try to keep abreast of legal developments. What is different about each case and every client is not the relevant law but the facts: the names, dates, places and people. Those are the things that must be learnt, forgotten and then learned afresh with every new case.

9.3   What's your message? Developing a case theory and themes

How do you prepare a case for a hearing in court? First, you sit down and read through the documents; there may be statements of case, statements from witnesses, a proof of evidence from your client and documentary exhibits. Then, you check that your legal knowledge is up to scratch. You consider what else you need to know, or to have available for court, and write an advice on evidence, calling for extra statements, other documents and so forth. You also have a conference with your client; there may be things you need to tell the client, almost certainly questions that you want to ask. Having prepared as thoroughly as you can, you begin to see where you are likely to be at the end of the trial or hearing, what evidence will be before the court, which issues need to be proved and the probable strengths and weaknesses of both your client's case and that of your opponent. What you need to do now is consider your theory of the case.

I say **your** theory, because you will have evolved it but we must be aware of ethical traps here. It is sometimes said that advocacy trainers are good on advocacy skills but worse on ethics. You must not put forward a theory of the case just because it seems to have a good chance of success. It must be supported by the evidence, it must further the objectives of your client and it must not mislead the court. You should always explain your proposed case theory to your client and get their agreement to use it. That is not to say that your case theory must be carved in stone, though. One important thing a novice advocate soon learns is that, when you get into court, things don't always turn out the way you expected them to. As each trial develops, so the way things are seen may change, witnesses become more (or less) credible, an anticipated strong point becomes a weakness; the advocate must respond to these shifts and so must your case theory.

An experienced practitioner at the Old Bailey used to say that he would start several hares running at the beginning of a trial and see which one the dogs chased. It is permissible to have more than one theory of the case, perhaps intended to meet a variety of possible outcomes. What the practitioner meant was that an advocate must retain adaptability until the end of the trial when, finally, any ambiguities must be resolved. He hoped that, when he advanced the case theory in its final form, he chose the one he felt confident would have the most appeal for the jury.

9.3.1   Themes

It is often said by prosecutors that the Crown does not need to show a motive, to explain why the accused committed the crime. There is no crime where the elements of the offence include greed, jealousy, revenge or anger. Nevertheless, when we are asked to determine whether a particular act was done, or a particular state of mind existed, then we automatically seek out clues that make such an act or state of mind more (or less) likely. If we can see a reason (ie motive) for someone saying or doing a particular thing, then we are more likely to find that the person did say or do that thing. Offering a reason is not necessarily conclusive when we have to persuade others, but it certainly helps. Themes are often put forward to enable the trier(s) of fact to assess properly the witnesses they see and hear, the documents they read and the arguments of the advocates. A witness may be accused of lying in court, a proposition easier to believe if there is evidence to show jealousy, say, against the advocate's client.

Suppose you want to say that an apparently credible eyewitness to a road accident is not to be believed. You could just say so but that is not very persuasive. If your theme is that the witness was too far away to have a proper view and is doing her best to help the court (not the party calling her, because we'll run into problems of showing partiality) but is nevertheless wrong, your theme for that witness is that she is honest but mistaken.

Compare, for example, what prosecuting counsel, Timothy Langdale, QC, was reported to have told the jury in opening the Crown's case against Sandra Wignall, charged with the murder of her husband, some 17 months after their marriage. The only elements of the offence that the Crown had to prove were that Sandra Wignall was a party to the unlawful killing of her husband and had an intention either to kill or to cause grievous bodily harm to him. Counsel told the jury (see *The Guardian*, 27 October 1993) that:

> lust and greed were the driving forces behind the murder . . . Sandra Wignall was a woman to whom sex was all-important and although she might fall for a number of men, there was one man who was a special object of desire to her, one man who seemed to have a hold over her so she would do his bidding [one of her co-accused, and her alleged lover, B] . . .

Later on during the trial, the prosecution called a witness, described in reports as a friend and neighbour of the accused woman, who testified that:

> Once she [Sandra Wignall] told me he [B] blindfolded her and tied her to the bed and brought a man in to have sex with her with . . . [B] present.

It is clear that, subject only to some apparent latitude by the court as to the relevance of this information, the prosecution's theme for Sandra Wignall was that she was besotted by her lover and would do anything for him, including playing an intimate part in the murder of her husband. Subsidiary themes that supported the 'rightness' of this theme were that the deceased man had a life insurance policy that would pay Sandra Wignall £21,000 on his death, that B had heavy debts, and that Sandra Wignall had previously discussed selling her house to raise money for him.

9.3.2 Case theory

This should be a short and simple statement that sums up how the issues in the case should be decided, based upon the evidence, and how that results in a verdict favourable to your client. To take the case of Sandra Wignall again, the prosecution's case theory was that the murdered man was taken for a night-time walk in local woods by his wife, that she 'in the hope of lulling him into a false sense of security . . . had gone so far as to perform oral sex upon him as the attackers came upon him' and that he was then set upon and stabbed three times with a knife, twice in the heart, dying before help could reach him. You can see there the essential allegations against Sandra Wignall:

(a) a man was killed (her husband);

(b) unlawfully (stabbed with a knife);

(c) with intention to kill (inferred from her role in the attack).

In a different case, the prosecution in 1994 of Gordon Foxley for corruption, Foxley had been a senior civil servant at the Ministry of Defence (MOD) when he allegedly took 'backhanders' of some £1.5 million from three foreign companies. Prosecuting counsel, Victor Temple, QC, told the jury at Snaresbrook Crown Court that the trial, expected to last two weeks, was almost entirely concerned with documents. You may think that with that amount of documentary evidence, the jury needed a peg to hang the prosecution case on. Counsel gave it to them:

The Crown say this defendant agreed to take a series of substantial backhanders, and in doing so took dishonest advantage of his position, breaching the trust bestowed upon him by his employers.

Again, the essential allegations are clear:

(a) this defendant (Foxley had already been identified as a senior official in the MOD: any person serving under the Crown would be covered by the relevant legislation);

(b) agreed to take (one can commit the offence of corruption by offering or receiving a bribe, in Foxley's case the latter);

(c) a series of substantial backhanders ('any gift or consideration' is what the law requires);

(d) took dishonest advantage of his position (the Crown did not need to show dishonesty, just that Foxley knew the payments were connected with the past or future performance of his duties, as reward or inducement but this is perhaps an example of a theme emerging within the case theory);

(e) breaching the trust bestowed . . . by his employers (again, directed towards showing that Foxley acted corruptly, that is purposefully doing an act that the law forbids as tending to corrupt, accepting any improper or unauthorised gift).

9.4 Delivering the message

The advocate should present himself or herself and their arguments in such a way as to convince the court of their merits. Let's not delude ourselves—sometimes cases are won **despite** the best efforts of the 'winning' advocate, not because of them. But it cannot hurt your client's prospects of success if you appear to be confident and in control. If the court can feel that you are to be trusted, then your credibility is likely to increase. That may help your client. What is confidence? It includes acting naturally (and not sweating unduly, or looking shifty), speaking clearly and naturally (no unnaturally long pauses, no inappropriate language) with variations of tone and pace to maintain interest and emphasise certain points.

The advocate should be seen to have a clear idea of what they are arguing for and to have an understanding of the relative strengths of their possible arguments. Have they sorted the relevant from the irrelevant and then **re-sorted** to refine the available material down to what the court really wants to know about? The effective advocate is the one who does not throw in everything including the kitchen sink but who, having done all the preparatory legwork, is prepared to dump most of it and focus their energies on what lies at the heart of that specific case.

Having identified what the client wants from the proceedings, and compared that with what the court is likely to give, the persuasive advocate thinks about how to 'sell' their arguments to the court, how to make them share what your client wants. In his book on advocacy, *Advocacy in Court*, Keith Evans describes defence counsel in a jury trial as having to 'show the jury the way home', that is how to arrive at the desired outcome by the least painful means. If you have a point that needs making but it is weak, then you should appreciate that and act upon it. Don't pretend it is not a weakness, you will be found out; better to acknowledge it as a weakness (again, you show you can be trusted and are acting practically), then produce a supporting argument to bolster it. If you can do all these things, then you have passed beyond the stage of novice advocate and are on the way to being really effective and persuasive in the courtroom.

9.5 Responding to the judge's interventions

As the use of skeleton arguments becomes more and more widespread in civil hearings, advocates are finding that judges enter the courtroom rather more well informed about the case and the arguments than perhaps they were in the past. Also, with the emphasis given in the Civil Procedure Rules to a proactive judiciary, advocates are finding judges much more interventionist than has traditionally been the case. No longer are judges prepared to sit silently as the advocates present their carefully crafted arguments. Now, judges have read the evidence, they have read the arguments in the skeletons, and they have questions to which they want the answers.

Some people might regard an interventionist judge with trepidation. Won't they ask all sorts of difficult questions? Well, yes, they will, and that should be welcomed with enthusiasm! An enquiring judge is not a problem for the advocate but is of potentially great assistance. No longer need you stand there, arguing away with no clues as to whether you are addressing the judge's concerns until he or she announces the decision. When a judge asks you a question, it usually indicates an issue that is troubling him or her. You now have the opportunity to target your arguments to maximum effect. No need to waste time talking about matters that are already sorted—instead spend your time helping the judge on those topics that are still to be determined. Of course, the potential pitfall for the advocate is that the interventionist judge makes greater demands on the advocate in terms of his or her grasp of the facts of the case and the relevant law. The judge's questions may be on a part of your submission that has not yet been reached— too bad, the judge wants an answer, now! The advocate really must be on top of the case, with excellent preparation skills. This should always have been the aspiration of the advocate, now it is a necessity.

The flexibility that this demands from the advocate is nothing new really. It is surely better to spend five minutes addressing a judge's real concerns than 15 minutes addressing everything that you think might possibly be of concern to the judge. Tackling the real issues and showing how to resolve them in a way that should ensure the success of your application must be what persuasion is all about. The opportunity to engage the court in a dialogue should be seen as a tremendous asset for any advocate. It is only a threat for the uninformed and under-prepared, two things an advocate should never be.

Part III

Preparing for advocacy

Your voice and speech

10.1 Introduction

Elsewhere in this book you will find references to the importance of speaking up, sounding confident and speaking positively, which are all to be encouraged. In this chapter you will find out how to take steps to achieve this as well as how your voice can communicate your thoughts more effectively. This will help your arguments and persuasive submissions to flow more easily. You will also discover that your voice is a primary instrument of your work as an advocate; you will learn how to look after it, support it and enable it to adapt to a variety of circumstances and environments. You are becoming a professional voice user with a vocal responsibility not only to yourself, but to your clients, colleagues, the court and the wider public who will hopefully not even notice your voice, but will be listening with interest to the content and wisdom of your words carried by your voice.

Before you embark upon the voice work contained in this chapter, it is worth making a short recording (about three minutes) of yourself, reading some of your prepared work aloud. Keep this recording and refer to it later, once you feel you have developed your voice somewhat. Re-record the same passage and identify and compare the changes. Later, you could set up a video recording, which will help you assess your body language as well as your vocal tone. You can objectively assess your progress. Your confidence will grow as you discover how you can improve your tone, intonation and clarity through following the guidelines set out in this chapter.

Here you will find a basic explanation of how your voice works and how speech is formed. There are exercises to help you learn how to support your voice, improve your articulation and intonation, enhance your posture and use your breath more effectively, all of which will combine to allow you to be more relaxed, interesting and effective in your speaking role.

By committing yourself to at least 20 minutes of practice a day by following a variety of the exercises described here, you can make a vast and positive difference to your voice by being aware of its possibilities and learning to use your voice with knowledge and respect. It will repay you in turn by helping you to appear stronger, sound more interesting and exude confidence.

10.2 How your voice works

The larynx is where the voice and body meet and where phonation begins. Phonation is the sound of your voice, created by the vocal folds in the larynx, powered by breath from the lungs. The type of sound we create with our voice is directly affected by what shape we are in physically and mentally and can be ameliorated by practice and conscientious application of vocal exercises.

Feelings can affect the quality of phonation through the pitch, volume, pace, clarity and tone of your voice. If you are not in control of your brief, or your case, the tension caused by stress could have a negative impact on your vocal tone, inadvertently damaging communication. Tension can cause a 'tight', disinterested, negative or preoccupied tone, which could misrepresent you as being bored or even contemptuous. Tension and anxiety can also make you speed up the delivery, to the extent that you cannot be understood.

When you are calm and on top of your brief, you are at your most effective. In that prepared state you can make full use of your voice. You will exude confidence and inspire trust. So the first rule is, know your work, and then you can apply yourself to the vocal presentation of it.

Like an athlete warming up before an event, your vocal musculature needs warming up before your performance. Below are important exercises to develop and release your voice. As J. Clifford Turner (*Voice and Speech in the Theatre*) said, 'What passes for an everyday voice will not stand the test of performance.' As an advocate, you are a professional voice user and your voice is being used for performance. This work will take time and commitment.

10.3 Looking after your voice and warming it up

Water Plenty of water should be available to you at all times to sip. The vocal folds and the intricate mechanics of your larynx are made of muscular tissue, which need plenty of lubrication in the form of H2O. Avoid alcohol before important speeches as this can cause dehydration and a dry throat causing your voice to falter.

Warming up your voice This is essential and failure to include this important step can result in voice strain or loss. You can achieve this by humming. Hum in the bathroom, in the street, in the car, for 5–10 minutes.

1. Press your lips lightly together, release your jaw, so the teeth are parted and let your tongue relax at the floor of your mouth, the tip resting behind your lower teeth.

2. Relax your shoulders, breathe in from the bottom of your lungs (so you feel your stomach getting gently pushed forward) and begin the hum on any note, as the air starts moving up and through your larynx and down through your nose.

3. You will feel a 'buzz' of vibration on your lips, behind your nose, in your neck and throat and maybe in your chest particularly on the lower notes.

4. When you have used up a breath, just wait for the next lungful of air to be drawn in and repeat the hum, on a slightly different note.

5. Repeat this for 10–15 breaths, just letting the air come out at its own pace, not pushing or forcing it and keep checking your jaw is relaxed, your tongue is low in the mouth and that your shoulders are also relaxed.

6. On the next breath, keeping everything relaxed and in the same position, try making a sound of approval, for instance when eating your favourite food—'Mmmm' with a higher sound in the middle.

7. Repeat, always waiting for your breath to come in naturally, beginning with a slightly lower note, going higher then lower again. Repeat five or six times.

8. Hum down from a high-ish note to a lower one, keeping everything relaxed. Repeat, beginning with a lower note and humming up to a higher pitch.

This exercise is literally warming up your vocal folds and encouraging your voice to find its way onto your lips, ready for the speech to come out audibly. You can encourage your jaw to release tension and relax during this exercise by gently rubbing the hinge area using small circular motions with your fingertips and stroking the jaw downwards.

Always begin to make your humming sound as soon as your lungs are comfortably full, so the humming sound lasts as long as your out-breath. The lungs will automatically refill as soon as they are empty and this process of linking phonation (voice) to breath is made easier with practice.

9. Next, on the out-breath, turn the 'Mmmm' sound into 'Mum-um-um-um-um . . .' to the end of the breath, keeping the jaw relaxed and away from the top teeth, noticing the vibration still on the lips with the 'Mmmm' part of the word. The sound of your voice is coming out from the front of your face, via the lips and nose, audibly and reaching towards your listeners.

10. Repeat using different notes or patterns up to ten times.

10.4 Breath and breathing

As you breathe in, oxygen fills your lungs and feeds your body, particularly your brain, providing inspiration of thought as you inspire (breathe in). As you exhale, you express yourself through speaking your thoughts thus 'expression' takes place.

Breathing in = inspiration = inspiring thought.

Breathing out = expiration = expression of that thought.

Keep your breath steady and regular, practise breathing down into the bottom of your lungs, as mentioned before. This will have the effect of displacing your stomach a little and you should feel it moving out. Your lower ribs will also be moving outwards, allowing your lungs to expand beneath. Keep the jaw relaxed and relax your shoulders, too. This takes patience and practice to achieve.

Now read your notes or submissions through silently, pausing at each comma—continue on the same out-breath, releasing what is left of the breath at every full stop. Read again, this time aloud, counting 'one, two' in your head when you come to a comma to create a pause and again, let the breath go completely at the end of the sentence. Take a new breath and begin speaking the next sentence as soon as your lungs are full. This will help you to slow down your words, giving you more opportunity for expression and your listener more time to digest the meaning of your words.

Your breath gives you power to speak. It also gives you the option not to speak. It gives you the occasion to pause. Following a significant statement, clause, even word—you can pause. It has the effect of underlining your words, giving the listener a chance to digest the meaning of what you have just described and can create great impact. Not speaking for a moment or two can be highly effective in focusing attention on what you have just said. You can also experiment with pausing just before and just after a key word or phrase to isolate them and thus to highlight their importance. Record a sentence with and without this technique and notice the effect of pausing.

To reap the maximum benefits of breath on your voice, it is essential to develop a good posture and this will be described next.

10.5 Posture and status

Your voice will be more effective with proper skeletal support that is the foundation of good posture. Furthermore, human beings are extremely adept at reading body language. As a professional speaker, your intention is to be listened to and respected, which can all the more easily be attained by transmitting positive messages about your professionalism. Good posture communicates confidence.

Meticulous research into the habits underpinning human posture was conducted by Frederick Alexander (1869–1955) and has been distilled into what is now known as the highly regarded 'Alexander Technique', which is still used extensively in drama schools and the theatre today.

Alexander noticed that the human skeleton naturally supports its weight and carries the body in the most effective way when it is free, released and aligned. He also noticed that the body develops habits which can be detrimental to good speech such as slouching, throwing the head back or overstretching the neck. Consider your spine with its curves supporting your head and protecting the vital organs via the ribs. Your voice will best function if the spine is allowed to be long, with your head balanced centrally above. When standing, allow your weight to be spread equally between your feet, which should be parallel and shoulder width apart. Your shoulders should be relaxed, wide and low. Your head should be up, so your eyes are forward and your chin straight (not tilted up or down). Imagine your head being raised from the crown, being lifted from your shoulders. Overall, your frame should be relaxed. Your voice benefits from the release of unnecessary tension in the body and for more individual help, an Alexander practitioner is recommended.

10.5.1 Standing posture

1. Using a full-length mirror, observe yourself standing in a casual way, as you might do in a coffee shop queue or when speaking with friends.

2. Next, imagine yourself in a courtroom environment, about to deliver an argument and notice any changes to your posture. It should change significantly. Moving from casual to professional, feet shoulder width apart, shoulders wide and low, spine long, head lifting away from your shoulders, your body language should be announcing 'confidence!'.

3. To help your relaxed, aligned posture and release tension, try this exercise: With feet shoulder width apart, squeeze your hands into balls, hunch your shoulders up tight, tense your stomach and tense your knee caps for a count of five. Then release all the tension and breathe out at the same time on a voiced sigh ('huhhh . . .').

4. Repeat twice more, remembering to tighten up all the muscles you can think of for a count of five, before releasing on a relaxed out-breath, 'huhhh...'. Check how you feel now. Then gently lift and rotate your shoulders three times forwards, then three times backwards and again, relax.

5. Notice your shoulders, are they a little lower than before? Are your hands warmer? Are your knees still relaxed with your weight centrally over your feet?

6. Repeat this in the comfort of your own home to develop the habit of a relaxed, aligned body and also in the privacy of a small room in every circumstance before going into a professional speaking situation.

7. You should notice your status rises as your posture moves into the professional stance. You should feel more confident and look the same.

10.5.2 Sitting posture

1. Place yourself in front of a mirror and notice what you look like when in a casual position. It is likely that you have your knees crossed, weight more on one side than the other, rounded spine, head to one side or tilted down.

2. Change your position as follows: Both feet placed on the floor, hip width apart, under your knees. Sit with the bottom of your back at the back of the chair so your lower spine is supported. You may need to have a plinth to support your feet, so your lower legs are at right angles to your thighs. Ensure your chair is close enough to your desk to easily rest your forearms.

3. Relax your shoulders, lengthen your spine and feel the top of your head lifting up from your shoulders. Compare this with your previous posture.

4. Practise changing between the two and notice how much more professional is the second way of sitting. You will also be able to maintain this posture for longer and resist distracting fidgeting activity to get comfortable.

During the rehearsal of your speeches, either standing or seated, keep checking your posture and bring it back to the new, professional stance of being perfectly aligned. It will take time to develop this new habit, it will need to be repeated and encouraged (by simply feeling a sense of achievement in accomplishing it) until it becomes second nature. By moving into your 'ready' position, your body will learn to become 'ready'.

When the body feels confident, when it is supported by good posture, your mind will also feel more confident, mirroring and augmenting your sense of professionalism.

10.6 Articulation

You have now covered the very basics of breathing, supporting your voice, warming it up, standing and sitting in a posture which will both help your voice to work effectively and assist in communicating a professional attitude. Clarity in your speech is vitally important and this is accomplished by your articulators, which shape the basic vowel sounds made by your voice. Your articulators comprise your tongue, teeth, soft palate and your lips. The function of your articulators is to break up your sounds into intelligible chunks that are understood by your listeners. The articulators' role is to create different sounds and to make sense of your voice by creating words. Together the consonants and vowels form intelligent speech. It is vital therefore that your articulation is clear and precise to make you intelligible to others. Mumbling and slurring words is not acceptable under any circumstances and basically will not win you cases, clients or success in the future.

Strength and precision in using your articulators will go a long way towards improving your speech and below are some exercises which will help develop spoken agility and clarity.

10.6.1 Tongue

The tongue is a large, flexible muscle, rooted at the base of the mouth and used to shape many sounds. You will benefit from using a mirror in the following exercises:

1. Drop your jaw away from your face so your mouth is open and let your tongue sit on your lower lip, completely relaxed. Flex the tongue so it becomes round like a sausage and relax to return to its flat state. At first this may be a challenge, but persevere and the muscle will awaken and respond well.

2. With the jaw still relaxed and dropped away from your face, curl the tip of your tongue to precisely touch the centre of the top lip, then touch the tip of the tongue to the centre of the bottom lip. Maintain the distance between the two lips to encourage the tongue to travel and grow in strength and accuracy. Relax your shoulders, keep your head free and centred between your shoulders.

3. Repeat the above exercise, and then move the tip of the tongue to the corner of the right side of the mouth, then to the left, so the tip of the tongue is bending up, down, right, left. Ensure you are very precise with the point of contact. It can help to touch the tip of your tongue with your finger then touch the centre top lip to match the two points of contact then allowing them to locate.

Then move the tongue to make contact *at that exact point* before moving to the next point and so on. Take your time—this is a new exercise and takes time to master.

4. Maintaining the position of the jaw dropped away from the face, put the tip of your tongue in front of your bottom teeth and inside your bottom lip. Move the tip of your tongue around the teeth in a clockwise direction, noticing the texture and shape of the teeth, then move up to the top teeth, all around, down to the bottom teeth and finishing back at the start point. Repeat in the other direction.

5. Repeat the exercise with the tip of the tongue on the lips themselves, clockwise then anticlockwise.

6. Stick your tongue out as far as you can in a straight line and pull back in until it is bunched at the back of the mouth. Keep the jaw dropped away from your face during this exercise.

7. Leave the tip of the tongue resting behind your bottom teeth, low in the mouth. Allow the wide middle of the tongue to come forward (rather like a frog action!) and bring back into the mouth again.

Repeat each of these exercises 5–10 times and *take your time*. Your body will find it new and it is your role to introduce the new demands slowly and build up strength and flexibility over a period of time. Relax your tongue by making a flappy 'blblbl' sound as your flick your tongue out and over your lips.

10.6.2 Lips

Your lips work in conjunction with your teeth and tongue to express your words clearly. They move in all directions, up and down, sideways, in and out, assisted by many facial muscles which grow stronger with exercise. Regularly warming up and strengthening these articulators is essential.

1. Give a wide, expansive smile that includes a sparkle in your eyes. Relax, and then bring the lips together in an exaggerated French-style pout. Pull the lips together so they can hardly be seen, then tuck the lips around the teeth, as though you have no teeth to show. Repeat several times in different combinations.

2. On an out-breath blow the 'Brrrr' sound out through your lips, 'horse lips' as it is sometimes called! It can also sound like an old car puttering along the country lanes. This relaxes the lips, keeps the sound at the front of the mouth while gently continuing to warm up your vocal folds in your larynx.

3. Give a gentle massage around your mouth area, using a light touch with your fingertips.

4. Read a challenging political speech aloud, over-articulating each word, exaggerating all articulator actions. Pause at punctuation and take a full breath with each new sentence.

10.6.3   Soft palate

Here is an opportunity to stretch and yawn which is rarely encouraged in a learning situation. This lifts, stretches and strengthens the muscles of the soft palate. Give an exaggerated yawn, using your voice and being conscious of lifting your soft palate at the back of the mouth. In the mirror, check how it moves up while you make the 'Aahhh' sound of yawning, until there is a large space at the back of the throat.

The front of the soft palate can be felt by the tongue by moving the tongue from the front top centre of the mouth and allowing the tip of the tongue to draw backwards along the hard palate ridge. The next section is the soft palate which culminates in the uvula, the dangly skin that hangs at the back of the throat which rises up as you yawn, or say 'Ah', as at the doctor's. Exercising the soft palate will strengthen your pronunciation and develop muscularity. The soft palate is used in conjunction with the back of the tongue, with consonants such as /k/, /g/ and the 'ing' sound, as well as what is known phonetically as 'dark L' in words such as 'shelf', 'tilt' and 'build'.

Identify and write down words which contain some of these consonants and practise clearly articulating them, being aware of the movement of your soft palate.

10.6.4   Teeth

The teeth are instrumental in forming sounds in partnership with the tongue or the lips. The lips and teeth create /f/ (no voice) and /v/ (voiced). The tongue and teeth create the 'th' (no voice, as in 'thick') and the sound 'th' (using the voice, as in 'those').

10.6.4.1   Practice sentences

1. These three thick things, those three thin things.

2. This, that, these and those; the victorious Colonel capitulated and threw them out.

3. Creaking kettles with thick, cracked, grey, fried goosefat.

4. I submit to his Lordship these final thoughts.

5. Clearly they were singing the praises of three quiet constituents.

6. Commit your thoughts and convince the court they have the convict.

Ensure you *finish the sounds at the ends of your words*. This is essential to carry the meaning clearly to the listener.

Practise re-reading these sentences out loud while over-articulating, really exaggerating your lip and tongue movements. This will strengthen your muscles and help to develop clearer speech.

10.7 Intonation

The tune of your voice plays a very important role in how you communicate with speech. Some British accents naturally use a wide range of 'notes' in everyday language, for example Welsh, while others habitually use a narrower band of variation. Using a wider vocal range of 'notes' adds interest, colour and texture to your words. Listen to BBC Radio 4 news presenters and journalists, they use their voices to emphasise words or phrases, using higher or lower pitch to command the attention of their listeners and to create interest in what they are saying. Increasing the range of your voice means that it will become more interesting and engaging to the listener's ear.

1. Record your voice speaking the following sentence:

'The actions of the council you say are deplorable yet you deliberately refused to cooperate with the third party.'

Punctuation has been purposely omitted in order for you to investigate the possibilities that exist through adding your own pauses where you wish. There are opportunities to add punctuation in several different places which will lend a variety of meanings especially when combined with varying intonation, all conveyed through your voice.

2. First of all speak the sentence as you would normally. Next, begin the sentence with a note slightly higher than one you would normally use and choose a word from the sentence that you wish to emphasise. Make the pitch of your chosen word sound either much higher or lower than the rest of your words in that sentence.

Combine with a pause just before or just after, then both; then listen to your voice recording and review the effect of this tune and pattern of speech.

You can continue with this exercise, with an almost limitless variation of possibilities.

3. Begin speaking the sentence on a low note, continue getting higher until the word, 'deplorable', then allow your voice to gradually lower again. The shape of the vocal journey, if you can imagine it as a drawing is like an inverted 'u' moving from low to high back to low (see Figure 10.1).

Figure 10.1   Shape of the vocal journey—low to high to low

4. Try the opposite of this, beginning with a higher note, working down to a lower note, for example landing on the word, 'deplorable' again, then let your voice move up in pitch until it is roughly where it started. Visually, this looks like a 'u' (see Figure 10.2).

Figure 10.2   Shape of the vocal journey—high to low to high

This pattern lends itself to a questioning tone at the end. Avoid the contemporary habit of 'upspeak', as follows: 'where almost every sentence lifts in pitch to what sounds like a question?' It is not appropriate for the professional speaker to use unless approbation is really required, since it gives the impression of insecurity and lack of knowledge and is irritating to hear.

5. As you gain confidence in moving your voice around, you can experiment with more complex intonation patterns. Again, make 'deplorable' the word where you first change direction of your vocal 'tune' or pitch (see Figure 10.3).

Figure 10.3   Shape of the vocal journey—intonation patterns

Continue recording and listening to your voice patterns and tunes while you make different choices of emphasis with your vocal tune. Actively interrogate what you hear back to determine which are the better choices and the ones you can adopt for your courtroom work. At first it will sound strange and unfamiliar as it will be outside your habitual comfort zone. With practice and familiarity, you will begin to use more of your vocal range and develop your 'tune'. This will enable you to pose questions, make assumptions and transmit confidence from your voice.

10.8 Projection

It is unlikely that early in your career you will be speaking much in the Royal Courts of Justice. However, as a professional speaker your voice needs to be prepared for a variety of environments and able to adjust accordingly. Your breath is the number one support system to your voice, together with water and a thorough knowledge of your subject. Always remember to gently warm up your voice. Below, you will find some exercises designed to help you understand your breath and use it to support your speech. In small rooms with few people you will need less breath inhaled at the beginning of your sentence than you will in a larger room with more people. As you speak, you transmit sound which is dissipated through the room. The sound will be louder if you use more breath to power your words, therefore you will need to take more air into your lungs before you begin to speak each sentence. All this work takes practice, preferably under the guidance of a voice coach. Eventually it will become habitual, and you will no longer consciously have to think about it. Commitment to using these breathing techniques will help you become more proficient and professional in your speech.

1. Breathe in to a (silent) count of two and at the same speed, breathe out while counting aloud to four (about one second per beat).
2. Breathe in to a count of three and count on the out-breath to eight.
3. Repeat, counting in to four and out to ten.
4. Repeat, counting in to two and out to ten.
5. Repeat, counting in to one and out to ten.
6. Repeat, counting in to one and out to 15.

Remember to breathe increasingly deeply into the bottom of your lungs as the sentence becomes longer and more breath is required. Be aware of the lower ribs expanding as the lungs fill, imagining you are inflating a fat tyre around your lower waist as you breathe in. With practice, you will be able to count out for much longer. You can also practise with the following sentence:

7. 'Where are you going in such a hurry?' Extend this phrase, saying lines 1 and 2, then 1, 2 and 3 and so on, until you are speaking this very long phrase on one breath:

   'Where are you going in such a hurry

   this fine Sunday morning

   when the bells are ringing

   the sun is shining

   and everything invites you to take your time

   and stay a short while for a sociable chat . . .'

Repeat the long phrase while you are standing, walking or sitting until you feel comfortable that you are easily supporting your voice with your breath for the duration of the whole phrase. Keep your jaw relaxed, shoulders wide and spine long. Feel the energy of your voice carrying the words out of your mouth.

This exercise demonstrates that with more air in the lungs, you can speak for a longer time. Try the exercise again, using a louder voice just allowing the breath to power your voice and being aware of how the diaphragm (the large muscle situated below the lungs) rises up to expel the air from the lungs. This air is used by the vocal folds to generate the sound. Try humming quietly then more loudly. Try saying 'Er . . .' as a teacher might to get a young class's attention. This loud buzz of resonance with a nice open jaw will carry sound quite a long way. Endeavour to keep that sense of loudness which is *powered by the breath from the diaphragm*. If your throat feels at all sore, stop. Sip water and go back to simply humming to get used to the volume increasing slowly and safely. An important point to mention here is clarity. The stronger your articulators, the more clearly you articulate your words, the more easily you will be understood. Therefore less volume is required.

Noticing your environment is important to help you prepare your voice for speaking. If the room has high ceilings, soft furnishings and many people, you will need to use extra power to project your voice, as it will be lost in the high spaces and absorbed by the room. If the room is large, and has hard surfaces like marble, concrete or plastic, you will need to slow your speech down significantly, in order to avoid 'bounce' where your voice has a slight echo which will overlay your next words and obscure them. Identify the person to whom you are speaking and imagine your voice carrying through the space to them—this will help avoid strain; use your breath to power your voice. In a small room with few people, speak more quietly but clearly and use small hand gestures so as not to overpower the listeners. Ensure you have good eye contact with the person(s) to whom you are speaking.

10.9   De-cluttering your speech

10.9.1   Excessive words

Listening to those around you, you may hear sentences interspersed with superfluous words that at best add little to the sense of the communication and at worse, impede understanding. Words and phrases such as 'like', 'sort of' and 'you know', together with hesitation sounds 'er', 'mm' and 'ah' are commonplace in ordinary speech but cannot be tolerated in performance arenas. Develop an awareness of your own and others' speech patterns as a first step to eliminating clutter or 'noise' which prevents clear understanding.

Instead of feeling pressure to keep speaking whilst you are thinking and struggling to find the correct word or phrase to utter; pause. Simply pause. Draw breath and then speak. This simple action will fulfil many functions. Taking a breath will allow you time to think. It will re-fuel your brain with oxygen, enabling faster thought. It will add gravitas to your last sentence, allowing your listeners time to absorb your words. It will also enable your next sentence to be spoken on a full breath, with all the opportunities for clarity, intonation and emphasis. This sentence can be delivered with a real sense of where it is going, given the benefit of the pause and time for thought.

10.9.2   Fidgeting

You will also observe other 'noise' obscuring the meaning of speech. This is in excessive body movement. Fidgeting, rocking backwards and forwards, making continuous hand gestures and head nodding are all captivating to an audience and will take centre stage and the limelight at the expense of the words of the speaker. If you have long hair, ensure it is tied up away from your face when you are speaking in a professional capacity. Resist any temptation to alter the fit of your clothes or position of your jewellery while you are speaking. If you can record yourself on video, do so. Make a note of any 'filler' words you use and habitual twitches and movements. Endeavour, over the course of the next few recordings, to gradually eliminate excessive movements and use of filler words. It will take time and practice to let go of old habits and to re-wire your brain to develop the new clear speech delivery methods, but it will happen. Give yourself time and opportunity to practise.

10.9.3   Accent

The British accent comprises many regional variations, all of which are valid and represent centuries of social history. The *Oxford English Dictionary* and others, use phonetics to assist pronunciation which is based on Non-Regional English Accent (NREA). This is known as Received Pronunciation (RP) or BBC or Queen's English. As long as your listener can understand you, then accent is **not** important. However, clear speaking, which includes well-articulated words, **is** important—and NREA can facilitate comprehension between people with different accents, which is the main objective of spoken communication.

Those who speak English as a second language can experience difficulty in pronunciation of sounds which do not exist in their own language. If this is the case, the help of a specialist voice coach may be required.

10.10 Confidence

Following all the above guidance will help with the mechanics of professional speaking, however, entering the courtroom can induce a sudden lack of confidence. Familiarity with the procedure eases nerves over time, but to begin with it will help to remind yourself that **you are there for a purpose** and you are **armed with the knowledge** to help your client. In addition to reassuring yourself that you know your work, your breath and posture will help you. Dedicate time and attention to practising your speeches at home several times, before you speak them in public. Words on the page do not always work easily in speech and may need revision. Consider which points you are going to emphasise and how you will do this using pause, intonation or volume.

Release tension: give permission to your shoulders to relax the muscles and drop (they easily rise up and become tense!). Relax your knees and further indulge in tensing and releasing shoulders, neck, jaw and stomach muscles before you begin to speak. This can be conducted inconspicuously before a meeting, presentation or court appearance. Remember to breathe steadily from the bottom of your lungs. If you get confused or lost, ask for a moment and use that time to take a new breath and gather your thoughts.

Whether you are seated or standing, keep your spine long, head lifted away from your shoulders, align your body by having your feet shoulder width apart under your hips (or under your knees if seated), head centred, shoulders relaxed. Be confident in your knowledge and enjoy the experience of speaking. When it is over, take time to reflect on what went well and be encouraged, as well as considering which areas you can improve upon next time. This process of self-evaluation is invaluable.

10.11 Recommended further reading

McCallion, M. *The Voice Book*, Faber & Faber, 1998.
Sharpe, E. and Haydn Rowles, J. *How to do Standard English Accents*, Oberon Books, 2012.
Houseman, B. *Finding your Voice*, Nick Hern Books, 2010.
Berry, C. *Your Voice and How to Use it*, Virgin Books, 2000.
MacDonald, G. *The Complete Alexander Technique*, Element Books, 1998.
Turner, J. C. *Voice and Speech in the Theatre*, Methuen Drama, 2007.

Memory and recall

11.1 Introduction

In **Chapter 2** the point was made that the able barrister has a wide variety of skills, several of which may need to be deployed at any one time. Some of these can be honed to your advantage so that they become almost second nature. One example is the ability to take accurate notes swiftly. Another is the ability to remember in a trial what a witness said five minutes/hours/days before.

It is of vital importance that the barrister can recall what a witness actually said in his or her testimony. An accurate note will help but, sometimes, you may not have the time to find your note. Also, in a trial you may be faced with a question like: 'Isn't there an authority on this point? A recent decision of the Court of Appeal?' It will be to your advantage to show that you are knowledgeable on current law but you cannot carry around an entire library. You have to rely on your memory.

This chapter contains some ideas on how you might improve your memory and recall, while **Chapter 12** has some tips on note-taking and shorthand.

11.2 Memory and recall techniques

You need to remember what you hear so that you can ask further questions in examination-in-chief, ask the right questions in cross-examination and re-examination, and, if you are making a closing speech, so you can emphasise those aspects of the oral evidence that support your theory of the case. Developing a good aural memory requires practice.

What can you do to help you remember what you hear? The following techniques can improve your ability to recall oral communications accurately.

Try to understand what you hear. Process the information you hear as you hear it. One of the problems that arises in processing the information as you hear it is that you may let your mind wander away from the speaker when the speaker is between words. This happens because you can think faster than anyone can speak and you will have processed the information as soon as, or even before, the last word is spoken. The pause in the speaker's communication to you then gives your mind time to dwell on other things that can interfere with the processing of the next piece of information. Try to keep your mind fully on the speaker even when the speaker pauses for thought. One way of maintaining your concentration is to predict what the speaker will say next and record mentally when you are correct and when you are wrong.

Trace the development of the ideas being communicated. Concentrate your attention and interest continuously on the speaker and what he or she is saying. Mentally repeat or summarise key ideas or statements, or associate related ideas as they are being communicated. Always remember that you can get the witness to summarise what he or she has said or to repeat what has been said. If possible, and a 'must' when you are cross-examining, take notes of the key ideas or facts. But do not take extensive notes as this will divert your attention away from what has been said. In the context of the cut and thrust of advocacy, you may not have time to refer to your notes of what the witness has said before you need to retrieve the information to use in examining another witness or in your closing speech.

11.3   Memory and recall exercises

The following exercises contain a number of passages taken from *Total Recall: Successfully Boost Your Memory Power* by J. Minninger, Thorsens, 1987, pp 206–9. Ask a colleague to read one to you and then see if you can list accurately the main points of the passage.

11.3.1   Exercise 1

Your wife or husband says:

We have a lot to do before the party tonight. I don't know if we have enough glasses. Could you call your brother, George, and ask him to bring ice when he comes if he's coming before 7.00. If he won't get here until later, ask Harriet to pick it up on her way home from work. The tablecloths are still in the dryer, and the folding chairs have to be brought up from the basement. I suppose George can do that if he comes early. I don't know if we have enough glasses. I better go get those tablecloths out of the dryer before they get wrinkled. Do you think your brother and Harriet will hit it off?

You have a lot of extraneous information. Your goals here are to decide what you were being asked to do and arrange them in proper sequence. Here's what you should have 'heard':

Call George and see if he is coming before 7.00 pm.

If yes:	(a)	Ask him to bring ice.
	(b)	Tell your wife he will be early, so he will bring the ice and can help carry the chairs up from the basement.
If no:	(a)	Call Harriet and ask her to buy ice on her way home from work.
	(b)	Tell your wife that Harriet is bringing the ice, and you will have to carry the chairs up from the basement.
Optional:		Count the glasses.

11.3.2   Exercise 2

That was a typical family situation. Now try one that you may have run into in your business life. Your boss, Mr Fickle, also likes to 'think out loud'. Mr Fickle says:

I need some cigarettes from the drugstore downstairs. Get me a pack of Camel Lights and charge it to my wife's account. Try to get Steve to take care of you because the older guy may give you a hard time. Before you go down, take this report to Mr Samson on the 13th floor in the annex and give it to his secretary. If she's not there, get somebody to sign for it. Last month some jerk lost the report and I got my ear bent. Make two Xeroxes of it just to be safe. One of those copies has to go to headquarters today, so drop it off at shipping, but tell them to send it second class. Mr Samson says we're spending too much on postage, so if it takes longer to get there, that's his sweet problem. Do you think something's wrong in his department? He's been crabby as the devil lately.

This was a hard one, but typical of many busy offices. Most of what was said were instructions, spoken and implied, but they certainly were not in order. You might even have had to grab a pencil and write down what was wanted to be sure you got it all. Here's what you were being asked to do.

(a) Address an envelope to headquarters (implied).

(b) Make two photocopies of the report. Place one copy in the envelope you just addressed.

(c) Deliver the original report to Mr Samson's secretary on the 13th floor in the annex. If she is not there, leave the report with someone else and get a signed receipt.

(d) Deliver the 'headquarters' envelope containing the photocopied report to shipping and ask them to send it second class.

(e) Buy a pack of Camel Lights at the drugstore and charge them to Mrs Fickle's account. Try to be waited on by the younger assistant.

(f) File the second photocopy of the report as a backup, in case one of the other copies is lost (implied).

11.3.3   Exercise 3

Remember that the skills acquired in one context will serve you equally well in another. Getting instructions from a teacher, colleague or sales assistant can be tricky. See how much of the following you actually need to remember, and try to organise it into a sequence.

The paint store sales assistant says:

Put the stain on with a soft brush and really rub it in. If you try to put it on too thickly, the surface will dry while the underneath part is still wet. Then you'll get a rippled surface because the hard top skates over the wet bottom. Did I tell you that you have to mix it well before you start? Don't use your best screwdriver. The lighter colours really look good in this finish, but I think the dark colour you've chosen will be OK. You have to seal it afterwards with two or three coats of polyurethane varnish, otherwise the rain will soak in and warp the wood. Oh, but you're using it inside, so that's not a problem, but be sure you clean the wood first to free it of dust and dirt.

You had to discard some of the information you got here. If you put the remainder in a working sequence, it should come out like this:

(a) Clean the wood first.

(b) Stir the stain if necessary.

(c) Rub the stain into the wood thoroughly with a soft brush.

(d) The sales assistant doesn't like dark stains.

As the exercises illustrate, an excellent means of ensuring that you remember things is to start by analysing and reorganising the information you need to remember.

There are many books that describe such techniques, including: Tony Buzan *Use Your Memory*, BBC Publications, 2006; Joan Minninger *Total Recall: How to Maximize Your Memory Power*, MJF Books, 1997; Peter Russell *The Brain Book*, E P Dutton, 1984.

11.4   Witnesses and the court

The exercises in **11.3** were designed to start you thinking about exactly how adequate your memory is and how you might set about improving it, as you almost certainly need to do. As advocates, though, we also rely on other people's memory skills.

11.4.1   Witnesses

If a witness cannot recall the events, words or documents that led to their being called as a witness, then it may be that some vital information is being lost to the court. While one might expect a witness who is being cross-examined to suffer a little from problems of memory, the same should not normally be said of a witness during their examination-in-chief. However, problems certainly do arise in-chief and one of the main causes is the requirement that you do not ask leading questions of your own witness. That is, you cannot ask the witness questions that suggest the desired answer to the witness. This frequently produces very open questions such as:

'What happened next?' or
'Did anything else happen?' or (just about the worst question you could ask)
'Is there anything else that you would like to say to the court?'

While the advocate who asks questions like these cannot be guilty of suggesting the desired answer to the witness, they are certainly not providing much help to them either. Let us suppose that a witness has already told us part of what they remember of an incident. You might ask a 'What happened next?' question but it does not specifically take the witness to that part of their story that you want them to talk about now. So, since the testimony of the witness might be compared to a spool of audio tape (or video film) gradually unwinding from their memory, you could offer some sort of marker to let them know where on the tape you want them to go. How about:

You have told the court that the claimant's car swerved across the road and onto the opposite carriageway. What happened next?

Now the witness has an idea of where you want him or her to take up the story, although still you have not indicated a particular incident or topic to him or her. If the witness is still stuck for an answer, you might then try (assuming it is not in dispute):

Were there any cars travelling along the road in the opposite direction from the claimant's car?

If you particularly want the witness to continue to talk about the claimant's car, you could ask:

Once the claimant's car crossed to the opposite carriageway, could you still see it?

Let's assume the witness answers 'Yes'; she now should have in her mind's eye that car on the wrong side of the road. So you might risk:

Q. Did you see what happened to the claimant's car then?
A. Oh yes, a white van drove into it and pushed it off the road completely.

Now the incident has come back to life for the witness and you should be able to get them talking more fluently. Witnesses' memories are like anyone else's, they sometimes need a bit of prodding to get them working and, like everyone else, they are more likely to respond to questions that give little bits of (non-contentious) information and start them visualising the incident at a particular point in what they saw or heard.

11.4.2   Judges, juries and magistrates

If the people who have to find the facts cannot recall your arguments or the important pieces of evidence when the time comes for their adjudication, you are in trouble (and so is your client). As with witnesses, the court will remember something best if they can visualise it. It is obviously more difficult for the court to do this than it was for the witness since the court may be unfamiliar with the scene, for example, and anyway the judge wasn't there when the incident happened and engraved itself on the witness's mind. This is an acid test of your skills as an advocate because you must bring the incidents to life for the court: not for nothing do we say that part of the function of an opening speech is to 'set the scene'. The better the court can get inside the head of the witnesses and almost see through their eyes, hear through their ears, the better your chance that the court will remember the evidence. Witnesses who are allowed the freedom to tell their own story are much more memorable than one who just has to answer 'Yes' or 'No' to a series of questions. Witnesses whose testimony is largely uninterrupted (or whose answers are not cut off by the advocate) are likely to be more clearly recollected later by the court, as well as probably seeming more credible. In your speeches or submissions to the court, try to concentrate on your strongest points: first, there won't be too many, which always makes things easier to remember; and second, you can get away with repeating yourself on a couple of points but not on a dozen. Repetition, whether of a word or phrase, or a verbal snapshot of a moment during an incident, always helps people to remember. If the court can remember your arguments, then you stand a chance of succeeding in the case; if it can't remember them, you have wasted your time and your client's money.

Note-taking

12.1 Note-taking in practice

One might assume that the work of a barrister is primarily about speaking, or about writing formal documents such as statements of case. Note-taking might seem to be a lesser skill of limited importance within the profession. In fact, as you move rapidly from one case to another, need to find a case you read some weeks ago within seconds, or need to recall exactly what a witness or judge said, you will quickly realise that high quality note-taking is a key professional skill. One might also assume that with the growing use of technology, the wider range of options for recording information would make traditional note-taking less important, but in practice electronic courtrooms are developing slowly. A note may be taken on an electronic notepad, but the underlying skill of note-taking remains an important part of professional information management.

Do not assume that your existing ability to take notes in a lecture will do. You now need to be able to take notes that meet much more demanding criteria:

(a) Are your notes always well structured so that you can find key points quickly?

(b) Are you able to identify what should go in the notes and what is not needed? Do you know when you do and do not need precise words?

(c) Are you good at noting references to other sources, so that you can use notes to find details and cases in other sources?

In the past, weak note-taking was usually no more than irritating, but as a professional barrister there is far more at stake. If your skills in taking notes are not good enough, the result may be that you fail to remember an important point that a client has told you, that you spend extra hours in a library because you cannot remember where you found a quote from a case, or that you do not have a sound basis on which to make a closing speech or an effective cross-examination.

From now on bad notes will cost time and money, and will have a real impact on how good a job you do for the client. In going into a profession where the accurate and efficient use of words is vital, you cannot afford to make do with inadequate notes.

Recall problems that you have had with notes you have taken in the past. Look back at notes you took as a student and examine them critically. Try to identify what the weaknesses were and start working on them **now**!

Even if your existing note-taking techniques are not too bad, they could still be more polished. In any event, you will still need to adapt your note-taking abilities for practice. In the past, you could always miss out bits if the lecturer was going too fast, but you are not going to be able to do that when a judge is giving judgment—you have to get it all and you have to get it right first time!

The rest of this chapter on notes is for guidance. It outlines where note-taking is important. It provides suggestions on how you might develop your skills. There are also some comments on how basic note-taking skills can and should be adapted for different purposes.

12.2   Essentials of good notes

The following checklist has some obvious ingredients, but it should be useful for reviewing how good your note-taking is, and may suggest some points on which you could work. A good set of notes needs to have:

(a) *Reasonable legibility*   It should be possible for you or someone else to read notes, even if taken at speed.

(b) *Good organisation*   You must be able to find something in a set of notes quickly. Points might be dealt with in groups or highlighted.

(c) *Clear layout*   Subheadings, under-linings, indentations, etc for easy reference.

(d) *Comprehensive coverage*   Every important point must be included. It is more important to get the sense and the understanding than to get every word down.

(e) *Selectivity*   You cannot write down everything, you must get down what matters without wasting space on what does not. If the exact wording does matter, it must be recorded.

(f) *Abbreviation*   To be able to get words down fast when necessary some form of coherent abbreviation, shorthand or speedwriting technique is essential. (See **12.9**.)

12.3   Research notes

You are probably already familiar with making notes of research. Anyone contemplating a career in the law needs to build a skill in taking notes from statutes and cases. In practice you will frequently need to identify the law in an area you are unfamiliar with, or the detailed and up-to-date law on a specific point. You are also likely to need to take notes from a variety of sources in order to build up a complete picture of the law, which adds to the complexity of the task.

Part of the skill of research is finding the best sources and knowing how to read them to extract the points that are most relevant, following a research trail. This is dealt with in the ***Opinion Writing and Case Preparation*** manual. Keeping coherent and comprehensive notes of your research is very important. When you are immersed in the research process it is easy to think that you only need to jot down a few key references and you will easily be able to find things again. In fact the moment you have finished the research you will move onto some other task, or go and do something completely different, and in very little time you are likely to find that you have forgotten quite a lot of what you found out, and that it is difficult to find the material again without spending almost as much time as you did doing the original research.

The reasons why good notes are an essential part of effective legal research and effective legal practice are:

• Legal research is often a task in itself, as you may be asked to do legal research for a pupil supervisor or an employer.

• It is very useful to keep a detailed note of your research with a brief for future reference so that no part of what you have already done needs to be repeated.

- You may need to do further research on a specific point in the light of further information from a client and it is useful to be able to go straight to the right source.

- You need a full list of sources for reference in an opinion or in advocacy.

Good legal research notes are not restricted to a list of sources, cases and statutory sections. You need to build the skill to write down exactly what is most useful, and know what level of detail will best serve a purpose. While it is not essential, there is merit in recording your notes in the form of a research trail rather than just noting what you have found. Research needs to follow a trail anyway as you look up key words and move to footnotes, cross-references and go from source to source. Briefly noting the trail can be very helpful in finding something again, and in reminding you what sources you used. There is more material on this in the ***Opinion Writing and Case Preparation*** manual.

12.3.1   Vital points in taking notes of research

(a) *Be systematic*   Never retain a point you have researched in your head or put it on whatever paper or electronic device is handy. Boring though it may be, all research should be systematically recorded.

(b) *Always keep clear references*   When researching an area of law in a textbook or in *Halsbury*, always make sure that you clearly note which book you are using and which page of the book the note comes from. When researching a case, make sure you write the name of the case and the reference at the top of the note accurately. It may be useful to quote references to the solicitor so that he or she can look the point up. If you are researching electronically, keep a precise note of the web page, not just the website.

(c) *Make full notes from each source*   Make sure you note all cases, statutes, etc that are mentioned in one source that will need to be followed up in another. If part of a judgment is particularly important, make sure you note down which judge gave the judgment and the page number of any quotation. In researching a statute, make sure you note the section and subsection exactly, and note whether you have written down the exact words of the statute or just a summary.

(d) *Note all points, not just those in your favour*   Always note points against you. Although you may not want to use them you must be prepared to meet them, and you must not mislead the court as to the effect of an authority.

(e) *Anticipate the future use of sources you research*   Make a clear note of which authorities you may actually wish to refer to in court. In some cases, as in magistrates' courts, or to support a skeleton argument, it may be necessary to have photocopies of an authority that you wish to refer to if it is not likely to be easily available at the court.

(f) *Make careful use of photocopies and saving material*   Photocopying sources is a useful way of gathering research material. If you take copies or a printout, ensure each is clearly labelled with the case to which it is relevant. Never assume that you have researched a topic simply because you have taken a photocopy of a relevant page and put it in the file—you must read it! If you save materials electronically, make sure you use a sensible and clear file structure.

(g) *Make up clear and coherent summaries*   In a complex case, research notes may need to be copied out more coherently for use. Making notes in a way you can easily word process may assist.

(h) *Always keep notes of research*   Never throw your research notes away. The case may come back or a similar case may come in. Do not send the notes back to the solicitor with the brief or they may get lost.

One way of keeping notes efficiently is always to take notes of research in the same notebook, starting a new page for each case you research and heading it clearly. Storing notes online can work well, but make sure you store notes systematically and choose file names with care.

Your notes of research should be good enough to be worth keeping. Good research notes ultimately save time and can become not only a resource but also a source of confidence and strength in constructing a case.

12.4   Notes made in preparing a case

Methods of information management in the preparation and presentation of a case are fully dealt with in the appropriate chapter of the ***Opinion Writing and Case Preparation*** manual. Only a few points are emphasised here. There is a tendency in preparing a case simply to make rough notes while working quickly and then throw them away. In fact good case preparation notes can be an important resource for a practitioner, and provide a sound basis for preparing each subsequent stage of a case.

Having said this, the first notes made on reading a brief or on reading a document may well only be of temporary use—they are simply first impressions of what is relevant. However, making notes that set up a full chronology, and grouping key information on parties and core events can provide a strong basis for getting to grips with a case again quickly when the case comes back for further consideration. Again attention to headings and storing will enable quick retrieval.

12.4.1   Vital points in taking notes in preparing a case

(a) *Prepare brief and clear notes on each aspect of the case*   Each aspect of a case should be summarised for easy reference. For example, most cases would need the following: a full chronology, a list of dramatis personae, lists of events, lists of documents, lists of evidence available and evidence required, etc.

(b) *Take care with layout*   A good layout will enable you to find a point quickly, and sooner or later you will appreciate how important that can be in court!

(c) *Appreciate the importance of good notes as a basis for a case*   Clear notes are the basis of the good and confident presentation of a case, in terms of advocacy and of writing and drafting. You must have a case at your fingertips if you are to present it clearly and coherently, and clear concise summary notes will be the best basis for this.

(d) *Appreciate the extent to which good notes save time and money*   Making good notes on all aspects of the case will save having to duplicate work on a brief when points have been forgotten.

(e) *Appreciate the extent to which good notes clarify thinking*   The more complex a case, the more difficult it is to get on top of it. Making good sets of notes about a case helps to bring it into focus.

(f) *Always keep a full set of notes*   As with legal research, it is important to put one's notes on a case together in a coherent and legible form, and to keep them for future reference. Many barristers will now store online key notes as well as documents such as opinions.

12.5   Notes made in preparation for writing

If you make good notes in the course of preparing a case, the thorough understanding gained will give you the soundest possible basis for clear writing. If you have good preparation notes, you do not need to rifle through the papers continually while you are writing an opinion or preparing a draft. If you have good notes of all the basic detail, there is much less chance that there will be errors in your writing, and the focus required for good notes will help you with analysis and structure. Good notes will save time where they can provide material to word process into the framework of a draft or opinion.

12.5.1   Vital points in making notes prior to writing an opinion or draft

(a) *Appreciate the importance of notes in ensuring clarity and coherence*   By making notes you can check that you have identified everything that should be included in the opinion or the draft.

(b) *Appreciate the importance of notes in providing a clear structure*   Making notes can help to give the clarity of structure that is vital, and should avoid the waste of time that often occurs if you start writing and then suddenly realise that you have left something out or failed to deal with it in the right place. Good notes should give you a framework for order of paragraphs and the proposed contents of each.

(c) *Appreciate the importance of notes for accuracy*   It is vital that an opinion or draft is completely accurate, or it will at least create a bad impression, and may weaken a case. Good notes should provide an easy source of reference to ensure accuracy.

12.6   Interview notes

There are particular difficulties in taking notes of an interview or conference, and yet such notes are important as they may be the only record of key details. The requirements of note-taking during an interview are rather different from those of taking notes from research or for written documents, and also more challenging. It is important that note-taking supports the interview rather than making it more difficult, the problem being that you must concentrate primarily on the client rather than on the notes.

(a) Take care to balance good note-taking with your focus on questions and answers.

(b) In making notes, you may look down quite often, losing eye contact with the client. Take care the client does not feel less involved and less communicative.

(c) In making notes, don't miss visual signs of how the client is reacting.

(d) You cannot write down everything, and must make instantaneous decisions about what is important enough to write down.

(e) In writing down one point, take care not to miss what is said next.

(f) Sometimes there will be physical difficulties in taking notes, for example when you talk to the client outside court and there is not even anywhere to sit down, let alone a table to lean on. The difficult circumstances do not make the notes any less important!

(g) The points that need noting will not necessarily come out in the right order, or with the right degree of emphasis.

(h) There is only one chance to take notes. Although you can to some extent go over notes to check that they are correct, there is only a limited extent to which this can be done without undermining the client's confidence.

Because of some of the difficulties of taking notes during interviews, there is a tendency to try to find alternatives, but the drawbacks of potential alternatives must be appreciated.

Recording an interview might appear relatively simple and avoid the need to take notes, but this can have drawbacks. You cannot refer back to points easily—it may be difficult to find the right point in the recording. If you later want the interview in written form then the whole recording must be typed out, which takes time and will produce a long manuscript that will take some time to read, especially if the client is verbose or wandering. If you do record an interview, you should get the permission of those present.

You can get someone else to take the note. A barrister taking a conference will often ask a solicitor or a pupil to take a note. This may well be a good decision as it leaves the barrister free to deal with the client, but the main drawback is that the resulting notes may fail to contain some items that the barrister needs. If someone else is to take the note, it should be made clear what points they should concentrate on, what form the notes should take, and so on.

12.6.1   Vital points in taking notes of an interview

(a) *Use a framework for the notes*   It may well be possible to have a framework in mind for the interview before it starts. This can provide a basic framework for the notes.

(b) *Decide who will take the note*   If a solicitor, a barrister and possibly a pupil or a trainee are at a conference, they do not all need to take a full note. Whenever there is a choice, it should be made clear who will take the full note. The barrister taking the conference may well still wish to take a few notes of particular points personally.

(c) *Have proper materials ready for taking notes*   This is easy enough in chambers, but may be more problematic if the interview is in a cell or a corridor. A proper notebook, paper with something to lean on, or suitable electronic device should be carried.

(d) *Keep a relationship with the client*   Try to avoid taking notes at the very start of the interview. It is important to establish a relationship with the client before starting to take notes, and to maintain it while taking notes. Explain to the client what you are taking notes of and why, and ask the client to pause while you write something down. However important the notes are, the client is more important.

(e) *Make selective notes*   You cannot write down everything the client says. You must be intelligently selective. Try to note the main issues briefly and clearly. It may help structure to make notes on the main points with large gaps that you can then fill in later in the interview, especially if you are using an electronic device. Beware the generalised summary where detail is required.

(f) *Note appropriate details*   Do not try to write down too much. Descriptions or figures can often be recorded with few words. If the actual words said matter, do make sure you get them down.

(g) *Make notes at the right time*   Try to judge when to write things down. It may not help if you take notes while a client is dealing with something he or she finds painful to deal with—knowing that everything is being taken down may discourage the client from speaking at all.

(h) *Check the notes before the interview ends*   Check your notes with the client before the interview ends. This will not involve pedantically running through every point, but summarising issues and checking details to ensure the notes are accurate.

(i) *Check the notes after the interview*   Try to reread your notes of the interview as soon as possible after it takes place to ensure that they are comprehensible and include all the relevant information. At that stage you may still remember enough of the interview to be able to make corrections—later you will not!

(j) *Keep a proper copy of the notes*   Do not leave the notes of an interview on odd pieces of paper, or in a relatively random file. If necessary, make a copy of the notes with everything set out clearly and in a suitable order. When you are preparing for trial, a note of an early interview can help to recall the details of the case that might otherwise be forgotten. Also keep a note of advice given—you may need to refer back to it later.

12.7 Notes in court

Taking notes during a court case may sound strange—the barrister is in court to talk, not to write. But there are various aspects of the case that will need recording for different purposes, and good advocacy is based on proper preparation and good notes.

Although some barristers make full notes for what they will say in court, it is generally better for good advocacy to make brief bullet point notes to which you can refer quickly and easily just to remind yourself what comes next. You should know your case well enough for this to be sufficient, and the advocate who is always shuffling papers or who appears to be just reading out notes will rarely look or sound convincing. You can also miss a lot if you are looking at papers rather than at people in court. Only a framework and the most important questions should generally be noted in advance. (See, eg, **21.2.2**.)

12.7.1 Opening speech

An opening speech will often be based on key point notes.

There are some special techniques for taking these notes.

(a) An appropriate order is vital. Perhaps consider including key opening points and key concluding points. It can also help to give the judge at the start a brief summary of the areas you will cover.

(b) Make the notes big and clear for easy use.

(c) Some form of highlighting may be used so that the notes can be glanced at quickly. You should know the case well enough for that glance to be sufficient.

(d) The points that must be made must be clearly emphasised so that none are forgotten.

(e) The notes can usefully include annotation on when to refer to your skeleton, the White Book, Archbold, etc as relevant so you make coherent use of sources.

12.7.2   Dealing with witnesses

Examination-in-chief   A witness statement will often stand as evidence-in-chief. Where it does, you only need to note any points on which you want to ask leave to add oral evidence. If the witness is to give detailed evidence, there are two basic approaches that tend to be taken by student barristers preparing an examination-in-chief. The first is to write out every question fully, and the second is simply to use the witness's witness statement without making notes. Both approaches have significant weaknesses. If you write out every question, or just follow an existing document, you will soon encounter the difficulty of not getting the answer you expect and not knowing how to proceed, or you will ask your next question rather than reacting properly to the witness's answer.

So an examination-in-chief should be based on notes properly prepared expressly for the purpose:

(a) Identify the areas on which the witness should be questioned and put them in a suitable order. These may be areas only where there is additional information to cover.

(b) Each of these areas and each change of issue should be emphasised in the notes to be easily followed.

(c) Identify the basic point of each question you consider asking and include that in the notes, but do not write out whole questions unless there are particular points where the exact wording is vital. If you read out questions the evidence may be much less convincing.

(d) You might annotate the notes with points about how to ask a question or what you are really trying to achieve by asking it.

(e) Always be ready to depart from your notes if reality requires it!

Cross-examination   There are two fairly common approaches to learning cross-examination. One is to write out long lists of hostile questions and the other is to lack focus and achieve little! In fact for the vast majority of people a good cross-examination is again most likely to be based on good notes.

In preparing notes for a cross-examination:

(a) List all the points that you need to put to the witness, either because they undermine the witness's testimony or because they are part of your own case.

(b) Put these points into a suitable order.

(c) With a clear focus on what you would like to get the witness to say or admit, note ideas for questions under each point.

(d) For cross-examination there may be some point in writing out whole questions, as there is more importance in the exact form of the question to make the point you want.

(e) Consider including in the notes some indication of how hard to push a point, depending on how im-portant it is to your case.

(f) Review your notes in detail during the examination-in-chief, being ready to add to them, delete from them or reorder them to most effect.

(g) Make sure your notes are clear enough for easy reference. For effective cross-examination it is especially important that you do not constantly refer to your notes. To be effective your concentration must be on the witness, not on a piece of paper.

(h) It is particularly important to be prepared to depart from your notes when the reaction of a witness demands it, but beware of being lured into a departure that may do your case harm!

Taking notes of what witnesses say   As well as making notes for questions to ask witnesses, it is also important to take notes of what a witness says. With any luck there will be important material to use with a later witness and/or in your summing-up. Do not just listen to what the witness says and hope you will remember—note what helps your case. You need to become adept at compressing a question and answer to note down what you need, and sometimes it is useful to note down verbatim what a witness says.

There are various purposes for which you may wish to take notes of what a witness says. While a witness is giving evidence-in-chief you may need to note a point where a witness says something that did not appear in any written statement, or where some point can be made about the exact words that a witness uses. During a cross-examination you may need to note what the witness says for re-examination or for your closing speech.

12.7.3 Closing speech

Basic notes for a closing speech will often be made while you are preparing the case for court—you can note what the main lines of argument and the main strengths of the case are, and organise a suitable order for dealing with them. Some notes must be made in advance as you will often have limited opportunity to work on your closing speech while the case is in progress, especially early in practice. Notes for what you want to be able to say in your closing speech will often form the basis for questions to witnesses. Notes for your closing speech will need to be reviewed during the case, in the light of arguments made by the other side and the evidence that is produced, as you continually review how you can present your case to best effect.

Some people say that good advocacy stems from a good closing speech—you decide what you will say and everything else is then constructed to build up to it. This emphasises the importance of coherent and detailed case planning.

12.7.4 Summing-up

While it is not necessary to take full notes of the summing-up by the judge in a criminal case, you should be ready to take notes of important points, not least because you may wish to refer to what the judge said on an appeal. While it may be possible to get transcripts from court, this will take time, and it can be valuable to have your own note to work with. On drafting grounds of appeal based on a summing-up, see the *Drafting* manual.

12.7.5 Judgment

Judgments are written out, and in some courts are recorded, so why should a barrister need to write them down personally? You only need to know if you won or lost, how much, and what is to happen about costs.

This reaction is to some extent true. You do not need notes of a whole judgment. But you frequently need some notes from a judgment, for example:

(a) to explain the details of a judgment to the client;

(b) to decide whether to appeal;

(c) to decide on what basis to appeal, if some grounds turn on precisely what the judge said.

Even when transcripts of judgments are available they take time and cost money, so you may well need a sufficient note on which to give immediate basic advice and take decisions. Notes may also be important for drafting grounds of appeal.

12.8 Note-taking in other contexts

The note-taking skills described in this chapter may be applied to other aspects of the lawyer's work. There is, for example, the need to take notes in carrying out a negotiation. It is important to make notes in advance of what your options are, what is the most and least you might achieve and so on. You also need to take notes during the negotiation, of anything that the other side reveals and of anything that is agreed.

There is also the need to take a proper note of a telephone conversation. It is increasingly common for barristers to give advice over the telephone, and it is necessary to have a clear written note of the key points made for the case file. When advising by telephone, or simply using the telephone to get further information, taking a full and clear written note is important.

Finally, there are two particularly important possibilities for the young barrister. First, your pupil master will almost certainly ask you to take notes during conferences, and a clear note that you can refer to quickly to check points or that you can hand over to be kept with the brief will impress. Second, in early practice one is often asked to do devilling work on a brief, which will frequently involve organising and making notes. Again, if this is done well it will impress.

12.9 Shorthand

The importance of an ability to take good notes in almost every skill the barrister uses has been outlined already. One central element of note-taking is a need to write quickly. You may already be able to write shorthand, or you may already have devised your own methods of abbreviation. However, many students will not be familiar with a speed-writing system, and others may well be able to improve their approach. This section gives guidance on speed-writing. It is adapted from C. G. L. Du Cann *Self-Shorthand*, 3rd edn, Council of Legal Education, 1982. The concept of shorthand may seem a little old fashioned, but for reasons pointed out earlier, while recording a conversation is initially easy, using a recording to retrieve information may be time consuming and inconvenient.

12.9.1   Why create your own system of self-shorthand?

It will enable you to take notes much more rapidly than, and just as accurately as, longhand. It may enable you to dispense with the drudgery of learning an established shorthand system, and yet gain for yourself all the advantages you personally need of shorthand. It will lessen your labours and save your time for more important use than mere transcription.

12.9.2   Elements of a system of self-shorthand

12.9.2.1   Initials

You already know, and probably use, hundreds of nationally recognised initials. This is the foundation of your extended use of initials.

Read the list given in any good dictionary, once or twice if you wish.

In general, you will find that those you might use will 'stick'. Besides, most of them speak adequately for themselves and cannot be confused with anything else.

These accepted initials are permanencies. That is a great advantage. Another great advantage is that they are generally understood.

Use initials with discretion. So long as it is not going to mislead, confuse, puzzle or delay you, they are invaluable. Remember that context is everything. If the word 'government' occurs over and over again and no other word such as 'God', which might be confused with it in interpretation and transcription, the letter 'G' will stand very well for 'government' and save the writing of nine letters wherever it occurs. In one piece of writing, hundreds of letters may be saved.

12.9.2.2   Abbreviations: national and professional

Abbreviations are of the utmost importance. Some which are nationally recognised you know already and have probably more or less accepted before you ever thought of self-shorthand.

'Abbreviate the abbreviations wherever practicable' says self-shorthand. Very often it **is** practicable. For the nationally recognised abbreviations were not scientifically thought out to the best advantage; they grew like a wild plant.

Applying the important principle of 'abbreviating the abbreviations' to the weekdays, for example, we can get down to 'MWF' for 'Monday, Wednesday and Friday', but 'T' and 'S' would equally stand for 'Tuesday' and 'Thursday' and 'Saturday' and 'Sunday'. Clearly then, you cannot abbreviate down to initials in this instance.

But by the aid of another principle, the small-letter principle—to be explained below—we may overcome this difficulty. M^y, T^y, W^y, Th^y, F^y, St^y, S^y will do very well indeed. Make a habit of this abbreviated abbreviation and think of the time and labour saved in a lifetime.

Never use an abbreviation, however conventional and nationally recognised, where a briefer and equally intelligible abbreviation exists. Be on the lookout for abbreviations that can be abbreviated, and cut them ruthlessly.

The set of professional abbreviations of the greatest general importance to the ordinary person is that of the journalistic and printing occupations.

There is a well-recognised list of these in all publishing, journalistic and printing establishments. Most of these were agreed as long ago as the International Shorthand Congress of 1887.

List of abbreviations for longhand

A	a	.(a dot on the line)
	about	abt
	according	acc
	account	acct
	advertisement	ad
	affectionate	aff
	affectionately	affl^y
	afternoon	aft^n
	again	ag^n
	against	agst
	American	Amer
	among	am^g
	amount	am^t
	-ance (suffix at end of words)	-ce
B	because	b^{ec}
	been	b^n
	between	b^{tn}
	brought	bro^t
C	caught	Ca^t
	chairman	ch^m
	circumstance	cir^{ce}
	committee	com^e (or cte)
	could	c^d
D	difference	dif^{ce}
	different	dif^t
	difficult	dif^{clt}
	difficulty	dif^{clty}
E	-ence	-ce
	England, English	Eng.
	especially	esp
	evening	ev^g
	ever	-r
	every	ev^r
	excellent	exc.
F	faithfully	ff^y
	for	f
	Friday	Fri
	from	f^m
	further	fur^r
G	general	gen
	generally	gen^y
	good	g^d
	government	gov^t
	great	g^t
H	had	h^d
	have	h
I	importance	imp^{ce}
	important	imp^t
	-ing	g
	-ion	n
L	large	lge

M	manuscript	Ms
	meeting	m^{tg}
	-ment	m^t
	Monday	Mon
	morning	m^g
N	notwithstanding	$notw^g$
O	objection	obj^n
	occasion	occ^n
	o'clock	o'c
	of	o
	opinion	op^n
	opportunity	pp^y
	other	o^r
	ought	o^t
P	page, pages	p. pp
	particular	$part^r$
	popular	pop
Q	query	q^y
	question	q^n
	quotation	quot
S	said	s^d
	Saturday	Sat
	several	sev^l
	shall	sh
	should	sh^d
	-sion	n
	specially	spec
	Sunday	Sun
T	that	t
	the	/(the first stroke of t)
	their, there	th^r
	though	tho
	through	thro
	Thursday	Thurs
	-tion	n
	together	tog^r
	truly	ty
	Tuesday	Tues
V	very	v or v^y
	very good	vg
W	Wednesday	Wed
	whether	wh^r
	which	wh
	with	w
	without	w^t
	would	w^d
Y	yesterday	$yest^y$ or y'day
	you	y
	your	y^r
	yours	yrs

These handsomely repay learning by heart. Many of them are self-suggestive so they are easy to master. Many of them, as already pointed out—notably the days of the week—can be further abbreviated.

But they will not only repay learning. They repay being studied. Note the *principles* behind them. Our initial principle is here. So is small-size and positional writing. So is the use of symbols like the dot for an 'a' and 'an' and the simple downstroke for 'the'.

12.9.2.3   Conventional spelling

As the Americans do, take the needless 'u' out of words like 'labour' and 'honour' at all times. But, of course, such words as these you can abbreviate further, for 'lab' and hon' are intelligible beyond confusion or mistake. Cut suffixes like 'ette' to 'et'. So write 'cigaret', 'suffraget' at the most, while you can at the least write 'cig' for 'cigar' and 'ci$^{gt'}$' for 'cigarette'.

You will have noted the superfluous apostrophe in words like 'don't' and 'can't' and others. It reminds us—unnecessarily—that a letter has been eliminated. In rapid writing the reminder is inopportune and distracting. So cut out the apostrophe as a set policy. Write 'cant', 'dont', 'wont', 'shouldnt'.

12.9.2.4   Fast-writing habits

Practice is the chief secret of success. But some people's writing lends itself to rapidity. A cursive or running style of handwriting is best. If you have a slow, crabbed hand through wrong teaching or wrong imitation when young, it may be difficult to adopt a new hand.

So eliminate unnecessary loops, for instance, both top and bottom. Journalists, who are fast writers from professional necessity, have a habit of joining words. This helps speed. It is a habit worth adopting, as it obviates delay caused by lifting the pen from the paper.

12.9.2.5   Small- and large-letter principles

In **12.9.2.2** you met the small-letter principle. It spoke for itself at once, and showed how useful and important it was.

The large-letter principle will cause you no difficulty.

For example, take the letter 'A':

Archbishop	Ab^p
Abridge	Ab^r
Absolutely	Abs^{ly}
Acceptance	A^{cc}
Acknowledgement	Ack^t
Affirmative	Afft^{ive}
Aeroplane	A^{pln}
Affidavit	Aff^{t}t
Agriculture	Ag^{ture}
Agent	Ag^t
Appendix	App^x
Archdeacon	Arch^d
Astronomy	Ast^y
Assistant	Ass^t
Average	Av^{ge}

Positional and small-size writing are useful in calling attention to abbreviated forms. You met with it in **12.9.2.2** at the ends of words like 'should' being written 'shd'. But it can be applied to beginnings as well as to ends of words, just as advantageously. Use it for prefixes as well as suffixes.

Thus the prefix 'con'—or 'com'—is frequent and can be indicated by a small 'c' positionally written, for example:

content may be written ^ctnt

compromise may be written ^cprme

And 'circum' can be equally well written by a small 'c'. If you feel you must distinguish it from the symbolic letter 'c' for 'con' or 'com' you can use 'cstroke' thus: 'c/'.

circumference—c/fmce

circumflex—c/flx

Other prefixes can be similarly reduced. Further examples are the very frequently occurring 'per' and 'pro'. Thus:

proposition—p/pstn

proposal—p/psl

while 'per' can take the small raised 'p' as in:

perspicuity—^pspct

thus clearly distinguishing it from:

prospect—p/spct

Prefixes and suffixes, in fact, are one of the most fertile fields for the ingenuity of the self-shorthand writer.

12.9.2.6 Eliminations

Often the words 'a', 'an' and 'the' can be omitted without loss. So can formal words like 'the member' or 'this ancient and honourable society', for the transcriber will recollect such formal adjectives.

Thus write 'hm' and 'hr' for 'him' and 'her', for such contractions cannot be mistaken for any other word.

Sometimes two or even more vowels can be dropped with real safety. Thus:

'plain' can be written 'pln'

'contentment' can be written 'ctmtt'.

12.9.2.7 Key words and recurrent expressions

This should remind the student that in self-shorthand one must always have regard to the context. It is the context that governs key words and recurrent expressions and how they are represented.

For example 'deft' is the recognised legal abbreviation for 'defendant', and a very useful abbreviation it is. But a note-taking judge, magistrate, barrister or non-phonographic reporter in court will not keep writing four letters when one will do all that is wanted. A capital 'D' is enough here—though on other occasions a capital 'D' might well mean something other than 'defendant'.

12.9.2.8 Arbitrary symbols

Do not be afraid of using arbitrary symbols, even if they are algebra to other people. Use them freely according to your convenience. But recollect that the more they spring naturally from the word or phrase they represent, the easier they are to decipher and to remember.

12.9.2.9   The commonest words

The self-shorthand writer needs, of course, to pay special attention to the commonest, that is to say the most frequently occurring, words in the English language. Obviously, to make and learn abbreviations for these is of special importance. The 12 commonest words are also 12 of the shortest. These 12 words, it is authoritatively stated, make up 25% of all normal English, whether written or spoken.

1. a or an	7. that
2. and	8. in
3. the	9. any
4. of	10. to
5. be	11. is
6. it	12. his

13

Modes of address

13.1 Introduction

Whenever you appear as an advocate you should always know the correct way to address the person or people who are in court to decide the issues of law and fact. Using an incorrect title is a sign of possible disrespect or inexperience. Most judges and magistrates will not object strongly to being addressed by an incorrect title, so you may not realise until later, if then, that you had risked upsetting the court. Of course, some judges do mind and will soon let you know if they think that your choice of title is inappropriate. You may find that their chosen response is to say, rather obscurely, 'I can't hear you, Miss Jones.' Your response may be simply to talk louder, assuming that either you are speaking too quietly or the poor old judge is a little deaf! What they mean by this expression is not that they can't hear you but that they won't—you sometimes get a similar response if a judge thinks you are dressed inappropriately for their court. With luck, your opponent will realise what the judge's objection is about and help you out, if possible.

If you are unlucky, the judge won't tell you about your gaffe, but will simply sit there and smoulder! Your chances of persuading the judge to decide in your client's favour may be diminishing with every fresh example of the slight. As a novice advocate, you will get much of your early experience in the magistrates' court or county court, so you will become used to addressing the court as 'Sir/Madam' or 'Your Honour'. Problems may then arise if you are sent to the High Court, and confusion may increase if your appearance there is before a Circuit judge, sitting as a judge of the High Court!

A few years ago, a very junior barrister appeared at the Old Bailey in a hearing with several more experienced barristers. He was the last one to address the judge and his task should have been a simple one; sadly, although most of what he said made sense, he addressed the judge several times as 'Sir'. This was a considerable slight since any Crown Court judge is entitled to be called 'Your Honour' and, even worse, anyone sitting as a judge in the Old Bailey is entitled to be addressed as 'My Lord/Lady'. The judge said nothing but sat there and glowered fiercely at the young barrister. The barrister eventually realised that something was up but could not think what, until he noticed that counsel sitting by his side was muttering something. The young barrister's first reaction was to think, 'How rude'; his second was to listen to what his colleague was muttering. It was 'My Lord—**my Lord**'. Realising his error, the barrister apologised at once, the judge recovered his previous complexion and everything went as planned thereafter.

In order to avoid similar embarrassment yourself, read the rest of this chapter with care.

13.2   Using the correct form of address

13.2.1   Vocative/accusative

The way in which you address the court may vary depending upon whether you are using the vocative case (ie calling upon the judge as if by name) or the accusative case (ie in place of 'you').

(a)   Where the correct form of address is 'Sir/Madam', 'Master' or 'Your Honour' there is no real distinction between addressing the court in the vocative or accusative cases.

Examples

Vocative:

'*Sir/Madam*, the defendant is content for the matter to be dealt with today.'

'In my submission, *Master*, the claimant has failed to show a total failure of consideration.'

'*Your Honour*, there are three affidavits in this case.'

Accusative:

'May it please you, *Sir/Madam*.'

'If you look at the document marked "A", *Master*, you will see that . . . '

'Does *Your Honour* have a copy of the defendant's antecedents?' (Note: you should avoid calling a Circuit Court judge 'you'.)

(b)   There is, however, a marked difference between the appropriate use of 'My Lord/ My Lady' and 'Your Lordship/Your Ladyship'. Use 'My Lord/My Lady' whenever you are addressing the judge in the vocative sense. Use 'Your Lordship/Your Ladyship' in place of 'you'.

Examples

Vocative:

'*My Lord*, the third defendant has taken no part in these proceedings.' 'I am obliged, *my Lady*.'

Accusative:

'*Your Lordship* may be minded to . . .'

'I am happy to tell *Your Lordship* that the parties have reached terms in this matter.'

'Does *Your Ladyship* have the claimant's affidavit sworn on the 13th March 2010?'

(c)   It is perfectly acceptable to combine both forms of address in one sentence.

Example

'*My Lady*, if I may deal with the points that *Your Ladyship* has raised . . .'

(d)   Use 'His Lordship/Her Ladyship' and 'His Honour/Her Honour' in place of 'him' or 'her', ie when referring to the judge in the third person.

Examples

'Describe the layout of the room to *His Lordship*.'

'Tell *Her Honour* what you saw when you entered the room.'

13.2.2 Hybrid situations

Figure 13.1 shows the way to address a person who is sitting as a deputy Circuit or High Court Judge. Some confusion, however, arises where a Circuit judge is sitting also as a deputy judge of the High Court in order to hear a mixed list, ie some county court and some High Court cases. In these circumstances, it is the case itself that determines the mode of address. If your case is a county court matter, address the judge as 'Your Honour'. If the case is a High Court matter, address the judge as 'My Lord/My Lady'. Note, however, that if a High Court judge hears a case that is listed as a county court matter, he or she must still be addressed as 'My Lord/My Lady' and not demoted!

Another hybrid situation occurs when it is necessary to see the judge in his or her private room, for example, to seek an indication regarding sentence (for the limited circumstances in which this might be appropriate see *R v Turner* [1970] 2 QB 321). In this situation, address the judge as 'Judge'.

Youth court **and** **magistrates' court**	District Judge (formerly Stipendiary Magistrate):	'Sir/Madam'
	Chairman of Lay Bench:	'Sir/Madam'
	Members of Lay Bench:	'Your colleagues'
Tribunals	Chairman:	'Sir/Madam'
	Other members:	'Your colleagues'
County court	Circuit Judge:	'Your Honour'
	Recorder or any person sitting as a deputy Circuit Judge:	'Your Honour'
	District Judge:	'Sir/Madam'
Crown Court	High Court Judge:	'My Lord/My Lady'
	Circuit Judge:	'Your Honour'
	Recorder or any person sitting as a deputy Circuit Judge:	'Your Honour'
	Exceptions [see: PD [1982] 1 All ER 320]:	
	Central Criminal Court—any person sitting as a Judge:	'My Lord/My Lady'
	Recorder of Manchester/ Liverpool:	'My Lord/My Lady'
High Court	Judge:	'My Lord/My Lady'
	Any Circuit Judge sitting as a Judge of the High Court:	'My Lord/My Lady'
	District Judge:	'Sir/Madam'
	Master:	'Master'
Court of Appeal	Lord Justice:	'My Lord/My Lady'
Supreme Court	Supreme Court Justice:	'My Lord/My Lady'

Figure 13.1 Modes of address

13.2.3   Referring to another judge

It is often necessary to refer the court to (the judgment of) another judge. In so doing, use his or her proper title.

Examples

Refer to 'Roper J' as 'Mr Justice Roper'.

Refer to 'Roper LJ' as 'Lord Justice Roper'.

13.2.4   Social occasions

Occasionally, you may meet a judge socially, for instance on the train to court. The proper form of address in these circumstances is simply 'Judge'.

14

The advocate as a storyteller

14.1 Introduction

We can often remember quite easily the earliest stories we were told and, if we have children, we are quite confident that we can recall and tell those stories to them. It may be that we can remember those tales just because we were young and our memories were very absorbent; it may also be because the stories were clear and had a simple structure. Also, the storyteller seemed to be familiar with the story so that they were fluent, had a confident manner and perhaps were able to do other things at the same time as telling the story (eg monitor the listener's attention—'Are you listening to me?').

We don't remember those stories because we can easily identify with their situations—mermaids and flying horses, talking animals and sentient toys—but the good storyteller will engage the listener's imagination. They are transported into a form of acceptance and we might call this a form of **persuasion**.

When telling a story, it is always a good idea to have a clear leitmotif (or recurrent theme associated with a particular person, idea or situation) and our childhood stories are full of those, even down to the names of the characters. What does the listener recall of the story later? All of it or just bits and pieces? If the 'story' is the evidence at a trial, then the advocate may want to ensure that the listener does indeed recall only bits and further that only those bits that favour the client are recalled. How might the advocate do this?

Perhaps the most important step is to decide whether the story is acceptable to the listener; does it 'fit' with the listener's idea of how the world and humankind work? Everyone who sits in court to adjudicate on competing versions of the 'facts' in a case brings with them some prior knowledge and beliefs about how things work, what makes people act in certain ways or what they mean when they say certain things. If your client's story fits better into that wealth of knowledge and beliefs than your opponent's story, you have the advantage in persuading your audience to find the facts as you allege them to be. Alternatively, since you are likely to have to present your client's story as it is, rather than as you might like it to be (an ethical requirement), you may need to think about strategies to adopt in order to alter the mindset of your listener, so that the story becomes more acceptable and so more credible.

Much has been written on the importance of storytelling as a part of the persuasive process. The rest of this chapter tries to put this into context for advocates.

14.2 Why should an advocate be able to tell a story?

It is a fact, sad but true, that advocates in England and Wales are not able to devote much time to consideration of stories and storytelling whilst undertaking their formal professional training.

Many barristers who appear in court will readily agree that stories are important to advocacy and that a good story can be very persuasive. You will often hear them talk of the importance, in examination-in-chief, of the need to get the witness to tell their story, or in a closing speech of the need to pull everything together into a convincing story. However, one may reasonably ask, is there much depth of knowledge beneath the surface? How much do these advocates actually know and understand about stories and storytelling? How much is there to understand? In an article written in 2005, it was suggested that storytelling was a crucial missing ingredient in professional legal education in England and Wales (see *The Law Teacher*, 2007, vol. 41). It still is—both crucial and absent. This is an important field for advocates to study and it would benefit their practice considerably if they took the opportunity to find out more and reflect upon it. In the rest of this chapter, we point out some of the advantages in learning more about storytelling and the reasons why you should seize every opportunity to do so.

(a) **How people give evidence**. This is probably the least contentious aspect of legal storytelling. When an event occurs, the usual rules of science apply and we know from our common sense how the world works. As advocates, when questioning our own witnesses, we strive to enable them to appear reliable and honest. One factor that fact-finders often associate with a witness's reliability is their apparent confidence in giving their evidence (although psychologists would say that this is an uncertain guarantee of reliability). Understandably, a witness is most confident when relating events as they actually occurred and were thus perceived by the witness. So, chronology is an aid to memory and helps to persuade fact-finders about the reliability of the witness. A second factor is detail—if a witness can provide the level of detailed information that we would expect if they *had* perceived the events they are now telling us about, this helps to show that they are honest. What we perhaps want most from our witnesses, then, is that they give an overview of their evidence initially—the basic picture of what happened—and then that we take the witness over that ground in more detail. Overlaying all of this is the basic story structure—a beginning, middle and an end.

The beginning for most examinations-in-chief comes with an introduction of the witness—who are they, why should we pay attention to them, how can they help us—and a setting of the scene. In a sense, this represents the 'once upon a time' element of their story. This is followed by the action—what happened, who did what, what was said or heard. This represents the middle or the substance of their account—why we are calling them as a witness. The end is represented by perhaps some reiteration of the key information and a pulling together of the account. Questions such as 'how did that make you feel?' or 'after he left the house, what did you do?' are perhaps attempts to impose a form of conclusion on the witness's account, before leaving them to await cross-examination.

(b) **How people understand evidence**. It has been suggested that when a fact-finder hears the evidence presented in court, he or she seeks to fit it within a story frame (often described as a 'stock story' or pre-existing template). This theory suggests that it is important to establish a story frame at an early stage, ideally within your opening address to the fact-finders. Three consequences follow from this.

First, the evidence subsequently given in the hearing is likely to be assessed according to the prevailing story frame and either accepted as consistent with the existing frame of reference, or rejected as incompatible with it. If it is incompatible—typically, with the opponent's account of what happened—then the party relying upon that evidence will need to work hard to persuade the fact-finders to change or at least amend their frame of reference, so that the new evidence 'fits'.

Second, there is the possibility that where there is information that the fact-finders expect to receive but that is not in fact given at the hearing, this 'omission' will count against the party whose story frame calls for such evidence. In other words, there is an expectation or external standard against which the fact-finders are assessing the completeness of the evidence that is produced at the hearing. It would be sensible to be aware of such expectations and either attempt to meet them or at least acknowledge them and explain why they are not being met.

Third, if such 'expected' information is not given, there is the possibility that the fact-finders may supply it themselves. This may happen unconsciously, with fact-finders thinking they have heard an answer or been given some information that in fact they have not. Therefore, if this 'omission' works in your favour—if it weakens the opponent's story frame—it may make sense tactically for you to highlight the absence of this evidence.

(c) **How advocates persuade**. Persuasion is of course at the heart of the advocate's work. In a closing address to the fact-finder, or decision-maker, the use of a story can be a powerful tool. It can impose a sense of order and unity on a mass of evidence, usually conflicting and contradictory. It can explain motives or goals for people to have said or done the things to which they lay claim, or that are alleged against them. It can therefore assist with establishing intention, knowledge or recklessness—often tricky issues to prove one way or the other.

Perhaps most important of all, it has been said that a story can help to give the fact-finder a reason to come down on one side rather than the other—a sense of 'doing the right thing'. Sometimes, in a case, the prevailing law may be against you; the only way to secure a verdict in your client's favour is to persuade the court to see things differently—perhaps select a legal framework from a different area, or maybe just change the law. Legal innovation or development may come about because judges are persuaded to see things differently. One example might be the change made to the defence of provocation to allow for a gradual build-up to the fatal act, rather than the traditional requirement for an overwhelming event and sudden 'snapping', where a woman had been the victim in an abusive relationship over a considerable period (see *R v Ahluwalia* (1992) 96 Cr App R 133).

If you think that this particular example represents a particular outlook—a feminist perspective on the defence of provocation—that may well be correct. One of the other aspects when considering stories within advocacy is that a 'stock story' may be widely accepted and yet outmoded or one that is unrepresentative of the situation in the particular case. This aspect of the study of legal stories has led over recent decades to a better appreciation of what are sometimes described as 'outsider' stories; these are stories that fall outside mainstream experience or the majority's knowledge of how the world works. Different social norms may be involved, or different experiences may be more relevant. We can see this idea emerge, for example, as the basis for an argument for an ethnically mixed jury in a trial—not one where race is necessarily an issue itself but perhaps where events may be interpreted differently depending upon one's worldview of how white police officers and a black suspect might interact. One can see this perhaps in England in the 1970s and 1980s, where police officers were alleged to have engaged in misconduct when investigating terrorist bombings carried out by those involved in the Irish Republican movement. Judges and juries found it impossible to imagine, at least publicly, that English police officers might behave in the ways alleged by some defendants. However, that worldview changed over time and cases such as those of the Guildford Four and Birmingham Seven are now acknowledged as miscarriages of justice. These cases are representative of how an unpalatable truth can gradually gain acceptance due, at least in part, to the central story being redefined into an alternative version.

So, in this chapter, we hope to have whetted your appetite to look further into the uses and theories of storytelling in the courtroom. There are many aspects to it, all of them useful for and relevant to your legal practice. Many sources of further information about storytelling are written by lawyers and academics who work outside the UK. Some sources are difficult to access or are out of print. That does not mean that you should not try to find them or others, and expand your knowledge. The short list that follows gives you some of the more accessible sources (particularly, for the articles, if you have access to HeinOnline).

14.3 Selective bibliography

Cotterill, J. *Language and Power in Court: A Linguistic Analysis of the O.J. Simpson Trial*, Palgrave Macmillan, 2003.

Hastie, R. and Davies, R. *Rational Choice in an Uncertain World: The Psychology of Judgement and Decision Making*, Sage Publications, 2010.

Lubet, S. 'The Trial as a Persuasive Story', 1990, *American Journal of Trial Advocacy*, vol. 14, 77–96.

Lubet, S. 'Persuasion at Trial', 1997, *American Journal of Trial Advocacy*, vol. 21, 325–56.

Lubet, S. 'Story Framing', 2001, *Temple Law Review*, vol. 74, 59–68.

Pennington, N. and Hastie, R. 'A Cognitive Theory of Juror Decision Making: The Story Model', 1991, *Cardozo Law Review*, vol. 13, 519–58.

Pennington, N. and Hastie, R. 'O.J. Simpson Stories: Behavioral Scientists' Reflections on the People of the State of California versus Orenthal James Simpson', 1996, *University of Colorado Law Review*, vol. 67, 957–76.

Rideout, J.C. 'Storytelling, Narrative Rationality, and Legal Persuasion', 2008, *Legal Writing: Journal of the Legal Writing Institute*, vol. 14, 53–86.

Sarmas, L. 'Story Telling and the Law: a Case Study of Louth v Diprose', 1994, *Melbourne University Law Review*, vol. 19, 701–28.

Singer, J. 'Persuasion', 1989, *Michigan Law Review*, vol. 87, 2442–58.

15

The course of a trial

15.1 Introduction

The most straightforward way to learn advocacy skills is through their performance, in a variety of tasks. Sometimes, however, to focus on the details of those tasks makes it harder to see the bigger picture and how each task fits into the overall pattern of the particular case. In this chapter, we have endeavoured to describe the usual running order of a trial, both in a criminal court and a civil court.

15.2 A criminal trial

The following numbered sequence charts the course of a trial on indictment involving two co-accused, D1 and D2 (named in the indictment in that order), and two offences, Offence X and Offence Y. D1 and D2 are jointly charged with Offence X. There is a separate count charging D2 alone with Offence Y.

The arraignment, as is now normally the case, took place at the Plea and Case Management Hearing. The counts in the indictment were put to D1 and D2 to plead guilty or not guilty. In the case of D2, a plea was taken on each count separately. D1 and D2 pleaded not guilty to Offence X. D2 pleaded not guilty to Offence Y.

Square brackets indicate stages that may or may not be taken depending upon the precise facts and circumstances of the particular case.

15.3 Course of a criminal trial

(1) Jury empanelled by clerk calling at random 12 names from the panel summoned to attend.

(2) [Subject to challenges for cause, the prosecution exercising their 'right' of standby and the judge's power to exclude jurors] each juror takes the juror's oath/affirmation.

(3) Clerk asks the jurors if they are all sworn and puts D1 and D2 in their charge, ie ' . . . D2 also stands charged with the following . . . (Offence Y). To this charge he [or she] has also pleaded not guilty. It is your charge to say, having heard the evidence whether he [or she] is guilty or not guilty.'

(4) Prosecution opening speech (which should exclude any references to evidence that is either clearly inadmissible or to which counsel for the accused have indicated, or either of them has indicated, that D1 and/or D2 will object).

(5) Prosecution evidence including, as appropriate, real evidence, documentary hearsay and formal admissions.

(6) [Each prosecution witness may be cross-examined by D1 and D2, in that order, and may then be re-examined by the prosecution.] Prosecution declares that that is all of its evidence—ie 'closes' its case.

(7) [Submission of no case to answer by D1 and/or D2. Note: the jury are asked to leave the court before any such submission is made. Defence counsel makes his or her/their submission(s) and prosecuting counsel is given an opportunity to reply. The judge announces his or her decision and the jury return to court. If the submission is upheld in relation to all counts on the indictment, the judge explains this to the jury and asks them to appoint a foreman, and the clerk takes from the foreman on each count a verdict of not guilty on the direction of the judge. If the judge decides that there is no case to answer on one count—for example, the count containing Offence Y—but that there is a case to answer on the other, the judge will direct the jury that (a) he or she will direct them, at the end of the trial, to return a verdict of not guilty on D2 in relation to Offence Y and (b) during the remainder of the trial they should ignore the count containing Offence Y. If the judge rejects the submission of no case on all counts, the jury are told nothing and the case continues.]

(8) Counsel for D1 (and D2) either (a) informs the court that D1 (D2) will give evidence or (b) does not so inform the court, or informs the court that D1 (D2) does not intend to give evidence. In the latter case, ie (b), the judge should then inquire of counsel whether he or she has advised his or her client about the fact that the jury may draw inferences from a failure to testify. If counsel replies in the affirmative, the case proceeds. If counsel replies in the negative, then the judge must direct the representative to advise his or her client on the matter, and should adjourn briefly for this purpose. See Criminal Justice and Public Order Act 1994, s 35 and Practice Direction (Criminal Proceedings: Consolidation) [2002] 1 WLR 2870, para 44.

(9) D1 presents his or her case: co-accused must present their cases in the order in which their names appear in the indictment.

(10) [D1's opening speech.] Note: if the only defence evidence is to be given by D1 or by D1 and witnesses speaking only as to his or her good character, D1 has no right to an opening speech.

(11) [D1 called to give evidence.] Note: Police and Criminal Evidence Act 1984, s 79: if an accused (D) intends to call two or more witnesses to the facts of a case and those witnesses include D, D must be called before the other witness(es) unless the court in its discretion otherwise directs.

(12) [If D1 does testify, after examination-in-chief he or she can be cross-examined by counsel for D2. Then the prosecution may cross-examine and counsel for D1 may re-examine.]

(13) [D1's other evidence, including, as appropriate, real evidence, documentary hearsay and formal admissions. Witnesses called by D1 will be examined-in-chief and then may be cross-examined by counsel for D2, then by the prosecution and counsel for D1 may re-examine.]

(14) D2 presents his or her case: see (9)–(13) above, reversing 'Dl' and 'D2' throughout.

(15) [Prosecution closing speech.] Note: the prosecution have no right to a closing speech if an accused (a) is unrepresented and (b) had no right to an opening speech—see (10) above.

(16) D1's closing speech.

(17) D2's closing speech.

(18) Judge's summing-up: functions of judge and jury; burden and standard of proof;

definition of offences charged; direction to treat D1 and D2 separately and to treat the separate counts separately; summary of evidence; directions on evidence as appropriate [eg effect of character evidence, effect of silence, etc]; advise appointment of foreman and retirement with a view to reaching a unanimous verdict.

(19) [If the jury return to court or are sent for by the judge after two hours and ten minutes or such longer period as the judge thinks reasonable, and the foreman, upon being asked whether they have reached a unanimous verdict, answers 'no', the judge may give a majority verdict direction: see Criminal Practice Directions part VI, 39Q and the Juries Act 1974, s 17.]

(20) Jury's verdict on each count:

(a) guilty (unanimous); or

(b) guilty (majority); or

(c) not guilty (unanimous); or

(d) not guilty (majority); or

(e) failure to agree upon any verdict.

Concerning (b) and (d), the procedure, following a majority direction and on the jury's return to court, is to ask if at least ten out of 12 are agreed; if yes, to ask whether guilty or not guilty; if guilty, to ask how many were in favour, how many against; if not guilty, simply to accept the verdict.

If the verdict is either (a) or (b), the court may adjourn for reports prior to sentence, in which event there is still a prima facie right to bail: see Bail Act 1976, s 4. If no reports are sought, there is usually no right to bail although an application for bail may be made pending appeal against conviction and/or sentence. The Crown Court judge will only be able to grant bail if he or she certifies the case is fit for appeal (rare).

If the verdict is either (c) or (d), the judge will direct the accused that he or she is free to leave the dock (provided, of course, he or she has not been found guilty on some other count and is not in custody on other matters).

Concerning (e), the judge may ask the jury to retire again [with or without a majority direction] or discharge the jury. Discharge of a jury in such circumstances is not an acquittal—there may be a retrial.

Mitigation should be prepared in advance: preparation during the jury's retirement may be interrupted by their early return to court!

15.4 A civil trial

The following numbered sequence charts the course of a civil trial involving two defendants, D1 and D2, who appear in the pleadings as First Defendant and Second Defendant. The material documents were collated into a trial bundle, with identical sets for everyone to use. If the case is proceeding in either the Queen's Bench Division or Chancery Division, there may also be a reading list, and there should be a case summary. This latter document is a short one, summarising the issues in the case and dealing with any relevant procedural matters. In a case proceeding in the High Court, counsel should provide the court with a list of any legal authorities, no later than 5 pm on the day before the hearing. Finally, the court should have skeleton arguments—these are compulsory in the High Court and optional but sensible for the county court. For more detail on this sequence, refer to *Blackstone's Civil Practice,* chapter 59.

15.5 Course of a civil trial

(1) The case may be tried by a District judge (small claims, cases in the fast track and some in the multi-track) or by a Circuit judge or Recorder in the county court or a High Court judge (most multi-track cases).

(2) The hearing will be in public generally. In exceptional situations, the court may decide to exclude members of the public. An example would be if privacy was needed to protect the interests of a child involved in the litigation.

(3) A trial timetable may determine time limits for making speeches and questioning witnesses. This will usually have been decided at a pre-trial review, if one has taken place.

(4) The claimant usually begins the trial, unless the burden of proof is on the defendant(s). The starting point is an opening speech. This may be dispensed with, particularly in a case where the judge has had the chance to read the trial bundle. If a speech is made, counsel for the claimant will set out the nature of the claim and use either the statements of case, or the case summary, or both, to identify the issues for resolution in the trial.

(5) Claimant's evidence is then called. This can include, as appropriate, real evidence, documentary evidence and witness statements, as well as oral testimony. Remember that hearsay is not inadmissible in civil trials (see Civil Evidence Act 1995). So, depositions or affidavits or witness statements may be used as evidence; usually, a witness statement will serve as the evidence-in-chief of its maker (see CPR, r 32.5).

(6) Further examination-in-chief may take place. For example, a witness may provide supplementary information, with the permission of the judge. Cross-examination can then take place, if necessary. Under the provisions of the Civil Evidence Act 1995, a witness statement may be relied upon as evidence even if its maker is not called as a witness or available for cross-examination. A witness's absence from the witness box will be a matter relevant to the weight of that evidence. If a witness is to be cross-examined then, if there is more than one defendant, the order of questioning will be determined by the order in which they appear on the court record, so—First Defendant, then Second Defendant. The witness may then be re-examined for the claimant. The claimant will finally declare that this is all of the evidence by 'closing the case for the Claimant'.

(7) Submission of no case to answer may be made now. This is less frequent than in criminal trials. It is usual for the judge to make a defendant choose between either making a submission of no case or calling evidence in support of his case. In exceptional circumstances, this choice may not have to be made.

(8) In the absence of a submission of no case, the defence may present its evidence. If calling evidence, counsel may begin by making an opening speech for the defence. In practice, defence counsel often forgoes this opportunity.

(9) The defendant and any other witnesses may be called to give their evidence to the court. Each witness may undergo examination-in-chief, cross-examination and re-examination. A number of defendants, if separately represented, will present their evidence in the order in which they appear on the court record. Thus, the evidence for the First Defendant will be presented before that for the Second Defendant, and so on. Eventually, all defendants will have 'closed their case'.

(10) The Defence closing speech may now be made, if the defendant has called evidence. This is clearly an important stage of the trial—if pressed by a time limit (imposed via a trial timetable), counsel may rely upon their skeleton argument for a fuller treatment

of the issues in the case. Where there are a number of defendants, their speeches will follow the usual pattern.

(11) Claimant's closing speech. The claimant usually has the last word before the judge determines the case.

(12) Judgment is given. This may happen immediately or later (in which case, it is described as a 'reserved' judgment).

(13) Costs are considered in light of the judgment. Arguments as to who should bear the costs should have been prepared in advance, to cover every likely outcome in the case (and see **Chapter 34**). As to how much the costs should be, a statement of costs should have been served 24 hours before the hearing. There may be a summary (or on-the-spot) assessment of costs by the trial judge; if so, that will be based on the statement.

Part IV

Opening and closing a case

Opening speeches

16.1 Introduction

The opening speech is the first opportunity that advocates have to set out the case theory that, in their opinion, will persuade the court to determine the issues in favour of their client. Very often, these days, the court will be quite familiar with the likely evidence in the trial—for example, in many civil trials now, there will have been a mutual exchange of witness statements. The judge will have a trial bundle consisting of those statements and the statements of case. Similarly, in the Crown Court the judge will have seen the indictment and the prosecution witness statements before the trial begins. The big difference is that the triers of fact in criminal trials are magistrates and juries. Crucially, they will have next to no knowledge about the case before the trial starts, apart from hearing the charge against the accused read out and hearing the plea of not guilty entered. Thus, for the triers of fact in criminal trials, the opening speech is the first real chance to become acquainted with the issues; whereas, in civil trials, the judge already has a good idea of what the case is all about before the advocate ever stands up. This may mean there are certain differences of emphasis when opening a case to a judge, rather than to magistrates or a jury. Nevertheless, there are some general factors that should be ever present in an opening speech.

16.2 The basic purpose of an opening speech

The opening speech serves as an introduction to your client's case. It should set out the essential facts on which your case is founded; it should fill in a little background so that the triers of fact begin to see the 'bigger picture'—otherwise there is a danger that the speech and the subsequent evidence will appear rather disconnected as if the witnesses were simply a group of people chosen almost at random; and, finally, the speech should introduce one (or more) possible case theories.

The opening speech comes at the very outset of the presentation of your client's case to the court. If you were writing a book, this speech would be an introduction or prologue to assist the reader and bring them up to speed with the plot and characters. If this were a restaurant and not a courtroom, the speech would be replaced by an enthusiastic maître d', talking the diners through the delights of the menu and offering an hors d'oeuvre or two to whet their appetite. Last analogy!—the triers of fact are about to board a bus, driven by you. It could turn out to be a mystery tour, where everyone finishes up at your intended destination (the end of the trial) but no one is quite sure how they got there or what they saw on the way. Indeed, some passengers may have seen different sights from the rest, some or all may have missed some very interesting sights along the way simply through ignorance. That's not what you want. Your opening speech must be like the very best guided tour—one where the travellers know from the off where they are going, how they are going to get there and what they are likely to experience along the way.

So, the speech is an outline and a guide. It is an introduction and it should introduce the circumstances that gave rise to the litigation, the parties who are involved in it, what your client seeks from the triers of fact and, most crucially, how the issues will be resolved in such a way as to make the outcome sought by your client the inevitable result of the trial. You should always take great care when preparing an opening speech, whatever the court, as what you say now will act as a template for the rest of the case. If you tell the court that a witness will say x in their evidence, and that witness fails to do so, your opponent is likely to draw the court's attention to that failure. It may not be a significant omission to you but the triers of fact may disagree. Also, if you advance a particular case theory in your opening speech and the evidence turns out not to support that but is fine for a different case theory that could also win the case for your client, you will have to work hard to persuade the court to let you walk away from your original theory.

This sounds like a recipe for caution, keeping things vague and talking in generalities. You can take this advice too much to heart but there is a great gap between what you **need** to say in an opening speech and what you **can** say by way of comment on the facts that you expect to prove. Too much caution is bad, but some caution is sensible; moderation is the rule. Never open a case 'higher' than you need to. It is a dangerous technique to be too bullish in your opening, bold assertions now that facts x, y and z will be proved may come back to haunt you later, what appear now as justified and confident predictions about the evidence may just turn out to be hostages to fortune. Take the example of prosecuting counsel in the obscenity trial concerning *Lady Chatterley's Lover* by D.H. Lawrence. Extracts from the speech to the jury show him saying:

> the heroine, Lady Chatterley, and the hero, the gamekeeper, are, you may think, little more than bodies, bodies which continuously have sexual intercourse with one another . . .
> . . . the story of the book . . . is little more than padding . . .
> . . . sex is dragged in at every conceivable opportunity . . .
> . . . the book puts promiscuous sex on a pedestal . . .

Each of the propositions was subsequently used by the defence as the basis for a question to the defence expert witnesses. They became ammunition for the defence to shoot back at the prosecution and no advocate can afford to supply his or her opponent with bullets. Of more concern, no client can afford to indulge an advocate who, through lack of foresight as to consequences (or maybe just lack of imagination), fails to see how what they perceive as strengths can swiftly become turned around into weaknesses. There is almost nothing your opponent will enjoy more than being given the chance to do this.

16.3 The elements of the speech

A competent opening speech consists of the following elements:

(a) introducing your role as advocate in the case, and that of your opponent(s), to the court;

(b) giving a clear summary of the facts of the case;

(c) giving a clear statement of the disputed issues between the parties;

(d) giving a brief outline of the evidence of witnesses, if the admissibility of that evidence is not challenged;

(e) addressing the court on the law, when appropriate;

(f) speaking clearly, using appropriate language;

(g) delivering the speech without reading from a prepared script;

(h) complying with the rules of professional conduct.

16.4 How to structure your opening speech

What follows are several suggestions on how to structure an opening speech in various contexts. They are not intended to be prescriptive and, when you become more experienced as an advocate, you will find that you prefer to do things in your own way. That is as it should be but you must always remember that the purpose of the opening speech is to put the essential facts of your client's case before the court and the basis for liability or its denial. Always try to keep your speech as concise as possible, appear to be decent and honest in your dealings with the court from the outset. Remember the rules of professional conduct.

16.4.1 Civil trials

The structure of speeches in civil trials will be largely the same, whether taking place in the county court or High Court (although in the latter forum, replace 'Your Honour' with 'My Lord/Lady'). The opening speech will usually be given by the advocate who represents the claimant but, occasionally, it may be the right of the defence to start the trial with a speech. It really depends upon who bears the burden of proof on the matters in issue in the trial.

It is quite usual in civil cases to have a skeleton argument prepared in advance of the trial. This document sets out, quite briefly, the issues that are in dispute between the parties (these may not be instantly clear from the individual statements of case and it requires an overview that can only be done after all statements of case are available). The skeleton argument should summarise the party's case on the issues and summarise the propositions of law that the party relies upon. Finally, it should contain cross-references to the statements of case, the court bundle (any documentary real evidence or witness statements), and the legal sources that support the propositions of law. The skeleton argument should underpin your opening speech; the written document is not intended to replace the oral speech. For more guidance on skeleton arguments, see **Chapter 25**.

In your opening speech, you should ensure that you do the following:

(a) **State the nature of the case**

For example, 'Your Honour, this is a claim for damages for personal injury arising out of a road traffic accident, caused by the defendant's negligence' or, 'Your Honour, this is a claim for damages based on an alleged breach of contract'.

(b) **State the issues in the case, ie the areas of dispute between the parties**

For example, 'The issue between the parties is whether the car was of merchantable quality' or, 'The issue between the parties is whether the defendant fell below the standard of care expected of a reasonable prudent driver when he overtook the lorry on the roundabout' or, 'There are three issues in this case: first, has the respondent committed acts of violence against the petitioner and, if so, is there a danger that he will do so again? Finally, if there is such a danger, should the respondent be excluded from the matrimonial home?'

(c) **Summarise the facts that have been established or will be established during the trial**

Thus, any significant factual matters that are relevant but not in dispute should be identified; you will want to identify the circumstances that gave rise to the events that are the subject matter of the litigation, as well as its aftermath.

For example, in a claim for damages for personal injury, you would want to set the scene, describe what was happening immediately prior to the injury being suffered, how the injury was sustained, what happened immediately thereafter and what the longer-term consequences were.

(d) **Read out the statements of case and the relevant parts of any documents whose use has been agreed by the parties**

This may seem unnecessary to you. After all, the judge has the statements of case and your skeleton argument. You may be right: the judge will often indicate that they will read the statements of case for themselves now or have already read them. If so, you should still take the judge to the key points in the statements of case (eg the allegations of negligence in a personal injuries case) as it remains important to ensure the judge has absorbed these important allegations.

(e) **Refer to any relevant legal principles contained in statute, regulation or case law**

Again, this may seem unnecessary. The judge will have considerable experience of handling cases like this and may be thoroughly familiar with the relevant law. Indeed, often the legal position will be agreed between the parties, and the court has to resolve only issues of fact. This may be where the skeleton argument comes into its own, particularly as no judge ever welcomes a lecture on the law! Unless the relevant law is quite esoteric, it is probably best to keep such references to a minimum.

(f) **Briefly state why, on the law and facts as you understand them, the claimant should succeed.**

16.4.2   Opening for the defence in a civil trial

It should be quite clear that much of what needs to be done in opening the case for the claimant need not be repeated by the defence. For example, the statements of case only need reading once. However, if the defence is calling evidence at the trial, it may be that an opening speech is desirable, in addition to any skeleton argument that the defence has prepared for the court. Remember that any opening speech for the defence will come after the evidence for the claimant has been presented to the court. Any defence opening should, therefore, concentrate on the matters that it is intended to establish through the evidence to be tendered on behalf of the defence, together with a summary of the case theory for the defence. This last point is important; up to this point in the trial, when defence counsel has cross-examined the claimant's witnesses, that has been done with two things in mind. The first is the statement of case entitled 'defence', which the judge has a copy of, the second is the defence theory of the case, which the judge does not have. A good judge can probably make a reasonably accurate guess as to the defence case theory, based upon the defence itself and the questions asked by defence counsel in cross-examination, but this is not the time to play guessing games with the judge. Use a short opening speech to clarify what your theory of the case is and why the defendant should succeed.

16.4.3 Criminal trials

A distinction must be drawn here between trials in the magistrates' court and trials in the Crown Court.

16.4.3.1 Magistrates' court

The basic rule here is that the prosecution advocate makes an opening speech and the defence does not (see Criminal Procedure Rules 2013, r 37.3). So, we don't have to worry about a defence opening speech—there won't be one. What about the prosecution?

We have to remember that, although justices of the peace are not professionally qualified for their position, they do adjudicate on many cases every year. The upshot is that they acquire plenty of judicial experience and don't need long lectures on the law (or only rarely). Also, factually they may be familiar with most of the scenarios that are likely to be played out in a summary trial. So what does the prosecutor say in the opening speech? The answer is next to nothing. A typical opening might run thus:

> Sir (or Madam), in this case I appear on behalf of the Crown and my learned friend, Miss Smith, represents the accused. This is a simple case of driving without due care and attention, contrary to the Road Traffic Act. I will now call PC Jones.

You could expand this if you wanted to, perhaps to identify the witnesses and their part in the proceedings, but that will seldom be necessary. This advice—to err on the side of extreme brevity—should be redoubled if you find yourself prosecuting in front of a district judge. They **are** legally qualified as well as hearing perhaps in excess of a hundred summary trials each year; they really have heard it all and, as there is no statement of case to refer the court to (unlike a civil trial) except maybe a quite uninformative charge sheet, you might as well get on with calling the evidence.

16.4.3.2 Crown Court

The prosecution opening speech Here, the prosecution is entitled to open the case to the jury and should always do so in a full and proper way. What follows is intended only as a starting point. You should always assess in each case whether or not the suggested structure is appropriate and, if not, you must alter it to suit the circumstances of that case (see also *Blackstone's Criminal Practice* D16.10).

The jury will probably find it helpful if your opening speech starts by setting out, very shortly, the essential facts that are the prosecution case. You might want to refer to the indictment here and, if it is a complicated one (perhaps it contains alternative counts covering the same behaviour), you might want the jury to look at it while you explain the counts to them. You should have ensured there are sufficient copy indictments for all the jurors to have sight of one. In simple cases, the jury will have heard the count(s) read out to the accused and his or her plea(s), or they will have been told what the counts are by the clerk to the court, so you won't need to spend much time on this part of the speech.

Typically, the prosecutor will then go on to review the facts in more detail. Of course, at this stage there are no facts usually, only allegations. But what you try to do is to set the scene, establish some sort of context in which to place the bald facts of the crime itself.

No offence occurs in a vacuum: crimes are committed by humans, acting on human impulses and emotions and with motives that other humans can understand. The jury need to be persuaded of the truth and, while the prosecutor is always there to see that justice is done rather than simply secure a conviction, the truth may become more identifiable if the jury are able to get a good feel for what was going on around the time of the offence. They may need to be given some understanding of the scene where the offence was committed, who was present and the relationship between them, and how the accused committed the offence. Into this (which is essentially a storytelling exercise), you could insert references to particular witnesses who will testify for the prosecution, as a prelude to their testimony. That is sensible and helpful but what you must avoid is overstating your case and, in particular, appearing to rely too heavily on specific witnesses to establish particular points for your case. If you are only calling a single witness, then you may want to indicate in quite explicit terms what he or she will say on oath; after all, if they don't then your case will collapse anyway. But, where you are calling several witnesses, be wary of setting expectations too high for them. It is much better to leave yourself some flexibility since you can never be quite sure how the evidence is going to develop during the trial. This is one of the hardest things for a novice advocate to grasp, ie that a trial is a dynamic, growing process of discovery. Of course, as the advocate you should have a better idea than most of exactly where you are all going and what is likely to happen by the end of the trial but you are mistaken if you believe that advocates are never taken by surprise by what witnesses say and never have to adapt their case to meet the situation as it confronts them. Your ability to respond is compromised if you have been too specific (and optimistic) in opening the case. There is also a risk that too much detail now will result in you losing the jury's attention; after all they are here to listen to the evidence and find the facts.

When you refer to specific evidence in your opening speech, you should always check first that your opponent does not challenge its admissibility. Now, you don't have to do that with every single piece of evidence but some items are almost certainly going to be challenged (eg police evidence of an alleged confession by the accused). You should always check with defence counsel, preferably before going into court, whether there will be an objection. This may have been dealt with at a pre-trial hearing but you should double-check. If the answer is no, then you can mention the evidence in your speech. If the answer is yes, then you must omit any reference to that evidence from your opening speech. If the issue was not resolved at a pre-trial hearing, the judge will usually have to determine the question of admissibility later, in the absence of the jury, and if you mention the evidence now, that determination will be otiose. It may be that the confession is really all the evidence that you have against the accused; in that situation, you can ask the judge to take the admissibility point as a preliminary issue before your opening speech. If so, the jury will be excluded while the point is argued. If you win the argument, you open your case as intended and refer to the confession; if you lose, you will probably not make an opening speech but offer no evidence and halt the case instead.

On a similar note, it may be that the defence disputes the identity of the offender, saying that while a crime may have been committed, the defendant was not the offender. If identification is a live issue in the trial, then you should not say that the accused was seen at a particular time or place, you may only say that a man (or woman) was seen at that time and place and that your witnesses will say that the man (or woman) was the accused.

It may be that you can anticipate with some confidence **what** the likely defence case will be. For example, the accused may have offered an innocent explanation during an interview with police, such as self-defence or alibi. The defence statement may have shed more light. Now, the burden of proof for most defences in criminal trials rests with the prosecution. While it is for the defence to raise some evidence to suggest, say, self-defence, if they do so then it is for the prosecution to prove beyond reasonable doubt that the accused did not act in self-defence. In such circumstances, it might be thought sensible to mention any such defences in your opening speech, so that you can knock them down again. In practice, your confident guess as to the nature of the defence case could turn out to be just that—a guess. Most of the time it is not worth spelling out to the jury what you think the defence case is going to be. It is much better to keep your guess to yourself, while planning accordingly.

The advice on the legal content of a prosecutor's opening speech given in previous editions of this manual can be summarised thus:

State what the elements of the offence(s) are and that the prosecution bears the burden of proof, which it can only discharge if the jury is convinced beyond a reasonable doubt of the defendant's guilt.

Further guidance on the subject has now come from the Court of Appeal (Criminal Division). In *R v Lashley* [2005] EWCA Crim 2016, Judge LJ stated that prosecuting counsel did not need to discuss relevant law with the jury when opening the case for the Crown. The crime alleged in *Lashley* was theft and the Court of Appeal agreed with the trial judge that 'everyone knows in general terms what theft is'. Judge LJ went on:

The presumption should be that an opening address by counsel for the Crown should not address the law, save in cases of real complication and difficulty . . .

This extended to the view that it was by no means in every case that a jury needed reminding of the burden and standard of proof. No further explanation was offered as to why such guidance would not be helpful to a jury.

Defence opening speech   The defence is only entitled to make an opening speech if calling witnesses to testify on the facts and the accused himself doesn't count for this purpose (see *Blackstone's Criminal Practice* D17.7). So, you may not have the right to make an opening speech at all and, even if you do, you may decide that it is sensible not to. It may be better to leave your arguments to the closing speech. As a general rule, perhaps you should not make an opening speech if you are not confident of what your witnesses will say on oath; better to wait and see, then your speech can be based on what the witnesses actually said and so, more importantly, can your theory of the case. Conversely, the longer the time that defence witnesses will spend testifying, the greater the need for some guidance for the jury before the witnesses start their evidence.

If you are going to make an opening speech, you should indicate that you are entitled to do so by informing the judge, 'Your Honour, I shall be calling witnesses of fact in addition to the defendant'. Then proceed to knit together the following five strands:

(a) *Comments on the prosecution evidence*   You may want to do this, especially because the prosecution could not. However, this is the sort of job that you will definitely want to do in your closing speech and the jury may wonder why you are just repeating yourself. It is usually best to keep your comments for your closing speech, then you can combine them with observations based on the evidence of the defence witnesses, too.

(b) *Outline the defence evidence*   This is quite similar to the job that the prosecutor had. As then, you should be alert to the fact that witnesses sometimes fail to say what we expect them to (and some even say things we never expected them to!). It is best to paint your picture with a broad brush; that way you leave some room to adapt your case as the evidence is given, and you avoid giving too much advance information to your opponent.

(c) *Your theory of the case*   Even applying a broad brush, you should still have a good idea of how the defence case is likely to unfurl in court. So you should have a case theory now (of course, you should have had a case theory before setting foot in the courtroom) and you may want to set it before the jury. A combination of the uncontested evidence in the case and your client's version of the matters in issue should enable you to present a theory of the case to the jury. You want to try to make the jury see that the only reasonable inference to be drawn from the evidence is that the defendant is not guilty and your case theory is the better/more appropriate/correct one. However, do this concisely and leaving some room for flexibility later, should the need arise. Of course, no one expects the defence case to collapse, as witnesses fail to deliver their expected testimony, but even if they all 'come up to proof', the jury won't want to hear you simply repeat your opening speech at the end of the trial.

(d) *Weaknesses in your case*   It is a very moot point whether you should mention these now. After all, you may be fortunate and the witness you had the least faith in does superbly. But in some instances you know that, even if everything goes well, a certain issue or incident will still be a source of potential danger for your case. Your choice is to say nothing now and try to deal with it when it arises in testimony and in your closing speech, or to raise it now. The latter strategy has a disadvantage in that you alert your opponent to the weakness, but it has the advantage of honesty. In the eyes of the jury, you will be seen as frank and open: the fact that you are prepared to acknowledge the flaws in your case, yet still demonstrate how the defendant is not guilty, may be quite persuasive. Openness now also shows that you are not being taken by surprise when the weakness becomes manifest during testimony, it shows control and confidence. If you do decide to be frank, never describe a weakness in those terms; simply state the point that is the weakness and try to put it in the best light that you can.

(e) *Burden and standard of proof*   You should take this opportunity, if making a speech, to remind the jury shortly that the prosecution brought the case and it is for them to prove it, beyond a reasonable doubt. The defendant does not have to prove his or her innocence, it is enough if they raise a question (or reasonable doubt) in the minds of the jury.

16.5 Dos and don'ts

16.5.1 Things to avoid doing in an opening speech

You should not:

(a) argue—now is not the time to discuss the pros and cons, nor is it the time to persuade—that will come later;

(b) state your personal opinions—either on the facts or the credibility of any witness—frankly, no one cares and it is not your job to waste time on this;

(c) overstate your client's case—the trier(s) of fact may remember what you say now, especially as they may be reminded of it by your opponent. Try to understate;

(d) read your speech from a prepared text—of course, you should have notes but if possible try not to look at them. If you are prepared properly, you should be able to make your speech with very little need to look at your notes; besides, there are other more important places to observe, for example, the jury box or the Bench.

16.5.2 Things you should consider doing in an opening speech

You should:

(a) consider the best way to enable the trier(s) of fact to empathise with your client—a typical example is by using your client's name, rather than his or her title in the proceedings (eg 'Mr Smith' and not 'claimant', or 'accused');

(b) decide on the best way to minimise any empathy the court may have for the opposing party—for example you may want to try to depersonalise them by using only a title when referring to them (eg 'the claimant');

(c) try to look at the trier(s) of fact—eye contact is desirable, although you don't want to stare. If addressing justices of the peace or a jury, try to make individual eye contacts rather than simply staring at a point on the wall above their heads. It is sometimes said that, for a jury trial, it is a good idea to forecast who the chairman of the jury will be and concentrate your efforts on them. I would not recommend that as you may be wrong and the other jurors may feel slighted.

16.6 Telling a story

The opening speech is your first chance to acquaint the court with your theory of the case, and the themes that give depth and colour to the cold, two-dimensional allegations between the parties. First impressions are very important and this will be the time when the court has its first real impression of you. As an advocate, your job is **to persuade** and one of the best ways of doing this is to recreate the moments (or longer) leading up to the matters that gave rise to the litigation and assist the trier(s) of fact to 'see' what happened. Most cases are decided on their facts, not on nice questions of law, and the sooner you knit 'the facts' (that is the uncontested facts and your client's version of those in dispute) into a single coherent story, the more likely it is to be remembered later. This 'storytelling' element of your speech is the best setting for your case theory to be introduced, but the story is more than just the theory. If your version makes sense as a story, it is likely to be persuasive. (See **Chapter 14**.)

16.7 Checklist for preparation

What should go into the introduction?

What are the main facts of the case? How will they be developed (that is through the testimony of witnesses, or documentary evidence, or other exhibits)?

What are the issues in the case? Which 'facts' are in dispute? What are the legal principles on which you will rely to establish your client's case?

What are your main themes in the case?

What are your subsidiary themes in the case?

What is your theory of the case?

What weaknesses are there in your version of the case, in your client's or in your witnesses'?

16.8 Further reading

Bergman, P. *Trial Advocacy in a Nutshell*, 3rd edn, West Wadsworth, 1997.

Du Cann, R. *The Art of the Advocate,* Penguin, 1993, revised, pp 72–91.

Evans, K. *Advocacy in Court*, 2nd edn, Blackstone Press (OUP), 1995.

Hyam, M. *Advocacy Skills*, 4th edn, Blackstone Press (OUP), 1999.

Mauet, T. et al *Trial Techniques,* Aspen, 2002.

Sonsteng, J.O., Haydock, R.S., and Boyd, J.T. *The Trial Book, A Total System for Preparation and Presentation of a Case,* West Publishing Co, 1984.

Closing speeches

17.1 Introduction

You will almost certainly have seen some great closing speeches without going anywhere near a courtroom. Many writers of stage plays, cinema films and television series have recognised the drama of the situation and the potential that it offers to stir the emotions with pleas for justice and the truth. Often these dramatic works are of American origin and involve jury trials. It cannot be denied that such scenes have tremendous appeal—they are exciting, moving and thrilling. How often is it like that at three o'clock on a hot June day in an airless courtroom in Acton? Not very often is the simple answer.

Although the closing speech does offer certain opportunities for counsel to indulge in an otherwise frustrated theatrical nature, it must be remembered that not every closing speech takes place in front of a jury (the vast majority will not), and that what may work in Hollywood won't be so effective in Cricklewood.

What you, as a barrister, must do is to consider your audience and what you are asking them to do. Closing speeches can be made in criminal trials and civil trials; they can be made to juries or to magistrates, to Crown Court judges or judges in the High Court or county court; they can be made for the claimant or the prosecution or for the defendant. What you have to do and the ways in which you seek to do it will vary, according to all of these factors. Your manner is also likely to be affected by the topic of the litigation—a closing speech to a judge in a personal injury claim may be quite different from another speech to the same judge when hearing a fraud trial (see, eg, *Blackstone's Criminal Practice* D18.15 etc). So, how should you go about making a closing speech?

17.2 The purpose of a closing speech

17.2.1 Persuasion

The purpose, at heart, never varies. You seek to persuade the person or people who have to decide the facts to come down in your favour. You should have put your theory of the case already, shown the court your story and your themes. Now you are trying to knit all these strands together into a coherent whole—to show them the picture as you want them to see it. This may sound like an incitement to distortion or deceit but it is not.

No barrister should ever mislead a court (specifically, whoever is responsible for determining the facts). You must never tell your audience that a witness said A when he or she really said B. You may need to remind the court of the times when a witness said something that made the going tough for your client, in order to explain it away (your opponent may remind the court without the favourable explanation!). But having said that, you are entitled to reinforce your client's story insofar as you have the evidence to back it up.

17.2.2 Unfavourable evidence

So the main purpose of a closing speech is to persuade your audience of the merits of your case, by interweaving your story with the appropriate evidence. Another major purpose has been alluded to—the necessity of dealing with the evidence that undermines your story, that knocks holes in your theory. Usually, this will be the evidence of your opponent's witnesses, perhaps unshaken by cross-examination. Sometimes, it will be evidence from your own witnesses—some damning admission made in cross-examination or an unexpected answer that just slipped out. Whatever its origin, do not ignore it. To do so runs the risk of misleading the court and since your opponent and/or the judge is almost certain to refer to this evidence, you will appear at best careless and at worst dishonest in the eyes of the court. If the court forms this opinion of your veracity, the client will be 'sunk without trace'.

17.2.3 The law

Having dealt with themes, stories and the evidence, what is left? Usually the law. The length of time and the detail that you devote to the legal points raised in the case will obviously depend on the nature of the case. You should not duck making submissions on the law but you should remember a few important points.

First, in a jury trial the judge decides questions of law and will direct the jury accordingly. Anything you say to the jury about the law is subject to whatever the judge says. (If he or she gets it wrong, the place to correct it is in the appeal court—don't have a slanging match in front of the jury.) Second, in a trial where a professional lawyer is adjudicating, whilst you can make sophisticated legal points in your speech, remember that the audience is human—he or she will eventually cease listening to you; and he or she is legally trained—make your points on law succinct and keep to the point, the court does not want a lecture on the law of nuisance (for example). Third, if you must quote from decided cases or statutes, you should do your utmost to ensure that the court has sufficient copies of the report to follow your remarks. (Curiously, it is not common to do this when addressing a jury, even though they are the audience most likely to be ignorant of the law.)

17.3 The content of a closing speech

17.3.1 Keep it to the point

Keep things short and to the point. It is often unnecessary to reiterate a great deal of evidence from the trial. Take what you need to remind the court of your themes and theory—use the evidence to reinforce the validity of your arguments. Remind the court of those things that you said you would demonstrate in your opening speech (if you made one), then highlight the evidence that (you say) makes your points.

17.3.2 Setting out the theory of the case

If you did not make an opening speech, now is the time to set out your theory of the case, how the evidence knits together to substantiate your assertions. Distil your arguments to a minimum—concentrate the minds of your audience on those few essentials that, if decided favourably to your client, will mean that judgment goes in your favour. Never appear to express your personal opinion of the evidence or of a witness. You should preface any comment on the evidence with an objective phrase such as 'Members of the jury, you may think . . .'.

17.3.3 The law

Deal with the relevant law but not in great detail or at length. When addressing an audience of non-lawyers (lay magistrates, jurors), remember that they may need points explained in quite straightforward terms. Do not labour any points. Always reiterate the appropriate burden and standard of proof. In a criminal trial, the defence barrister, when confronted by apparently watertight prosecution evidence that is directly contradicted by the defence, will remind the jury (or magistrates) that a 'Not Guilty' verdict does not mean that the defendant has proved his or her contentions, simply that they have been left in doubt and must give the defendant the benefit of it.

17.3.4 Order of presentation in your speech

It is normal in a civil trial to deal first with the claimant's case and then with that of the defendant, regardless of whether you are making a closing speech for the claimant or defendant. Similarly, in criminal trials your speech will usually start by reviewing the case for the prosecution and then that for the defendant. So you follow the sequence in which the evidence was presented. This is because, generally, it is the claimant or prosecution who has the legal burden of proof—their case will be lost if the evidence in their favour is not up to the requisite standard. Because the claimant (or prosecution) started the litigation, it is usually they who have defined the issues in the case or 'chosen the battleground' and it is sensible to set out those issues within the context of their 'case'.

17.3.5 Preparation

If possible, do not make a closing speech without a chance to prepare it fully. This is so obvious that you may think it does not need saying. In a trial, it is not always possible to predict precisely when you will be called upon to make your closing speech. Often it will be straight after the last witness has finished his or her testimony and the defence has closed its case. If you have been occupied in examining witnesses, you may not have your closing speech in anything like its ideal state. It now becomes important to see who has 'the last word'.

17.4 Order of speeches

17.4.1 Civil trials

Closing speeches always occur in an established sequence. In a civil trial, the defendant's counsel goes first, followed by the claimant's barrister. So, the barrister appearing for the claimant gets more time to marshal his thoughts and the evidence, and to perfect a plan. (If there is more than one claimant or defendant, speeches go according to numerical order: 1st defendant, 2nd, 3rd, etc.)

17.4.2 Criminal trials

In a criminal trial, the basic principle is that the defence closing speech goes last. After that, you must distinguish between trials with magistrates and with a jury.

17.4.2.1 Magistrates

Under the Criminal Procedure Rules 2013, r 37.3, the prosecution may make a closing speech ('make final representations in support of the prosecution case') where the defendant is legally represented or, whether represented or not, the defence has called evidence other than just the defendant. The defence may always make a closing speech to the magistrates and should have the final word.

17.4.2.2 Trial by jury

If you are in a trial by jury, then usually both the prosecution and defence can make a closing speech, regardless of whether an opening speech was made. The prosecution barrister may forgo a closing speech if he or she made an opening speech and either there was no defence evidence or the only witness was the accused—counsel may feel that there is nothing to add to the opening (see *Blackstone's Criminal Practice* D18.17). A defence barrister should never surrender the chance to make a closing speech. Often, the defence do not make an opening speech (either through choice or because of the rules) but, even if the defendant's case was opened with a speech, the chance to have the last word to the jury is generally seen as a vital asset. See further *Blackstone's Criminal Practice* D18.19–18.20.

17.4.2.3 More than one defendant

If there is more than one defendant in a criminal trial and each is represented separately, the closing speeches for them will take place in the order in which they are named on the indictment. The defendants have no say in determining this order: sometimes the least important defendant is last, sometimes the most important. Whoever's name appears last gets the plum position for their closing speech. (Note that in this situation, the prosecution makes a single speech, dealing with all the defendants.)

17.4.2.4 Value of the final speech

When making the final speech that the jury hear (subject to the judge's summing-up) before they consider the verdict, you can deal cogently with all the issues in the case, whether raised by the prosecution or any co-defendant. Those barristers who preceded your speech could only guess what you were going to say and how you would say it; you have the advantage of knowing what they said.

17.5 Planning your speech

It should be clear that you need to think about the content and structure of your closing speech (if one is to be made) before the trial starts. It can only be a rough plan but you should have it ready for the beginning of the trial. As the trial progresses and witnesses substantiate (or undermine) the points you want to make, keep a record of what they said (highlight it in your notes or put an asterisk by it) so that it can be found easily. Try to refine and fill in the detail of your plan after each witness, or during adjournments. Such 'free' time is often limited in a trial, especially those lasting a day or less, so make the most of every chance you get to polish your speech. Even if you do so, you will inevitably have to carry a lot of material in your head.

This is no bad thing. You should be able to recall the really important pieces of evidence quite clearly. It will help you to do this if you have chosen a few key words or phrases (or even mental pictures) taken from your theory of the case and its themes. This will help you when making the speech to get your message over—as key words stick in your mind, so they will with the jury, judge, etc. The fewer points you ask your audience to think about, the more likely they are to do so and with reasonable recollection of the relevant evidence.

17.6   Delivering your speech

'May it please you, Your Honour/Sir/Madam/members of the jury . . .'. This is the traditional, courteous way to start a closing speech. Some judges deprecate use of the phrase 'may it please you'. After that, the manner in which you present your speech is really a question of individual style. You will develop your own style with time but it is a good idea to watch more experienced barristers when you go into court during your pupillage. You may see good and bad examples of a closing speech—be discriminating. Think about the sequence of events used in the speech, about the tone used by the barrister and the pace of delivery. Then consider how effective it was.

Just as you watched the judge's pen while examining a witness, so you must observe your audience during your speech. Make sure that you don't go so fast that they lose track of your arguments; but don't go so slowly that their eyes start to glaze over! Remember to look the jurors (or whoever is deciding the facts) in the eye but don't stare at individuals. Don't look wildly around the room—you are talking to a specific group of people and it is legitimate to concentrate on them. The best advocates will establish such a rapport with their audience that, for both sides, there is no one else in the courtroom.

Some barristers like to use hand gestures, others don't. You will probably do whatever is natural to you; but remember, you want your listener(s) to recall your arguments and evidence, not the fact that you looked like a Punch and Judy performer without the puppet! So if you are going to use gestures, do so sparingly and to emphasise your points. Judges generally prefer the more detached approach, with points made calmly and rationally, without appeal to the emotions. You will almost certainly 'lose' a judge if you indulge in too many gestures or any 'purple' prose. Remember that Horace Rumpole is a creature (of fiction and) of the Old Bailey—he works with juries, not in the Chancery Division of the High Court.

17.7   Further reading

Du Cann, R. *The Art of the Advocate,* Penguin, 1999, pp 189–218.
Evans, K. *Advocacy in Court,* 2nd edn, OUP, 1995, pp 66–7, 80–7.
Stone, M. *Cross-examination in Criminal Trials,* 3rd edn, Tottel Publishing, 2009.

17.8   Checklist for a closing speech

(a) Prepare a plan before the trial. (Once you know where you want to be at the end of the case, it will help you to concentrate on how you are going to get there.)

(b) Use key words or phrases to encapsulate the important points of your case. (Both you and your audience are more likely to remember a few simple phrases.)

(c) Remind the court (especially non-lawyers) of the appropriate burden and standard of proof on the contentious issues in the case.

(d) Make any concessions that seem appropriate in the light of the evidence given in the case. (It helps to focus attention on the real issues and may make you seem quite a reasonable person.)

(e) Using your key words, review the important points in a sensible order. Refer to the evidence that supports or undermines your case.

(f) If there is evidence that damages your case, deal with it. You might be able to offer an explanation for it that is consistent with your case; you might suggest that the witness is mistaken or lying; you might argue that, even if the evidence is accepted by the court, it does not prove what your opponent says it does.

(g) Watch your audience. Try to keep their attention. Think about how they might see the evidence and arguments, then try to present your speech in a manner that makes your points comprehensible to them.

(h) Decide before you begin what your closing words will be. If need be, write them down. Nothing reduces the impact of a speech more than the sight and hearing of an advocate who runs down at the end of a speech simply because he or she does not know how to end it. It saps the life out of everything that precedes it. It gives an unmistakable appearance of a lack of confidence in the advocate in the case he or she is presenting. It is easily avoided.

(i) Don't go on for too long.

17.9   Epilogue

'My poor client's fate now depends on your votes.'
Here the speaker sat down in his place,
And directed the judge to refer to his notes
And briefly to sum up the case.
But the judge said he never had summed up before;
So the Snark undertook it instead,
And summed it so well that it came to far more
Than the witnesses ever had said!

(From 'The Barrister's Dream' in Lewis Carroll's *The Hunting of the Snark.*)
Note: the Snark should not be used as a role model!

Part V

Witnesses

18

The task ahead

The following five chapters (**Chapters 19** to **23**) look at how advocates deal with witnesses. The chapters concentrate on the practical issues of technique and objectives. Please read them all carefully and use case studies as the raw material to practise them on (see, eg, *R v Heath* in the **Appendix** to this manual). Try working with your friends and colleagues, taking turns to play the role of the witness.

At The City Law School, we use a set of advocacy training criteria to measure the competence of an individual advocate when questioning a witness. These criteria are set out in full in **Chapter 19**. You will get a better understanding of the following chapters if you read **Chapter 19** first. Whenever you practise questioning a witness, try to apply these criteria to your work and consider the results. Equally valuable will be the comments of your friends and colleagues if they can base their feedback to you on those criteria. Of course, you can also apply them to any example of questioning a witness that you *see*, for example when visiting a court on a mini-pupillage or whilst watching a training video. The best advocates reflect upon their work frequently and think about ways in which they might improve.

One of the criteria that you should pay particular attention to is that which deals with questioning technique. For an advocate to abide by professional rules and the rules of evidence, the questions that he or she asks should appear in an appropriate form. An example of this is that, when you question your own witness, you should not 'lead' them. This means that the witness should be enabled to tell their own story in their own words. **Chapters 20** and **21** explain more about that and other questioning techniques that are appropriate for examination-in-chief. Conversely, when you question an opponent's witness, you should aim to exert considerable control over the witness. In cross-examination, you should not give the witness an opportunity to repeat the damage they have just inflicted on your case when they were questioned by their advocate; nor should your questions allow the witness to elaborate or give more details in ways that simply strengthen the case against your client. Competent cross-examination demands that you put your case to the witness, in an affirmative fashion, and that you exert control over the witness by asking plenty of closed, 'leading', questions. These questions should restrict the witness's freedom by severely limiting the range of answers that he or she can possibly give. **Chapter 22** tells you more about the techniques of cross-examination, and its aims and objectives. **Chapter 23** looks at the important, and often overlooked, skill of re-examination. This aspect of questioning is becoming even more important in civil cases as the opportunities to examine-in-chief are restricted. Re-examination often becomes the only significant chance that the advocate gets to question their witnesses at all, in court. We mentioned earlier the need for any advocate to abide by professional rules when questioning witnesses. This includes the need to comply with relevant rules of professional conduct, of course. It also includes the need to behave properly and sensitively towards witnesses. **Chapter 3** drew your attention to these important matters, since to proceed in ignorance of them may affect not just your own professional obligations but also your client's prospects of success in the instant case. If necessary, reread **Chapter 3** before continuing.

Basic components for witness handling

19.1 Introduction

You have already encountered some of our basic components in this manual. In **Chapter 4**, we introduced the criteria that can be used to gauge the effectiveness of advocacy in the context of applications and submissions. These were then considered in more detail in the rest of **Part II**. It is now time to introduce the criteria that we use at The City Law School when advocacy involves questioning a witness. For our purposes, this consists of two contexts—examination-in-chief and cross-examination. Although there is a third context for questioning—re-examination—this does not really raise any different skills or techniques (see further **Chapter 23** on the topic of re-examination).

The next point to bear in mind is that we are not starting from scratch. Many aspects of the criteria that were relevant to advocacy in applications and submissions are just as relevant now, when questioning witnesses. There is still the need for thorough preparation, for a clear and logical structure and for the advocate to communicate clearly in the courtroom. However, examination-in-chief and cross-examination both introduce new criteria that are of great importance if witnesses are to be questioned properly and effectively. Let's start by setting out the criteria.

19.2 Advocacy training criteria for examination-in-chief

In order to question your witness satisfactorily, you must show your ability in these areas:

(1) **Law and analysis**—prepare the case effectively, understanding:

    (i)   the case that has to be proved;

    (ii) the issues in the trial;

    (iii) the issues on which this witness can give evidence;

    (iv) the rules of evidence and procedure;

    (v) the principles of examination-in-chief.

(2) **Questioning content**—ask questions that:

    (i)   seek only relevant and admissible evidence;

    (ii) enable the witness to establish all of the relevant, admissible evidence he or she can give (including the production of exhibits).

(3) **Structure** the questions in a way that:

    (i)   is clear and logical to the witness/jury/tribunal;

    (ii) is responsive to the witness's answers;

    (iii) takes into account the relevance of this witness to the case as a whole and the client's interests.

(4) **Delivery**—speak clearly and fluently, at an appropriate pace, using appropriate language and manner, referring to notes when necessary or desirable.

(5) **Questioning technique**—control the witness and elicit evidence using appropriate questioning techniques, which:

    (i)   enable the witness to give his or her evidence in as coherent and persuasive a way as possible;

    (ii) respond as appropriate to the witness's answers.

Remember that the rules of professional conduct should always be observed.

19.3 Advocacy training criteria for cross-examination

In order to question an opponent's witness satisfactorily you must show your ability in the following areas:

(1) **Law and analysis**—prepare the case effectively, understanding:

    (i)   the case that has to be proved;

    (ii) the issues in the trial;

    (iii) the issues on which this witness can give evidence, in particular those on which this witness is helpful, damaging or neutral to your client's case;

    (iv) the rules of evidence and procedure;

    (v) the principles of cross-examination.

(2) **Questioning content**—ask questions that:

    (i)   seek only admissible evidence;

    (ii) seek only relevant evidence (whether to an issue or to credit);

    (iii) cover all relevant evidence of the witness including that relating to exhibits;

    (iv) enable the witness to assist your client's case insofar as he or she is able to do so;

    (v) insofar as it is necessary to do so:

        • put your client's case to the witness;

        • undermine the testimony of the witness;

        • undermine the credibility of the witness;

    (vi) make appropriate use of contradictory material.

(3) **Structure** the questions in a way that:

    (i)   is clear and logical to the tribunal;

    (ii) is responsive to the witness's answers;

    (iii) takes into account the relevance of this witness to the case as a whole and your client's interests.

(4) **Delivery**—speak clearly and fluently, at an appropriate pace, using appropriate language and manner, referring to notes when necessary or desirable.

(5) **Questioning technique**—control the witness and elicit evidence using appropriate questioning techniques, which:

    (i)   confine the witness's testimony appropriately to the evidence you seek to adduce;

    (ii) respond as appropriate to the witness's answers.

Remember that the rules of professional conduct should always be observed.

19.4 Planning to work with witnesses

In this section, we examine the matters that the advocate should consider before going into court for a trial, or other hearing that involves calling witnesses.

19.4.1 Thinking about the evidence

As with any appearance in court, you must identify several matters:

- What are the appropriate legal tests that will be applied?
- What are the facts in issue in the case? (In a civil case these should be clear from the statements of case; in a criminal case, a plea of not guilty requires proof of all the elements of the offence and one should then consider the possible/probable defence case as disclosed by the defence statement.)
- What evidence do you intend to adduce to ensure each issue is resolved in favour of your client?
- How do you intend to adduce that evidence?

This final point lies at the nub of how we start to prepare for calling witnesses. Will the evidence be in the form of answers given by a witness to questions asked by the advocate? Will the evidence emerge from a document, such as an affidavit, or from examination of an exhibit, such as a sketch plan or the alleged weapon, stolen property, etc? If so, who will produce the exhibit in court? Might the admissibility of the evidence be challenged?

What you need to do is to plan how the evidence needed to prove each material issue can be put before the court. Look at your papers critically to determine each place where a material fact can be proved with the use of a witness and/or an exhibit. You can set out your conclusions in tabular form, using a column to identify each fact in issue, then another to show that there is evidence to prove that fact (maybe just a tick would do), then a third to identify the source(s) of that evidence. There could be more than one source—for example several eyewitnesses to an accident who can each speak about what they saw happen. If one source is open to challenge—for example a confession in a criminal trial might be excluded—that point should be recorded and alternative sources to supply the same evidence should be shown. That way, you can identify in advance all the possible ways to prove your case (or attack the opponent's case), consider the arguments for and against issues of admissibility, and think about your best response if your preferred source of evidence on an issue fails to do the job that you wanted.

In the courtroom, when questioning witnesses, try to be as flexible and responsive as you can be. We have just considered one way to do this—by plotting different routes by which you can reach the same conclusion. Another way to resist inflexibility is to avoid using a detailed list of questions. By all means, have a concise note of those facts that you want the witness to tell the court about, and an idea of how you want to present this witness to the court (if it is your witness, they should appear to be reliable, truthful and accurate).

You should have a structure when working with witnesses. You need to think about the order for calling the witnesses, if you have more than one, and you always have to think about the structure of each witness's testimony.

19.4.2   Preparing the evidence in your case

There are some conventions that are used in deciding the order in which several witnesses may be called into court to give their evidence. In criminal cases, it is usual to call the victim first. In cases of violence, they will usually establish that the assault took place, what injuries were suffered and perhaps identify the assailant. In cases of dishonesty, where property has been taken, the victim can assert that they did not give permission for their property to be dealt with in that fashion. In cases involving illicit drugs, the prosecution will need to prove the nature of the substance, requiring expert evidence of the testing of a sample recovered from the accused. They will also need to prove that the sample of substance tested by the expert was the one taken from the accused—this requires the prosecution to show a chain of possession, with the substance being taken into lawful custody, put into a sealed container, labelled and initialled and then transported through various pairs of hands until it reached the expert. The prosecution should be ready to call every person who provides a link in this chain, if it becomes necessary to do so.

The order of witnesses for the defence in a criminal trial is not wholly a matter of choice for the advocate and the client. The Police and Criminal Evidence Act 1984, s 79 prescribes that if the defendant is to testify at trial, they must be the first witness to be called for the defence. This is subject to the court's discretion to allow another defence witness to be called into the witness-box before the accused testifies; the discretion is only likely to be used where the other witness will talk about non-contentious facts and there is some good reason for taking their evidence out of the usual order. Generally, witnesses in criminal cases are kept out of court until the time comes for them to testify. The objective that lies behind s 79 is that, as this rule cannot be applied to the accused, there is a risk that the accused may modify his or her testimony to 'fit' what evidence has already been given. This risk (which arises because the accused can see and hear all of the testimony in the case, up until he or she testifies) can be kept to a minimum if he or she is the first defence witness. Defence witnesses who will talk only about the character of the accused should always be called after the accused has testified.

Within these limitations, the advocate must still consider the best running order for the presentation of the evidence that he or she will rely upon. One excellent rule of thumb is to put yourself into the position of the trier(s) of fact—what would best enable the tribunal of fact to understand your client's case? Will the court be able to see how each witness contributes to your case? Will the significance of their testimony be clear? How do you want the story to unfold? These are all important questions but perhaps the most practical one is—who is available? Witnesses sometimes fail to turn up at court when they should. This may be due to nerves, illness, or even forgetfulness. Unless you are granted an adjournment by the court to secure the witness's attendance, you will have to do the best you can with what you have. That is one reason why you should have identified already the various alternative sources of evidence that you could use to establish each contentious issue in the case. Now you are able to stay calm and use your flexibility to your advantage—your advance planning is already paying dividends!

19.4.3 Planning the testimony of individual witnesses

Having determined the (probable) sequence for calling the witnesses, we must now look at each witness individually. The order in which you explore topics with a witness will depend in large measure upon whether they are called to support your client's case or that of the opponent.

19.4.3.1 Planning for examination-in-chief

For examination-in-chief of 'your' witness, you will be concerned to see that:

(a) the witness is encouraged to recall the events;

(b) he or she can express their recollection clearly;

(c) the witness can talk about matters in the required degree of detail; and

(d) the court can follow and recall the evidence easily.

You can usually achieve these aims by helping the witness to go through the material events in a chronological order. After all, that is the sequence in which the events occurred so it should seem quite natural to the witness and the court to talk about them in that order. It may be that you do not get the necessary amount of detail about a particular matter from the witness when they talk about it for the first time. That can happen because you must not 'lead' your witness but use open questions that prompt them to tell the story in their own words. This will mean that, from time to time, you will need to interrupt their narrative in order to go back and cover a topic in more detail. For example, 'You have told the court that you arrived at the bus stop at about 10.30 am. Can you recall what the weather was like then?' and then, 'After you arrived there, how many people were at the bus stop?' If the witness is the first to be called for your client, you may want to get their story out quite swiftly, so that the court can see what happened, in broad terms. Having established the backdrop, as it were, you can then backtrack and enable the witness to fill in more of the detail.

Sometimes, you will decide that the court will have a better understanding of events (or perhaps be more sympathetic to your client) if they learn first what happened to bring the parties to court at all, and then find out what events led up to that conclusion. Having settled the witness with the usual questions, such as, 'Please tell the court your full name' or 'What do you do for a living?', you might then ask the witness, 'Do you know why you are in court today?' When the witness replies affirmatively, you can then ask, 'Please tell the court what happened'. The witness is likely to start talking about the conclusion of a sequence of events, for example, 'My car was stolen.' or 'I was hit over the head and had to go to hospital.' or 'This man came up to me in the club and said I'd been talking to his girl.' You can then concentrate on those events with the witness, before turning to more preliminary matters.

Finally, we should also consider the use made of witness statements in civil cases. In both civil and criminal cases, witnesses usually provide statements to the parties calling them, in advance of the hearing. Generally, these statements will be exchanged between the parties before the trial, so that there are no surprises at the hearing itself (one significant exception to this is with defence witnesses in a criminal trial). In criminal cases, such statements will usually be disclosed only to the parties and their lawyers, and the judge in Crown Court trials; the witness's evidence at trial will be what they say in the witness-box rather than what they said in the previous statement. In civil cases, the witness's previous statement will often be ordered to serve as their evidence-in-chief (see eg, CPR, r 32.5(2)). This has consequences for any examination-in-chief by the advocate.

The start of the (civil) examination-in-chief will look something like this:

Having asked the witness to identify themselves, the advocate will have the court usher show the witness 'a document'.

Advocate:	'Do you see a signature on the document?'
Witness:	'Yes.'
Advocate:	'Whose signature is it?'
Witness:	'Mine.'
Advocate:	'When did you make that statement?'
Witness:	[replies]
Advocate:	'Were its contents true when you made it?'
Witness:	'Yes.'

At this point you (as the advocate) may sit down, leaving your witness to be cross-examined. However, you may wish to ask the witness to augment the evidence that is in their statement. You will need to ask the judge for leave to do so. The judge may refuse and suggest that you can pick up any points during your re-examination of the witness, after cross-examination. If you are given permission, then you may build on the witness's earlier statement. For example, 'Mr Smith, in paragraph 3 of your statement, you say that, "Because the weather was so hot, I took the safety guard off the machine that I was operating." What did you do with the safety guard?'

Because, in effect, you are combining the written statement with the oral testimony, you can be more selective with the topics that you ask the witness to deal with in the witness-box. Concentrate on those topics that are central to your case, and that will help the court to form a view of the witness's reliability and recollection. It is probably helpful to work through those topics in the order in which they appear in the written statement. As you will often use the statement as the 'springboard' for a question, the witness should understand clearly what you want them to talk about. Another reason to question your witness in court is where their statement is now out of date. Here, strictly speaking, you do not need to get leave from the court before asking questions but you should tell the judge what you are proposing to do. The judge may be concerned that a second, up-to-date statement should have been taken from the witness and served on your opponent before the trial. Since your aim now is to bring out new information, rather than looking at known events in greater detail, you should probably follow a chronological sequence, as we saw earlier.

19.4.3.2 Preparing for cross-examination

Your aims are rather different when you question the witnesses that have been called by your opponent. For one thing, you do not expect that they will support your client's case (although they may do in some topics). It is usual for a cross-examiner to want to undermine either the testimony of the witness (or the credibility of the witness) or to show its irrelevance to the issues in the trial. Further, as the witness's recollection of events is likely to be significantly different from the one that you seek to establish, you want to make their recollection more obscure than clear. You are also under a duty to question the witness on issues where your client's case differs from their recollection (known as 'putting your case to the witness'). In cross-examination, you are allowed to ask questions that suggest things, or put propositions, to the witness. So, you might say, 'But the man in the green jacket never had a knife in his hand, did he?' or 'You never saw his hand.' or 'The man in the green jacket had left by then.' In other words, you have a different story to tell and you do not want to give the witness a second chance to repeat their evidence-in-chief.

In cross-examination, then, your order of topics should be clear to the court. You want the tribunal of fact to understand why you are asking the questions that you use: you want the court to appreciate the discrepancies between the competing versions of events. But you do not always want the witness to see where you are going or what you are trying to do. The order of topics needs careful consideration, as does the order of questions on a particular topic.

You may wish to try to bait a trap for the witness, rather than immediately confront them with the proposition that you would like them to accept. So, for example, you may want to cast doubt on a witness's earlier testimony that when they saw the man in the green jacket, he was holding a knife in his hand. If you simply say to the witness, 'The man in the green jacket never had a knife in his hand, did he?', the likely answer you will get is, 'He did.'; blatant confrontation seldom produces agreement. If you begin by exploring the circumstances in which the observation took place, you may find either that the witness accepts that your proposition is reasonable or the court may well decide it is reasonable and not accept the witness's testimony on the matter. So, you might suggest (if to do so is consistent with your instructions) that the venue was dark, or busy, or the witness's attention was distracted, or something of that sort that might lead onto the witness acknowledging at least the possibility that they might be mistaken, in all the circumstances.

19.5   Asking questions—the purposes of questioning witnesses

This is the equivalent of 'content', the second criterion for applications to the court. However, it is a more complex topic in relation to witnesses than it is for applications. You might want to turn to **19.2** and **19.3** and re-read the advocacy training criteria on examination-in-chief and cross-examination with specific reference to 'questioning content' in both lists.

19.5.1   Your witness

What you ask a witness will be governed by several considerations. First, you must not ask your witness leading questions on matters in dispute (see **Chapter 21**). If you do, then although the subject matter of the question may be 'relevant' and based on a sound understanding of the law and allegations, it may not be 'appropriate'. Thus, you should use appropriate questioning techniques.

In any hearing where witnesses are called to testify, you should have identified what evidence they can give that will help to establish your client's case. This will decide the relevance of your questions and their answers. If you don't ask questions to make the optimum use of the witness and get all of the relevant evidence that they could give, you probably have not conducted an examination-in-chief that is wholly appropriate to the circumstances of that case. Further, you should not ask a question that requires the witness to speak about inadmissible matters; such questions may be logically relevant but are not legally relevant (see, eg, *R v Blastland* [1986] AC 41). Finally, you should try to insulate your witness from attack by your opponent in cross-examination. That may mean getting the witness to talk about topics relevant to your opponent's case as well as your client's case. Such topics may not be of direct legal relevance to your client's case but it could certainly be appropriate to canvass them at this point.

19.5.2 Your opponent's witness

As before, what is required here will be fact-specific to the individual case, as determined by the issues between the parties and what evidence the witness can give. You should use appropriate questioning techniques here, too, but what is appropriate has changed (see **Chapter 22**). In general terms, examination-in-chief is about **trust**, the advocate allowing the witness the freedom to tell their story in their own words, but cross-examination is about **control**. The cross-examiner doesn't want the witness to tell their story in their own words; instead, the cross-examiner asks leading questions designed to convey the story of the cross-examiner's client in words chosen by the cross-examiner. In one sense, it does not matter what answers most witnesses give in cross-examination because the cross-examiner never expected the witness to agree with the proposition in the question anyway. One of the functions of cross-examination is to put your client's case to the witness (see **Chapter 22**) and such 'questions' are unlikely to produce much agreement between the advocate and the witness. The degree of control exerted on witnesses in cross-examination can often be seen if you keep a note of the questions and answers; typically, the questions contain the detail while the answers are just 'Yes' or 'No'. Questions asked during examination-in-chief are generally not so detailed but can produce quite lengthy and complex responses from the witness.

Other aims of cross-examination, which make certain questions appropriate, are the need to use the witness to assist your client's case and the possibility of undermining the witness and/or their evidence. On the former point, it is not always the position that a witness called by the opposing party will be 100% damaging to your client's case, more often than not the witness may be a source of assistance on at least some topics. If you can see a way in which your opponent's witness could supply answers that help your client, it is appropriate to ask the questions that produce those answers; evidence given by opposing witnesses that supports your case always seems to be more persuasive. On the latter point, undermining, you might ask questions that attack the credibility of the witness themselves (eg to show they are biased) or of their version of events (eg comparing it with other evidence given in the cases that is inconsistent with their version).

19.6 The structure of questions to a witness

19.6.1 Your witness

During examination-in-chief, you should be using each witness to tell the court what they know of the story of the case. In each trial there are one or more issues that the parties dispute and that the court must resolve; sometimes these are disputes of law but much more often they are disputes of fact. You should structure your sequence of questions to a witness with a primary objective of getting the witness to speak clearly and logically about the 'facts'. Your questions should assist the witness to achieve a good communication with the trier(s) of fact. That means that you go through topics in a sensible order, that the witness is enabled to give all of the evidence that they could give (and that is useful to your client's case) and they do so by telling their story in their own words, as much as possible. Studies of witness credibility have shown that juries are likely to find a witness much more credible (and persuasive) if they demonstrate a good understanding of what they are testifying about and appear confident in what they are saying. It also helps, apparently, if the advocate does not interrupt very often.

What you need to do to start the examination-in-chief is to settle the witness. They need to get used to their surroundings, to being the focus of attention, and to the sound of their own voice projected across the courtroom. So you start them with easy, short questions to which they know the answers and that allow them to talk a little. For example, in a case where the witness's job or workplace is relevant:

- Please tell the court your name.
- What is your occupation?
- Where do you work?
- How long have you worked there?

Such questions pose no major test for a witness and so they help to take the pressure off. Once the witness has relaxed, you can move onto the substance of their evidence. What sequence might you adopt there?

You will usually find that, as the witness is telling a story, they will recollect it best (and the trier(s) of fact will remember it better) if you enable the witness to work through their story in a chronological order. As this is your witness, you should not ask leading questions, even if you wanted to (see **Chapter 21**). Open questions that allow the witness some freedom to tell their story are the ones that should be in the majority at the beginning of the examination-in-chief. Obviously, the lack of direct control that you have when using open-type questions means that sometimes the witness says something ambiguous or obscure and further explanation is required. Then you have a choice; either you interrupt the 'flow' of the witness's narrative, as in:

Stop there, please, Sergeant. You just said that Mr Jones was drunk. What led you to that conclusion?

and immediately seek further clarification from the witness. Or you can let the witness continue to answer open questions until they have concluded their narrative, and then return to topics raised by the witness earlier, getting the detail through more specific questions. The former tactic is acceptable (it is sometimes called the 'funnel' technique; and see **20.8**) but you must be careful not to go into so much detail now, through overuse of closed questions, that the court cannot see the wood for all the trees.

As well as using your witnesses to establish your client's case, you may also want to use them to cast doubt on your opponent's case and you may want to protect your witness from a damaging attack in cross-examination. Both objectives are likely to result in you asking questions that are not an obvious part of your client's theory of the case. In order to minimise any confusion that may arise in these circumstances, it is usually better to leave these topics to later in the witness's evidence, after they have done their best to establish the evidence favourable to your client.

The other consideration is that you should be responsive to a witness's answers. You cannot simply plough on, making it appear to others that you are paying no regard to the answers the witness is giving. The sequence of questions and answers should flow in a clear and logical fashion. When breaks occur, and there is a change of subject, that should be clear from the first question on the new topic, as in, 'I want to turn now to the moment when the ambulance arrived. What did . . .?'

So you see that, when thinking about the sequence of your questions for examination-in-chief, you should have a clear idea of the basic running order of topics through which to take the witness. The sequence in which specific questions are asked may be better left until you are actually on your feet questioning the witness, otherwise you risk being too tied to a plan and not responding appropriately to the witness's answers.

19.6.2 Your opponent's witness

When cross-examining a witness, your aims are a little different. Now you are likely to be less concerned with assisting the witness and allowing them to tell their story. In fact, you probably don't want them to tell their story (again). You won't be able to finalise your running order for the topics you need to cross-examine on until the moment that your opponent concludes the examination-in-chief. That doesn't give you a lot of time! Obviously you need a list of all the topics you might need to question the witness about, and you should think about a sensible order in which to raise those topics. But suppose the witness never gave an anticipated and crucial piece of evidence? A large part of your intended cross-examination may just have become redundant. You must be able to respond to the evidence actually given by the witness in-chief. If they haven't hurt your case, don't cross-examine them, leave them well alone.

You need to analyse each opposing witness to see on each issue in the case:

(a) do they have evidence relevant to this issue;

(b) if so, does it hurt my client's case; or

(c) does it help my client's case; or

(d) is the witness effectively neutral?

Once you have done that, you will have an overall picture of the witness as potentially harmful, helpful, neutral, or a mixture of these depending on the particular topic. In turn, that will help you to decide on your likely running order for the topics. If you think the witness can help you on a particular topic, it might be best to deal with that at or near the start of your cross-examination, especially if you think you may have to attack them on other topics. They may be less willing to agree with your questions towards the end of your cross-examination if you have given them a tough time earlier on.

Finally, as with the examination-in-chief, listen to the witness's answers and respond to them. Your response will probably be different since the answer may be a damaging one, but you should constantly be reassessing what questions you need to ask this witness. One difference between the sequence of questions in examination-in-chief and in cross-examination is this: in examination-in-chief, you want to help the witness and so you raise topics in a clear and logical order (typically chronological). In cross-examination, you want your questions to be structured in a way that makes them clear and logical to the trier(s) of fact but maybe not so clear to the witness—at least until it is too late for them to do anything about it! The key here may be to have a gentle and patient build-up, through a series of relatively innocuous questions, until you have painted the witness into a corner. Then you ask the key question (probably putting some part of your client's case to the witness), saying something like, '. . . That must be right, mustn't it, Miss Smith?' If you have built up the previous questions and answers sensibly and patiently, the court is likely to agree with your proposition even if the witness does not.

19.7 Speaking and delivery

You should refer to **Chapter 8**, which dealt extensively with the subject of communication, and that has not altered in this context. However, you will need to bear in mind that, as well as having to communicate with one or two sets of listeners in the courtroom—judge, magistrates, jury—there is now an additional recipient of your communications—the witness in the witness-box. When you question a witness, he or she must hear and be able to understand your question. Equally, the judge and any other fact-finders must be able to hear your question, usually in order to make sense of the answer from the witness. This places an added burden on you to speak clearly and at the appropriate pace and volume. You must also assist the witness to communicate clearly with the judge or magistrates and jury (if there is one). For example, remind your witness that his or her answers should be directed towards the judge (or magistrates or jury) and not towards you. Tell them to speak at a comfortable pace and suggest perhaps that they watch the judge as he or she takes a note of their evidence, to ensure the pace is comfortable for the court, too. You will still need to monitor the pace of the witness's answers—don't leave it up to the witness to judge! You will also need to consider the pace of the exchanges between yourself and the witness. Is it too fast/too slow? If you are asking a lot of closed questions, say in cross-examination, and the witness is just responding with 'Yes' or 'No', the exchanges can get quite fast. In that situation, you may need to build in an occasional pause.

19.8 Controlling the witness and using appropriate questioning techniques

Control is essential whether dealing with your own witness or one called by an opponent. A witness is not in the witness-box to say just what they want, how they want. They are there for a purpose. The party calling the witness wants to use them as a source of credible and helpful evidence that is relevant to the facts in issue. The party who has not called the witness often wants to limit the damage done to their case by this witness. The cross-examiner may want to exert quite overt control over the witness, typically by the use of leading, closed, questions. The examiner-in-chief will exert control more subtly, usually, through selection of topics, interventions when a witness strays into inadmissible or irrelevant evidence, and courteously stopping an answer when too much information is being given for the court to absorb. **Chapters 21** and **22** contain very helpful guidance on the aims and techniques of examination-in-chief and cross-examination, which are unnecessary to duplicate here. In summary, though, examination-in-chief avoids the use of leading questions, whilst these are quite acceptable in cross-examination. Open questions, which allow the witness to give relevant evidence in their own words, are the main staple for examination-in-chief.

20 | Basic questioning skills

20.1 Introduction

This chapter provides a brief introduction to the different types of questioning techniques that you will need to apply when conducting the examination of witnesses in civil and criminal cases.

20.2 The open-ended question

This is a question that does not limit the scope of the answer. This type of question allows the witness to either give a short or full narrative answer. The witness will usually give a narrative answer.

Examples

Q: 'What happened after he struck you?'

Q: 'Why did you telephone her?'

Q: 'Where did you go after you left the police station?'

Q: 'How did you cope at work with one arm in plaster?'

This type of question is particularly useful when you want the witness to tell the story or part of it in his or her own words. It helps to move the story along. It can, however, allow the witness too much scope for 'rambling' off the point and the story may come out in a confusing way. A series of open questions runs the risk of losing control of the witness.

20.3 The closed question

This is a question that limits the scope of the answer. It is particularly useful when you are seeking to elicit a particular piece of information or detail from a witness. It allows much greater control of the witness than an open question.

Examples

Q: 'What time was it?'

Q: 'How far away were you at that point?'

Q: 'In which hand was he holding the gun?'

20.4   **The transition**

Transitions are a means of moving the witness from one piece of evidence or topic to another. They communicate a change of topic or place to the witness and also to the court. They may take the form of a statement such as 'I want to turn now to the moment when the ambulance arrived', or a question (either open or closed) such as 'After that day, when did you next see the defendant?' Transitions are a useful way of structuring the testimony, controlling the witness and moving from irrelevant to relevant information.

Suppose, for example, you wish to elicit two pieces of evidence from the witness:

(a) that she was present in the doctor's surgery on the day in question; and

(b) approximately 20 minutes after her arrival, she heard the defendant threaten the doctor.

After establishing the witness's presence in the waiting room at the doctor's surgery, you might ask:

Q: 'What, if anything, happened then?'

A: 'Well, I picked up a magazine from the table, you know one of those fancy ones, I think it was *Country Life*. As I was reading it, they have such beautiful pictures in it you know, Mrs Reid from down my road came in with her Sandra who had this awful chest cold. Mrs Reid was telling me about the arthritis in her hands and the pain she was in. Then we heard this commotion and all of a sudden, Brian Peters came storming out of the doctor's room shouting that he'd be back and that next time he'd make sure the doctor never practised again. . .'

Although you got there in the end, it would have been much more effective if you had used a transitional question instead, for example:

Q: 'Did there come a time when something unusual/unexpected happened while you were sitting in the waiting room?'

A: 'Oh yes. I was sitting chatting to Mrs Reid about her arthritis' (there is a limit to the extent you can control some witnesses!) 'when we heard this terrible commotion. All of a sudden, Brian Peters came storming out. . .'

20.5   **The point of reference (or 'piggy-back' question)**

This is the method of including in your question a fact or facts that have already been elicited from the witness. It provides a context for the question and is a useful technique for emphasising an important fact, clarifying the evidence, obtaining greater detail from the witness, controlling the witness and/or providing a transition.

Examples

Q: 'What happened directly after you heard Miss Jones scream?'—emphasis and detail.

Q: 'When you said he left, to whom were you referring?'—clarification.

Q: 'Describe the knife you saw in the defendant's hand'—emphasis and detail.

Q: 'Did you see Mr Green again after he left your office that afternoon?'—transition and control.

Note that a point of reference can be included in either an open or closed question and form part of a transitional question. This method of questioning should not be used simply to get the witness to repeat a clear answer to an earlier question(s).

Examples of how not to use 'piggy-back' questions

A: 'I heard Miss Jones scream.'

Q: 'You said Miss Jones screamed?'

A: 'Yes.'

20.6 Leading questions

A leading question is one that suggests or tends to suggest its own answer. It often assumes a fact that has not yet been established. It sometimes calls for a 'Yes' or 'No' response.

Examples

'Were you in Manchester on 5 May 2014?'

'Did you see the knife in his hand?'

'Was she standing three feet away from you?'

A non-leading question in the same circumstances would have been:

'Where were you on 5 May 2014?' (date not in dispute).

'What did you see?'

'How far away was she?'

The witness's role is to tell his or her account to the court. As a general rule, it is therefore not permitted to elicit evidence in **examination-in-chief** by the use of leading questions. There are two exceptions to this general rule.

20.6.1 Circumstances in which a leading question may be asked during examination-in-chief

20.6.1.1 A leading question may be asked when the subject matter of the question is not in dispute.

Example

There is no dispute that the parties met at the claimant's office on the evening of 10 March 2014.

Q: 'Did you meet the defendant at your office on the evening of 10 March 2014?'

Sometimes one piece of information is agreed while another is not.

Example

There is no dispute that the parties met on the evening of 10 March 2014. The time of the meeting is in dispute.

Q: 'Did you meet the defendant on the evening of 10 March 2014?'

A: 'Yes.'

Q: 'What time did you meet?'

Example

There is no dispute that the parties met one evening at the claimant's office. The date is in dispute.

    Q: 'Do you recall an evening when you met the defendant at your office?'

    A: 'Yes.'

    Q: 'What date was that?'

Counsel often use a leading question when the subject matter is unlikely to be contentious. For instance, where there is unlikely to be any dispute that a conversation took place, counsel might ask 'Did you have a conversation with the defendant?' It is important to differentiate between the fact of a conversation taking place and what was said during that conversation. One may be in dispute while the other is not. If in doubt, check with your opponent before you go into court.

20.6.1.2   **A leading question is permitted when you are seeking to elicit a denial from your witness as to his or her own alleged conduct or actions**

For example your witness's version of events for examination-in-chief may be very different from the case presented by the prosecution. In order to obtain your witness's response to a material allegation that is not part of **their** case, it may be necessary to ask a leading question to elicit a denial.

Example

    Q: 'On 4 January did you stab your wife with a carving knife?'

    A: 'No.'

Example

    Q: 'Did you tell Mr Smith on 4 January 2014 that he was "dead meat"?'

    A: 'No.'

What is in reality a leading question may appear to be non-leading by the simple device of offering the witness limited choices. As a matter of common sense, the answer must be one or the other.

Example

    Q: 'Were you in this country or abroad on 6 February last?'

In this example, the answer is suggested in the question, in the sense that the witness will select one or other option. This type of question is leading but has the advantage of enabling you to guide the witness where you want him or her to go. Note that the non-leading version is to ask 'Where were you on 6 February last?'

20.7   Non-leading questions

How then do you formulate your questions so as to avoid asking your witness a leading question? There are two basic methods you can use:

(a) Start your questions neutrally with one of the following interrogatives:

Who. . .?

What. . .?

Why. . .?

When. . .?

Where. . .?

How. . .?

Or with a neutral invitation:

Tell   Describe

Explain   Demonstrate

These will enable you to elicit the answer from the witness. Generally avoid asking questions that start with the words 'Did you. . . ?', 'Were you. . . ?', or 'Was it . . . ?' —these will normally contain suggestion(s) and tend to lead!

(b) Another basic way is to think of the answer you wish your witness to give and then omit any reference to the answer when framing the question. The question should come quite naturally.

Example

Answer required: 'Sunday'. Q: 'What day was it?'
NOT: 'Was it a Sunday?' (a leading question).

Answer required: 'Blue jeans and a white t-shirt.'
Q: 'Describe what he was wearing.'
NOT: 'Was he wearing blue jeans and a white t-shirt?'

Answer required: '(He left) three weeks ago.'
Q: 'When did he leave?'
NOT: 'Did he leave three weeks ago?'

The above illustrations show the advantage of preparing by using short headings or points. Try using a simple note form with subheadings and 'bullet point' words. A note might just state: 'Setting the scene—Sun/8 pm/wet?' Avoid writing a long list of all the questions you wish to ask the witness, as you will focus on your notes rather than listening to the response of the witness. If you are not listening to the witness's reply you may miss the opportunity to ask transition questions or reference point ('piggy-back') questions.

20.8   Combining questioning techniques

If you use too many open-ended questions, you run the risk of losing control of the witness and too much irrelevance clouding his or her testimony. If you use too many closed questions, you will leave the court with the impression that the witness is a robot whom you have pre-programmed. Instead, achieve a balance by combining these techniques for the maximum effect:

(a) ask open questions to allow the witness to tell his or her story;

(b) ask closed questions to elicit details from the witness or emphasise part of the story;

(c) ask open questions to enable the witness to continue with the next part of the story;

(d) ask closed questions to elicit details, and so on.

This is sometimes referred to as the funnel technique. You start with open questions and then gradually restrict the answers the witness can give by asking a series of closed questions.

20.9 In summary

Leading questions	*Non-leading questions*
(Avoid in examination-in-chief; use in cross-examination)	(Use in examination-in-chief; avoid in cross-examination)
You said. . .?	Who?
You saw. . .?	What?
You did. . .?	Why?
You were. . .?	When?
It was. . .?	Where?
Did you?	How?
You did not...?	Tell/Describe
Were you?	Explain/Demonstrate
Was it?	

21

Examination-in-chief

21.1 Introduction

Examination-in-chief is the process of eliciting evidence from your own witness and is the first opportunity the court has to assess the witness. A strong impression made at that stage will give the witness credibility and may withstand any attack in cross-examination.

21.1.1 The aims of examination-in-chief

The aims of conducting any examination-in-chief should therefore be threefold:

(a) to establish your case or part of it through the evidence elicited from the witness;

(b) to present the evidence so that it is clear, memorable and persuasive;

(c) to insulate the evidence, insofar as possible, from anticipated attack in cross-examination.

Before turning to look at how these aims can be achieved, let us first consider some preliminary matters.

21.2 Preparation and planning

21.2.1 Establishing an order

While preparing your case (see *Opinion Writing and Case Preparation* manual), you will have already identified what you need to prove or disprove at the trial and have determined the facts and legal principles that are relevant to establishing your case. You will have also selected the theory of your case and the key elements of the evidence that support it.

You are now ready for the next step in your preparation. This involves:

(a) selecting the order of the witnesses;

(b) selecting the order of the evidence to be elicited from each witness.

21.2.1.1 Selecting the order of the witnesses

(a) It is preferable to start and finish your case with a witness who makes a strong impression. Avoid calling as your first witness one whose evidence is particularly vulnerable to cross-examination (eg because it contains many inconsistencies or the witness's recollection is poor).

(b) In a large proportion of cases, it is usual to start with the witness whose evidence is first in time. This may, however, create difficulties where a number of your witnesses deal with matters that are relevant to the whole of your case. It may then be preferable to call as your first witness the one who gives the greatest overview of your case. This is likely to be your client, although not necessarily so.

(c) As a general rule, you do not have to call your client as your first witness. The one exception to this is provided by the Police and Criminal Evidence Act 1984, s 79. As defence counsel in a criminal trial, you must call the accused (if he or she is giving evidence) before any other witness of fact unless the court directs otherwise.

(d) Avoid calling your client in the middle of your witnesses. It makes a stronger impression if you call him or her either first or last. If you call your client as your final witness it may give him or her an opportunity to settle down and familiarise himself or herself with the atmosphere of the court.

(e) Corroborative witnesses should be called as close as possible to the evidence they are corroborating in order to support and insulate that evidence.

(f) Beware of calling too many cumulative witnesses or of seeking to over prove your case. This may backfire (you may even be penalised in costs on detailed assessment). Calling six witnesses who claim to have seen the same incident may give your opponent the opportunity of highlighting inconsistencies between their various accounts. If you must call a number of cumulative witnesses, particularly where you are prosecuting in a criminal trial, simply tender some of them for cross-examination.

(g) Where your expert opinion evidence is based on establishing certain facts it would be more sensible to call the expert after witnesses of fact have given evidence. Note, however, that the availability of your expert witness might determine when you call him or her. Expert witnesses called at the end of your case will enable you to finish on a strong note and may provide you with an opportunity to recap and/ or emphasise the evidence you have already elicited from your previous witnesses. In civil cases, active case management may have already determined which experts will give evidence, what expert evidence is to be heard at the trial and on what issue(s).

21.2.1.2 Selecting the order of the evidence to be elicited from each witness

Your aim should be to organise the key elements of the witness's testimony in a logical order so that the judge, jury or tribunal can understand how each part fits into the overall theory of your case. This will normally result in a strict chronological presentation of the evidence, particularly in the case of a witness to a specific incident. For example, in a claim for damages for personal injuries sustained at work, the claimant's witness statement might be structured to give evidence in this order:

(a) his or her background;

(b) his or her training and experience;

(c) safety instruction in the job;

(d) description of the site where the accident occurred or of the machinery being used at the time;

(e) what occurred just before the accident;

(f) how the accident actually occurred;

(g) what happened immediately after the accident;

(h) initial treatment, pain and suffering;

(i) continued treatment, pain, suffering, loss of amenity;

(j) present disabilities: physical, mental, emotional;

(k) financial losses to date.

Not every case, however, lends itself to a strict chronological presentation of the witness's evidence. If a chronological presentation will not be effective you should structure the evidence so as to emphasise the key elements that establish or support your case. For example, imagine you are representing a father seeking a residence order of his child. Your aim is to elicit evidence from the family's au pair regarding the mother's financial irresponsibility, alcoholism and physical abuse of the child. You could deal with everything the witness has to say, in a strict chronological order, from the moment she entered the household; but it will be more effective if you elicit the evidence by topic. This does not prevent you from dealing with the subject matter of each topic in a chronological order. However, by eliciting the evidence by topic you will leave the trier of fact with a much stronger cumulative picture of each aspect of the behaviour.

21.2.2 Written preparation

Many novices prepare for examination-in-chief by writing out all the questions they propose to ask each witness. This is usually done as a confidence booster in case they forget to ask the relevant questions or are unable to form their questions spontaneously.

If you have your face in a notebook, you will probably pay scant regard to the witness's answer in your anxiety to find and read the next question. You may lose the vital opportunity of watching the witness, his or her reaction to the question, the manner in which he or she responds and the impression he or she makes upon the court. You may miss what your opponent has seen, the telling gesture, the judge's expression and the jury members' looks of incredulity. You may convey an impression of disinterest in your witness's account. Most important of all, if your preparation is too rigid, you will find it difficult to adapt your questions to suit the witness's answer(s), to cope with an unexpected answer (witnesses do change their stories!), or a piece of evidence that has emerged during the trial.

Therefore, while recognising that the practice varies at the Bar, you will be encouraged, during the Bar Professional Training Course, not to rely upon a prepared script of written questions. If you need to write out some of your questions as a confidence booster, you will be encouraged to restrict these to a couple on the most important or complicated issues in the case. It is normal practice to use the witness's proof of evidence (in criminal cases) or witness statement (in civil cases) as the basis of examining him or her in-chief.

This does not mean that you should not prepare for examination-in-chief; preparation and planning are vital. Rather than writing down a string of questions, you will be encouraged to write down a note of the topics you want to deal with, broken down into subheadings or points, where appropriate. Preparing your case in this way, using 'trigger notes' or 'bullet points', will enable you to concentrate on the issues, the key elements of the evidence and allow you greater flexibility. You can then see at a glance where you wish to guide the witness.

21.3   Presenting the evidence

21.3.1   Calling the witness

It is time to call your first witness! You normally do so as follows:

'Sir/Madam, I (now) call Mrs Mary Brown';

or, as a matter of courtesy, just after you have finished your opening speech/statement:

'With your permission Sir/Madam' or 'With your Honour/Your Lordship's permission, I call Mrs Mary Brown'.

While the witness is taking the oath, you must stay both silent and still. Do not shuffle papers!

21.3.2   Getting started

Start examination-in-chief by settling the witness. Help the witness to get used to their surroundings, to being the focus of attention, and to the sound of their own voice projected across the courtroom. So you start with one or two easy, short questions to which they know the answers and that allow them to talk a little. For example:

Q: 'What is your full name, please?'
Q: 'What do you do for a living?'/'Where do you work?'
Q: 'What is your position in that company?'
Q: 'What are your responsibilities?'

The circumstances of the case will dictate the extent to which it is necessary to elicit personal background information from the witness. Personal background information is not always relevant to the case so move to a few easy questions in a relevant area. Once the witness has relaxed, you can move onto the substance of their evidence.

21.3.3   The initial hurdles

You must now guide the witness to the starting point of his or her evidence. This will normally establish his or her connection with the case. Much now depends upon the extent to which the facts are in dispute as this will dictate the extent to which you may or may not lead at this stage. It may be clear from the statements of case/affidavits/witness statements that a matter is non-contentious. If it is not apparent, check with your opponent before you go into court. You must frame your question(s) so as not to lead on disputed matters.

21.3.3.1   Where there is no dispute

Q: 'Did you let a room at your home to the defendant in July 2014?'
Q: 'Did you examine the claimant in your surgery on 15 May 2014?'
Q: 'Did you meet the defendant in the "Horse and Hounds" public house in Ealing during the evening of 6 October last?'
Q: 'Were you employed by the claimant, Mrs Gray, as a housekeeper during the period from October 1998 to June 2014?'
Q: 'Did you attend at the security office in Harrods store during the afternoon of 3 August 2014?'

21.3.3.2   Where a matter is only partially in dispute

Q: 'Where were you during the morning of 4 September 2014?' (date and time not in dispute)

Q: 'When did you let a room at your premises to the defendant?' (tenancy not in dispute but date in dispute)

Q: 'In what capacity were you employed in October 2010?' (job not in dispute but job role in dispute)

Q: 'Where did you meet the defendant during the evening of 6 October last?' (meeting not in dispute but place in dispute)

21.3.3.3   Where there is a disputed matter

There are some occasions, however, when it is clear that a matter is entirely in dispute or when your opponent asks you not to lead on a particular point. The way in which you deal with this varies in every case. As a general rule look for some common ground or begin with an uncontentious matter (this may be apparent from the statements of case/ witness statements). It may be necessary to generalise or ask the witness about an event that occurred at an earlier time.

Example 1

Q: 'Where do you work?' (working not in dispute)

A: 'At Lloyds Bank, Charing Cross Road.'

Q: 'How long have you worked there?'

A: 'About two years.'

Q: 'How do you get to work in the mornings?'

A: 'I catch the tube to Charing Cross and then walk down the road to the bank.'

Q: 'During the last two years, has anything exceptional happened in that vicinity on your way to work?'

A: 'Yes. I once saw a car crash.'

Q: 'Where precisely was that?'

Example 2

Q: 'Do you know Mr Jones?'

A: 'Yes.'

Q: 'When did you first meet him?'

A: 'We met at an office party about a year ago. He came with one of the girls I work with.'

Q: 'How long was your meeting?'

A: 'We were introduced and chatted for about ten minutes at the party. He and his girlfriend then gave me a lift home.'

Q: 'Did you ever see Mr Jones again?'

A: 'Yes.'

Q: 'When was that?'

A: 'It was 11 June 2014, the night I was burgled.'

Example 3

Q: 'Do you recall an occasion when you spent a weekend in Manchester?'

A: 'Yes.'

Q: 'When was that?'

A: 'The beginning of May last year.'

Q: 'On what date did you return home?'

A: 'I came back on 5 May.'

Q: 'Did you notice anything in particular on your return?'

A: 'As soon as I got to the house, I noticed that the front door had been kicked in and was hanging off its hinges...'

21.3.4   Setting the scene

Having guided the witness to the start of his or her evidence, it will probably be necessary to 'set the scene' further by eliciting details of the surrounding or background circumstances. This is particularly so in the case of a witness to an incident.

Examples

Q: 'Describe the weather/traffic/road surface conditions.'

Q: 'Where were you standing?'

Q: 'Who else was present at the meeting?'

Q: 'When did you first meet the defendant?'

The nature of the case will determine the extent to which you need to develop a picture of the surrounding/background detail.

21.3.5   Witness statements

The preparation and exchange of full witness statements, directed to stand as the witness's evidence-in-chief, has increasingly replaced the need for examination-in-chief in civil cases. In such a case, it is unnecessary for the witness to repeat the content of his or her statement. The start of the (civil) examination-in-chief will look something like the following.

Having asked the witness to identify himself or herself, the advocate will ask the following:

Q: 'Mr Smith can you please turn to page 6 of the trial bundle?'
A: 'Yes.'
Q: 'Do you recognise that document?'
A: 'Yes, it is my witness statement.'
Q: 'Can you please turn to the end of that document on page 12?'
A: 'Yes'.
Q: 'Do you see a signature on the document?'
A: 'Yes.'
Q: 'Whose signature is it?'
A: 'Mine.'

It is not necessary to invite the witness to confirm the making and truth of the statement as the statement of truth is already endorsed at the end of the statement. The witness is then asked to remain in the witness-box for cross-examination.

Note that the judge retains a discretion to override a direction that the witness statement stands as the evidence-in-chief. The judge will therefore indicate if there are matters on which he or she would like to hear oral testimony despite the fact that they are dealt with in the witness's statement. This will normally occur where there is a factual dispute between two parties and the judge wishes to hear the oral testimony so that he or she can assess the credibility of each witness as they set out the evidence in their own words in examination-in-chief. In the majority of civil cases the witness statement will stand as the evidence-in-chief.

You may only adduce evidence of additional matters in-chief, the substance of which was not contained in the witness's statement, if (i) the other party consents, or (ii) such additional evidence relates to new matters that have arisen in the course of the trial or recently and there has been insufficient time to serve a supplemental witness statement, and (iii) you obtain permission of the court because you wish to amplify or clarify the witness evidence. Where additional evidence is available after a witness statement is prepared and there is sufficient time, it is normal practice for a supplemental witness statement to be produced and disclosed to the other side in civil cases. The supplemental witness statement will be in the trial bundle. The witness will be asked to prove the supplemental statement after proving their first statement in the same manner as described in the example given earlier.

21.3.6   The heart of the testimony: achieving the aims of examination-in-chief

We considered briefly at the start of this chapter the three aims of examination-in-chief:

(a) establishing your case;

(b) making the evidence clear, memorable and persuasive;

(c) insulating the evidence, insofar as possible, from anticipated attack in cross-examination.

How can these aims be achieved? Unfortunately, there is no single 'magic' answer to this question but if you observe the following basic principles, you should begin to master the skill of conducting a successful examination-in-chief.

21.3.7   Twenty basic principles

21.3.7.1   Know your objective

Concentrate on the key elements of the witness's testimony and keep them to the forefront of your mind. You should be asking yourself questions such as: What am I seeking to show through this witness's evidence? What part of my case does this witness (help to) establish/support? What is it that I want him/her to deal with? In what order do I want to cover these matters?

21.3.7.2   Do not rush

The trier(s) of fact will be listening to the evidence for the first time. It takes longer to absorb new information when hearing it rather than reading it. The main points can be submerged if drowned in too much peripheral detail.

21.3.7.3   Do not lead on a fact that is disputed (or that may be disputed)

Avoid questions that suggest or tend to suggest the answer to the witness where the subject matter is in dispute. Do not assume facts are in evidence before they have been elicited from the witness. Where a fact is clearly not disputed, you may adduce evidence of it by using a leading question.

21.3.7.4   Know the answer before asking the question

In general, you should avoid asking questions to which you do not know the answer. There is always a danger that the answers to such questions may damage your case. There is no rule that you cannot ask such questions. You can, and sometimes must, ask them *but* only where the (unknown) answer will not, or cannot, damage your case *and* it will assist the judge/jury to understand the case.

21.3.7.5 Scene first, then action

Before the trier(s) of fact can understand what happened, they will need the background or context against which to understand the action. Set the scene first.

21.3.7.6 Keep it clear

Break the evidence down into intelligible pieces. Ask one question at a time. Avoid jargon or legalese. Keep your questions short and simple: seven to eight words per question is a good length. Plant a firm question mark at the end of each question and allow the witness time to answer. Cut out unnecessary preamble, for example, 'Could you please tell the court what the registration number of the car was?' Ask instead 'What was the car's registration number?' Use plain English, for example, 'see' rather than 'perceive', 'car' rather than 'vehicle'.

21.3.7.7 Organise the key elements of the testimony

A logical progression or structure to the order in which the information is introduced will make it easier to follow. You will usually find that, as the witness is telling a story, they will recollect it best (and the trier(s) of fact will remember it better) if you enable the witness to work through their story in a chronological order. Do not hop backwards and forwards from one subject to another. Structure the testimony rather than merely presenting it in a haphazard fashion. The aim here is to enable the trier(s) of fact to understand how each part fits into the overall theory of your case.

It may be that you do not get the necessary amount of detail about a particular matter from the witness when they talk about it for the first time. That can happen because you must not 'lead' your witness but use questions that prompt them to tell the story in their own words. This will mean that, from time to time, you will need to interrupt their narrative in order to go back and cover a topic in more detail. For example, 'You told the court that you arrived at the party at about 10.30 pm—how did you get there? Who did you see when you first arrived? What was he doing at that time?' and so on.

Sometimes, you will decide that the court will have a better understanding of events (or perhaps be more sympathetic to your client) if they learn first what happened to bring the parties to court and then find out what events led up to that conclusion. Having settled the witness with the usual questions, such as 'Please tell the court your full name' and 'What do you do for a living?', you might then ask the witness, 'Do you know why you are in court today?' When the witness replies affirmatively, you can then ask, 'Please tell the court what happened.' The witness is likely to start talking about the conclusion of a sequence of events, for example 'My car was stolen', or 'I was hit over the head and had to go to hospital', or 'I fell over a broken paving stone and cut my leg'. You can then concentrate on those events with the witness, before turning to more preliminary matters.

21.3.7.8 Get the witness to tell the story

Allow the witness to tell the story in his or her own words. The witness was there—they saw, heard, or perceived what happened. It is much more effective and memorable if they relate their experiences to the trier(s) of fact than if they simply answer a series of questions in monosyllables.

21.3.7.9   Let the testimony flow

Try to avoid constant interruption of the witness. A fractured account may leave little impression on the trier(s) of fact. Allowing the witness to tell their story 'in paragraphs' rather than 'sentences' can help to build a picture of the events in the mind of the trier(s) of fact. As indicated later, detail can always be picked up afterwards.

21.3.7.10   Listen to the answers and respond accordingly

Do not give the impression that you are not listening to the answers the witness is giving. Look at the witness and listen to their reply. You may need to ask a follow-up question to ensure the testimony is clear and complete or that a technical word needs explaining. Or you may need to stop the witness answering your question if, for example, he or she begins to introduce inadmissible material.

21.3.7.11   Exercise control, keep it relevant

Control the witness by using transitions, a point of reference, or by asking a closed question to cut out irrelevant information. If the witness is talking too fast or is dealing with irrelevant matters, interrupt the flow in a firm but polite manner, for example, 'I'm afraid, Mr Smith, that you are going too fast for His Honour to take a full note of what you are saying. Try and watch His Honour's pen . . .' or 'pausing there for a moment, Mr Smith, I would like to deal with. . .'. Then follow this up with closed questions, keeping them as short as possible.

21.3.7.12   Combine questioning techniques

Vary the types of questions you ask, combining the questioning techniques you have learned—open and closed questions, transitions and points of reference—this should lead to clarity of presentation and enable you to exercise control when required.

Example

Q: 'Did you see Mr Green again after he left your office that afternoon?' (not in dispute)

A: 'Yes, I saw him two days later.'

Q: 'Where was that?'

A: 'He called at my home.'

Q: 'Were you expecting him?'

A: 'No, I was not.'

Q: 'At what time did he call?'

A: 'About 10.30 pm.'

Q: 'Was he with anyone else?'

A: 'No, he was alone.'

Q: 'Who else was at home?'

A: 'No one. My wife was out visiting her mother.'

Q: 'What happened when Mr Green arrived?'

A: 'As I opened the front door to let him in he pushed past me, knocking me against the wall. He started shouting that he was going to teach me a lesson. Then he pulled a gun out from underneath his jacket and threatened me with it.'

Q: 'Pausing there, how would you describe Mr Green's demeanour when he arrived?'

A: 'He was angry, almost mad.'

Q: 'Please describe the gun.'

A: 'Yes, it was a small black pistol.'

Q: 'Where were you when he pulled out this small black pistol?'

A: 'I was still against the wall where he had pushed me.'

Q: 'Approximately, how far away was Mr Green at that time?'

A: 'At first, he was about two feet away but then he came closer.'

Q: 'What happened as he came closer?'

21.3.7.13 Use pace to keep the story vivid

Use pace as an effective means of emphasising important evidence or conveying the speed with which something happened. You and not the witness choose the pace at which the evidence flows from the witness. Keep an eye on your audience—you need them to understand and follow the witness's account.

Example

Q: 'What happened as he came closer?'

A: 'He came right up to me, mouthing obscenities, pinning me against the wall. He spat on my face.

Then he stepped back and struck me in the face with the metal pole. I could feel blood on my cheek.'

Q: 'How did you react?'

A: 'I tried to push him away but he kept coming at me, trying to hit me again with the metal pole. I was screaming for him to stop, trying to get the metal pole away from him, he was fighting like a maniac . . .'

In the above series of questions, the questioner has let the evidence flow, allowing the witness to tell the important part of the story with little interruption. He or she could have interrupted, for example to obtain greater detail of the 'obscenities' or of how 'Mr Green had pinned the witness against the wall' but it would have spoilt the effect, 'fractured' the witness's own account of what happened and slowed down the pace. Such detail can be elicited at a later stage, for example:

Q: 'You stated that Mr Green was mouthing obscenities. Do you recall the words he used?'

21.3.7.14 Use frequency for emphasis

A number of specific questions on the same subject emphasises its importance and builds a picture of the event in the mind(s) of the trier(s) of fact.

Example

A: 'Then the defendant hit me.'

Q: 'With what did he hit you?'

A: 'His fist.'

Q: 'Which fist did he use?'

A: 'His right fist.'

Q: 'Can you show the court how he held his hand?'

A: 'It was with a closed fist, like this [demonstration].'

Q: 'Where did he hit you with this closed fist?'

A: 'In my face.'

Q: 'Whereabouts in the face?'

A: 'My right cheek.'

Q: 'How many times did he hit your cheek?'

A: 'Twice.'

21.3.7.15 Make the connections

Tie the evidence up. Do not leave loose ends. Do not leave it to your closing speech to make or show the connections between one fact and another or a series of facts and the conclusion they support. Develop the specific facts and then the conclusion that rests upon them or elicit the conclusion and then fill in the supporting facts.

Example 1

(Supporting facts first; conclusion second.)

A: 'The defendant tried to get out of the car.'

Q: 'How?'

A: 'He opened the car door and put one leg out. He couldn't get any further without my assistance. He could hardly stand up on his own.'

Q: 'Did you have any conversation with the defendant?'

A: 'Well I tried to but he kept slurring his words. He stank of alcohol.'

Q: 'Officer, did you form any opinion as to the defendant's condition?'

A: 'Yes, I did. He was drunk.'

Example 2

(Conclusion first; supporting facts second.)

A: 'The defendant tried to get out of the car.'

Q: 'Officer, did you form any opinion as to the defendant's condition at that time?'

A: 'Yes, I did. He was drunk.'

Q: 'Upon what did you base that opinion?'

A: 'He stank of alcohol and kept slurring his words. He couldn't get out of the car without my assistance. He put one leg out but could hardly stand up on his own.'

The first example makes a lasting impression. It is persuasive. The second example probably makes less impact although it has the advantage of conveying at an early stage the point of the witness's testimony.

21.3.7.16 Fill in the gaps

Do not leave holes in the witness's evidence. Think about what you might ask if you were in your opponent's shoes. For example, in the case of an identification witness, establish (in respect of each occasion he or she has seen the subject) such details as the lighting conditions, distance, angle, length and quality of observation. In this way, you may insulate the evidence from attack in cross-examination to the effect that the witness only got 'a fleeting glance'.

21.3.7.17 Be realistic

For instance, do not expect a witness to repeat verbatim a conversation that took place a long time before or one that is lengthy. The risk with asking 'What did he say to you?' is that you may get an 'I don't remember' response. If this is likely to happen, avoid it in this way:

Q: 'Do you remember exactly what the defendant said?'

A: 'No, it's too long ago.'

Q: 'Do you remember the substance (or gist) of what he said?'

A: 'Oh yes. He said something to the effect that . . .'

21.3.7.18   Illustrate the evidence

Use illustrative aids where they will assist the trier of fact to follow the evidence, for instance a sketch plan of the scene of the accident, a floor plan of the store, a schedule of figures. See **21.3.8** for the introduction of exhibits. Remember the witness needs to verbalise their evidence when using a plan. Simply asking the witness to point to a position on a plan will not be sufficient if the witness does not articulate his evidence. The witness will need to describe the position he or she is pointing to; for example, 'Mr Jones with the help of the sketch plan can you describe where you were standing?' Reply 'Yes, I was standing by the second door to the right of the main counter marked "P" on the sketch plan.'

21.3.7.19   Avoid bad habits

Do not comment on the evidence or give your opinions on the witness's response to your question. Avoid irritating habits such as thanking the witness or stating 'I see' or 'Yes, I see' after every answer. It is equally irritating to keep repeating everything the witness has just said. Do not make a lot of noise or shuffle papers while the witness is giving his or her evidence; it is distracting. This behaviour creates an impression of disinterest in the witness's answer or of lack of preparation or both.

21.3.7.20   Establish as much of your case as the witness can testify to

Before you sit down, check that you have elicited from the witness all the relevant evidence that he or she can give to help you establish your case or part of it.

21.3.8   Introducing real evidence

'Real evidence' is evidence in a tangible form such as a weapon, an article of clothing, a document (letter, contract, diagram, lease), or a photograph. There are several matters to consider before introducing such evidence during the examination of a witness.

(a) Location of the exhibit—it may be contained in one party's bundle of documents or exhibits, in an agreed bundle of documents or exhibits, it may be in the possession of a witness or you may have the original in your possession.

(b) Disclosure—ensure that the item/document has been properly disclosed to your opponent and/or that your opponent has had the opportunity to inspect it.

(c) Admissibility—ensure that the item/document is admissible and can be introduced by the witness in question. It may be necessary to lay a proper foundation before it can be admitted in evidence, for example, by satisfying the requirements of the Civil Evidence Act 1995, s 9 in respect of business records.

(d) Continuity—ensure that, if necessary, you can show continuity of possession, for example, in a drugs case, unless the defence concedes the issue, you will need to prove that the substance analysed in the laboratory was the same substance as that found in the defendant's possession. You can do this by eliciting evidence as to the taking of the drugs from the defendant; the packaging of the drugs in a sealed bag and the recording of the seal number; the transmission of the sealed bag to the forensic laboratory; and the analysis of the substance by seal number. (In most drugs cases, however, continuity is admitted. The issue normally relates to whether or not the defendant was 'in possession' of the drugs.)

21.3.8.1 Marking the exhibit

The introduction and use of exhibits is different in the criminal and civil courts. You must not get the two different systems confused.

Criminal system

An item can only be used as part of the evidence in a trial if it has been formally exhibited. To exhibit an item you must give the court all of the information it needs to understand it and use it properly. The item can then be given an exhibit number. In a criminal trial there may be a jury bundle including exhibits, but the court will still need information about how to understand it and use it. That information could be contained in a statement admitted under the Criminal Justice Act 1967, s 9 or in a formal admission under s 10 of that Act. Even where the evidence is included in a jury bundle, it will often be necessary to have it exhibited through the oral testimony of a witness.

21.3.8.2 Introducing the evidence: no dispute

What information the court needs about an exhibit will depend upon what the exhibit is, what the trial is about and what the court knows from the evidence already given. If you wish to exhibit a photograph of the scene of a crime, for example, you may need to establish (amongst other things) the vantage point of the photographer, the time of day that the photograph was taken and the distance the photographer was from the subject when they took the photograph; these things will assist the court to understand the content of the exhibit and how it can be properly used.

The first piece of evidence exhibited in a criminal trial will be exhibit 1. Subsequent exhibits will be numbered sequentially. No reference is given based on which party asked for the item to be exhibited.

Example 1

A: 'That's when I entered the shop.'

Q: 'Usher, could Mr Smith be handed the document marked JS/1 please?'

Q: 'Mr Smith, what is the document you have just been handed?'

A: 'It is a drawing of the inside of the shop.'

Q: 'Who drew it?'

A: 'I did.'

Q: 'When did you draw it?'

A: 'On the same day as I made my statement to police.'

Q: 'Is it to scale?'

A: 'Not really, but it shows the rough layout.'

Q: 'Your Honour, could that be exhibit number 1, please?'

Example 2

A: 'At that point I asked Mr Smith to empty his pockets and he produced a gun.'

Q: 'What did you do with the gun?'

A: 'I took it from Mr Smith and sealed it in an exhibit bag with the unique reference number 1234567.'

Q: 'What happened to that exhibit bag?'

A: 'I gave it to the exhibits officer, Sergeant Khan.'

Q: 'Usher, could you hand this item to the witness, please?'

Q: 'What is the item you have just been handed?'

A: 'It is a sealed exhibit bag.'

Q: 'What is the reference number?'

A: '1234567.'

Q: 'What does it contain?'

A: 'The gun that I seized from Mr Smith.'

Q: 'Your Honour, could that be exhibit number 2, please?'

21.3.8.3 Disputed or agreed evidence

Whether the parties agree or dispute that the item should be exhibited or what, as a matter of evidence, the item is, does not have any impact on what information the court needs to understand or use it. Where the status of the item is agreed between the parties, it is possible to admit it by **leading**:

Example 3

A: 'At that point I asked Mr Smith to empty his pockets and he produced a gun.'

Q: 'Is it right that you seized that gun and placed it in a sealed exhibit bag reference number 1234567.'

A: 'Yes.'

Q: 'Usher, could you hand this item to the witness, please?'

Q: 'Is that exhibit bag 1234567 containing the gun you seized from Mr Smith.'

A: 'Yes.'

Q: 'Your Honour, could that be exhibit number 2, please?'

Civil system

In civil cases the exhibit is often a document such as photographs or a plan which is exhibited in a witness statement. The exhibit will have the initials of the person making the statement and bear a number. For example Mr Paul Jones has a plan exhibited to his witness statement; this will usually be marked PJ 1. Subsequent documents will be numbered sequentially, in our example, PJ 2 and PJ 3 etc. Mr Jones when giving evidence will be referred to the exhibit PJ 1 in his witness statement, contained in the trial bundle.

Sometimes the parties agree that exhibits may form part of a separate agreed bundle of documents, each exhibit is numbered, there is an agreed index and the witness giving oral testimony is asked to turn to the relevant exhibit in the agreed bundle.

In civil proceedings there is no need to deal with the preliminary matters of formally introducing the exhibit (as happens in the criminal system) and the process of referring to exhibits is much simpler. You will however still require the witness to explain how the document was produced, explain any information that is recorded in the exhibit that is not obvious and its relevance to any matters in dispute.

Example 1

Q: 'Please look at page 3 of the trial bundle. Do you see a letter referred to a JP1.'

A: 'Yes.'

Q: 'Did you write that letter?'

A: 'Yes.'

Q: 'Can you explain why you wrote that letter?'

Example 2

Q: 'Did you send the defendant a notice to quit the premises?'

A: 'Yes.'

Q: 'Please turn to page 8 of the trial bundle. Is that a copy of the notice you sent.'

A: 'Yes.'

21.3.9   The final question

When you come to your final question, try to make it an important one. Let the witness finish on a strong note. It can be useful to let the court know you are about to finish by starting your last question with the words, 'Finally, Mrs Brown . . .'.

At the end of the witness's answer, a simple 'Thank you, Mrs Brown' will suffice although it is perfectly acceptable to add such words as 'Just wait there, would you?'/'Please wait there.'/'You will now be asked some questions by the defendant's counsel.'

21.4   Special aspects of examination-in-chief

21.4.1   Affidavit evidence

There are occasions where the witness has already sworn an affidavit dealing with the relevant issues. If you call the witness to give evidence, it is rarely necessary to examine the witness fully on the contents of his or her affidavit. Unless the judge requests it, he or she will not normally wish to hear a repeat of the matters already set out in the affidavit. It is, however, usual to give the witness the opportunity to explain any change in his or her circumstances since the affidavit was sworn, expand upon any matter that is not comprehensively covered, clarify any ambiguity and/or deal with any matters that have arisen since the affidavit was sworn.

Examples

Q: 'Did you swear an affidavit in these proceedings on 6 September 2014 (you may add "dealing with . . . for example, your financial means/your involvement with the defendant company") . . .?'

Q: 'Has there been any change in your income/position since you swore that affidavit?'

Q: 'In paragraph 4 of your affidavit you refer to a Miss Styles. Who is she?'

Q: 'You deal in paragraph 8 with an incident in which the defendant threatened you. Was anyone else present at the time?'

Q: 'Have you had any further contact with the defendant since you swore your affidavit?'

Two further points about affidavit evidence. The court may have already directed that the affidavit is to stand as the witness's evidence-in-chief. If not, and you are unsure whether or not to take the witness through matters already dealt with in the affidavit, seek an indication from the judge, for example 'Unless your Lordship/Your Honour considers it would assist, I do not propose to deal (at any length) with the matters already covered in the applicant's affidavit.' The judge will normally give you the required indication.

You may hear counsel at some stage inviting a witness to verify the contents of his or her affidavit, for example:

Q: 'Did you swear an affidavit in these proceedings on 6 September 2014?'

Q: 'At the time you swore it, were the contents of that affidavit true to the best of your knowledge, information and belief?'

The second question is unnecessary. The witness has already taken an oath to that effect at the time of swearing the affidavit. It is a bad habit to invite a witness to verify the contents of his or her affidavit—it is best to avoid it.

21.4.2   Memory-refreshing documents

During oral testimony a witness in a criminal trial may be allowed to refresh their memory from a statement made by them at an earlier time. This rule is created by the Criminal Justice Act 2003, s 139. The rule requires the witness to assert that: (1) the earlier statement records their recollection of the matter at the time it was made, and (2) that their recollection at that earlier time is likely to have been significantly better than now. A witness may refresh their memory at any point during their examination. It is for the judge to decide whether the requirements of the rule are met as a matter of fact.

The witness, particularly if it is a police officer, may need to refer to their notebook or statement in order to refresh their memory of the events or part of them. This is allowed if the statement records the witness's recollection at the time he made it and his recollection was likely to be better than it is now. Often police officers pool their recollections of the events and then only one police officer writes out the notes. The others may be permitted to refresh their memories from the same notebook provided they read and checked the notes at the time and were satisfied that the notes contained an accurate record of what they also saw or heard at the time.

Example 1

Q: 'What was the man wearing?'

A: 'I can't remember.'

Q: 'Did you make a statement to police on the day of this incident?'

A: 'Yes.'

Q: 'In that statement did you set out the facts as you remembered them on that day?'

A: 'Yes.'

Q: 'Was your recollection of the matter on that day likely to have been significantly better than now?'

A: 'Yes.'

Q: 'Usher, could you hand the witness a copy of his statement?'

Q: 'Is that your statement?'

A: 'Yes.'

Q: 'Is it dated the day of the incident?'

A: 'Yes.'

Q: 'Could you read through the second paragraph to yourself and let me know when you have finished?'

A: 'Yes, I have read that.'

Q: 'What was the man wearing?'

A. 'Grey trousers, a white shirt and black shoes. He was also wearing a tweed flat cap.'

The witness's notes/statement may contain inadmissible evidence. Warn the witness in advance to omit any reference to the offending part. When the witness comes to that part of the evidence, help him or her over it and onto the next admissible part by intervening with a question such as 'Did you then/subsequently. . .?'

Note that when referring to a memory-refreshing document, the witness should use it merely to refresh memory. Some witnesses, particularly police officers, use it as an opportunity to read out their evidence; this is objectionable and the witness should be reminded not to do so, for example:

'Officer, refreshing your memory, if necessary, from your notes, what happened upon your arrival at . . .?'

The above rule is not only applicable where a witness states that they cannot remember a thing, the requirements could equally be satisfied where the witness has remembered something incorrectly. There are occasions when you may wish the witness to refresh his or her memory from a statement made at the time. Where the witness has remembered something incorrectly, some explanation may be required from the witness so that their credibility is not undermined.

Example 2

Q: 'What was the man wearing?'

A: 'Jeans, a t-shirt and trainers.'

Q: 'Did you make a statement to police on the day of this incident?'

A: 'Yes.'

Q: 'In that statement did you set out the facts as you remembered them on that day?'

A: 'Yes.'

Q: 'Was your recollection of the matter on that day likely to have been significantly better than now?'

A: 'Yes.'

Q: 'Usher, could you hand the witness a copy of his statement?'

Q: 'Is that your statement?'

A: 'Yes.'

Q: 'Is it dated the day of the incident?'

A: 'Yes.'

Q: 'Could you read through the second paragraph to yourself and let me know when you have finished?'

A: 'Yes, I have read that.'

Q: 'What was the man wearing?'

A. 'Grey trousers, a white shirt and black shoes. He was also wearing a tweed flat cap.'

Q: 'You told us earlier that he was wearing jeans, a t-shirt and trainers. Can you explain that?'

A: 'Oh, yes. I have seen him several times since and on those occasions he was always wearing jeans and trainers.'

In civil cases the matter of a witness refreshing their memory is much easier, as they will have a copy of their witness statement in the trial bundle. If a witness cannot recall matters or remembers an incident incorrectly in their oral testimony they should be taken to the relevant part of their witness statement and asked to read it. The witness will read the statement in the witness-box. Wait quietly whilst the witness does this. You will then need to ask some supplemental questions to explain their state of recollection at the time the statement was made, as in the example above.

21.4.3 Alibi evidence

It is particularly important in the case of an alibi witness not to lead on the date or time. Do not ask an alibi witness 'Where were you on the evening of 9 March 2014?' Elicit the date from the witness.

Example

> Q: 'Did there come a time when you heard that the defendant had been arrested and charged?'
>
> A: 'Yes.'
>
> Q: 'When was that?'
>
> A: 'The day of his arrest. His brother telephoned and told me.'
>
> Q: 'Do you recall the exact date?'
>
> A: 'Yes. It was the 10 March 2014.'
>
> Q: 'What did you understand was the nature of the charge?'
>
> A: 'He was supposed to have burgled a house the evening before.'
>
> Q: 'Where were you during that evening?'
>
> A: 'I was at a party with the defendant and two other friends . . .'

21.4.4 Expert reports

Where there has been a direction for the disclosure of expert reports, the expert witness's evidence will already be contained in the report and any subsequent joint statement with other experts (which identifies the areas on which they disagree and their reasons). If the report is not agreed, it will be necessary to call the expert as a witness at the trial which requires the court's permission. The expert at trial will need to adopt the evidence contained in the report and any joint statement. The fact of prior disclosure is not sufficient for this purpose. It is necessary to elicit details of the expert's qualifications and experience at the outset (in order to satisfy the court that the witness is an expert) and then proceed in this way:

Example

> Q: 'Did you examine the claimant at your surgery on 14 July 2014?'
>
> A: 'I did.'
>
> Q: 'Are your findings/are the results of that examination/is your evidence of the claimant's medical condition/ contained in your report dated 17 July 2014?'
>
> A: 'Yes, they are/it is.'

In civil cases, do not invite the expert witness to repeat what is contained in his or her report save for the purpose of clarification, expansion or updating his evidence. It is then usual to turn to the other expert's report and/or the joint statement produced by the experts (which identifies the areas they disagree on) to deal with disputed matters.

Example

> Q: 'Have you read the report prepared by Dr Smith on 14 October 2014?'
>
> A: 'I have.'
>
> Q: 'Dr Smith's measurements of the degree of mobility in the claimant's left ankle are greater than yours. Can you account for that?'
>
> A: 'Yes.' (Note: make sure you know the answer before asking this type of question!)

In criminal cases where the expert report (or part of it) is agreed, it (or the agreed parts) will be admitted. An admission (CJA 1967, s 10) will be read to the jury, setting out the agreed parts. Where there are disputed matters, the evidence of these must be adduced in the normal way in examination-in-chief.

21.4.5 Previous convictions

If, in a criminal trial, you decide to refer to the defendant's previous convictions in order to take the 'sting' out of the anticipated cross-examination, it is usually preferable to do this at an early stage in your examination-in-chief. Elicit the details of the defendant's past record in a business-like fashion, emphasising any favourable aspects such as the fact that the defendant pleaded guilty on each previous occasion.

21.4.6 Tendering for cross-examination

If the witness is a cumulative witness in the sense that he or she is giving the same evidence as has already been elicited from the previous witness(es), it is preferable to tender him or her for cross-examination. This often arises where, for example, you are calling several police officers to deal with the same incident. Establish who the witness is and his or her presence at the scene, for example:

Q: 'Officer, please give the court your full name and rank.'
A: 'Police Sergeant Richard Smith attached to Marylebone police station.'
Q: 'Were you on duty at the police station during the evening of 12 January 2014?'
A: 'Yes.'
Q: 'Were you present when the defendant was charged?' (no dispute)
A: 'Yes, I was.'
Q: 'Wait there, the defence may have some questions for you.'

Cross-examination

22.1 Introduction

Cross-examination is the name given to the process of examining the witness(es) called by your opponent or by another party in the case (eg a co-defendant in either civil or criminal proceedings). It is the most challenging and, for the new advocate, the most intimidating of the tasks he or she has to perform. If successful, it provides an advocate with one of the most satisfying moments of his or her work.

First of all, forget what you have seen in films—the witness is not likely to break down in the witness-box and confess all! You must accept that not all your cross-examinations are going to be successful. Try to keep your facial expression neutral and professional. The witness should not be able to 'read' your thoughts or see an emotional response to his or her replies by the expressions on your face. Think of playing a game of cards, you have a bad set of cards but do not want the other card players to know this; cultivate a 'poker face'.

Second, contrary to popular belief, cross-examination is not, nor should it be, 'cross' in the sense of angry, confrontational or controversial. Apart from applying the cardinal rule set out at **22.3**, cross-examination should be viewed as a constructive art and not necessarily a destructive one. There is no need to shout or adopt an unpleasant, sneering manner in cross-examination. Nor is it necessary to harangue a witness in order to be effective. This will probably only serve to antagonise the jury or the judge. While you must exercise control over the witness, the most effective way is to adopt a polite, courteous approach, use a combination of closed and leading questions and deliver them in the spirit of an inquiry. Appear business-like and quietly confident.

Consider, by way of example, the case of Lizzie Borden:

Lizzie Borden took an axe,
Gave her father forty thwacks.
When she saw what she had done
She gave her mother forty-one.

The murders occurred when she was alone in the locked house with her parents. Much blood must have been spilt when the axe was used and would have splattered the assailant. The prosecution case was that Lizzie must have taken her clothes off (this was the 1890s) while committing the murders and then washed and dressed again afterwards for there was no blood found on her clothing. Lizzie claimed to have been ironing and to have seen or heard nothing of the crimes until after they were committed. A neighbour was called and cross-examined:

Q: 'We have been told you were the first neighbour into the house.'
A: 'I have been told so.'

Q: 'Did you go into the room where Miss Borden was ironing?'
A: 'I did.'
Q: 'Was there an ironing-board in place?'
A: 'There was.'
Q: 'And an iron on the board?'
A: 'Stood on edge.' (This was the age of the flat-iron.)
Q: 'And was the ironing completed?'
A: 'There was a small pile of handkerchiefs which from so nearly as I could see had been ironed.'
Q: 'And ironing yet to do?'
A: 'There was a basket of handkerchiefs ready dampened.'
Q: 'Did you feel the iron?'
A: 'I did. It was warm.'

Note:

(a) the lack of hostility;

(b) the directness;

(c) the simplicity;

(d) the lack of comment;

(e) the preparation for the closing speech: a woman halfway through ironing, the most domestic of tasks, breaking off to murder her parents?

The objectives for this cross-examination were clearly identified before it began, pursued throughout the cross-examination and achieved. It was conducted in the spirit of a courteous enquiry into the facts rather than in a confrontational manner.

22.2 The aims of cross-examination

22.2.1 Aim 1: To advance your own case

This means asking questions that seek to establish facts fitting in with or corroborating your case. For this your manner will not appear hostile. You will, at least in the first instance, be seeking the cooperation of the witness. If the witness proves intransigent or difficult you may eventually need to apply pressure, but don't begin by doing so.

22.2.2 Aim 2: To undermine your opponent's case

Of course, these two aims overlap, at least in the sense that anything that advances your case at the same time undermines your opponent's. However, while preparing for cross-examination you should keep the two aims distinct. Your approach to the witness may depend on your aims and this may change during your cross-examination.

Remember too there is a substantial difference between seeking to undermine the witness's evidence and seeking to undermine the witness. In the former case you will probably need to go about your work without letting the witness know what you are about; in which case your manner will be neutral. In the latter case it may or may not be so. The choice is yours alone. You will set, maintain or choose to adapt the tone of the cross-examination.

22.3   The cardinal rule of cross-examination

You must put your case. You must challenge all material parts of the evidence given by witnesses called by your opponent that your client (or his or her witnesses) does not accept. If the witness says that your client 'orally agreed to pay him £4,000' and your client denies both the agreement and the fact that the conversation ever took place, you must put these points to the witness. If you fail to do this, the judge will refuse to allow you to challenge your opponent's version in your closing submission. He or she will tell you that your failure to challenge that version is the equivalent of accepting it. This can inflict fatal damage to your case.

In addition, if you do not challenge the disputed parts, or put your client's version of the events to the witness, and then call evidence that contradicts your opponent's evidence in material particulars, you may find that your client and/or his or her witnesses are accused of inventing their evidence—on the basis that if their version of events was known before the trial began it would be known to you and you would have been obliged to cross-examine and 'put the case'. You did not cross-examine; therefore the version now given is a late invention. This is sometimes correct—in which case you can only sit and squirm. If, however, it is your fault because you have failed to comply with the rule, you must immediately stand up and say so—and apologise to the court!

The rule is one that admits of no exceptions. Our adversarial system of trial requires that witnesses be given the opportunity while in the box to answer the case presented contrary to their account of the facts. This does not mean that you have to challenge every unessential detail but you must cross-examine on material particulars.

22.4   Questioning technique

Cross-examination should not be a repeat of the examination-in-chief. You must avoid giving the witness the opportunity simply to repeat unfavourable testimony that he or she has already given in-chief. (The one exception to this may be where you suspect that the witness has memorised his or her testimony or has planned with another witness to tell an identical story. In that case, you may be able to highlight the fact that the witness is using identical phrases or repeating his or her or another witness's words verbatim.) Your twofold aim is to use the witness to advance your case and undermine your opponent's. The focus should therefore be on your case rather than allowing the witness the freedom to repeat theirs.

In the chapter on questioning techniques, **Chapter 20**, we saw that open-ended questions with neutral starts (who, what, how, which, when, where, why, tell and describe) give the witness a chance to give a narrative account, to tell the story in their own words. This is not what you want your opponent's witness to do when you are cross-examining—you want the focus to be on your questions and to retain control over the answers.

In cross-examination, there are therefore two golden rules:

(1) Tell: don't ask! Include the answer you want in the question.
(2) Lead, lead, lead—avoid open-ended questions wherever and whenever possible.

Of course, these rules do allow for exceptions and the more experienced the advocate, the more one might risk an open-ended question. But, at this stage, it is best not to do so unless the matter is peripheral or you are clear that the answer is unlikely to damage your case.

A combination of leading and closed questions will best enable you to control the witness. For example, imagine you represent the wife in a disputed maintenance case. Your aim is to show that her estranged husband is extravagant with money that ought to be spent on household bills:

Q: 'You go to the pub after work sometimes, don't you?'
A: 'Yes.'
Q: 'Usually with your work colleagues?'
A: 'Yes.'
Q: 'On average, two to three times a week?'
A: 'Yes.'
Q: 'And when there, you drink beer?'
A: 'Yes, usually bitter.'
Q: 'About six or seven pints each time?'
A: 'Well, sometimes but not always.'
Q: 'You normally stay until closing time?'
A: 'Yes.'
Q: 'From about 6.00 pm?'
A: 'Yes.'
Q: 'So it would not be unusual to drink six or seven pints during the four or so hours you are there?'
A: 'I suppose not.'
Q: 'A pint of beer costs about £5?'
A: 'Yes.'
Q: 'You sometimes grab a bite to eat too while in the pub?'
A: 'Yes although I usually have my main meal at lunchtime.'
Q: 'So, it would not be unusual for you to spend £45 during a full evening at the pub?'

During cross-examination, transitions and points of reference can also be used to good effect in moving from one topic to another or referring to the witness's evidence in-chief. (Note that if you are co-defending, although you may use leading questions when cross-examining the co-defendant, it may be wise not to do so where you are using the same defence. A series of leading questions in this situation will give the impression that you do not trust the witness to give favourable evidence without your careful prompting.)

22.5   Achieving the aims of cross-examination

22.5.1   Advancing your case

There are two basic ways of advancing your own case in cross-examination.

22.5.1.1   Eliciting favourable testimony

Frequently you will find that part of a witness's evidence is in fact helpful or potentially helpful to your case. Not everything a witness says is necessarily damaging. For example, a witness to an alleged shoplifting offence may agree that the store was very crowded;

a witness to a road traffic accident may agree that the road surface was wet or that the other driver was driving fast; a witness in a child care case may agree that on the occasions when she saw your client and the children together, the children appeared happy and content or that it was usually your client who took the children to their doctor's appointments.

It is therefore important to approach each witness's testimony in the first place with an open mind—avoid dealing with the damaging part(s) of the evidence until you have considered the potentially helpful parts. Ask yourself: Is there any area of consensus between the witness's observation/recollection and my client's? Can the witness say anything that will assist/support my theory of the case? Does the witness say anything that can be expanded upon to assist my case? Is the witness silent on a matter that would have been mentioned if it was detrimental to my case? What must the witness admit if he or she was present at the time of the alleged incident? If having considered the evidence in this way there are positive aspects to the witness's testimony, these are the parts that you want to emphasise.

Generally it is accepted that it is tactically better to elicit any favourable testimony that the witness can provide before attempting to discredit the witness's evidence. This will enable you, at the very least, to obtain some positive help from the witness before he or she reacts in a negative or antagonistic way to the rest of your questions.

22.5.1.2 Developing your case

Both when 'putting your case' (cardinal rule, see **22.3**) and pursuing one or other or both of the aims (see **22.2**) you have the chance to develop your case in the sense that you can begin to show your audience the way you want them to look at all the facts. It is usually better to let the facts speak for themselves depending, obviously, on the nature and quality of the audience. It is very tempting to adopt the styles of advocates seen in films or TV who add plenty of running commentary to their questions but you should avoid this.

In putting your case, it is not necessary to use the words 'I put it to you that . . .'. Although you may hear counsel using this expression on occasions, many consider it unnecessarily formal. It can also alert the witness that you are about to challenge their evidence. If you say to a witness 'I put it to you that you have come here to tell the court a pack of lies', the answer will invariably be 'No, I haven't'. How far has that got you? It is equally unimpressive to argue with a witness—such as 'You did', 'I didn't', 'Yes, you did', 'No, I didn't'.

Be subtler when putting your case. Although, in most cases, the witness will not agree with your client's version of events, at the very least you will introduce and develop your theory of the case and prepare the way for your witnesses to give evidence in support of it. Aim to do this without labouring your points or making them in a heavy-handed way. Consider this example:

> Q: 'Since Mrs Smith left home, have you taken any steps to encourage the children to keep in contact with her?'
> A: 'Well, I tried to but they refused.'
> Q: 'Is it right that Mrs Smith used to telephone the household twice a week?'
> A: 'Yes'.
> Q: 'And on each occasion you put the telephone down on her?'
> A: 'I had nothing to say to her and the children wouldn't come to the telephone.'
> Q: 'Was that the reason why you changed your telephone number in May?'
> A: 'I wanted to stop her bothering me.'
> Q: 'Bothering you or the children?'
> A: 'Just me.'

Q: 'Was that why you also changed the locks on the front door of the house?'

A: 'Yes. She'd left—she had no right to come back when it suited her.'

Q: 'Not even to see the children?'

A: 'I told you, the children didn't want to see her.'

Q: 'Mrs Smith sent the children several letters and cards, didn't she?'

A: 'A few.'

Q: 'And you returned them unopened?'

A: 'Yes. The children asked me to.'

Q: 'Do you always do everything the children ask you to?'

A. 'No, not always.'

Q: 'Did you consider that it was very rude to return mail unopened without the courtesy of a response?'

A: 'Not really.'

Q: 'Did you consider contacting Mrs Smith and explaining to her that the children were upset by her correspondence?'

A: 'No. It wasn't necessary.'

Q: 'It's right, isn't it, that you told Mrs Smith when she left you would ensure she never saw the children again?'

A: 'No, I didn't. I told her if she left, I wouldn't have her back.'

Q: 'And, in fact, since she left, despite her attempts, you have ensured she has not seen, spoken to or heard from the children?'

A: 'That was of her own making, not mine.'

Certain types of witness, for example police officers, may give identical, or similar, evidence on one or more aspects of the case. It is not usually necessary to put the same challenges to every witness unless:

(a) you consider that in doing so you are likely to achieve a different or inconsistent response; or

(b) you consider that by putting your case more than once it will leave a greater impression upon the mind(s) of the trier(s) of fact.

If you do not wish merely to repeat the same challenges, indicate to the judge that you have already put your case to the previous witness(es) and that you do not propose to put the same challenges again to this witness unless the judge considers it necessary.

22.5.2 Undermining your opponent's case

This is the second aim of cross-examination. In order to undermine your opponent's case, you must successfully meet the unfavourable testimony given by his or her witness(es). This can be achieved in one or more of the following ways.

22.5.2.1 Limiting the testimony

Witnesses frequently observe only part of an incident or overlook the fact that their evidence leaves many unexplained or inconsistent gaps. Try to meet the unfavourable testimony by showing its limitations. Consider such evidence in the wider context of the case. Stress what the witness did not see; highlight the absence of matters that you would ordinarily have expected the witness to see/hear if he or she had witnessed the whole event or those matters that you would have expected to find if the situation was as the witness suggests/believes. For example:

(a) In the case of an alleged assault, a witness gives evidence that he or she saw your client strike the victim. If your case is that the blow was struck in self-defence, you may be able to get the witness to agree that he or she was not present prior to that moment or that his or her view was momentarily obstructed and that he or she was therefore not in a position to see a blow struck first by the alleged victim.

(b) In the case of an alleged burglary, a police officer gives evidence that he or she arrested your client outside the burgled premises. You may be able to limit his or her evidence by establishing that your client's fingerprints were not found at the scene of the crime, yet no gloves/socks were found in the vicinity of the premises or in the defendant's possession at the time of his or her arrest.

(c) In the case of an alleged identification witness, you may limit the evidence by stressing the dissimilarities between the defendant and the description originally given by the witness to the police.

(d) In a dispute about contact arrangements in a family case, the mother gives evidence of the child's apparent distress after Sunday visits to the father. You may undermine her evidence by establishing that there have been no reported problems from the school as to any change in the child's behaviour particularly on Mondays.

22.5.2.2 Discrediting the testimony

The assumption that in every case at least one person is lying to the court is a false one. In many cases, the truth lies somewhere between the witnesses' accounts and/or is obscured by misconception, mistaken/selective recall or simply a different interpretation of the facts. Your purpose in discrediting the evidence is to show or suggest that it is probably less true/reliable than appeared at the end of the examination-in-chief; the emphasis here is not upon seeking to destroy the witness. Challenging the reliability of the testimony is the most common form of cross-examination. Blatant confrontation rarely results in a witness conceding an issue and simply reinforces their opposition. The following are the basic methods for exposing the weaknesses in the evidence:

(a) *Testing the limits of the witness's perception,* ie the witness's ability and opportunity to observe the matter in question. It is quite common for a witness to 'fill in' the gaps in his or her observation/memory so as to present a complete picture of events. If a witness hears a car crash and then sees the angle of the cars, he or she may jump to a fairly quick assumption/conclusion as to what in fact happened. He or she replaces the missing gaps in his or her knowledge with what he or she believes to be the best explanation of what must have occurred. He or she then convinces himself or herself that this is what he or she actually witnessed and the more he or she repeats it, the more he or she believes it. It is not a deliberate attempt to lie or mislead the court. Most of the time this is done subconsciously.

To test the witness's perception, probe what the witness actually perceived or heard, for example, his or her angle of observation, distance from the events, any factor that may have interrupted, obstructed or distorted his or her view/hearing/powers of observation (eg presence of other persons, bad weather conditions, fear, anger); the length and nature of his or her involvement/observation; consider what the witness ought to have seen/heard if he or she had witnessed the whole of the incident; elicit whether there has been any discussion with others since the event occurred that may have influenced the witness's perception.

(b) *Testing the witness's memory,* ie the witness's ability to remember the details and his or her efforts to record them. Probe the witness's memory of peripheral matters, those facts that the witness ought to remember if he or she had seen the whole incident or was involved to the extent that he or she suggests. Concentrate on the time lapse since the event, the lack of record of the events, the absence of reference to a particular fact in the record of the events, the number of similar incidents that the witness has experienced that may affect his or her ability to remember (eg the number of invoices that a secretary has typed/sent since the one in issue; the number of arrests that a police officer has made since the event in question), the fact of any conversation with others that may have influenced the witness's recollection.

(c) *Testing the witness's powers of communication/appreciation,* ie the witness's ability to articulate what he or she observed or heard, and the witness's interpretation of what he or she perceived. Probe the witness's ability to record/assess information especially of a technical nature, to estimate distance, time, etc.

22.5.2.3 Discrediting the witness

On occasion, it may be necessary and possible to discredit the witness. The emphasis of this type of cross-examination is demonstrating that he or she is unreliable or unworthy of belief. There are three ways to discredit the witness:

(a) *Discrediting the witness's conduct:* Some witnesses give their evidence in a reasonable and persuasive manner that belies the inconsistency of their conduct or behaviour at the time of or after the events in question. For example, a woman seeking an injunction to restrain her husband from using violence against her gives evidence of an assault she suffered two weeks beforehand and her fear of her husband since that occasion. She fails to mention the fact that she went out for dinner with him the following week. Or a driver, who denies that his negligent driving was the cause of a collision, fails to mention that he left the scene of the accident in a hurry, refusing to call the police. Look for inconsistencies between the evidence and either the acts or omissions of the witness. Consider what a reasonable person would have done in the witness's position, how you (and the trier(s) of fact) would have expected the witness to behave as a matter of common sense. You should, however, be prepared for the witness to offer an explanation—either in response to your questions or during re-examination.

(b) *Showing the inconsistencies in the testimony:* The witness's account may contain a fact that is inconsistent with a previous statement of the witness, contradicts other facts, is an exaggeration or is inconsistent with the evidence of another witness.

Many novices approach a prior inconsistent statement like a 'bull in a china shop'. In their anxiety to show that they have caught the witness out they fail to appreciate that the manner in which they show this may well spoil the effect; it may give the witness time to realise his or her error and either correct or explain it away.

The best technique for exposing a previous inconsistent statement is to structure your approach and execute it simply and swiftly. First, commit the witness to the fact that he or she asserts or asserted during examination-in-chief. Second, close the door on any possible explanation—consider how you might try to explain it away if you were the witness. Finally, contrast his or her answer with the previous inconsistent statement. For example:

Q: 'Miss White, you say that the man you saw was well over 6 foot tall?'
A: 'Yes.'
Q: 'How tall are you, Miss White?'
A: 'I'm 5 foot 5 inches.'

Q: 'Do you normally wear high-heeled shoes?'

A: 'Most of the time, yes.'

Q: 'Were you wearing them on that evening?'

A: 'Yes.'

Q: 'Approximately how high were the heels?'

A: 'About two inches.'

Q: 'That would have made you about 5 foot 7 inches—wasn't the man you saw about that height?'

A: 'No, he was much taller.'

Q: 'Didn't you tell Detective Constable Myles that the man you saw was about your height?'

A: 'I don't remember saying that.'

Q: 'You remember making a statement to the police a few hours after the incident?'

A: 'Yes.'

Q: 'Is that the statement you made?' (copy handed to witness)

A: 'Yes.'

Q: 'You made it shortly after the incident while everything was fresh in your mind?'

A: 'Yes.'

Q: 'Look at paragraph 2, third line: "the man was about my height . . . " That is what you told the officer at the time?'

A: 'Yes.'

You may also show inconsistencies in the evidence by exposing embellishments/exaggerations in the witness's account, by highlighting any self-serving conclusions or explanations and/or by uncovering differences between the various witnesses' accounts.

(c) *Impeaching the witness:*   In some cases, you may be able to show that the witness himself or herself is unworthy of belief or that little weight should be attached to his or her evidence. The ways of limiting/discrediting the evidence in this manner are to establish:

(i)   bias;

(ii)   interest in the outcome of the proceedings;

(iii) motive for testifying in a particular manner;

(iv)   previous convictions or bad acts.

This must be done carefully. For example, the fact that a witness is related to a party does not automatically mean that he or she has deliberately come to court to tell lies. For example, do not begin a cross-examination of a parent giving alibi evidence for a son by baldly accusing him or her of coming to court to tell lies on behalf of their child. Instead, develop the possible bias of a parent in favour of the child so as to show or at least to give the foundation to suggest that the parent is incapable of being impartial.

Q: 'Mr Reynolds, your son was living with you at the time he was arrested for assaulting Miss Clancy?'

A: 'Yes.'

Q: 'You enjoy a good relationship with your son?'

A: 'Yes.'

Q: 'You were surprised when he was arrested?'

A: 'Yes, I was.'

Q: 'As far as you are concerned, this must all be a dreadful mistake?'

A: 'Yes.'

Q: 'You've discussed it with your son?'
A: 'Yes.'
Q: 'On more than one occasion?'
A: 'Yes.'

Three points emerge from this examination:

(i)   the closeness of the relationship between father and son;

(ii) the father's inability to believe anything bad of his son; and

(iii) the fact that the father and son have discussed the matter in issue and may have influenced each other.

These points can then be emphasised in your closing speech. But remember that if it is your case that the witness could not be mistaken about the alibi evidence that he has given, and so must be telling lies, it is your duty to put that to him in cross-examination. The same questions also lay a good foundation for examining the details of the alibi to see how reliable it is. Remembering the cardinal rule (**22.3**), and applying it to a short and simple example like this, it will be necessary before finishing the cross-examination to decide whether you are suggesting simple unreliability in the parent or untruthfulness. If the former, you could finish:

Q: 'Are you sure you are right about the date/time/place?'

If the latter, you could finish:

Q: 'Are you more concerned to help your child escape the charge than help the jury with the truth?'

22.6 Preparation for cross-examination

Provided your questions are relevant and you do not seek to elicit inadmissible evidence, you are generally free to ask whatever questions you consider appropriate. The only restrictions upon your conduct of the cross-examination are the limitations imposed by the Code of Conduct, for example you must not ask questions that are 'merely scandalous or intended or calculated only to vilify, insult or annoy either a witness or some other person'.

Now that you appreciate the aims of cross-examination and the basic ways of achieving those objectives, you are ready to prepare for cross-examination.

The first step is to ensure that you have the issues clear in your mind.

(a) What must you prove or rebut?

(b) What is your theory of the case?

(c) What are the key elements of the evidence that will support or undermine your case?

Make a note of the above and keep them to the forefront of your mind at all times.

The next step is to decide whether it is necessary to cross-examine the witness at all. Never cross-examine just because you think the client expects you to or in order to justify your fee or because you think that is what your job as an advocate is all about.

You may already have a good idea of the evidence the witness is likely to give either from the witness statements, reports, and/or documents disclosed pre-trial. This is your starting point.

(a) Look at the potential evidence with a critical eye. Can the witness assist your case in any way? Can he or she give evidence that may undermine/harm your case? Which of the essential elements of your case does the witness support/dispute/contradict? It may help to make a note of this.

(b) If the witness neither assists nor harms your case (ie is neutral), will that be apparent to the trier of fact? Particularly in the case of a jury trial, will the jury appreciate, without a brief cross-examination, that the witness does not take the case against your client any further, for example, that the witness was not present at the time of an alleged conversation? Does this need emphasising?

(c) Consider whether you can elicit the favourable testimony or limit/meet the harmful part of the testimony more effectively in any other way, for example, through another witness/documentary evidence.

(d) Now apply the test: what is your purpose in cross-examining this witness? What do you hope to achieve? There must be a purpose to your cross-examination, even if it is only to 'put your case' to the witness. If you have no reason to cross-examine, no clear objective or identified purpose, then stay glued to your seat.

(e) Remember that this is the preparation stage. It will be necessary to reassess the situation after the witness has given any oral evidence. This is to guard against any unexpected turn in the case or in the witness's testimony. You must be able to respond to the evidence actually given by the witness in-chief. What if, for example, the witness never gave an anticipated and crucial piece of evidence? A large part of your intended cross-examination may just have become redundant. If they haven't hurt your case, and there is no other reason to cross-examine them, leave them well alone.

22.6.1 Written preparation

Try to get used to jotting down bullet or 'trigger' points for cross-examination rather than the whole questions themselves. Although there are times when it may be necessary to write out (some of) your questions in full, for example when dealing with an expert witness or a particularly difficult or important matter, it is preferable not to cross-examine from a prepared set of questions. To do otherwise may well impair your ability to watch the witness and adapt your questions to suit the manner of the witness's response. If you are restricted by a rigid set of questions, you will probably find it difficult to engage in the 'parry and thrust' of cross-examination.

This does not mean that you should not prepare for your cross-examination. On the contrary, preparation and planning are vital. You should map out the purpose of your cross-examination, the points you wish to deal with and the order in which you propose to deal with them.

22.6.2 Structure of cross-examination

You are not restricted to following the order in which your opponent examined the witness in-chief. Nor are you limited to asking questions that arise out of the examination-in-chief. In cross-examination, you want your questions to be structured in a way that makes them clear and logical to the trier(s) of fact but maybe not so clear to the witness—at least until it is too late for them to do anything about it! The key here may be to have a gentle and patient build-up, through a series of relatively innocuous questions, until you have painted the witness into a corner. It is important that the build-up is not too long or appears to be on completely irrelevant matters as the judge may ask you to get to the point if it appears your foundation questions are not relevant to the matters in dispute. Keep your foundation questions relevant to the topic then you ask the key question, probably putting some part of your client's case to the witness. As a general rule, elicit the favourable testimony before dealing with the unfavourable. Aim to finish on a strong note.

22.6.3 Useful tips

Here are some general hints for conducting your cross-examination:

(a) Formulate your questions so that they contain one fact at a time. Use short questions. Do not recite facts at length and then ask the witness 'Is that right?' Be clear and concise.

(b) Do not misquote the witness's evidence in-chief.

(c) Avoid getting bogged down in too much minute detail unless it is really necessary.

(d) Know the probable answers to your questions; if you must risk a question to which you do not know the answer, frame it in a closed manner.

(e) Ensure you listen to the answer before asking the next question.

(f) Keep it relevant—limit the areas of your cross-examination to the aspects of the witness's evidence that concern the key elements of your case. Do not pursue pointless cross-examination or get sidetracked by irrelevancies.

(g) Constantly reassess what questions you need to ask the witness.

(h) Keep a structure. Do not jump backwards and forwards from one topic to another. You may succeed in unbalancing the witness in this way but you will also confuse yourself and the trier of fact at the same time!

(i) Lay the foundations first before putting the conclusion to the witness. If you put it to the witness that he was drunk, he may deny it. If you build a picture, step by step, through your questions, showing that the witness had spent all afternoon in the pub, and had drunk several beers and whiskies, had not eaten anything, and had been unable to drive home, the witness may still deny the conclusion you put to him (ie that he was drunk) but the court will have formed its own view!

(j) Be a good actor, keep a poker face if the witness's evidence harms you and try not to show your reaction by your face, manner or voice.

(k) Know when to finish and avoid the temptation to ask one question too many. When you have elicited the evidence move on to the next topic. Avoid dealing with the same matter several times or, if you are not making progress, consider whether the time spent is justified. Do you have more important matters that you need to move on to deal with? Leave the concluding argument to your final submission.

22.7 Special types of witness

22.7.1 The expert witness

The cross-examination of an expert witness is often the key to the whole case. Some expert witnesses are extremely difficult to deal with and, on occasions, you may find that you make little headway in cross-examination. All the more reason to ensure that you are fully prepared and have consulted your own expert on the possible weaknesses of your opponent's expert and/or in his or her opinion/reasoning/methods.

In addition to the cross-examination techniques we have already looked at, there are several other techniques that may be used effectively when cross-examining an expert witness. The aim is to cast doubt upon the expert's experience, methods or opinion. This may be achieved by:

(a) limiting the witness's apparent expertise. Narrow the extent of his or her expertise/experience by showing that it is not directly applicable to the case in question or, perhaps, by contrasting it to the experience of your expert;

(b) showing that the witness has had less involvement/contact with the case than your expert, for example, has only examined a party once; or viewed the machinery long after the accident;

(c) showing your knowledge of the expert's subject. Using your knowledge of the technical terms involved or the way in which any tests were carried out, the expert will be less inclined to avoid your questions. Contrast this approach with the way you may deal with an ordinary witness of fact by simplifying technical terms;

(d) inviting the witness to define technical terms and sometimes in highly complex matters it may be necessary to invite the expert to use common language;

(e) challenging his or her methods, for example, showing that there were other tests that the expert could/should have carried out that might have produced a different result. Remember to check that the expert's facts, calculations and methods do actually produce the results set out in his or her report and, if they do not, challenge the expert as this may undermine the confidence and credibility of the expert's evidence;

(f) inviting the witness to agree with the propositions that form the basis of your expert's opinion—he or she is unlikely to disagree with everything your expert says and you should know from your own expert those areas that are in dispute. Remember to 'put your case' to the expert by inviting him or her to deal with your expert's methods/opinion/conclusions;

(g) inviting the witness to agree that, in his or her field, legitimate differences of opinion frequently occur between qualified experts. This shows that the witness is not infallible and that his or her evidence is 'opinion' only;

(h) using hypothetical facts to test the strength of the expert's opinion. Testing whether a different interpretation of the same facts or a slight change in those facts would affect the expert's opinion.

22.7.2 The evasive witness

You may well find that some witnesses, who gave straightforward responses during examination-in-chief, become evasive during cross-examination. Such evasion can take many forms, for example the witness may avoid answering the question directly, respond to an entirely different question, ask you to keep repeating your questions, or continually respond with 'I don't know/remember', 'I might', 'I could', 'I would/would not'.

You may deal with this in a number of ways. You can try to pin the witness down by repeating the question. If really necessary, invite the judge to direct the witness to answer the question. Or you can enquire whether the witness is having difficulty understanding or hearing your questions. Or let the witness make a terrible impression upon the trier(s) of fact. You can then follow this with a reference to the witness's demeanour in your closing speech, for example, 'Members of the jury, you may think that Mr Smith was rather evasive . . .'.

22.7.3 The belligerent/argumentative witness

Some witnesses try to 'have their say' at length and either ignore the question or cover matters that you did not ask them; or they answer your question with another question; or become abusive or accuse you of not knowing what you are talking about.

Control the witness by using closed, leading questions. If a witness insists on talking, try to cut him or her off by interrupting the flow with your next question. Make each question short. This will contrast with the witness's response and show the trier of fact what the witness is doing. If the witness asks you a question, for example, 'What would you know about it?', or is abusive, simply ignore the remarks and/or just repeat your question. You will usually find that the judge admonishes the witness. Never get involved in an argument with the witness.

22.8 A famous cross-examination considered

22.8.1 The cross-examination of Dr Crippen

The following is an edited version of the cross-examination of Dr Crippen, who was charged with the murder of his wife, Cora Crippen (also known as Belle Elmore). This extract is taken from *Notable Cross-Examinations* by E. W. Fordham. It illustrates many of the points that we have looked at in this chapter.

22.8.2 The background

Mrs Crippen disappeared from the matrimonial home at 39 Hilldrop Crescent at the end of January 1910. In the course of that month, Dr Crippen had bought (for his practice) five grains of hyoscin hydrobromide, a drug used only in minute proportions by the medical profession. He alleged that his wife had gone to America. Shortly after his wife's disappearance, he pawned jewellery of hers for £195. He gave some of her jewellery to Ethel Le Neve, a girlfriend who came to live with him in March 1910. Shortly afterwards, he announced that he had received a cable informing him of his wife's death.

Suspicion was aroused and Dr Crippen was interviewed by the police. He admitted that he had not, in fact, received any news of his wife's death and had not seen her since February 1910. A description of Mrs Crippen was circulated describing her as 'missing'. Two days later, Dr Crippen and Miss Le Neve sailed for Montreal under the disguise of a father and son named 'Robinson'. A warrant was issued for Dr Crippen's arrest, which was effected on board the ship.

Number 39 Hilldrop Crescent was thoroughly searched and human remains were found under the floor of the cellar. Death had resulted from hyoscin poisoning. A scar on part of the remains was one such as would have been caused by an operation that Mrs Crippen had undergone.

Two issues concerned the jury: were the remains those of Mrs Crippen? If so, was she murdered by her husband?

22.8.3 The cross-examination

In reading the cross-examination of Dr Crippen by R. D. Muir, you will see that he followed a distinct plan, progressing logically from one subject to another. The underlying purpose of his cross-examination was to show that Dr Crippen knew his wife was dead. He therefore directed his questions to exposing (a) the implausibility of Dr Crippen's assertion that his wife was still alive, and (b) the inconsistencies between Dr Crippen's account and his conduct at the time of and subsequent to both his wife's disappearance and his arrest. Note Mr Muir's courteous manner and his use of short questions, each containing only one fact at a time. Note also Dr Crippen's tendency to give evasive answers.

Q: 'On the early morning of the 1st February you were left alone in your house with your wife?'

A: 'Yes.'

Q: 'She was alive?'

A: 'She was.'

Q: 'And well?'

A: 'She was.'

Q: 'Do you know of any person in the world who has seen her alive since?'

A: 'I do not.'

Q: 'Do you know of any person in the world who has ever had a letter from her since?'

A: 'I do not.'

Q: 'Do you know of any person in the world who can prove any fact showing that she ever left that house alive?' (*Note: This is central to the prosecution case.*)

A: 'Absolutely not; I have told Mr Dew exactly all the facts.' (*Mr Dew was the Police Inspector who arrested Dr Crippen.*)

Q: 'At what hour did you last see her on February 1st?'

A: 'I think it would be about between two and three some time that we retired; that would be the last time I saw her.'

Q: 'Did you breakfast at home?'

A: 'I did.'

Q: 'Who prepared your breakfast?'

A: 'I prepared my own breakfast; I nearly always did.'

. . .

Q: 'We have heard that you were a kind and attentive husband?'

A: 'I was.'

Q: 'Preparing the breakfast in the morning, did you usually take her a cup of tea?'

A: 'Not often; once in a great while I took her a cup of coffee, but very seldom.' (*Note: Line of enquiry unfruitful—Not pursued.*)

. . .

Q: 'What time did you come home on that night when you say you did not find your wife there?'

A: 'The nearest I should say is, it would be my usual time, about 7.30.'

Q: 'Do you not recollect on that momentous night what time it was you came home?'

A: 'I would not like to say. It was somewhere near 7.30, it might have been 7.25, it might have been 7.35, but it was close to 7.30.'

Q: 'Did you tell Inspector Dew that you got home between 5 and 6?' (*Note: Previous inconsistent statement being put to the witness.*)

A: 'I do not remember telling him that hour.'

Q: 'Listen: "I came back to business the next morning, and when I went home between 5 and 6 pm I found she had gone." Is that right?'

A: 'If I said that to him, that was probably right. I cannot trace it back.'

Q: 'That was a Tuesday?'

A: 'A Tuesday, yes.'

Q: 'The 1st February?'

A: 'Yes.'

Q: 'Where did you think your wife had gone?'

A: 'I supposed, as she had always been talking about Bruce Miller to me, that she had gone there. That was the only thing I could make out.' (*Dr Crippen alleged that his wife had been friendly with this man who, at the time of her disappearance, had returned to America.*)

Q: 'That is to America?'

A: 'To America.'

Q: 'Have you made enquiries?'

A: 'No.'

Q: 'As to what steamers were going to America on or about that date?'

A: 'No, I have not.'

Q: 'At no time?'

A: 'At no time.'

Q: 'Not since your arrest?' (*Note: Counsel showing the inconsistency between Dr Crippen's assertion that his wife was alive and his behaviour, ie his lack of effort to substantiate it.*)

A: 'Not at all.'

Q: 'What?'

A: 'Not at any time.'

Q: 'Not to find out whether there was some steamer sailing for America in which there was a woman answering the description of your wife?'

A: 'I have not.'

Q: 'Nobody has made those enquiries?'

A: 'No.'

. . .

Q: 'Going to America on the 1st February, did your wife take any of her furs with her?' (*Note the use of a point of reference to make a transition to another topic.*)

A: 'That I could not say. She had any quantity of furs—any quantity of dresses.'

Q: 'Did she take any of her boxes with her?'

A: 'I believe there is one missing. There were a lot of trunks and boxes in the house; I do not know how many, because she bought several lately—well, not lately, but early last fall. I believe she bought two or three boxes.'

Lord Chief Justice:

'You must kindly listen to the question; it is a very important one. You are not asked whether she bought them. Are you able to say whether she took any boxes with her?' (*Note: Judge admonishing the witness for an evasive answer.*)

A: 'I am not able to say definitely.'

Q: 'Is there a cabstand near your house?'

A: 'There is one round the corner somewhere—round in York Road there is a cabstand.'

. . .

Q: 'Did you go to the cabstand to enquire whether any cabman had come to take away a box for your wife?' (*Note: Counsel asks a series of questions designed to highlight Dr Crippen's failure to seek proof that his wife was alive.*)

A: 'I did not.'

Q: 'At any time?'

A: 'At no time.'

Q: 'Not since your arrest?'

A: 'No.'

Q: 'Had you any neighbours at 39 Hilldrop Crescent on either side?'

A: 'Yes, we had neighbours on either side.'

Q: 'Have enquiries been made of the neighbours to know whether a cab or box was seen to leave your house on the 1st February?'

A: 'I have made none.'

Q: 'And, as far as you know none have been made?'

A: 'Not as far as I know.'

Q: 'You do not suggest that your wife, on a voyage to America in February, would walk away from the house?'

A: 'I am sure I do not know what she would do. She was a very impulsive woman.'

Q: 'But you have made no enquiries?'

A: 'I have made no enquiries.'

. . .

Q: 'Have you enquired of the milkman whether he saw your wife alive after you had left the house on that morning of the 1st February?'

A: 'I have already said that I made no enquiries.'

. . .

Q: 'It would be most important for your defence in this case on the charge of murder if any person could be found who saw your wife alive after the Martinettis saw her alive; you realise that?' (*The Martinettis dined with the Crippens on the evening of 31 January.*) (*Note: This is central to the theme of the prosecution case.*)

A: 'I do.'

Q: 'And you have made no enquiries at all?'

A: 'I have not conducted my own defence.'

Q: 'Of tradesmen, or neighbours, or cabmen? You say you have not conducted your own defence?' (*Note: Counsel picking up on the witness's answer.*)

A: 'I have not.'

Q: 'You have been consulted about it, I suppose.'

A: 'Certainly.'

Q: 'Did you suggest enquiries of that kind?'

A: 'I did not.'

. . .

(*Note: The following is a series of questions, designed to show that Dr Crippen knew his wife was dead.*)

Q: 'Have you made any suggestion to Mr Newton or anyone as to enquiries being made anywhere?' (*Mr Newton was Dr Crippen's solicitor.*)

A: 'That is a point that did not occur to me, so I have not made any such suggestions.'

Q: 'Did you know that any such enquiry would be fruitless?' (*Note: Counsel 'putting his case' in a very subtle manner.*)

A: 'I know nothing of the kind.'

Q: 'Supposing that your wife had written for her furs and jewels, what would have happened?'

A: 'I would have kept them. I paid for them, and I should not have given them up—after (her) leaving me.'

Q: 'Did you know that she would not write for them?' (*Note: Again, Counsel 'putting his case'.*)

A: 'I did not.'

. . .

Q: 'Where do you suppose your wife was going to get the money to pay her passage to America?'

A: 'She always had plenty of money, apparently.'

Q: 'Did you give her any?'

A: 'I did not give her any, no; I asked her if she was provided with money, if she wished any, and she said, "No, she wanted nothing off me".'

Q: 'You asked her if she wanted any money?'

A: 'Yes.'

Q: 'When did you ask her that?'

A: 'I asked her at the time she said she was going to leave me.'

Q: 'How many times had she said she was going to leave you?'

A: 'Numerous times.'

Q: 'Did you always on those occasions ask her if she wanted money to go away with?'

A: 'I never paid any attention because she had never carried it out to such an extent.' (*Note the evasive answer.*)

Q: 'She said she did not want money from you?'

A: 'Yes.'

Q: 'Were you in want of money?' (*Note: Counsel prepares to expose an inconsistency in the witness's conduct.*)

A: 'I was not.'

Q: 'What did you do with the money that you got from pawning your wife's jewels?'

A: 'I used it for advertising a new scheme I was starting—a new preparation I was putting on the market.'

Lord Chief Justice:

'Do you mean the whole £200—the £80 and the £115 [sic]?'

A: 'Yes, probably I used most of it.'

Lord Chief Justice:

'You are not asked "probably"; you were asked what you used the money for.' (*Note: Judge again admonishing the witness for an evasive answer.*)

A: 'For paying for the advertising.'

Q: 'Anything else?'

A: 'Well, I also bought some new dental instruments with it.'

. . .

Q: 'Why were you in such a hurry to pawn your wife's earrings and marquise rings?'

A: 'Because when I contracted for the advertising I would have to pay cash.'

. . .

Q: 'On the 2nd February you began to raise money (for this scheme) on your wife's jewels.'

A: 'Quite so.'

Q: 'Had you never pawned jewellery of your wife's before?'

A: 'I never pawned my wife's jewellery before.'

Lord Chief Justice:

'Had you ever pawned jewellery before?'

A: 'I had pawned jewellery before, yes.'

Q: 'Of your wife's?'

A: 'No, of my own.'

Q: 'Were February the 2nd and 9th of this year the only two occasions on which you ever pawned jewellery of your wife's?'

A: 'I refuse to accept the idea that it was my wife's.'

. . .

Q: 'Did you say this to Inspector Dew, "I have never pawned or sold anything belonging to her before or after she left"?' (*Note: Previous inconsistent statement.*)

A: 'I did, but I did not consider it was her property. I considered myself justified in answering in that way.'

Q: 'You told the truth (to Inspector Dew) according to your view about the property?'

A: 'Yes.'

Q: 'Did you account for your wife's jewellery by producing those exhibits which you showed to Inspector Dew at the house?'

A: 'I showed him some she had left.'

Q: 'That she had left behind?'

A: 'Yes.'

Q: 'And did you tell the Inspector that she had other jewellery, and must have taken that with her?'

A: 'She did have some, as I have already said; she had some rings and a watch that belonged to her before she was married.'

Q: 'Did you intend the Inspector to believe that you were accounting for the whole of your wife's jewellery?'

A: 'Certainly.'

. . .

Q: 'When you found your wife had gone you say you sat down to think how you could cover up the scandal?'

A: 'Yes.'

Q: 'You did your best to cover up the scandal?'

A: 'I did.'

Q: 'Is that your letter written on March 20th at 39 Hilldrop Crescent?' (*Letter handed to Crippen.*)

A: 'It is.'

Q: 'At that time was Ethel Le Neve living with you at that address?'

A: 'I would not be sure whether she came permanently to live with me at that time or not, but she had been on and off there.'

Lord Chief Justice:

'When do you say Miss Le Neve came to live at 39 Hilldrop Crescent?'

A: 'The first time she came there was 2nd February, the Wednesday night. From that time on she was with me probably two or three nights or perhaps more out of the week, but when she came permanently I would not like to say, except that it was shortly before Easter.'

Q: 'On the night of February 2nd did Ethel Le Neve sleep at Hilldrop Crescent?'

A: 'She did.'

(*Counsel now read out Crippen's letter to Mr and Mrs Martinetti of the 20th March*: 'Dear Clara and Paul, Please forgive me for not running in during the week, but I have been so upset by very bad news from Belle that I did not feel equal to talking with anyone. And now I have just had a cable saying she is so dangerously ill with double pleuro-pneumonia that I am considering if I had better not go at once. I don't want to worry you with my troubles, but I felt I must explain why I had not been to see you . . .')

Q: 'Had you, when you wrote that letter, arranged to go to Dieppe with Ethel Le Neve for Easter?'

A: 'Yes, I believe I had.'

Q: 'And did you want to wipe your wife off the slate before you went?'

A: 'It was not a question of that kind. It was that I felt something was necessary to stop all the worry I was having with the enquiries.'

Q: 'Did you want to announce your wife's death before you started for your holiday with Ethel Le Neve on the following Thursday?'

A: 'I do not think that follows a logical sequence.' (*Note the evasive answer.*)

Q: 'That is what you intended to do at the time you wrote that letter?'

A: 'I do not know whether I had at that time fixed the time when I would say that the other cable had arrived or not.'

Q: 'You prepared an advertisement of your wife's death for the Era?'

A: 'Yes.'

Q: 'When did you do that?'

A: 'I cannot tell you.'

Q: 'On the 24th March you sent a telegram to Mrs Martinetti saying that you had had a cable that your wife had died the previous night.'

A: 'Yes.'

Q: 'You sent that from Victoria Station on the eve of your departure with Ethel Le Neve?'

A: 'Yes.'

Q: 'Then you went off and took your holiday with her?'

A: 'Yes.'

Q: 'And you came back?'

A: 'Yes.'

Q: 'And you had to play the role of the bereaved husband?'

A: 'Yes.'

Q: 'Did you do it well?'

A: 'I am sure I could not tell you that.'

(*A letter from Crippen to a friend on black-edged paper is put to the witness, recording his sorrow for his wife's death.*)

Q: 'Sheer hypocrisy?'

A: 'I am not denying any of this.'

Q: 'Do you ask the jury to believe that, not knowing that your wife might write to those people, you told them she was dead?' (*Note: Counsel showing the implausibility of Dr Crippen's position.*)

A: 'Yes.'

Q: 'Where did you think she was?'

A: 'I thought she had gone to Chicago where Bruce Miller lived.'

Q: 'If she were alive she might call at any moment on her sisters?'

A: 'I did not think she would. If she went off with some other man I did not think she would have the face to go there.'

. . .

Q: 'You had been a tenant of 39 Hilldrop Crescent for five and a half years?'

A: 'Yes.'

Q: 'Had the floor of the cellar of that house been disturbed during the whole of that time?'

A: 'Not to my knowledge.'

Q: 'You were familiar with the cellar; you knew where the place was?'

A: 'I have not said that I was not.'

Q: 'You know, of course, that those remains were found in the cellar?'

A: 'I was told when I returned to England by my solicitor.'

Q: 'So far as you know, they could not have been put there while you were tenants?'

A: 'Not that I know of; of course . . . I would not say it was impossible, because there were times when we were away.'

. . .

Q: 'When did you make up your mind to go away from London?'

A: 'The morning after Inspector Dew was there—the 8th or 9th.'

Q: 'Had you the day before been contemplating the possibility of your going away?'

A: 'I would not like to say that I had made up my mind. When Inspector Dew came to me and laid out all the facts that he told me, I might have thought, well, if there is all this suspicion, and I am likely to have to stay in jail for months and months, perhaps until this woman is found, I had better be out of it.'

Q: 'What crime did you understand you might be kept in jail upon suspicion of?'

A: 'I do not understand the law well enough to say. From what I have read it seems to me I have heard of people being arrested on suspicion of being concerned in the disappearance of other people.' (*Note the evasive answer.*)

Q: 'You thought you were in danger of arrest?' (*Note now the effective use of short, leading, concise questions to highlight Dr Crippen's conduct and its consistency with guilty knowledge.*)

A: 'Yes.'

Q: 'And so you fled the country.'

A: 'Yes.'

Q: 'Under a false name?'

A: 'Yes.'

Q: 'Shaved off your moustache?'

A: 'Yes.'

Q: 'Left off wearing your glasses in public?'

A: 'Yes.'

Q: 'Took Le Neve with you?'

A: 'Yes.'

Q: 'Under a false name?'

A: 'Yes.'

Q: 'Posing as your son?'

A: 'Yes.'

Q: 'Went to Antwerp?'

A: 'Yes.'

Q: 'Stayed in a hotel there?'

A: 'Yes.'

Q: 'Stayed indoors all day?'

A: 'Oh no . . . we went to the Zoological Gardens and walked all over the place.'

Q: 'Enjoying yourselves?'

A: 'Certainly.'

Lord Chief Justice:

'What name did you give at the Hotel?'

A: 'If I gave any name anywhere it would be Robinson.'

Q: 'The second description (in the hotel register) is that of Miss Le Neve?'

A: 'Yes.'

Q: 'Disguised as a boy?'

A: 'Yes.'

Q: 'Passing as your son?'

A: 'Yes.'

. . .

Q: 'When you got to Quebec on board the steamer, or near Quebec, Inspector Dew came on board?'

A: 'Yes.'

Q: 'You were much surprised to see him?'

A: 'I did not expect to see Inspector Dew.'

Q: 'Did you recognise him at once?'

A: 'Yes . . . but not until he came into the cabin.'

Q: 'Did the Inspector say "Good morning, Dr Crippen, I am Inspector Dew"?'

A: 'Yes.'

Q: 'And did you say, "Good morning, Mr Dew"?'

A: 'Good morning, Mr Dew.'

Q: 'Did the Inspector then say, "You will be arrested for the murder and mutilation of your wife, Cora Crippen, in London, on or about February 2nd last"?'

A: 'I would not say that I took that in, because I was so very much surprised and confused that I did not quite have my right senses.'

Q: 'Did a Canadian officer, Mr McCarthy, caution you?'

A: 'He did.'

Q: 'And you realised you were being charged?'

A: 'Yes.'

Q: 'With what?'

A: 'I realised I was being charged.'

Q: 'With what?' (*Note: Counsel repeats the question which the witness has evaded.*)

A: 'Well, I realised that I was being arrested for murder; I remember hearing that.'

Q: 'The murder of your wife?'

A: 'Yes.'

Q: 'Up to that time did you believe she was alive?'

A: 'I did.'

Q: 'Did you put any question to Inspector Dew as to whether she had been found?' (*Note: Counsel showing the inconsistency in Dr Crippen's behaviour.*)

A: 'I did not put any question at all.'

Q: 'As to how he knew she was dead?'

A: 'No.'

. . .

Q: 'As you left the cabin did you say to the Inspector, "I am not sorry, the anxiety has been too much"?' (*Note: Counsel 'putting his case'.*)

A: 'Yes.'

Q: 'Anxiety for what?'

A: 'Anxiety thinking I might be pursued from London.'

Q: 'For what?'

A: 'For the same reason that I ran away.'

. . .

Q: 'Of course you understand that if your wife is alive there is no foundation for this charge at all?' (*Note: Counsel reinforcing his previous examination to show that Dr Crippen knew his wife was dead.*)

A: 'Decidedly not.'

Q: 'And that if she could be found you would at once be acquitted of it?'

A: 'Oh, rather.'

Q: 'What steps have been taken by you to find your wife?'

A: 'I have not taken any steps.'

. . .

(*Note: Change of subject*—Counsel showing that Dr Crippen had the means to kill his wife.)

Q: 'When did you first think of prescribing hyoscin for your patients?'

A: 'The first I knew of it was in 1885.'

Q: 'Here in London?'

A: 'Yes, it was early in January this year I first prescribed it for patients.'

Q: 'You can give the names and addresses of the persons to whom you sent your remedies?'

A: 'If I went and looked them up.'

Q: 'Were you prescribing hyoscin for any of those patients?'

A: 'Yes.'

Q: 'As a medicine?'

A: 'Yes.'

Q: 'To be administered through the mouth?'

A: 'Decidedly.'

Q: 'For what disease?'

A: 'Nervous disease—coughs of a septic character and asthmatic complaints.'

Lord Chief Justice:

'If there is any book in which hyoscin is prescribed for use in this way, you had better produce the book.' (*No such book was ever produced.*)

. . .

Q: 'Will you answer this question, have you got anywhere left any homeopathic preparation into which you put this hyoscin?'

A: 'They were all sent out as they were made.'

Q: 'You have none left?'

A: 'I have none left.'

Q: 'Have you got any patient to whom you sent such homeopathic preparations?'

A: 'Mr Newton has been looking the matter up; I do not know.'

The skill of Mr Muir's cross-examination was such that he made it appear easy! It is no surprise that the jury found Dr Crippen 'guilty'.

23

Re-examination

23.1 Purpose

As soon as the cross-examination of your witness has been completed, you have the opportunity to re-examine the witness. The purpose of re-examination is to clarify, explain or develop matters arising out of cross-examination so as to limit, where possible, any damage to your case.

23.2 The cardinal rules

The cardinal rules of re-examination are:

(a) You have the right to re-examine only on matters that arise out of cross-examination. Re-examination is therefore not an examination-in-chief all over again, nor is it an opportunity to ask questions on some matter that you forgot to ask about in-chief and on which your opponent has not asked questions. If you realise during the cross-examination that you omitted to ask in-chief about some point that could be important and you want to repair your own self-inflicted damage, then you must ask the judge for permission to do so. This will, of course, give your opponent the right to further cross-examination, so you ought to do this before you begin your re-examination. Remember to apologise, it is your mistake, not your client's.

(b) Never re-examine just for the sake of it. Never re-examine unless you are clear about what you can achieve by doing so. Ask yourself 'Does the evidence need clarifying or explaining?'; 'Can I achieve that by my question(s)?'; 'Can the matter be developed further so as to shed a different light upon it?'; 'Can I meet the attack on the witness's credit?' Unless you are satisfied that the answer to one or more of these questions is 'Yes', leave well alone.

(c) Never use leading questions to elicit evidence from your own witness in re-examination (see the exceptions in **20.6.1**).

(d) Avoid asking a question in re-examination to which you do not know the answer. This is a dangerous practice at any time: it could destroy your case at this late stage.

23.3   Is it necessary to re-examine?

The most common situations where it may be necessary to re-examine arise where:

(a) the cross-examiner has elicited only that part of a conversation or an occurrence that is favourable to his or her case; **or**

(b) he or she has attacked the witness's conduct/character; **or**

(c) he or she has highlighted an inconsistency in the witness's evidence or has impeached the witness with a prior inconsistent statement; **or**

(d) the witness has become muddled or confused or you think the audience has become muddled or confused. In either event, order and clarity need to be restored.

23.4   Examples of re-examination

If you must re-examine, make it short and business-like. Beware of the 'just one more question' syndrome.

Example 1

A mother, who is opposed to contact between her children and their father, is cross-examined to the effect that she stopped the visits only after the father reduced the maintenance he was paying her. She denies that the money had anything to do with her decision to stop contact between the children and their father.

Re-examination

Q: 'How much is your weekly income?'

A: '£102.'

Q: 'How is that figure made up?'

A: 'I get £27 in child benefit and £50 a week now from my ex-husband. The rest is made up from Income Support.'

Q: 'How much was your ex-husband paying you before he reduced it?'

A: '£75 a week.'

Q: 'What was your total income at that time?'

A: 'With the child benefit, it was the same, £102 per week.'

Example 2

The defendant is charged with taking and driving away a motor vehicle without the owner's consent. The owner is cross-examined to the effect that he had loaned his car to the defendant, his neighbour, on a previous occasion and had told the defendant he could take it at any time. The owner admits the former but not the latter allegation.

Re-examination

Q: 'You told the court, in answer to my friend, that you had let the defendant borrow your car on a previous occasion.'

A: 'Yes.'

Q: 'When was that?'

A: 'About six months beforehand.'

Q: 'What were the circumstances?'

A: 'It was the day of the tube strike. He asked me if he could borrow the car or he'd miss an important job interview. He brought it back a few hours later.'

Q: 'What happened to your car keys on that occasion?'

A: 'He returned them to me.'

Q: 'Did you give him your car keys at any other time?'

A: 'No.'

Q: 'Did you give him permission to borrow your car on any other occasion?'

A: 'No, I did not. It was a one-off.'

Example 3

The cross-examination of an assault victim has emphasised the fact that she originally told the police she did not know her attacker. It was only two weeks later that she 'pointed the finger' at the accused.

Re-examination

Q: 'Why did you tell the police initially that you did not know your attacker?'

A: 'I was frightened. He told me he knew where I lived and he would come and get me.'

Q: 'Why did you subsequently change your mind.'

A: 'I managed to find another place to live. I felt safer.'

23.5 In conclusion

If you decide not to re-examine, you can simply say 'I have no further questions (of this witness) Your Honour/Sir/Madam'.

Whether you decide to re-examine or not, it is proper to give the judge or magistrate the opportunity of asking the witness any question he or she deems necessary.

'Unless your Lordship/Your Honour has any questions?'/'Have you any questions, Sir/Madam?'

If the judge or magistrate does question the witness, he or she must give both you and your opponent the opportunity of asking further questions **arising out of** what he or she has asked.

23.6 Releasing the witness

Unless the witness is a party to the proceedings or the defendant in a criminal trial, you must ask the court to release the witness from continued attendance at court.

'My Lord/Your Honour/Sir/Madam, may this witness be released?'

The judge or magistrate will ask your opponent whether he or she objects to the witness being released. The answer is usually 'No'. The judge or magistrate will then indicate that the witness is free to go.

It is time to call your next witness or to inform the court: 'That is the case for the prosecution/claimant/defendant.'

Part VI

How-to-do-it guides

24

Using this Part of the manual

The chapters in this Part are all about making your life easier. They are a set of how-to-do-it guides that cover some of the most common types of applications that you may face as an advocate at the start of your career. Usually they are written by practising barristers with considerable practical experience of the matters they are writing about. The matters range from the sort of hearing where your application is the sole purpose for the hearing (eg an application for summary judgment) to those applications that have to be made as and when the need arises, in the context of other proceedings in the case (eg applying for bail when a criminal case is remanded). Some of these guides are necessarily more extensive than others.

As we have already noted in the manual, in practice different barristers may well have different styles that they use, different structures or techniques that they find work well for them. The aim of these guides is to give you an insight into how a particular application or hearing might work and what needs to be covered in it. As we said earlier in the context of observing barristers in court—never slavishly follow what you see and hear, always think critically about it. Did that work? Why? Could I do that? Could I improve on that? The same advice should be borne in mind when reading any of these guides—they are simply one starting point for you.

The aim of these chapters is not to render you competent to make such an application overnight. You should read them in conjunction with the other BPTC manuals and relevant practitioner works, as appropriate for the application. The aim is to give you some advance notice of what happens in court when a particular application is made: who starts, what documents are needed, how many copies must be provided and so forth.

After reading this material, you should have a basic idea of how to plan for a particular application, rather than making your first one in a state of '**un**blissful' ignorance! Never neglect the other resources at your disposal, though. You should always feel able to ask other, more experienced barristers for advice or hints when you are in chambers. If possible, try to get to court early so that you can watch how similar applications are being made; note the judge's likes and dislikes.

The chapters start with a general guide to the preparation of skeleton arguments, which may be used in civil and criminal cases. Next, you will find some guides for work in the civil courts and tribunals. It is hoped that these are of particular assistance as civil interlocutory matters so often take place in private, with only the parties and their advocates present, so there is limited opportunity simply to observe them. These are followed by some guides to work in the criminal courts.

25

Skeleton arguments

25.1 General

25.1.1 The importance of skeleton arguments

The ability to draft a strong, persuasive and yet precise skeleton argument in support of the case you are putting forward is now a fundamental skill required of an advocate. Owing to the importance increasingly placed by judges on skeleton arguments, the skill of preparing them should be seen by the junior barrister as one that is every bit as important as the skill involved in undertaking other forms of written work, such as drafting the statements of case at the start of the claim, or advising in writing during the lifetime of the claim.

A skeleton argument is designed to assist the court with a written outline of the main points to be put forward by a party at a subsequent oral hearing. It is produced by that party's advocate, and given to the judge, before the oral hearing. At the hearing, the judge will expect the advocate to follow it. The use of the word 'skeleton' is significant and its meaning in this context should be understood at the outset and never forgotten. The purpose of a written skeleton argument is to provide you with a structured framework on which you can hang your oral submissions to the court. It is, quite literally, the bones upon which you later build the flesh of your argument. It follows that all the main issues with which you will seek to deal at the hearing should be covered.

It is now common practice for advocates to draft skeleton arguments, whether for use at interim applications or to form the basis of final submissions at trial after the evidence has been heard. The strict timetables imposed by the CPR have led to the ever more widespread use of written argument.

In criminal proceedings skeleton arguments are frequently used to form the basis of pre-trial argument, such as applications to exclude evidence or to sever an indictment. They are also used at the conclusion of the prosecution case if a submission of no case is to be made.

From time to time, in practice, advocates are asked to provide the judge with written submissions. These should be distinguished from skeleton arguments. A written submission is intended to be an *alternative* to oral argument (see *Sleeman v Highway Care Ltd*, The Times, 3 November 1999). A skeleton argument is an *aid* to oral argument.

25.1.2 Practice Directions and guidelines

In 1995, Lord Chief Justice Taylor issued a *Practice Direction (Civil Litigation: Case Management)* [1995] 1 All ER 385, which applied to all lists in the Queen's Bench and Chancery Divisions, except where other directions specifically applied. The purpose of the Practice Direction was to improve case management, and to reduce the costs and delay of civil litigation. It required, not less than three clear days before the hearing of a claim or application, each party to lodge with the court (with copies being provided to the other parties) a skeleton argument concisely summarising that party's submissions in relation to each of the issues, and citing the main authorities relied upon, which may be attached.

Now that judicial case management takes place under the CPR, you will find in practice that for all multi-track cases in which a case management conference takes place, the court will give detailed directions for the steps to be taken up to the trial and for the trial itself. Those directions will inevitably include a provision requiring the parties to file skeleton arguments a certain number of days prior to trial or before any application of substance to a judge.

In addition, under PD 28 (the fast track) and PD 29 (the multi-track), the parties will be required to file a case summary prior to trial in the fast track and prior to a case management conference in the multi-track.

Skeleton arguments are also required when filing a notice of appeal (PD 52, para 5.9).

There is guidance on the drafting of skeleton arguments in PD 52A, para 5.1, Appendix 7 to the *Chancery Guide*, para 7.11.12 of the *Queen's Bench Guide*, and Appendix 9 to the *Admiralty and Commercial Courts Guide*. No matter what court you are appearing in, and for whatever type of hearing you are preparing your skeleton argument, it would be wise to follow the requirements of PD 52A, para 5.1, which reads as follows.

5.1

(1) *The purpose of a skeleton argument is to assist the court by setting out as concisely as practicable the arguments upon which a party intends to rely.*

(2) *A skeleton argument must—*
  - *be concise;*
  - *both define and confine the areas of controversy;*
  - *be set out in numbered paragraphs;*
  - *be cross-referenced to any relevant document in the bundle;*
  - *be self-contained and not incorporate by reference material from previous skeleton arguments;*
  - *not include extensive quotations from documents or authorities.*

(3) *Documents to be relied on must be identified.*

(4) *Where it is necessary to refer to an authority, a skeleton argument must—*

  (a) state the proposition of law the authority demonstrates; and
  (b) identify the parts of the authority that support the proposition.

  If more than one authority is cited in support of a given proposition, the skeleton argument must briefly state why.

(5) *The cost of preparing a skeleton argument which—*

  (a) does not comply with the requirements set out in this paragraph; or
  (b) was not filed within the time limits provided by this Practice Direction (or any further time granted by the court),

  will not be allowed on assessment except as directed by the court.

But follow also the guidance in the *Chancery Guide*:

Appendix 7   Guidelines on Skeleton Arguments and Chronologies

1. *A skeleton argument is intended to identify both for the parties and the court those points which are, and those that are not, in issue, and the nature of the argument in relation to those points which are in issue. It is not a substitute for oral argument.*

2. *Every skeleton argument should therefore:*

  (1) identify concisely
    (a) the nature of the case generally, and the background facts insofar as they are relevant to the matter before the court;

(b) the propositions of law relied on with references to the relevant authorities;

(c) the submissions of fact to be made with reference to the evidence;

(2)   be as brief as the nature of the issues allows—it should not normally exceed 20 pages of double-spaced A4 paper and in many cases it should be much shorter than this;

(3)   be in numbered paragraphs and state the name (and contact details) of the advocate(s) who prepared it;

(4)   avoid arguing the case at length;

(5)   avoid formality and make use of abbreviations, eg C for Claimant, A/345 for bundle A page 345, 1.1.95 for 1st January 1995 etc.

Take heed also of the *Queen's Bench Guide*, which says:

7.11.12   A skeleton argument should:

(1)   concisely summarise the party's submissions in relation to each of the issues,

(2)   cite the main authorities relied on, which may be attached,

(3)   contain a reading list and an estimate of the time it will take the Judge to read,

(4)   be as brief as the issues allow and not normally be longer than 20 pages of double-spaced A4 paper,

(5)   be divided into numbered paragraphs and paged consecutively,

(6)   avoid formality and use understandable abbreviations, and

(7)   identify any core documents which it would be helpful to read beforehand.

25.1.3   The length of a skeleton argument

As the Practice Direction makes clear, the purpose of a skeleton argument is solely to identify and summarise the points at issue. It is an aide-memoire for convenience of reference before and during the hearing. A skeleton argument should therefore be as succinct as possible. It is not the function of a skeleton argument to argue the case on paper. The guidance set out above suggests a normal maximum of 20 pages of double-spaced A4 paper, but in many cases skeleton arguments can and should be much shorter than this. It is wrong to assume that longer cases justify proportionately longer skeleton arguments. In the case of interim and shorter final appeals in the Court of Appeal, it should normally be possible to do justice to the relevant points in a skeleton argument of considerably fewer than ten pages. For short hearings before the district judge in the county court, of the type often undertaken by junior counsel in the early years of practice, and that might, for example, involve applications on disclosure issues, or seeking permission to call a particular expert witness, it is suggested that the skeleton argument should rarely exceed five pages.

In the case of *Tombstone Ltd v Raja* [2008] EWCA Civ 1444, [2008] All ER (D) 180 (Dec), the Court of Appeal was scathing about the length and quality of Tombstone's skeleton argument. In an appeal from a relatively short judgment, it ran to 110 pages plus 64 pages of appendices. Mummery LJ said (para [124] and following):

The length of Tombstone's skeleton did not assist the court. In fact, it tended to detract from Tombstone's case . . .

Practitioners who ignore practice directions on skeleton arguments . . . are well advised to note the risk of the court's negative reaction to unnecessarily long written submissions . . .

We remind practitioners that skeleton arguments should not be prepared as verbatim scripts to be read out in public or as footnoted theses to be read in private. Good skeleton arguments are tools with practical uses: an agenda for the hearing, a summary of the main points, propositions and arguments to be developed orally, a useful way of noting citations and references, a convenient place for making cross references, a time-saving means of avoiding unnecessary dictation to the court and laborious and pointless note-taking by the court.

Skeleton arguments are aids to oral advocacy . . . Too many practitioners, at increased cost to their clients and diminishing assistance to the court, burden their opponents and the court with written briefs. They are anything but brief. The result is that there is no real saving of legal costs, or of precious hearing, reading and writing time . . .

This criticism by Mummery LJ should be remembered by all advocates when determining the amount of detail to be advanced in a skeleton argument. Accordingly, the first and foremost rule for the preparation of any skeleton argument must be to 'keep it concise'.

25.1.4 The content and structure of a skeleton argument

There is no strict formula, but a good skeleton argument will usually:

(a) set out the nature of the application/submission;

(b) state briefly what the case is about (if necessary);

(c) summarise the issues between the parties (if necessary);

(d) set out the argument in the form of a series of legal propositions and submissions supported by authority and by evidence (with page/paragraph references as necessary);

(e) assist the court to assimilate your argument with ease;

(f) assist you to persuade the court to grant the order you seek; and

(g) identify precisely what the court is being asked to do.

The content of the skeleton argument will inevitably vary according to the complexity of the issues and the stage in the proceedings at which the submissions are made. You should bear in mind that your skeleton argument will be read in advance by the judge and your opponent. It is therefore your first opportunity to influence the outcome of the hearing. The structure should be logical, with clear paragraph numbers and sub-headings. Although your skeleton argument should be informative, it should also be concise and easily absorbed. Above all, a *skeleton* argument should be just that: the argument should not be fully fleshed out. It is for the advocate to develop the submissions orally. Finally, it is good practice, particularly in civil proceedings, to assist the court by handing up a chronology in a separate document.

In the same way as you develop a style for drafting statements of case, similarly you will develop a style for the preparation of skeleton arguments. The precise form for a skeleton argument will be very much a question of personal choice, which you will develop in your own good time. Nevertheless, one can provide some very basic 'dos' and 'don'ts', which must always be adhered to.

In the case of points of law, there should be a list of the propositions of law that are going to be advanced. The skeleton argument should clearly state the point being contended for and cite the principal authority or authorities in support, with reference to the particular page(s) where the principle concerned is enunciated.

Thus in a medical negligence claim, for instance, one might see early on in the skeleton argument the proposition: 'a doctor cannot be guilty of negligence if he acts in accordance with a responsible body of medical opinion (see *Bolam v Friern Hospital Management Committee* [1957] 1WLR 582 at 587)'.

Imagine you are acting for a claimant in a trial involving an epidural injection of anaesthetic into the client's spine, which it was alleged by the claimant (and supporting medical expert opinion evidence) had been negligently administered by a young and inexperienced doctor, in the wrong place, and not by a senior consultant as contended for by the defendant health authority. The local anaesthetic has escaped into surrounding tissues where it should not have been allowed to go, causing severe long-term injury.

In dealing with breach of duty, a skeleton argument might well have a subheading 'Breach of Duty' and then choose to list the central factual issues to be determined by the judge at trial as follows:

(1) Who performed the injection?

(2) Where was the needle sited?

(3) Where was the anaesthetic's intended target?

(4) Was the needle site appropriate?

(5) Was the local anaesthetic released at the target site in the spine?

(6) If the answer to question (5) is 'Yes', how did the local anaesthetic escape to the site of injury?

(7) If the answer to question (5) is 'No', where was the local anaesthetic released?

If such a list of questions were to feature in a skeleton argument being handed in at the start of the trial in this imaginary claim, clearly it would be of immense assistance to the judge when it came to understanding the case in opening, and also when deciding the case later on. If a skeleton were being prepared for a trial at first instance, obviously there would be no transcripts of evidence to be referred to. Reference would, however, have to be made within the skeleton argument to the evidence within the trial bundle (both lay witness statements and reports from the medical experts), which would assist the trial judge in answering the questions you have posed.

25.1.5 Citing authorities in a skeleton argument

There are some important requirements set out in a *Practice Note* [2001] 2 All ER 510, as follows.

Methods of citation

8.1. *Advocates will in future be required to state, in respect of each authority that they wish to cite, the proposition of law that the authority demonstrates, and the parts of the judgment that support that proposition. If it is sought to cite more than one authority in support of a given proposition, advocates must state the reason for taking that course.*

8.2. *The demonstration referred to in para 8.1 will be required to be contained in any skeleton argument and in any appellant's or respondent's notice in respect of each authority referred to in that skeleton or notice.*

8.3. *Any bundle or list of authorities prepared for the use of any court must in future bear a certification by the advocate responsible for arguing the case that the requirements of this paragraph have been complied with in respect of each authority included.*

8.4. *The statements referred to in para 8.1 should not materially add to the length of submissions or of skeleton arguments, but should be sufficient to demonstrate, in the context of the advocate's argument, the relevance of the authority or authorities to that argument and that the citation is necessary for a proper presentation of that argument.*

25.1.6 Other requirements

The Court of Appeal's Practice Direction specifically states that in the case of an appeal on a question(s) of fact, the skeleton argument should state briefly the basis on which it is contended that the Court of Appeal can interfere with the finding of fact concerned, with cross-references to the passages in the transcript or notes of evidence that bear on the point.

In the Court of Appeal, it is mandatory for the appellant's advocate's skeleton argument to be accompanied by a written chronology of events relevant to the appeal, cross-referenced to the core bundle or appeal bundle. Chronologies are also strongly recommended by the *Queen's Bench Guide* and *Chancery Guide*. The point to note here particularly is that the chronology is a separate document, and is not to be found within the skeleton argument. It is important that the chronology is kept as a separate document from the skeleton argument, in order that it may easily be consulted in conjunction with other papers.

25.2 Skeleton argument for use at a civil trial

Given the very nature and purpose of a skeleton argument, in that it seeks to present an overview of a whole claim and the party's fundamental case to be presented, it is very difficult, if not impossible, within the space available here, to provide any really useful 'model' skeleton argument.

However, there is an example of a skeleton argument provided below. It involves an imaginary case in which a hospital cleaner is alleging she fractured her wrist whilst at work following a fall down some stairs. The defendant NHS Trust's case is that there was no accident suffered at work at all! There is no real issue as to the law and the trial will turn on the resolution of the factual dispute. You should note the basic structure of the skeleton argument, namely an introduction, a list of the issues contended for, how the defendant puts its case with regard to the accident, and also what the defendant says about the injury sustained.

25.2.1 Skeleton argument

IN THE HIGH COURT OF JUSTICE   Claim No 2008 HC 6312
QUEEN'S BENCH DIVISION

BETWEEN

MRS SANDRA LOCKWOOD   Claimant

and

HARLEY NHS TRUST   Defendant

DEFENDANT'S SKELETON ARGUMENT

INTRODUCTION

1. The Claimant claims damages arising out of an accidental fall at work with the Defendant on 2nd October 2007 ('the Material Accident') when she allegedly suffered a fracture of the scaphoid of the left wrist. The Claimant was working as a cleaner at the time of the alleged accident. Her case is that she fell down some stairs having tripped up on a defect at the top of the staircase.

2. A default judgment for damages to be assessed has been entered and, accordingly, the hearing on 26th June 2012 is an assessment of damages. The question is what damages—that is, for personal injuries and consequential financial losses—can the Claimant prove she has suffered, if any, as a result of the material accident?

THE ISSUES

3. The Defendant contends that the principal issues are as follows:

(1) Did the Claimant in fact suffer a fracture to her left scaphoid or indeed any injury to her left wrist in the Material Accident on 2nd October 2007?

(2) If the Claimant injured her left wrist in the Material Accident, what was the nature of the injury, did she have a pre-existing degenerative condition of the wrist and, if so, did the injury merely bring to light and/or exacerbate a condition that would in any event have caused the Claimant the troubles complained of and, if so, to what extent?

(3) Which absences from work (if any) have been attributable to the Material Accident and was the Claimant's medical retirement from the Defendant's employment in July 2009 (on the grounds of 'scaphoid bone cyst') attributable to the Material Accident and, if so, to what extent has the Claimant's employability thereafter been restricted as a result of matters properly attributable to the Material Accident?

THE ACCIDENT

4. The Defendant's case is that in the Material Accident the Claimant suffered no injury to her left wrist (which is the *only* injury in respect of which she claims: see Particulars of Claim, para 7, Particulars of Injury, at Trial Bundle, page 8, 'TB 8').

5. Trial Bundle, pages 191–199 ('TB 191–199'), to which reference is made below, are annexed to this Skeleton.

6. On the day of the Material Accident, Tuesday 2nd October 2007, at 14.00 hours first aid was given to the Claimant when she was found to be suffering from a 'badly bruised right upper arm and back of shoulder resulting from an accident at rear staircase'. The Claimant returned to duty at 14.15 hours; see First Aid Report at TB 191.

7. On Friday 5th October 2007, the Claimant herself completed an Accident on Duty Report recording that on 2nd October 2007 at 14.00 hours on the rear staircase 'I slipped on top stair' and described her injury as 'bruised right upper shoulder': see TB 192.

8. The same day, 5th October 2007, a supervising officer's Accident on Duty Report and an entry in the Accident Book were completed (see TB 193–194 and TB 195 Entry No 935, respectively). The contemporaneous description of the Claimant's injury in both cases was 'bruised right shoulder'. The words 'plus wrist fracture' at paragraph 10 of the supervising officer's Accident on Duty Report, TB 193, were added at a later date, after, the Defendant will contend, the Claimant had attended hospital on 15th and 16th October 2007. The same contention is made in relation to the words 'fractured left wrist', which were added to and then deleted from the Accident Book entry at TB 195.

9. The Claimant did not cease work until 15th October 2007: see her computerised sick absence record at TB 199.

10. The Claimant did not attend her general practitioner in respect of the Material Accident or any injury to her left wrist: see the clinical record cards at TB 125.

11. The Claimant attended the Accident and Emergency Department of the Burton General Hospital on Monday 15th October 2007, when she complained of

'Injury left wrist fell down stairs at work on Friday. Painful ever since.' (Friday would have been 12th October 2007.) She gave the history 'Friday: fell down stairs at work and hurt left wrist? mech [mechanism] of injury unable to recall how landed.' See the Casualty Officer's contemporaneous A & E Department records at TB 66–67.

12. The following day, Tuesday 16th October 2007, the Claimant returned to the Burton General Hospital as an outpatient, where she gave the history 'Had a fall 4/7 [ie four days ago] landed on left outstretched hand. Seen at A/E Department 1/7 [ie one day ago].' On clinical and radiological examination, she was found to have a left scaphoid fracture. Scaphoid type POP [plaster of Paris] was applied. 'Today POP is satisfactory circulation is okay X-ray cyst in left scaphoid (fracture) through it': see the clinical notes at TB 68.

13. The Claimant has never reported or complained to the Defendant of an accident at work on Friday 12th October 2007: see the Accident Book at TB 195, which records accidents up to 15th November 2007.

14. In the circumstances, the Defendant will contend that the Claimant suffered no injury to her left wrist in the Material Accident on 2nd October 2007 and, therefore, her claim fails in its entirety, as the whole of her claim for both general and special damages is based upon an alleged injury to her left wrist.

15. In the event of this Court finding that she did injure her left wrist in the Material Accident, the Defendant's alternative arguments are outlined below.

THE NATURE OF THE INJURY

16. The contemporaneous clinical notes at the Burton General Hospital quoted above record that when X-rays were first taken they showed a cyst in the left scaphoid with a possible fracture running through it (TB 67 foot and TB 68). A further entry on 1st December 2007 noted, inter alia, 'X-ray no definite (fracture)': TB 69.

17. In the circumstances, if there was in fact a fracture to the left scaphoid the most it can be blamed for is bringing to light and exacerbating an existing degenerative condition in the wrist that would, in any event, have caused such problems in due course.

18. The Claimant was off work initially from 15th October 2007 to 1st December 2007 and then from 19th December 2007 to 1st May 2008 with problems related to her left wrist injury. Thereafter, she returned to work and had no further absences attributable to her left wrist for nearly nine months until 29th January 2009: see the computerised sick absence record at TB 199. During those nine months her only substantial absences were in August and November 2008, 34 days with back pain, and January 2009, a total of 19 days absence, again related to back pain.

19. When in 2009 the Claimant again complained of problems relating to her left wrist these were said to have arisen from an injury to her wrist in February 2009 when she was 'pulling a bucket': see the memorandum from Dr Sheridan, the Defendant's Area Medical Adviser, dated 25th April 2009 at TB108, the middle of the page. In the circumstances, the Defendant will contend that the Claimant's eventual medical retirement in July 2009 on grounds of 'scaphoid bone cyst' (see the Medical Retirement Certificate at TB 116) and her subsequent restricted working ability is not attributable to the Material Accident but to the pre-existing degenerative condition and/or a further accident, in February 2009.

20. If necessary, the Defendant will contend that in the light of the Claimant's full sick absence record (TB 196–199), irrespective of the material accident, the Claimant's employment with the Defendant would not have continued beyond her actual retirement date in July 2009 in any event.

21. In so far as may be necessary, in relation to the calculation of damages claimed the Defendant will rely upon its Counter Schedule dated 1st June 2012 (TB 175–181).

BESS TOFFER

25.2.2   Commentary

The above skeleton argument, when set out in the conventional way, double-spaced on A4 paper, with generous margins, is seven pages long. This is well within the guidelines on length.

It is not easy to read and understand quickly, since you cannot follow up the references to the trial bundle, and the chronology needs to be clear in your mind. But read it again carefully in conjunction with this commentary and you will find it has a compelling clarity and logic. It is a good skeleton argument.

Note above all that it does not attempt to duplicate any other documents: it is not in any way setting out what would be found in the statements of case, the witness statements, the exhibits, the medical reports or the schedules of loss, but it draws on all of these to construct the argument.

It is fully headed, and the title of the document identifies whose skeleton argument it is ('Defendant's').

Introduction   Paragraph 1 is a very brief statement of what the case is about, setting the facts out far more briefly than they would be in the particulars of claim. The chief function of this paragraph is to identify and define the material accident, which is an essential point of departure for the argument that follows. Paragraph 2 simply states the broad issue before the court.

Issues   It is essential to summarise the issues at the outset, so that the judge can know what point the argument is addressing. It is more accurate to say 'the Defendant contends that the issues are' than 'the issues are', since the claimant may well have a different set of issues in her argument. Paragraph 3 then subdivides into the three main issues. Issue (1) is the most important and comes first: it is very clear. Issue (2) is arguably several sub-issues rolled into one, but it becomes clear when they are argued (in paragraphs 16 and 17) that they are inseparable. Issue (3) also raises several sub-issues, but they are closely connected and interdependent, so they can be identified as one.

The structure of the remainder of the skeleton argument is based on these three issues. Paragraphs 4–14 contain the argument on issue (1); paragraphs 16 and 17 contain the argument on issue (2); and paragraphs 18–21 contain the argument on issue (3).

Paragraphs 4–14   The argument on issue (1). This section begins by making a clear statement (in paragraph 4) of the proposition the argument is intended to prove, namely that there is no causal link between the accident complained of and the injury complained of. Paragraph 5 is then a formal statement of the pages annexed for the judge's convenience.

From paragraph 6 onwards the argument is built up step by step in a logical way. Note how every step in the argument is supported by evidence. The defendant is not saying what it would like to prove, but what it contends it actually can prove. Obviously, the argument is based on evidence that has not yet been accepted by the court or tested by cross-examination, and it may be that when it comes to oral argument counsel for the defendant will need to make adjustments and recognise different strengths and weaknesses. But at this stage, the skeleton argument can only be based on the evidence that will go in as evidence-in-chief, and so it is.

In essence the argument is as follows:

(1) The accident on 2nd October 2007 did not cause any injury to the claimant's left wrist. Evidence in support of this:

    (a)   first aid report says right shoulder (paragraph 6);

    (b)   claimant's accident on duty report says right shoulder (paragraph 7);

    (c)   supervisor's accident on duty report says right shoulder (left wrist added later) (paragraph 8);

    (d)   accident book says right shoulder (left wrist added and then deleted later) (paragraph 8);

    (e)   claimant did not cease work after accident (paragraph 9);

    (f)   claimant did not consult GP regarding accident (paragraph 10).

(2) If her left wrist was injured at all, it was injured in a separate accident on 12th October 2007. Evidence in support of this:

    (a)   casualty notes from hospital including claimant's own complaint (paragraph 11);

    (b)   further casualty notes including same complaint by C (paragraph 12).

(3) Any accident on 12th October is not alleged to be the fault of the defendant. Evidence—no entry in accident book (paragraph 13).

Paragraph 14   Sums up the argument by repeating the defendant's contention and stating the consequence that flows from it, namely that the claimant's claim fails in its entirety.

Paragraph 15   Acknowledges the fact that if the defendant succeeds on issue (1), issues (2) and (3) will not need to be argued or decided.

Paragraphs 16–17   The argument on issue (2). The argument here will depend on favourable medical opinion, but if the medical opinion is favourable, the argument is straightforward. The X-ray results showed a cyst (see paragraph 12) and no definite fracture (paragraph 16), so even if there was a fracture to the left wrist, and even if it was caused by the material accident, it only produced a condition that the claimant would have suffered from in due course in any event.

Paragraphs 18–21   The argument on issue (3). This argument addresses the quantum of damages for lost earnings and seeks to show that even if the wrist was injured in the material accident, and even if the defendant is liable for that injury, most losses of earnings claimed stem from other causes. The only concession, made at the start of paragraph 18, is that two periods of loss were due to the wrist injury. Thereafter she had periods off work due to back pain (paragraph 18), which the defendants will contend are irrelevant (it is not clear whether the claimant has claimed in respect of this loss anyway).

The main loss of earnings results from the claimant's retirement from work, which the defendant contends was due either to the pre-existing condition or to yet another accident (paragraph 19). As a last resort the defendant says the claimant's sickness record taken as a whole was such that she would probably have retired when she did in any event for one reason or another (paragraph 20). The figures that flow from these contentions are to be found in the counter-schedule of loss (paragraph 21).

The skeleton argument should be signed by counsel.

25.3 Skeleton argument in support of an interim application

The following is an example of a skeleton argument that might be used in an application to set aside judgment in default. The particulars of claim in this case can be found in the *Drafting* manual at **9.5.1**, and the witness statement in support of the application can be found in the same manual at **20.8.1**.

25.3.1 Skeleton argument

IN THE HIGH COURT OF JUSTICE   Claim No 2012 HC 98744
QUEEN'S BENCH DIVISION
MANCHESTER DISTRICT REGISTRY

BETWEEN

SHILTON MACHINE TOOLS LIMITED   Claimant

and

BANKS PLASTIC MOULDINGS LIMITED   Defendant

SKELETON ARGUMENT OF THE DEFENDANT

Introduction

1. This is an application on behalf of the Defendant for judgment entered in default, under **CPR, Part 12,** to be set aside under **CPR, r 13.3** and for transfer of the proceedings to Leeds County Court.

Evidence

2. In support of the application the Defendant will refer to the witness statement of Brian Parkes (**'WS/BP'**) dated 15th November 2012, together with the following exhibits:

Exhibit BP1: Contractual documentation with United Plastic Containers Plc

Exhibit BP2: Corres

Exhibit BP3: Defence and Counterclaim.

Background

3. The claim is for the sum of £70,500, being the price of moulding machines sold and delivered by the Claimant to the Defendant. The Defendant contends that the machines were defective.

4. Claim form/particulars of claim issued: 22.09.12

Date of Service: 03.10.12

Expiry of time for filing acknowledgement of service/defence: 17.10.12

Judgment in default entered: 07.11.12

APPLICATION TO SET ASIDE DEFAULT JUDGMENT

The court's discretion

5. The court has a discretion to set aside judgment entered in default of a defence: 'if the defendant has a real prospect of successfully defending the claim': **CPR, r 13.3(1)(a);**

   or

   'if it appears to the court that there is some other good reason why judgment should be set aside': **r 13.3(1)(b)(i);** or

   'the defendant should be allowed to defend the claim': **r 13.3(1)(b)(ii).**

6. The four machines delivered to the Defendant by the Claimant were defective in that they were the subject of frequent breakdowns. A consulting engineer has advised the Defendant that two of the machines are so badly designed that they are incapable of meeting industry standards and cannot be repaired. Consequently, the Defendant has lost a lucrative supply contract with United Plastic Containers Plc: **WS/BP, paras 2 and 3; exhibits BP1 and BP3.** It is submitted therefore that the defence has a real prospect of success.

7. It is submitted that the following are matters that the court may take into account in the exercise of its discretion and that they amount to good reasons why the judgment should be set aside or the Defendant should be allowed to defend the claim:

   (a) The Claimant's engineers had notice of the defects in the machines after delivery: **WS/BP, para 2.**

   (b) The Defendant sought the opinion of an expert in respect of the defects: **WS/BP, para 2.**

   (c) The Defendant responded promptly upon receipt of the Particulars of Claim: **WS/BP, para 3; exhibit BP2.**

Matters to which the court must have regard

8. In considering whether to set aside or vary judgment entered under **CPR, Part 12** the matters to which the court must have regard include whether the application to set aside is made promptly: **CPR, r 13.3(2):**

Judgment entered 07.11.12.

Application dated 15.11.12.

It is submitted that the Defendant has acted promptly in making this application and that in the interests of justice judgment should be set aside.

APPLICATION TO TRANSFER

9. The power to transfer from High Court to County Court: **County Courts Act 1984, s 40(2).**

Matters to which the court must have regard

10. These are set out in **CPR, r 30.3(2).**

The Defendant relies upon the following factors:

(a) the financial value of the claim;

(b) whether it would be more convenient or fair for hearings (including trial) to be held in some other court; and

(c) whether the facts, legal issues, remedies or procedures involved are simple or complex.

11. Although the value of the claim exceeds the usual jurisdiction of the county court of £50,000, the facts, legal issues, remedies and procedures involved are not complex. The machines that are the subject of the dispute between the parties are located on site at the Defendant's address in Leeds. The Defendant's expert is based in Leeds.

12. It is submitted therefore that, if the court is minded to grant the Defendant's application to set aside judgment, the case should be transferred from the Manchester District Registry to the Defendant's local court, namely Leeds County Court.

15th November 2012
4 Gray's Inn Place   BESS TOFFER

25.3.2 Commentary

This is shorter than the previous example (not surprisingly, since this is for an interim application, whereas that one was for a trial). It is much more the sort of thing that students on a Bar Professional Training Course will need to draft.

Introduction   As previously suggested, the skeleton begins by stating what the application is for. There are two applications to be made, and they need to be identified and in due course dealt with separately. Paragraph 2 draws the judge's attention to the relevant evidence to be looked at in conjunction with the skeleton argument.

Background   Paragraph 3 states the nature of the case and gives a brief chronology. The chronology is too short to be worth setting out in a separate document.

Paragraphs 5–8   Set out the argument in support of the first application. Since the order sought is a discretionary one, regulated by the CPR, Part 13, the argument must be based on the powers of the court and the circumstances in which the court may exercise its discretion in the defendant's favour. There are only two such circumstances, set out in r 13.3(1). The skeleton argument seeks to show that each of these circumstances exists. The precise sub-rule is identified in each case.

First, the skeleton argument tries to show (in paragraph 6) that the defendant has a real prospect of successfully defending the claim. This contention must, of course, be justified by the evidence, so the argument refers in outline to the relevant evidence and cites the sources of it. It concludes by stating the inference that the court will be invited to draw.

Second, the skeleton argument tries to show (in paragraph 7) that there is some other good reason why judgment should be set aside or the defendant should be allowed to defend the claim. It refers to the evidence upon which the argument will rely, picking out three specific points that the defendant contends are good reasons. It submits that in the light of these three points the 'good reasons' requirement is satisfied.

But as well as showing that the court has power to set aside judgment, the argument must also show why it should do so, and this is dealt with in paragraph 8. There are two submissions. One matter that the court must have regard to is stipulated by r 13.3(2), so the argument must address this issue. The fact that the application was made promptly can be shown simply by referring to the relevant dates, so these are stated, followed by the obvious submission. The second submission (the interests of justice) is not separately argued, but will obviously be supported by the matters set out in paragraphs 6 and 7.

Paragraphs 9–11   Set out the argument in support of the second application. The skeleton argument must, of course, begin by identifying the court's power to make the order sought (paragraph 9). Then it needs to address the criteria to which the court *must* have regard (paragraph 10). Rule 30.3(2) sets out seven such matters, of which the defendant relies on three. If an argument is to be based on rules, it is clearly essential to refer to the rules first.

The defendant then puts forward three arguments in favour of transfer, relying on the factors already stated (paragraph 11). The precise relationship between the facts and the rules will doubtless be elaborated on orally, but for the purposes of the skeleton there is enough apparent connection for the judge to understand the outline submission.

Finally, the skeleton restates the conclusion that the court is to be invited to reach (paragraph 12).

25.4 Skeleton argument in a criminal case

The following is an example of a skeleton argument that might be used in a criminal case. It forms the basis of an application to exclude evidence of pre-arrest questions and answers and of two police-station tape-recorded interviews. The defendant, Julia Smith, was charged with robbery jointly with Jason Barnes and Brian Lewis. The prosecution case was that on 30 April 2012 the three defendants met at an address and agreed that Smith would telephone a friend of hers, Rose Dean. The two females then arranged to meet at Dean's address. The three defendants then took a taxi to the address. Barnes remained in the car and the other two went to the front door. Smith rang the bell, spoke to Dean via the entryphone and when the door latch was released Lewis burst in with Smith, who then pretended to be a victim. Lewis then terrorised Dean, threatening her with a handgun and stole about £100 in cash from her. He then ran off and escaped with Barnes in the taxi, leaving both the females behind. Smith surrendered voluntarily to the police on 1 May 2012.

DC Jones gave evidence of the following:

(a) a conversation with Smith preceding her arrest on 1 May 2012 in which she denied all knowledge of Lewis and stated that she went to Dean's address by bus;

(b) an interview with Smith on 1 May 2012 in which Smith admitted knowledge of the plan to commit a robbery, that she assisted Lewis to gain entry and that she was present throughout. She stated that she knew Lewis and that she went along with the plan because she was frightened;

(c) a second interview on 3 June 2012 in which Smith still maintained she was frightened but made a number of inconsistent and incriminating remarks.

25.4.1 Skeleton argument

IN THE CROWN COURT AT WOOLWICH   Indictment No T101234

THE QUEEN

v

JULIA SMITH

DEFENDANT'S SKELETON
ARGUMENT

<u>APPLICATION TO EXCLUDE EVIDENCE UNDER S 78, POLICE AND CRIMINAL EVIDENCE ACT 1984 [BLACKSTONE F2.21]</u>

<u>Submissions</u>

1. <u>Failure to caution—Conversation preceding arrest/caution 1st May 2012</u>

Statement of DC Jones [**Statement Bundle p 65**]:
Smith: It was terrible, as I got to her flat a masked man put a gun to my head and pushed me into Rose's flat.
DC Jones: <u>Do you know this man?</u>
Smith: <u>No, I have never seen him before.</u>
DC Jones: <u>How did you get to Rose's?</u>
Smith: <u>The 35 bus.</u>

DC Jones then went on to say that he had grounds to believe that Smith was involved in the offence and arrested and cautioned her.

It is conceded that the first remark made by the defendant is an unsolicited comment. It is submitted, however, that the subsequent questions and answers (underlined) should be excluded because DC Jones failed to caution the defendant before putting the questions.

Code of Practice C:10.1 [Blackstone Appendix 1; D1.83 etc.]
<u>R v Sparks [1991] Crim LR 128 CA</u>
<u>R v Pall [1992] Crim LR 126 CA</u>
[Blackstone F2.48]

2. <u>Failure to caution after break in questioning—Interview 1st May 2012—2nd tape</u> [**Interview bundle p 44**]
DC Jones: I must remind you that you are still under caution. Do you understand?
Smith: Mm.

It is submitted that, after the break in the interview, DC Jones should have cautioned the defendant in full and should have ensured that she was aware that she remained under caution.

Code C:10.1, C:10.8 [Blackstone Appendix 1; D1.83 etc.]
3. <u>Failure to explain the caution—Interview 3rd June 2012</u>

DC Jones: [Caution given in full] Do you understand the caution?
Smith: Yes.
DC Jones: Can you give me a brief explanation of what you understand by the caution, say how it affects you.
Smith: Well, if I don't say nothing now and I need to say something when I get to court I won't be able to say it because I should have said it now.
DC Jones: Right.

It is submitted that:

(a) the defendant did not understand the caution;

(b) DC Jones did not explain it in his own words; and

(c) DC Jones allowed the defendant to continue to misunderstand the caution, thereby appearing to endorse her understanding of it.

Code C:10D [Blackstone Appendix 1; D1.83 etc.]

4. **Sufficient evidence for prosecution to succeed before interview 3rd June 2012**

>   (a) Interview 1st May 2012: defendant admitted knowledge of plan to commit robbery, that she assisted Lewis to gain entry and that she was present throughout.
>
>   (b) Statement of Rose Dean (victim) 1st May 2012: stated that it was a 'set-up' (p 3).
>
>   (c) Statement of Mel Stokes (taxi driver) 18th May 2012: stated that all three passengers were relaxed and happy (p 12); female not unhappy or afraid (p 13); she had plenty of opportunities to escape or alert him (p 13).

It is submitted that by 18th May 2012 there was sufficient evidence for this prosecution to succeed and therefore on 3rd June 2012 there should have been no further questioning of the defendant.

Code C:11.6; 16.1 [Blackstone Appendix 1; D1.89]

1st February 2013

4 Gray's Inn Place   ELIZABETH BLAKE

25.4.2 Commentary

You have now seen three different ways of laying out skeleton arguments. Do not assume that there is only one right way, or even that a barrister will always adopt the same format in every case. Choose a format that suits the structure of your argument.

As always, the skeleton argument begins by stating clearly what submission is being made.

You must identify for the judge the power under which you are inviting him to act, so there follows a reference to the paragraph in *Blackstone's Criminal Practice* where s 78 of the Police and Criminal Evidence Act 1984 is printed. You will have noticed there are numerous such references in this skeleton argument. *Blackstone* is in wide use in criminal courts, and whatever you may say the judge will want to look it up, so be helpful by giving the references. You could alternatively give references to *Archbold*.

There are then four numbered submissions, each of which, you will argue, should lead the judge to the conclusion that some part of the evidence should be excluded.

Submission 1   The headline tells the judge the nature of the submission—failure to caution. The argument must, of course, be based on the evidence, so the skeleton sets out the relevant part of the evidence (after identifying where it comes from). There is no easy way to refer to the precise words in question other than by copying them out, so it is helpful to do so. This is followed by the submission itself and the authorities that will be cited in argument. PACE Code C, para 10.1 says that 'A person whom there are grounds to suspect of an offence . . . must be cautioned before any questions about an offence . . . are put to them if either the suspect's answers or silence . . . may be given in evidence.' The cases of *R v Sparks* and *R v Pall* hold that a failure to caution should be regarded as a 'significant and substantial breach' of the Code.

Submission 2   The structure of this submission is exactly the same as that of the first. There is a headline, reference to the source of the evidence, quotation from the evidence, the submission itself and legal citation. Code C, para 10.8 contains the main point: 'After any break in questioning under caution, the person being questioned must be made aware they remain under caution. If there is any doubt the relevant caution should be given again in full when the interview resumes.' This is not perhaps your strongest point.

Submission 3   This is the first of two submissions to the effect that the whole of the interview of 3 June should be excluded. The exchange between the officer and defendant is again quoted and it is self-evident that the defendant did not correctly understand the caution, and that the officer endorsed her misunderstanding. This not surprisingly justifies the first and third submissions. The second submission is based on Code C, note 10D: 'If it appears a person does not understand the caution, the person giving it should explain it in their own words.'

Submission 4   The interview of 3 June is also challenged on the basis that the police had sufficient evidence to charge the defendant before the interview took place and so should not have proceeded with it. The argument begins by identifying the evidence available to the police after 18 May (together with its sources) and then states the conclusion to be drawn and the relevant legal sources. Code C, para 11.6 says 'The interview . . . of a person about an offence with which that person has not been charged . . . must cease when . . . (c) the officer . . . reasonably believes there is sufficient evidence to provide a realistic prospect of conviction for that offence.' By Code C, para 16.1, when similar conditions are satisfied, the defendant should be brought before the custody officer with a view to his being charged.

25.5   Exercises

25.5.1   Exercise A

You are instructed to appear on behalf of the claimant, Baildon Garages Ltd, on the claimant's application for summary judgment at Bromley County Court on 17 January 2014. The brief facts are that on 15 November 2013 the defendant, Harold Spencer, purchased a Ford Mondeo from the claimant for the sum of £8,500. Mr Spencer paid by cheque and took the car away the same day. On 19 November the garage presented the cheque for payment but it was dishonoured, payment having been countermanded by Mr Spencer. The garage commenced proceedings in respect of the cheque on 3 December 2013. In his defence (filed 17 December 2013) Mr Spencer stated that he stopped the cheque because:

(1) the following day the car broke down;

(2) he took it to a different garage and was told that:

    (a)   the repairs would cost £1,500;

    (b)   the car was unsafe to drive; and

    (c)   it appeared to have previously been involved in a collision;

(3) when he tried to return the car to Baildon Garages the salesman, Robert Miller, refused to take it back.

Mr Spencer is alleging breach of implied terms in the contract and total failure of consideration. Your instructions are that:

(1) Mr Miller has no knowledge of any previous collision or any defects in the vehicle;

(2) the car had a full service history; and

(3) before he bought the car Mr Spencer had a full AA inspection carried out.

Copies of the relevant documents are exhibited to Mr Miller's statement. You advise that Baildon Garages are entitled to summary judgment because a mere right of set-off can never constitute a defence to a claim on a dishonoured cheque: *Jackson v Murphy* (1887) 4 TLR 92; *Esso Petroleum Co Ltd v Milton* [1997] 1WLR 938. You are of the opinion that, although the defence relied upon (total failure of consideration) might, in principle, be recognised by the court, on these facts it would have no real prospect of success: CPR, r 24.2(a)(ii). You further advise that, in your opinion, there is no other reason why the case should be disposed of at trial: CPR, r 24.2(b).

Draft a skeleton argument that will form the basis of your application for summary judgment.

25.5.2 Exercise B

You represent a defendant, Joseph Palmer, who is charged with an offence under s 17(2) of the Firearms Act 1968, which provides as follows:

> *If a person, at the time of his committing or being arrested for an offence specified in Schedule 1 of this Act has in his possession a firearm or imitation firearm, he shall be guilty of an offence under this subsection unless he shows that he had it in his possession for a lawful object.*

The relevant offence in Sch 1 in this case is assaulting a constable in the execution of his duty, contrary to the Police Act 1996, s 89(1). The indictment alleges that Palmer had the firearm in his possession at the time of committing the assault.

At his trial at Maidstone Crown Court on 3 February 2014, the evidence of the police officer (PC Anderson) is as follows.

(1) He stopped Palmer because he was running from the direction of a burglary.

(2) He wanted to search him for stolen property.

(3) During the course of the search Palmer punched PC Anderson in the face.

(4) PC Anderson then arrested Palmer for assaulting a constable in the execution of his duty.

(5) Palmer tried to escape and was seen to drop an object in a dustbin.

(6) He was caught and a firearm was recovered from the dustbin.

In cross-examination PC Anderson admitted the following:

(7) Although he identified himself as PC Anderson from Croydon Police Station, he did not state the object of the search or the grounds for the search.

(8) Although he was not in uniform (because he was off duty) he did not produce his warrant card.

Having researched the law, you decide to make a submission of no case to answer at the conclusion of the prosecution case. Your researches indicate as follows:

A submission of no case should be allowed when there is no evidence upon which a reasonable jury, properly directed, could convict. The judge will stop the case if there is no evidence that the crime alleged has been committed by the defendant: *R v Galbraith* (1981) 73 Cr App R 124 (see *Blackstone* D16.65).

It was held by the Court of Appeal in *R v Nelson* [2000] 2 Cr App R 160 that it is not necessary to show that an offence in the schedule has been committed; see *Blackstone* B12.99. But it seems to you that *R v Nelson* is distinguishable.

Furthermore, you take the view that the offence under s 89(1) has not been committed. PC Anderson acted in breach of the Police and Criminal Evidence Act 1984, s 2 and PACE Code A, paras 3.8–3.9, which set out what a police officer must do before carrying out a search. You conclude that the search was unlawful and that the prosecution have therefore not proved an essential ingredient of the scheduled offence, namely that PC Anderson was acting in the execution of his duty.

You believe on the basis of this research that you can construct an argument to the effect that the prosecution have failed to establish the offence under s 17(2).

Draft a skeleton argument that will form the basis of your submission.

Default judgments

26.1 Setting aside default judgments—an introduction

A common type of interim application is that made to set aside a judgment that has been entered in default. A default judgment is simply a judgment obtained by one party as an administrative act (ie by presenting the necessary forms to the court staff, ordinarily with no consideration of the application by a judge, Master, or district judge) because the other party has not taken some step required by the rules. In ordinary Part 7 claims most default judgments are obtained by a claimant because a defendant has not filed an acknowledgment of service or defence. However, default judgments are also regularly obtained on a CPR, r 20 counterclaim, because a claimant has not filed a defence to that counterclaim.

There is no requirement on the party entitled to enter the default judgment to do so quickly. The only time limit to bear in mind is CPR, r 15.11. If a default judgment has not been entered, it used to be thought that all the party in default had to do was take the necessary step late, and judgment could not be entered. However, in *Coll v Tattum* (2001) The Times, 3 December 2001, [2001] All ER (D) 320 (Nov) the court had to consider whether an extension of time was required for the party in default to file the document late. The court concluded that an extension of time was required, so a defaulting party could not simply file the document late as of right. The court observed that in most cases the extension would be granted, but it was a matter for the discretion of the court applying the overriding objective.

The label 'default judgment' is sometimes applied to a judgment obtained as a result of breach of a peremptory order of the court. A peremptory order is a specific order addressed to one or more parties specifying that in default of taking a certain step in the action within a specified time, judgment may be entered against that party. Peremptory orders are commonly referred to as 'unless' orders. Applications to set aside a judgment in default of an 'unless' order are considered separately at **26.6**.

The test for setting aside a true default judgment is to be found in CPR, r 13. The test for setting aside judgment entered for breach of a final or 'unless' order is to be found in CPR, r 3.9. Although the tests are not the same, the key factor in setting aside a default judgment is whether there is a defence to the claim. A default judgment entered in proceedings that a defendant actually knows nothing about (eg because he has never seen the proceedings that are merely deemed served under CPR) will not be set aside if there is no defence: *Akram v Adam* [2004] EWCA Civ 1601. Similarly, where there is a clear failure to comply with an 'unless' order, relief from sanctions has historically depended upon there being a defence: *CPL Industrial Services Holdings Ltd v R & L Freeman & Sons* [2005] EWCA Civ 539. Although, the new CPR, r 3.9 regarding relief from sanctions now robustly sets out that the court will consider **all the circumstances of the case**, so as to enable it to deal justly with the application, including the need (1) for litigation to be conducted efficiently and at proportionate cost; and (2) to enforce compliance with rules, practice directions and orders, the old CPR, r 3.9 criteria are still potentially relevant in an application for relief from sanction: *Michael and another v Middleton and another* [2013] All ER (D) 124 (Oct).

The effect of a decision on an application to set aside a default judgment was clarified by the Court of Appeal in *Mullen v Conoco Ltd* [1997] 3 WLR 1032, which held that a decision on an application to set aside a default judgment would give rise to a final determination (subject to any appeal) on whether a judgment was regular or not, but it would not be a final decision on any discretionary element. A discretionary refusal to set aside a default judgment because the proposed defence of set-off of a counterclaim was thought too weak did not give rise to a plea of *res judicata* or issue estoppel. A fresh action based on the proposed counterclaim was not an abuse of the process of the court and could not be struck out on that ground. This decision is one that ought to be followed despite the introduction of the Civil Procedure Rules.

26.2 Civil Procedure Rules

The distinction between irregular and regular judgments is maintained by the CPR. Irregular judgments are known as wrongly entered judgments. Wrongly entered judgments are those falling within CPR, r 13.2, and the court *must* set them aside. In all other cases the court has discretion whether to set aside or vary the default judgment (CPR, r 13.3(1)). The defence must have a prospect of success that is better than merely arguable (International Finance *Corporation v Utexafrica Sprl* [2001] CLC 1361). Delay remains relevant to the exercise of the discretion (CPR, r 13.3(2)). The court can still attach conditions to an order setting aside a default judgment (CPR, r 3.1(3)) and also order a party to pay a sum of money into court under CPR, r 3.1(5).

26.3 Making the application

You should familiarise yourself with the requirements of CPR, Part 23 for all interim applications, for evidence and for selecting the court in which the application should be made. These are set out in your ***Civil Litigation*** manual.

If the judgment was for a specified sum of money then the application to set aside will be transferred to the defendant's home court, unless the case was commenced in a specialist list: CPR, r 13.4.

26.4 Documents required to set aside a default judgment

The documents required to set aside a default judgment are:

(a) an application notice (commonly an N244 or for Commercial Court claims an N244CC, complying with CPR, Part 23), which should as a matter of good practice state the irregularity where it is alleged that the judgment was wrongly entered;

(b) evidence in support of the application (ordinarily in the form of a witness statement), unless the application to set aside is only based on the judgment being wrongly entered;

(c) it is good practice (although not strictly necessary) to attach a draft order and draft defence to the application notice.

26.5 The hearing of the application

At the hearing of the application it is for the party applying to set aside judgment to open the application. In the Queen's Bench Division the Master will probably not have seen any of the papers in advance of the hearing, so the party applying must hand in to the Master the original application notice and evidence in support and take the Master through the evidence in support. The party opposing the application should then take the Master through any evidence in answer. If the party applying has further evidence, the Master should be taken through that additional evidence. When the evidence stage is completed it is for the party applying to make submissions (if required to do so), then for the party opposing to make submissions (if required to do so) and finally for the party applying to respond (if required to do so).

In the Chancery Division and in the county court there will be a court file, which should contain the application notice and the evidence (provided it has been filed by the parties). Where there is a court file, it is appropriate to ask the Master or district judge whether he or she has had an opportunity of reading any of the papers, before the parties go through the stages set out in the preceding paragraph.

It is sometimes convenient to deal with any question of wrongly entered judgment before considering any alternative application to set aside as a matter of discretion. This is particularly useful where the argument that the judgment is wrongly entered is strong. If the hearing is divided in this way it may save court time as, if the judgment is set aside as being wrongly entered, it is not normally necessary to consider the merits at all. If the judgment is set aside, the party applying should seek its costs and directions. If the judgment is not set aside as being wrongly entered, the Master will have to dismiss that application and go on to consider any alternative application on the merits.

A chronology is often required to show the court the sequence of events and any period of delay in making the application to set aside the default judgment. The only delay that is relevant is delay after issue of proceedings (*Thorn plc v MacDonald* [1999] CPLR 660). Note the words of Moore-Bick LJ in *Standard Bank plc v Agrinvest International Inc* [2010] EWCA Civ 1400 that state, 'promptness now carries much greater weight than before [the CPR].' Usually some evidence explaining the delay is required but, if the period of delay is short, the absence of an explanation is not now fatal to the exercise of the discretion to set aside. At the end of the submissions the Master or district judge should give a reasoned judgment. After judgment, if the application to set aside is dismissed, the only issues are likely to be the costs (which should follow the event), and any application by the party applying for a stay of execution pending any appeal. Permission to appeal will also be required. It is often a good idea to check with those instructing you whether they wish for you to seek permission to appeal in the event of your application not succeeding.

If the application is successful and the judgment is set aside, there may be discussion about the directions to be given (eg when the defence is to be filed by and other directions); about the conditions (eg how long should be given for any money to be brought into court as a condition of the judgment being set aside); and costs. If the judgment was irregular, the party applying should be awarded his or her costs unless there is an exceptional feature such as substantial delay. If the judgment was regular, the party applying will normally have to pay all the costs of the entry of judgment, or any execution, and of the application and will usually be ordered to pay those summarily assessed costs forthwith rather than in any event.

Where there is a discretion to set aside the default judgment, the most common condition imposed (apart from requiring the costs thrown away to be paid by the party in default) is that some or all of the money claimed has to be paid into court as a condition of permission to defend the claim. The order will then provide that the judgment is only set aside if that condition is fulfilled within a specified time.

If the court decides that the default judgment ought to be set aside, it should not impose a condition that cannot be complied with: see *Yorke Motors v Edwards* [1982] 1 WLR 444 and, post-CPR, *Training in Compliance plc v Dewse* [2001] CP Rep. 46, CA. The test is one of impossibility and not mere difficulty raising the money. The party applying for the default judgment to be set aside faces a choice: should evidence be filed that establishes that it could not pay any of the money into court or not? Without clear evidence of impecuniosity (and the burden is on the party alleging this), there must be a risk that the court could impose a condition that cannot be complied with. If evidence of impecuniosity is filed, it can create the impression that the application is merely a delaying tactic in relation to a judgment that cannot be paid. In most cases, the court will not adjourn the hearing of the application to allow further evidence to be filed on this point.

26.6 'Unless' orders

Under CPR r 3.1(3) the court is empowered to make an order subject to a condition, with a sanction that will automatically trigger on a party's failure to comply with the condition. Such an 'unless' order should be absolutely clear in describing the action required to be taken by the party, the date and time by which it is to be taken and the sanction to be imposed if that order is not complied with. The sanction should be proportionate to the potential default and can consist of striking out part or all of the claim or defence (CPR, r 3.5, PD 40B, para 8.2). It is even possible for parties to agree to an 'unless' order in the form of a consent order, although see *Chiu v Waitrose Ltd* [2011] EWHC 1356 (TCC), where the court did not enforce an 'unless' order to which the parties had consented, following consideration of all the circumstances.

Although an 'unless' order is not the same as a default judgment, there is some similarity regarding procedural advocacy matters in making applications to either set aside default judgment or obtain relief from sanctions following the breach of an 'unless' order. It is therefore briefly addressed here, although a detailed consideration of the interpretation of the new CPR, r 3.9 falls beyond the remit of this manual.

26.6.1 Challenging the 'unless' order

Once the 'unless' order has been made it should be treated in the same way as any other interim direction of the court: it should be complied with or promptly challenged by way of application to vary or appeal. It is unlikely that the courts will, save in exceptional cases, allow a party to ignore an 'unless' order or escape the sanction merely because the order is not in proper form. However, an unrealistic or impossible requirement may be subject to challenge. The order should either be appealed or challenged by way of prompt application to the court which imposed the order to revoke or vary it under CPR, r 3.1(7). A requirement for money to be paid into court under an 'unless' order that can plainly not be complied with on the evidence of the applicant is not a mere administrative decision but 'a final decision which may be of considerable consequence to a defendant' (per Longmore LJ in *Rajval Construction Ltd v Bestville Properties Ltd* [2010] EWCA Civ 1621, 17) and should therefore be challenged. It is important to note that in any event, the parties cannot agree to extension of time (CPR, r 3.8(3)) and as such an application would still need to be made to the court, even if parties were both disposed to agreeing an extension of time.

26.6.2 Non-compliance with the order

Subject to the right to seek an extension of time for compliance (either before or after the deadline), the sanction set out in the order will take effect if the party fails to comply with it (CPR, r 3.8).

26.6.3 Disputed non-compliance

Where an 'unless' order has been made and the time for compliance has expired, it will usually be obvious whether there has been compliance or not. If, for example, an order is made that unless the claimant file a list of documents by 4.00 pm on 1 March the claim be struck out—either a list will have been filed by that date or it will not. If a list is filed then, on the face of it, the order is complied with. If the list is not filed then the claim is struck out without any further order being made.

However, there can be cases of purported compliance—for example, filing a list of documents that contains only the pleadings and party correspondence and no other documents. In that situation, the case has not been automatically struck out, because there is a list. The court would have to determine whether there was sufficient compliance or not, or whether to make any further order or to impose any other sanction. Application should then be made under CPR, Part 23, or on notice at the next case management conference for this issue to be determined.

26.6.4 Relief from sanctions

CPR, r 3.9 governs the courts' discretionary powers to grant relief from sanctions, including relief from sanctions set out in an 'unless' order. An application will be made in a similar way to an application for setting aside a default judgment, using an application notice N244, supported by evidence. This evidence can either be contained within the application notice itself or by way of a separate witness statement. The revised CPR, r 3.9(1), as set out at **26.1**, is applicable to all applications seeking relief from sanctions issued on or after 1 April 2013. It indicates a move to a 'tougher, more robust approach to rule compliance and relief from sanctions ... intended to ensure that justice can be done in the majority of cases': *Mitchell v News Group Newspapers Limited* [2013] EWCA Civ 1537, para 39.

Because of this more rigorous approach that is now taken to relief from sanctions, counsel acting in such applications must ensure that their preparation and legal argument is well thought through and that the evidential application is precise. In *Mitchell* the Court of Appeal stated that an application for relief from sanctions presupposes that the sanction has been properly imposed and that therefore an applicant should not make the argument on the basis that the order should not have been made in the first place. An application for variation or revocation of the order is different to relief from sanction, although both applications **can** be made at the same hearing, as set out in *Mitchell*, para 45.

In arguing a case for relief from sanctions, counsel should ensure that their argument is conversant with the new overriding objective and that due regard is given to (i) proportionate cost and (ii) the move towards enforcing compliance. The authority of *Durrant v Avon & Somerset Constabulary* [2013] EWCA Civ 1624 makes it clear that the court 'must approach the exercise with the focus or degree of toughness called for by the guidance in Mitchell'. It is probable that once this new, more rigorous approach filters through the litigation process over the coming years, counsel will find that there are fewer instructions given to attend hearings for relief from sanctions. The greater importance for counsel will be to ensure that advice is given at the relevant early stage to ensure timely compliance with the order in the first place. Should an application be made though, counsel attending a hearing of this type should ensure (as always) that the application is made promptly, that the latest authorities dealing with the procedure and interpretation of CPR, r 3.9 are consulted, and that a concise skeleton argument is drafted and used as appropriate. An application will no doubt be hard fought. The authority of *Adlington & 133 others v Els International Lawyers LLP (in administration)* [2013] EWHC B29 (QB) will be of assistance, particularly the words of HHJ Oliver-Jones QC at para 34 which state that, 'the circumstances do not have to be exceptional to attract the granting of relief, but a decision as to whether or not relief should be granted does involve the "change of balance" implicit in the new wording of CPR 3.9 . . . bearing in mind that the relationship between justice and procedure has not changed so as to transform rules and rule compliance into trip wires, and "nor has it changed it by turning the rules and rule compliance into the mistress rather than the handmaid of justice"'.

26.7   Checklist for default judgment

What you should have:

- copy of relevant practitioner work (here, *Blackstone's Civil Practice*, the *Green Book*, or the *White Book*);
- relevant paperwork (here, application notice compliant with CPR, Part 23 and supporting evidence or evidence to counter the application, a draft order and draft defence);
- possibly a chronology along with a very succinct skeleton argument, to show the court the sequence of events, including the time between the default judgment and the initiation of this application to set aside;
- a schedule of costs for the application.

Your court will be:

- a Queen's Bench Division Master (addressed as 'Master'); or
- a district judge in a High Court District Registry or the county court (addressed as 'Sir' or 'Madam').

Before the application:

- Tell the court staff that you are present and who you represent.
- Identify your opponent and introduce yourself to him or her.
- If it is your application, make sure that you know your opponent's name so that you can introduce him or her to the court.

What should happen in the application:

- If it is your application, you start.
- Introductions—for example, 'Master, I am Miss Jones and this is my application to set aside. Mr Smith appears for the Respondent/Greenways Ltd.'
- Hand in the application notice and evidence in support.*

* If the application is made in the county court or in the Chancery Division, the application notice and the evidence should all be contained in a court file. If so, ask the judge if he or she has had the chance to read any of this paperwork before embarking on your exposition of the evidence as it may be unnecessary or you may be able to abbreviate it.

- Take the judge through your evidence.
- Sit down/stop so that your opponent can take the judge through their evidence.
- After the evidence has been presented to the judge, you may make submissions in support of the application (if required), either:
  o set aside because judgment wrongly entered; or
  o set aside by exercise of discretion ('on the merits').
- Answer any questions the judge asks. Indicate clearly when you have finished, usually by saying something like 'That is my application, Sir' or 'Those are my submissions, Master'. Your opponent may then be called upon to put their arguments.
- If you feel that a response to your opponent's arguments is needed, you may ask for permission to address the judge once more, saying something like 'If I might reply briefly on the issue of . . .'.
- The judge will give a reasoned judgment. Ensure you take as careful a note of this as possible.
- If the application succeeds, the applicant's advocate should ask for an order that the respondent pay the costs of the application and seek further directions (these may need to be discussed by the judge and both advocates).
- If the application fails, the respondent's advocate will ask for their costs. The applicant's advocate may ask for a stay of execution pending an appeal.
- Regardless of which party you are appearing for, endeavour to prepare at least one or two succinct submissions for costs that are specific to your case and fall outside the generic discretion of the court. Given that many judges are reticent to grant costs orders in interim applications such as this, you will ordinarily need a more compelling reason to persuade a judge to award costs at the hearing rather than simply reserving them to be decided in the substantive case. To this end, also ensure that you have a discrete schedule of costs for the hearing in order to make it easy for the judge to summarily assess the costs for the order.

Summary judgments

27.1 Introduction

The Civil Procedure Rules 1998 (CPR), Part 24, sets out a procedure whereby the court may decide a claim or a particular issue without a trial. The purpose is to deal summarily with issues that do not need full investigation or trial. Applications can be made by a claimant or by a defendant or of the court's own motion.

27.2 Before attending court

Check that the procedural requirements have been complied with, for example:

(a) When acting for a claimant ensure that the claimant has complied with any relevant pre-action protocol and usually that the defendant has filed an acknowledgement of service or a defence (CPR, r 24.4(1)(b)); in cases against the Crown a claimant cannot apply for summary judgment until after expiry of the period for filing a defence (CPR, r 24.4(1A)).

(b) When acting for a claimant ensure the claim is one to which summary judgment is available, ie not proceedings for possession of residential premises against a tenant, a mortgagor, or person holding over after the end of his tenancy, nor proceedings for an admiralty claim *in rem*; (see CPR, r 24.3(2)). Small claims *are* open to summary judgment.

(c) Has the respondent been given at least 14 days' notice of the date fixed for hearing and of the issues that it is proposed that the court will decide at the hearing?

(d) The contents of the application notice:

(i) the application notice must include a statement that it is an application for summary judgment made under CPR, Part 24;

(ii) it must state what order the applicant is seeking and why the applicant is seeking the order;

(iii) it must identify the written evidence on which the applicant relies unless no evidence is relied on or the application notice itself contains all the evidence relied on;

(iv) it must draw the respondent's attention to the time limit for filing and serving its own written evidence (at least seven days before the summary judgment hearing).

(e) Written evidence:

(i) an applicant may rely on written evidence set out in his claim form, statement of case, application notice, or in a witness statement. Each item of written evidence relied on must contain a statement of truth. Affidavit evidence is also permissible but is subject to cost implications;

(ii) the applicant's written evidence must be served at the same time as the application notice;

(iii) the respondent must file and serve his written evidence at least seven days before the summary judgment hearing;

(iv) if the applicant wishes to rely on written evidence in reply, this must be filed and served at least three days before the summary judgment hearing;

(v) the application notice or the supporting evidence must identify concisely any point of law or provision in a document on which the applicant relies and/or state that it is made because the applicant believes that on the evidence the respondent has no real prospect of succeeding on the claim or issue or of successfully defending the claim or issue to which the application relates, and in either case state that the applicant knows of no other reason why the disposal of the claim or issue should await trial.

(f) Check that any directions given by the Master or district judge in relation to the hearing have been complied with. The time limits for filing evidence are varied if the summary judgment application is fixed by the court's own motion (see CPR, r 24.5(3)).

Note: if a procedural requirement has not been complied with, consider whether the defect could be cured, for example, by an application to the court under CPR, r 3.10 for an order to remedy the error.

Familiarise yourself with the contents of the statements of case and the written evidence in support, so that you are able to refer the court to specific passages and points quickly and smoothly, even though this may not follow the set order you planned for your submissions. It is unlikely that the court will allow you to develop all your submissions without interruption—the court will strive to get to the heart of the issues as quickly as possible.

Take with you spare copies of the statement of case, the application notice and the written evidence. Although these should have all been filed, occasionally documents go missing from court files.

27.3 At court

The hearing will be either before a Master in the High Court at the Royal Courts of Justice or before a district judge, if in a High Court District Registry or in the county court. However, the Master or district judge may direct that a summary judgment hearing should take place before a High Court or a county court judge (see CPR PD 24.3). The hearings are likely to be in public (even though it is most unlikely that any members of the public will be present) but no robes are required.

27.3.1 Before a Master

Fill in a case slip outside court to enable the Master to have a note of the advocates' names. Don't forget to introduce yourself and your opponent to the court notwithstanding having completed a slip. Address the Master simply as 'Master'.

If you have a short appointment you are likely to have to address the Master from a standing position. Stand close to the Master's desk and use the shelf or ledge for your papers. Longer appointments are taken with the advocates sitting. As a rule of thumb, if there are no chairs in position facing the Master's desk, be prepared to make your submissions standing. The Master will indicate that you can bring chairs forward from the back of the room if she or he is minded to permit counsel to be seated.

27.3.2 Before a district judge

A member of the court staff is likely to be on hand to take your name and/or to ask you to fill out an advocate's name slip. Address the district judge as 'Sir' or 'Madam' as appropriate. The advocates will make their submissions seated however long or short the application is.

27.3.3 The hearing

Unless or until the court invites argument on a specific point or issues, the claimant's counsel should be prepared to give a brief outline of the application by referring to the particulars of claim and the terms of the application notice. She or he should ask whether the Master or district judge has had the opportunity to read the written evidence and if not whether the court would like them read now. Usually a Master or district judge will prefer to read such material themselves but it is courteous to enquire whether they wish to do this or to have the written evidence read aloud. If the written evidence is to be read aloud, the respondent's counsel should read the respondent's written evidence. Once the written evidence has been read the claimant's counsel will make his or her submission. In reply the respondent's counsel will make his or her submissions and the claimant's counsel will usually be given an opportunity to make further submissions after that. Do not be surprised if the court selects only certain points from your submissions or if the Master or district judge departs from the usual order of submissions. Do not be afraid to emphasise or reiterate what you consider to be your best point (or points) if the court seems to have ignored it or misunderstood it. When preparing your submissions or indeed making them remember how difficult it will be for a Master or district judge to pick up the issues in all the cases listed before him or her each day if advocates are over-elaborate or verbose. Clear, succinct submissions will be welcomed.

27.3.4 The court's approach

Where a claimant applies for judgment on his claim the court may give that judgment if:

(a) the defendant has no real prospect of successfully defending the claim or issue; and

(b) there is no other compelling reason why the claim should be dealt with at trial.

Where a defendant applies for judgment in his or her favour on the claimant's claim, the court will give the judgment if it considers that:

(a) the claimant has no real prospect of succeeding on the claim or issue; and

(b) there is no other compelling reason why the claim should be dealt with at trial.

Where it appears to the court possible that a claim or defence may succeed but improbable that it will do so, the court may make a conditional order.

27.3.5 The order

The court will give judgment orally, setting out reasons for the order and declaring the terms of the order. Make a verbatim note of both aspects. The court may order:

(a) judgment on the claim or on any issue therein;

(b) the striking out or dismissal of the claim or of an issue therein;

(c) the dismissal of the application;

(d) a conditional order that requires a party to pay a sum of money into court or to take a specified step in relation to his or her claim or defence and provides that the party's claim will be dismissed or his or her statement of case struck out if he or she does not comply;

(e) an order relating to costs.

After judgment is given the question of costs has to be decided. Costs are very important. Be prepared to make submissions on the appropriate order as to what the costs should be and why. See further **34.8.6** on costs.

The court is empowered to give further directions about the management of the case when it determines a summary judgment application (CPR, r 24.6; PD 24, para 10). Be prepared.

27.4 Appeals

In order to appeal a summary judgment order it is necessary to obtain permission to appeal either from the court that made the order or the court to which the appeal is to be made. You need either to apply at the summary judgment hearing or make an application for permission in an appeal notice within 21 days from the initial hearing.

The appeal notice must be filed at the appeal court within such period as directed by the lower court or, in the absence of a direction, within 21 days of the date of the decision to be appealed. Copies have to be served on the respondents to the appeal not later than seven days after the appeal notice is filed. If you do wish to appeal, consider whether you need a stay pending appeal.

Note that permission is granted only where:

(a) the court considers that the appeal would have a real prospect of success; or

(b) there is some other compelling reason why the appeal should be heard.

See generally CPR, Part 52.

27.5 Checklist for the hearing

Materials essential or useful at the hearing:

- your brief;
- counsel's notebook containing a skeleton or plan of your intended submissions;
- at least three pens;
- spare copies of the application notice, the written evidence in support such as witness statements, and the statements of case (in case papers have gone missing from the court file);

- copy of relevant practitioner work (*Blackstone's Civil Practice,* the *Green Book,* or the *White Book* would be sensible but, whatever you take, it must contain a full copy of the Civil Procedure Rules in case you have to argue about associated matters such as the appropriate track, directions or costs);
- three copies of any authorities you seek to rely on;
- a fully charged mobile phone with a reasonable amount of credit and a note of the telephone number of your instructing solicitors (in case they send no representative and you need to seek instructions or impart information quickly);
- reading glasses, if you use them;
- a working calculator.

Additional materials essential or useful in order to attend the hearing:

- an adequate amount of cash and/or debit card and/or credit card for transport costs and emergencies;
- a note of the telephone number of the court (in case you are delayed and need to inform the court or chambers);
- a train timetable if you are travelling by train;
- a map extract indicating the precise location of the court you are seeking to attend if you are unfamiliar with the area.

Your court will be:

- a High Court Master (addressed as 'Master'); or
- a district judge in a High Court District Registry or the county court (addressed as 'Sir' or 'Madam');
- if an injunction is being sought, the application will usually go before a High Court or county court judge (addressed as 'My Lord/Your Lordship' or 'Your Honour' respectively); robes are not required.

Before the application:

- Tell the court staff that you are present and who you represent (this may mean that the usher writes your name on their list and/or that you fill in your details on a slip of paper and hand that back).
- Identify your opponent and introduce yourself to him or her.
- If it is your application, make sure that you know your opponent's name so that you can introduce him or her to the court.

What should happen in the application:

- If it is your application, you start.
- Introductions—for example, 'Madam, I am Miss Jones and this is my application for summary judgment. Mr Smith appears for the Respondent/Greenways Ltd.'
- Hand in the application notice, the statement of case and any evidence in support.
- Briefly outline the application, referring to your statement of case and the application notice.
- Ask whether the judge has already read the written evidence—'Have you had the chance to read the evidence in support, Madam?', for example. If the answer is 'No', offer to take the judge through your evidence.

- The judge will often say that she would prefer to read it while you continue with the application; alternatively, she may say that you can take her though it, which you will then do by reading it aloud.

- Sit down/stop so that your opponent can take the judge through their evidence.

- After the evidence has been presented to the judge, you may make submissions* in support of the application:
  - that the claimant/defendant has no real prospect of successfully pursuing/defending the claim or issue; and
  - there is no other compelling reason why the claim should be dealt with at trial.

* The judge may indicate that she wants to hear you address only a specific point or points, in which case that is what you will do.

- Answer any questions the judge asks. Indicate clearly when you have finished, usually by saying something like 'That is my application, Madam' or 'Those are my submissions, Master'. Your opponent may then be called upon to put their arguments.

- If you feel that a response to your opponent's arguments is needed, you may ask for permission to address the judge once more, saying something like 'If I might reply briefly on the issue of . . .'.

- The judge will give a reasoned judgment (which you should make a note of, both as to the order itself and the reasons).

- If the application succeeds on the whole claim, the applicant's advocate should ask for an order that the respondent pay the costs of the matter.

- If the application succeeds on an issue, the applicant's advocate should ask for an order that the respondent pay the costs of the application and seek further directions (these may need to be discussed by the judge and both advocates).

- If the application fails, the respondent's advocate should ask for an order that the applicant pay the respondent's costs for the application.

- If summary judgment is ordered, the respondent's advocate may ask for permission to appeal there and then (or it can be sought from the court to which the appeal will be made, within 21 days).

28

Interim payments

28.1 Introduction

An order for interim payment is one of a number of interim remedies that a court may grant; CPR, r 25(1)(k). In the course of litigation it may be apparent that one party will receive an award of a sum of money from his or her opponent at the conclusion of the trial, but that the amount is hotly disputed. The courts have established an interim payment remedy to prevent a party from being kept out of the entirety of his or her money for too long. Thus an interim payment application seeks a payment on account of any damages, debt or other sum (excluding costs) that the respondent may be held liable to pay to or for the benefit of the applicant.

An order for interim payment can be obtained in all proceedings where the claim includes a claim for some form of money save for cases proceeding on the small claims track (CPR, r 27.2(1)(a)). However most interim payment applications will be made in multi-track cases as the timetable for fast track proceedings does not usually provide significant scope for acceleration of payment.

28.2 Procedural requirements

(a) An application must be made by filing and serving an application notice at any time after the time limit to acknowledge service has expired.

(b) A copy of the application notice must be served at least 14 days before the hearing of the application and must be supported by evidence; CPR, r 25.6(3). The evidence should usually be by witness statement; CPR, r 32.6(1).

(c) The written evidence must deal with the following:

    (i)   the sum of money sought by way of interim payment;

    (ii) the items or matters in respect of which the interim payment is sought;

    (iii) the sum of money for which final judgment is likely to be given;

    (iv) the reasons for believing that the conditions set out in CPR, r 25.7 have been satisfied;

    (v) any other relevant matters. This includes what the money will be used for. Although normally the court is not concerned with this aspect there are occasions when the urgency of the requirement or the amount that should be awarded would be assisted by such particulars;

    (vi) the exhibit of any documentary evidence relied on in support of the application, including in personal injuries claims the medical reports.

(d) In a Fatal Accidents Act 1976 claim the written evidence must give details of the persons on whose behalf the claim is made and the nature of the claim.

28.3   The basis of the application

28.3.1   Liability

The court may make an order for interim payment only if:

(a) the defendant against whom the order is sought has admitted liability to pay damages or some other sum of money to the claimant; or

(b) the claimant has obtained judgment against that defendant for damages to be assessed or for a sum of money (other than costs) to be assessed; or

(c) the court is satisfied that if the claim went to trial the claimant would obtain judgment against the defendant from whom the interim payment is sought for a substantial amount of money (other than costs) whether or not that defendant is the only defendant or one of a number of defendants to the claim; or

(d) in a claim for possession of land, the court is satisfied that if the case went to trial the defendant would be held liable (even if the claim for possession fails) to pay the claimant a sum of money for the defendant's occupation and use of the land while the claim for possession was pending; or

(e) in a claim in which there are two or more defendants and the order is sought against any one or more of those defendants, the following conditions are satisfied:

    (i) the court is satisfied that, if the claim went to trial, the claimant would obtain judgment for a substantial amount of money (other than costs) against at least one of the defendants (but the court cannot determine which); and

    (ii) all the defendants are either—

        (a) a defendant that is insured in respect of the claim;

        (b) a defendant whose liability will be met by an insurer under the Road Traffic Act 1988, s 151, or an insurer acting under the Motor Insurers Bureau Agreement, or the Motor Insurers Bureau where it is acting itself; or

        (c) a defendant that is a public body.

28.3.2   Quantum

Once satisfied regarding liability, the court has a discretion whether to make an interim payment and if so of what amount:

- CPR, r 25.1(1)(k): 'The court may grant an order for an interim payment . . .'
- CPR, r 25.7(4): 'The court must not order an interim payment of more than a reasonable proportion of the likely amount of the final judgment.'
- CPR, r 25.7(5): 'The court must take into account (a) contributory negligence; and (b) any relevant set-off or counterclaim.'

28.4 The hearing

In the High Court the appointment will be before a Master but in public (unless directed otherwise). Address the Master simply as 'Master'. No robes will be required in whatever court the application is proceeding.

Outside London if the action is proceeding in the High Court the interim payment application will be directed to a district judge sitting in the District Registry of the High Court. The hearing will prima facie be in public. A district judge will be addressed as 'Sir' or 'Madam'.

In the county court the application will be made to a district judge sitting in public (unless directed otherwise) who should be referred to as 'Sir' or 'Madam' as appropriate. It is possible for the hearing of an interim payment application to be conducted by telephone but the principles that apply are the same.

Your basic tools in an interim payment application will be the statement of case and the witness statements or other written evidence in support. Any evidence that is not included in the filed and served written evidence will be inadmissible and will require an adjournment, if you can get it, so that a supplemental statement can be provided.

The first step, if it is your application, is to introduce yourself and your opponent to the court. Then introduce the case by declaring what the application is for and briefly mentioning the claim in the main action and how it arises. The next step is to place the evidence before the court. Enquire whether the Master or district judge has had an opportunity to read the written evidence. The likelihood is that he or she will have read such material in advance. If not, direct him or her to the passages that he or she should read. Usually the Master or district judge will find it easier to read to himself or herself, but if in doubt, ask.

Prepare your submissions by dealing with liability first. In some cases this will require only a sentence or two if interim judgment has already been obtained or there is a clear admission in the statement of case. However, in other cases, liability will be a much greater problem. The standard of proof required is to the civil standard, but compare 'would succeed' with 'would be likely to succeed' (*British & Commonwealth Holdings plc v Quadrex Holdings Inc* [1989] QB 842; *Andrews v Schooling* [1991] 3 All ER 723). It is often useful when dealing with quantum to outline the overall size of the claimant's claim and then to deal with any heads of damage where the claimant is either bound to succeed or where the possibility of failure is remote. In personal injury actions the court may be assisted by a valuation of the damages for pain, suffering and loss of amenities. Take the *Judicial Studies Board Guidelines* (11th edn, OUP, 2012) or *Kemp & Kemp on Quantum of Damages etc* to court plus photocopies of what is relevant.

It is a requirement that the written evidence sets out the amount you are asking for. You will need to justify the sum as a fraction or percentage of the overall claim. The courts are sometimes wary of giving an interim payment when no specific need for the money has been dealt with in the written evidence or when the interim payment may be a payment on account of general damages in a personal injury action.

There was clear authority that there was nothing under the old Rules requiring the claimant to show a specific need (*Stringman v McArdle* [1994] 1 WLR 1653). You may need to be prepared to argue this, not so much as a requirement, but as an aspect that the court can take into account when considering its discretion. Also bear in mind that, with the expected improved speed of getting cases to trial, you may have to argue why the claimant should be awarded some money now rather than have matters disposed of in one go at trial.

It is easier if you can justify your interim payment against special damages, but there is no reason why a payment in respect of general damages cannot be obtained. Remember, the court is primarily concerned to see that there is no risk of overpayment at the interim stage, since return of the money if the claimant has spent it can often be problematic.

28.4.1   The interim payment order

The court will give judgment orally setting out reasons for the order and declaring the terms of the order. Make a verbatim note of both aspects.

In a personal injury case where there are repayments to be made to the Compensation Recovery Unit, the order should set out the amount of the relevant deduction. Payment of the net amount only will be made to the claimant.

As the fact of an interim payment should be kept from the trial judge if another application is made at the same time that results in an order, there should be two separate orders drawn up, not one. Don't forget that you will have to deal with costs at the end of the application.

28.5   Appeals

In order to appeal an interim payment order it is necessary to obtain permission to appeal from the court that made the order or the court to which the appeal is to be made. You need either to apply at the interim payment hearing or make an application for permission in an appeal notice within 21 days from the initial hearing.

The appeal notice must be filed at the appeal court within such period as directed by the lower court or, in the absence of a direction, within 21 days of the date of the decision to be appealed. Copies have to be served on the respondents to the appeal not later than seven days after the appeal notice is filed. If you do wish to appeal, consider whether you need a stay pending appeal.

Note that permission is granted only where:

(a) the court considers that the appeal would have a real prospect of success; or

(b) there is some other compelling reason why the appeal should be heard.

See generally CPR, Part 52.

It is therefore usually easier to obtain the order you seek on the first hearing than it is to correct it on appeal.

28.6   Checklist for the hearing

Materials essential or useful at the hearing:

- your brief;
- counsel's notebook containing a skeleton or plan of your intended submissions;
- at least three pens;
- spare copies of the application notice, the written evidence in support such as witness statements, and the statements of case (in case papers have gone missing from the court file);

- copy of relevant practitioner work (*Blackstone's Civil Practice,* the *Green Book,* or the *White Book* would be sensible but, whatever you take, it must contain a full copy of the Civil Procedure Rules in case you have to argue about associated matters such as directions or costs);

- three copies of any authorities you seek to rely on, such as from *Kemp & Kemp* or the Judicial Studies Board Guidelines on quantum (currently in their 11th edition, see *Guidelines for the Assessment for General Damages in Personal Injuries* (OUP, 2012));

- a fully charged mobile phone with a reasonable amount of credit and a note of the telephone number of your instructing solicitors (in case they send no representative and you need to seek instructions or impart information quickly);

- reading glasses, if you use them;

- a working calculator.

Additional materials essential or useful in order to attend the hearing:

- an adequate amount of cash and/or debit card and/or credit card for transport costs and emergencies;

- a note of the telephone number of the court (in case you are delayed and need to inform the court or chambers);

- a train timetable if you are travelling by train;

- a map extract indicating the precise location of the court you are seeking to attend if you are unfamiliar with the area.

Applying for an injunction

29.1 Introduction

This chapter considers the *procedure* at the hearing of an application for an interim injunction in civil proceedings (other than family proceedings). For the substantive legal principles regarding the granting of an interim injunction, students should consult a relevant practitioner text such as *Blackstone's Civil Practice*, the *Green Book*, or the *White Book*.

Whether you are in practice or merely a regular visitor to a county court you will soon notice that a very large number of applications for injunctions are made in family cases. While interim injunctions are less common in other civil litigation, they are by no means rare. It is important to be familiar with the basic procedure for applying for an interim injunction in non-family cases as injunctions are, by their very nature, often required quickly, and in the case of without notice (formerly *ex parte*) applications extremely quickly.

29.2 Some expressions explained

A number of expressions are used in connection with injunction applications with which you ought to be familiar. The main expressions are:

ancillary orders	refers to any order that is connected with the main injunction or injunctions (eg an order to disclose the whereabouts of an object or asset);
American Cyanamid	refers to the leading authority of *American Cyanamid v Ethicon Ltd* [1975] AC 396 which sets out the factors to be considered by the court in deciding whether or not to grant an interim injunction;
Angel Bell	an order within a freezing injunction permitting the payment of certain (usually specified) business debts or commitments or living expenses. The order is named after *Iraqi Ministry of Defence v Arcepey Shipping Company SA (The 'Angel Bell')* [1981] QB 65;
Anton Piller	the old name for a search order (see later in list);
freezing injunction	the name for what used to be called a *Mareva* injunction, which freezes the use of some or all of the assets of a person, firm or company;
interim injunction	a temporary injunction or order granted for a specified period of time 'until the . . . day of . . .' or 'until trial or further order'. Formerly known as an interlocutory injunction;

Mareva injunction	the old name for a freezing injunction (see earlier in list);
ouster order	colloquial expression for an 'occupation order' removing (ousting) a person from property (usually a home), which is most commonly made in family proceedings under the Family Law Act 1996, ss 33–41 but can also be obtained in other disputes;
quia timet	'because he apprehends', an expression used in relation to a threatened wrong that has not yet taken place;
radius order	an order prohibiting someone from entering a specified area near a building or home, commonly used in family proceedings but can be obtained in other proceedings; see *Burris v Azadani* at **29.3**;
return date	the date fixed for further consideration of the injunction (usually the with notice hearing fixed after a without notice injunction has been granted);
search order	the name of what used to be referred to as an *Anton Piller* order, an order that requires the giving of access to premises and of immediate delivery up of documents or property. Order originally named after *Anton Piller KG v Manufacturing Processes Ltd* [1976] Ch 55;
short service	an order obtained (usually without notice, which permits an application to be considered when the other party has not been given the full notice required by the Rules);
penal notice	a notice on the court order that warns the person injuncted of the consequences of a breach of the order.

29.3 The nature of the order

An injunction is an order of the court requiring a person or company to do a specific act or acts (a mandatory injunction) or to refrain from doing some act or acts (a prohibitory injunction). The distinction between a mandatory injunction and a prohibitory injunction depends not upon the wording of the order but upon its substance. Do not waste time trying to make a mandatory order look as if it is prohibitory merely because the latter are more likely to be granted at an interim stage. Individual injunctions will be either mandatory or prohibitory (although both may appear in the same order).

Quite separately, injunctions can also be divided into final and interim (historically known as interlocutory) injunctions. This distinction is often based upon when they are obtained in the proceedings. An interim injunction is usually obtained before any trial and a final injunction is obtained at the end of the case (usually, but not always at a trial). The statutory power for the High Court to grant an injunction is contained in the Senior Courts Act 1981, s 37 and gives the power 'in all cases in which it appears to the court to be just and convenient to do so'. In the county court the statutory power is now to be found in the County Courts Act 1984, s 38 which gives the county court power to make any order that the High Court could have made.

The traditional view is that injunctions are not a cause of action in themselves but a relief granted in support of an existing legal or equitable right (*The Siskina* [1979] AC 210).

In many cases the 'right' to be enforced by a proposed injunction will be obvious. However, the courts seem prepared to extend the concept of 'rights' where necessary. The House of Lords qualified the strict approach to be found in *The Siskina* on more than one occasion. Since then, the House of Lords has doubted whether the strict approach to 'rights' in *The Siskina* is correct; see, for example, the speech of Lord Browne-Wilkinson (with whom Lords Keith and Goff agreed on this point) in *Channel Tunnel Group Ltd v Balfour Beatty Construction Ltd* [1993] AC 334. To make matters more complex, the Privy Council refused to uphold a wholesale challenge to *The Siskina* in *Mercedes-Benz AG v Leiduck* [1995] 3 WLR 718. However, it seems that the approach in *The Siskina* may now be limited to cases involving private law rights, and not the wider interests of the public, in cases such as those brought between a trustee in bankruptcy and the bankrupt (*Morris v Murjani* [1996] 2 All ER 384).

Thus, while *The Siskina* may be a good starting point, take care to consider the statutory power to grant an injunction 'in all cases in which it appears to the court to be just and convenient to do so' before deciding that there is no power in the court to make the particular order sought.

In the light of attacks made on the traditional view in *The Siskina,* it is becoming more and more difficult to decide the exact circumstances in which the court may grant an injunction. Six historic examples may assist in demonstrating the way in which the traditional view of 'rights' has been extended by the courts:

TSB Private Bank International SA v Chabra [1992] 1 WLR 23. In this case the court granted a *Mareva* (now freezing) injunction in a claim under a guarantee that covered, *inter alia,* assets being sold by a UK company of which the defendant was the majority shareholder. The court, of its own motion, joined the company in the action as a necessary party under RSC O 15, r 6(2)(b)(ii). The court then held that where a claimant has a right against one defendant, it had power to grant an injunction against a co-defendant against whom no cause of action lay.

Aiglon Ltd v Gau Shan Co Ltd [1993] BCLC 132. In this case the court found that the claimant's evidence disclosed a strong prima facie case under the Insolvency Act 1986, s 423 which gave the claimant a direct cause of action under s 425(1)(d) of that Act, but also held that the court had jurisdiction under s 238 of that Act to grant the worldwide *Mareva* (now freezing) injunction even though that section gave no direct cause of action or claim.

Khorasandjian v Bush [1993] QB 727. In this case the majority of the Court of Appeal granted a *quia timet* injunction restraining persistent unwanted telephone calls as the inconvenience to the recipient constituted an actionable interference with the ordinary and reasonable use of property that could be restrained without proof of damage.

The Mercantile Group (Europe) AG v Aiyela [1994] 3 WLR 11167. In this case the Court of Appeal continued a *Mareva* (now freezing) injunction against a person who was not a judgment debtor, and against whom the claimant had no surviving cause of action, as the order was ancillary to the order against the judgment debtor and was properly made in the interests of justice.

Burris v Azadani [1995] 1 WLR 1372. In this case the Court of Appeal upheld the making of an injunction restraining the defendant from approaching within 250 yards of the claimant's home distinguishing (on grounds that are somewhat tenuous) the well-known earlier decision of the Court of Appeal in *Patel v Patel* [1988] 2 FLR 202.

Morris v Murjani [1996] 2 All ER 384. In this case the Court of Appeal limited the requirement that there be an existing cause of action as the basis for granting an interlocutory (now interim) injunction, to cases involving a violation of private rights. Thus an injunction restraining a bankrupt from leaving the country before the hearing of an application for his committal for breach of the Insolvency Act 1986, s 333 could properly be made.

The court will not simply grant any order that is sought, as two further examples will illustrate.

Law Debenture Trust Corporation v Ural Caspian Oil Corporation Ltd [1993] 1 WLR 138. In this case the Court of Appeal accepted that a purchaser of property who acquired it in the knowledge of some contractual covenant binding the vendor might be restrained by negative injunction from breaching that covenant, but refused to extend that approach so as to grant a mandatory injunction against the purchaser to perform the covenant.

Caterpillar Logistics Services (UK) Ltd v de Crean [2012] EWCA Civ 156. In this case the Court of Appeal refused to grant an injunction restraining the defendant from misusing her former employer's confidential information when the claimant failed to establish 'any arguable case that she [the defendant] has broken or intends to break or even that there is a real risk that she will break the terms of the confidentiality agreement'.

Frequently, an injunction will be sought to prevent repetition of a wrong that has already taken place, or the undoing of the wrong (eg removal of a trespass or obstruction). However, it is not necessary to wait until the proposed defendant has committed the wrong before applying to the court. A *quia timet* injunction can be obtained if a wrong is merely threatened; see, for example, *Redland Bricks Ltd v Morris* [1970] AC 652. Two criteria normally have to be satisfied: first, that there is a threatened wrong; second, that the wrong infringes some right that the claimant already has (although this second criterion may now have to be reconsidered in cases involving some public duty).

It must be remembered that an injunction remains a discretionary remedy of the court to which equitable principles are still applied. Even if a clear right has been infringed, an injunction will not necessarily be granted at trial or at the interim stage. An injunction (like the remedy of specific performance) will be refused where it serves no useful purpose, but the mere fear that the defendant will not obey is not sufficient to justify the refusal to grant an injunction (*Castanho v Brown and Root (UK) Ltd* [1981] AC 552). An injunction may be refused where there is only a trivial infringement or threatened infringement of a right; where there would be undue hardship to the party being restrained; where the party seeking the injunction has been guilty of some equitable fraud or has unclean hands; or where there has been undue delay or acquiescence on the part of the person seeking the injunction.

The Civil Procedure Rules have not changed the discretionary nature of the injunction remedy. The general criterion for the grant of an interim remedy is now whether it will give effect to the overriding objective (CPR, r 1.2). Detailed provisions appear in CPR, Part 25 and PD 25 (Interim Injunctions). In practice the court will generally consider the principles outlined in *American Cyanamid Co v Ethicon Ltd* [1975] AC 396; whether there is a serious question to be tried, if so, would damages be an adequate remedy for the applicant or whether the respondent can be adequately compensated by damages in the event of the injunction being wrongly granted, and if there is doubt as to the adequacy of damages available to either party or both, consideration of where the 'balance of convenience' lies.

29.4   Enforcement of the order

As an injunction is an order of the court, breach of its terms constitutes a contempt of court punishable by imprisonment, sequestration of assets or a fine. It is beyond the scope of this chapter to set out the detailed procedure for applying to commit a person for breach of a court order as regulated by CPR, Part 81. However, it should be noted that as the defendant's liberty may be in jeopardy, a technical approach is always adopted by the court both on the procedural aspects of the application and in interpreting the wording of the order. Although most injunctions are complied with, without any applications to commit being made, it is extremely important that the wording of the order is crystal clear and that the order that is served has a 'penal notice' included (see **29.11**). Finally, in some cases it is essential that the order has been properly served upon the defendant.

29.5 Jurisdiction

When applying for any interim injunction, it is important to consider both the jurisdiction of the court in which you intend to make the application and the jurisdiction of the judge hearing the application to grant the order.

29.6 The undertaking as to damages

If a party wishes to obtain an interim injunction, it is normally necessary to give an undertaking in damages, as set out in Practice Direction—Interim Injunctions PD 25A, para 5.1. which states that 'Any order for an injunction, unless the court orders otherwise, must contain (1) ... an undertaking by the applicant to the court to pay any damages which the respondent sustains which the court considers the applicant should pay.' The undertaking is a promise to the court to pay damages to the party restrained by the order if the court subsequently finds that (a) they have suffered any damage by reason of the order and that (b) the party obtaining the order ought to pay for that damage.

The courts do not require such an undertaking in every case. The main exceptions are:

(a) family injunctions under the Family Law Act 1996 involving conduct rather than money or property (such as a non-molestation order);

(b) applications by public bodies charged with enforcement of some area of law (*Kirklees Metropolitan Borough Council v Wickes Buildings Supplies Ltd* [1993] AC 227).

In most cases the undertaking is only invoked by an inquiry as to damages either upon discharge of the order shortly after it is granted (eg on discharge of an order without notice) or at the trial of the action when the parties' true rights are established. Upon discharge of an injunction prior to the trial the court will have to decide whether to order an immediate inquiry or leave the decision until the conclusion of the case. The practice to be followed has been considered by the Court of Appeal in *Cheltenham & Gloucester Building Society v Ricketts* [1993] 1 WLR 1545.

Five practical points need to be noted:

(a) Although it may not be absolutely essential that the court be given information about the financial status of the party seeking the injunction, it is good practice to do so in the evidence in support of the application.

(b) If you are aware of any factor that makes the undertaking in damages of doubtful value or worthless, that fact should be made known to the court. In *Schmitten v Faulkes* [1893] WN 64, a solicitor, who failed to disclose to the court that the undertaking was worthless because he had commenced bankruptcy proceedings against his own client, was ordered to pay the costs and damages personally.

(c) The fact that the undertaking is of limited value is not an absolute bar to obtaining an injunction; see the unusual case of *Allen v Jambo Holdings Ltd* [1980] 1 WLR 1252 in which the Court of Appeal reinstated a *Mareva* (now freezing) injunction although the undertaking in damages was virtually worthless.

(d) In some cases the court may require an undertaking to be fortified by a guarantee or deposit of money or by an undertaking from someone else (eg a parent company of a newly formed or impecunious subsidiary). Obviously you should ensure that you have actual authority to give an undertaking from someone else before doing so. In *Udall v Capri Lighting Ltd (In Liquidation)* [1988] QB 907, the Court of Appeal ordered an inquiry into the conduct of the solicitor for the defendant and any losses occasioned by that conduct. The solicitor had given an undertaking that the defendant's directors would provide security for its liabilities towards the claimant by creating second charges in the claimant's favour on their personal properties but, when the judge subsequently ordered the solicitor to carry out his undertaking, the evidence showed that the directors were unable to fulfil the commitment. If the solicitor's failure to implement the undertaking was inexcusable and merited reproof, the judge could make a compensatory order of a disciplinary nature. A requirement for security may be imposed either at the without notice stage or at any later stage prior to discharge of the order as a condition of continuing the order. When a deposit or security is sought by the party restrained, the court would require evidence in support of the application to show that there is a risk of substantial loss being caused by the order and some sound basis for the belief that the undertaking given may be insufficient (*Bhimji v Chatwani* [1992] 1 WLR 1158).

(e) Although there is no question of a party buying an injunction merely by being wealthy enough to give a valuable undertaking in damages, if the person or company applying for the injunction has assets it will not harm them to say so. In the case of a company, filed accounts can be exhibited. In the case of an individual, some estimate or statement of net worth can be made.

If undertakings are given to the court and accepted in lieu of an injunction, take care that you note the difference in practice over the undertaking as to damages between (a) the Chancery Division and (b) the Queen's Bench Division and the county court set out at **29.12**. It is vital that it is clearly understood whether an undertaking as to damages has been given or not.

29.7 A without notice application

A without notice application can only be made pursuant to CPR, r 25.3 in cases where 'it appears to the court that there are good reasons for not giving notice', for example where there is some imminent danger that the court is being asked to prevent. The 'good reason' should be clearly set out in the evidence in support of the application, which should also state when the facts that are the foundation of the application became known to the party applying or to his or her advisers. (In cases where the good reason relates to urgency, it is particularly important to state when those facts became known if they occurred some time before or if you cannot state exactly when they occurred.) The authority of *National Commercial Bank Jamaica Ltd v Olint. Corp Ltd (Practice Note)* [2009] UKPC 16 is of assistance in emphasising the importance of giving notice.

There is a duty of full and frank disclosure in applications made without notice and failure to make proper disclosure may lead to any order being set aside without consideration of the merits of the case. The duty extends to factors affecting the value of the undertaking in damages (see **29.6**). In *Intergraph Corporation v Solid Systems CAD Services Ltd* [1993] FSR 617, the court stressed that merely exhibiting a large number of documents to the evidence does not constitute disclosure. Unless the judge reads the document on a without notice application it has not been disclosed.

A without notice application will often be made before proceedings have been started. Under CPR, r 25.2, the court may only grant an interim remedy before a claim has been made if the matter is either urgent or it is otherwise necessary to do so in the interests of justice. These factors should also be addressed, both in the supporting evidence and in counsel's submissions to the court. It is routine for the court to give directions requiring a claim to be commenced where it has granted an injunction before proceedings have been issued pursuant to CPR, r 25.2(3)–(4), but it need not do so as a point of absolute necessity. For example, in cases where the application is made for an order for disclosure of documents or inspection of property before commencement of a claim, it would not necessarily follow that a claim would **have** to be commenced, depending on the practical outcome of the injunctive proceedings, as set out in CPR, r 25.4.

29.7.1 Arranging the hearing

Your solicitor or your clerk may make the arrangements for the hearing of an application without notice. However, you should be familiar with the procedure, particularly for out-of-hours applications.

In cases of the utmost urgency it is possible to arrange for application to be made to the duty judge at any time outside court hours by telephoning the officer on duty at the Royal Courts of Justice on 020 7947 6000. There is always a duty judge who will hear the application. The practice in the Queen's Bench Division is to be found in the *Queen's Bench Guide,* which explains the requirements for listing an interim application. The specific requirements of the Chancery Division appear in the *Chancery Guide* and for the Commercial Court in the *Admiralty and Commercial Courts Guide.* The judiciary. gov.uk website also contains very straightforward guides to interim hearings in the Chancery Division and Queen's Bench Division, aimed at explaining the basic procedure to litigants in person. In all divisions a hearing can be arranged at the High Court, at the judge's home or in extreme cases application can be made by telephone; see, for example, *Allen v Jambo Holdings Ltd* [1980] 1 WLR 1252. If you seek a prohibitory injunction, it is effective and binding on the person restrained as soon as he or she is notified of it (even before personal service of the order). When making an out-of-hours application, applicants should bear in mind *R (on the application of Hamid) v Secretary of State for the Home Department* [2012] EWHC 3070 (Admin) which warns that such applications should be made as early as possible and before the out-of-hours service becomes necessary.

In cases that do not require an application to be made outside normal court hours, the hearing is arranged by contacting security at the Royal Courts of Justice and leaving details for a return call from the judge's clerk.

In the county court, the papers should be lodged prior to the hearing. If time permits, they can be lodged the day before the without notice application, but more commonly they will be lodged only when the court office opens on the day of the application. Take care if you are told that your application will be heard by the judge at 10.00 am as most county court offices do not open until that time and it will be difficult to lodge the papers at the court office and be heard by the judge at the same time (particularly if the judge is not sitting in the same building as the court office). Obviously appearing before the judge is likely to be more important than issuing the proceedings, as an undertaking to issue forthwith can be given to the judge if an injunction is granted. Whichever court you are making the application in, the standard documents required will be the application notice, claim form (issued or in draft), any particulars of claim or other statements of case, the evidence in support of the application and the draft order.

29.7.2 Procedure at the hearing

In the Chancery Division, the hearing will normally be in open court and the procedure will be the same as for other applications (see **Chapter 30**). The applications judge may go through the applications in the order in the daily list for that day to ascertain which are 'effective' (ie agreement has not been reached between the parties on all the matters in dispute) and which are 'ineffective', and in each case the time estimate for the application. The judge is likely to indicate the order in which he or she will dispose of the applications when he or she has gone through the list that first time.

In the Queen's Bench Division and the Commercial Court, the hearing will be in private with counsel not wearing their robes. The judge will normally allow you to address him or her seated if the application is heard in a room, but not if heard in court.

In the county court, applications are usually heard in private but the practice varies from court to court so you should ensure that you have your robes with you in case they are needed.

You should open your application by briefly describing the injunction you seek such as, 'My Lord [or "My Lady"], this is an application for an injunction without notice restraining a trespass to the claimant's land . . .'. The judge should be taken to:

(a) the statements of case or draft statements of case to show the cause of action;

(b) the evidence or draft evidence in support of the application and to any exhibits; and

(c) the draft order that is sought indicating, if necessary, that only certain parts of the order are being sought at the without notice stage. The formal parts (eg any undertaking to issue and the undertaking as to damages) can usually be dealt with very briefly.

If the judge has read the papers in advance (do not be afraid to ask whether that is the situation) you may not be required to go through the statement of case or evidence.

It should not be necessary to explain to the judge the test to be applied if you are relying upon *American Cynamid v Ethicon* [1975] AC 396. You should be familiar with the decision of *Series 5 Software Ltd v Philip Clarke* [1996] FSR 273, which reconsiders or explains the factors to be taken into account in granting an injunction, as well as any other up-to-date authorities on the factors to be considered in granting an interim injunction. If your case falls within an exception to the test in those cases, you may have to explain why it is exceptional and the test that is then to be applied. Your legal argument should always be very practically focused, with real attention given to the core evidence and the workability of the specific wording of the order.

You should end your submissions by asking the judge to make an order in the terms of the draft. There is almost always discussion about the draft order before the judge announces what order, if any, he or she is prepared to make. If you are seeking several different orders you should be able to link each part of the order sought to the evidence justifying the part of the order. For example, if you are seeking a freezing injunction and want an order that evidence be sworn setting out the defendant's assets, you may have to explain why the order requires that a particular officer of the company is to swear the evidence.

There will often be discussion about the duration of the without notice order. Liberty to apply to the court on specified notice to your solicitors to vary or discharge the order is almost always given. You should remember to put the name, address, telephone and facsimile numbers of your solicitors in the draft order when dealing with liberty to apply (in a freezing injunction or search order an out-of-hours contact number is frequently required to be given). Even where liberty to apply is given, the court may still wish to fix a date for further consideration of the order, which will then appear in the order itself (a return date). In the Chancery Division and in the county court it is still common practice to fix a date for further consideration of the order. In the Queen's Bench Division and in the Commercial Court it is less common to fix a date for further consideration, the liberty to apply provision being thought adequate for most cases.

The judge will then announce the terms of the order that he or she is making. It is rare for anything approaching a formal judgment to be given for a without notice application. The judge will normally merely state that an order is being made in the terms of the draft order, as amended in some stated respects.

If you are refused any form of without notice relief, you can still properly ask for permission to serve an application on short notice. If such an order is given, the judge will normally specify that there be a with notice hearing on a particular day provided that you serve the defendant quickly, often by a stated time later that day.

If you obtain any injunction or an order for short service, you must deal with costs. Normally at this stage costs should be reserved to the return date (if any) or to the trial. If you are refused both the injunction and permission to serve on short notice, there will be little point seeking any with notice costs order.

Your solicitors will have to arrange for the order to be drawn up and sealed by the court (except in the Chancery Division and county court, where the orders are drawn up by the court itself). In every case your solicitors will have to arrange for service of the order, normally personal service of an order endorsed with a penal notice.

29.7.3   Procedure at the hearing for freezing injunctions and search orders

Freezing injunctions and search orders are, by their very nature, orders that are almost invariably required without giving any notice to the defendant. The procedure when applying for a freezing injunction and/or search order will be similar to that for any other without notice injunctions.

The procedure has been made much more straightforward as a result of the adoption of standard form orders for both types of injunction (CPR, PD 25 (Interim Injunctions)). The following additional points should be noted:

(a) If a defendant is outside the jurisdiction, you will have to satisfy the requirements of Council Regulation (EC) No 44/2001, so that service outside the jurisdiction can be effected without permission or you must obtain permission when you obtain the injunction.

(b) Great care should be taken in giving full and frank disclosure as most of the applications to discharge for breach of this duty arise in freezing injunction and search order cases and the court seems to take an even more stringent view of the duty than it does with less draconian orders.

(c) There is normally a requirement to inform third parties of a freezing injunction order that affects them and to pay any costs of the third party in complying (such as the costs of a bank inquiring whether the defendant holds any accounts and whether those accounts are in credit).

(d) A freezing injunction order should normally have a maximum sum to which the injunction applies (calculated by reference to the proper value of the claimant's claim).

(e) A freezing injunction order should allow the defendant to draw reasonable living expenses and legal costs up to a stated sum, often with a proviso that the sum can be increased by written agreement between the parties' solicitors to save the time and expense of applying to the court for every variation of that amount.

(f) In both freezing injunction and search order cases the variety of ancillary orders is extremely wide and needs to be considered with great care particularly if a writ *ne exeat regno* is sought (see **29.7.4**).

Although the adoption of standard form orders has made the task of preparing the draft order simpler, the standard wording may not always be appropriate. It seems that the judges of the Queen's Bench Division are more prepared to vary the standard wording than other judges and some commonly accepted variations can be found in the editorial notes in the *White Book*. In error the standard forms make no provision for costs.

29.8 The opposed without notice application

As it is now possible to send documents worldwide very quickly by email there is an increasing tendency (particularly in the Chancery Division) to notify a defendant or proposed defendant that application is being made for an order without notice. This practice is not used where giving the defendant prior notice of the order will enable him or her to defeat it (eg in most freezing injunction and search order cases).

At an opposed without notice application the role of the defendant will be either to sit silently and take no active part in the proceedings, or to treat the hearing as a hearing with notice even if there has been no time in which to prepare evidence in answer. A defendant given notice of a hearing faces a considerable dilemma. If the defendant takes an active part in the hearing, he or she may encourage the court to make an order at that stage by, for example, being wholly unable to offer any explanation for some apparently obvious wrongful or unlawful act. If the defendant fails to attend or takes no part, it may appear to the court that the defendant has little interest in the outcome of the application. Finally, by attending, there may be additional pressure on the defendant to offer some undertakings rather than face the prospect of an injunction being granted.

The main disadvantage to the claimant in giving notice is that, if the application is dismissed, the claimant is likely to be ordered to pay the defendant's costs whereas, if the application were made without giving notice, the claimant would only be responsible for his or her own costs.

29.9 Applications to vary or discharge

An order may be made (whether with or without notice) giving liberty to the defendant and to third parties to apply to vary or discharge the order. If there is to be a hearing with notice shortly after the without notice hearing, you are less likely to find an express power to apply to discharge.

In some circumstances application may be made without notice to vary or discharge an injunction but the power will only be used in cases that are exceptionally urgent.

If there is an application to vary or discharge the injunction or some parts of the order, it should be supported by evidence setting out the reasons for the variation or discharge. The application can be made simply by giving notice but the usual course is to issue an application. The other documents required will be those used at the initial hearing, save that the draft order will be an actual order of the court. If time permits, there may be further evidence from the claimant. There are three main reasons for seeking an early variation or discharge:

(a) there has been some non-disclosure by the claimant that entitles the defendant to have the order set aside;

(b) the injunction should be varied or discharged because of some facts not known to the court or the claimant at the time of the grant of the order; and

(c) the defendant wishes the court to impose conditions upon the continuation of the injunction (such as security for the undertaking as to damages).

Applications for discharge are sometimes made at a much later stage (eg if the claimant, having obtained the injunction, does not proceed diligently with the action or because of a change in circumstances).

At the hearing of the application to vary, the defendant should have the right to open and close his application. The judge may be prepared to treat the hearing as if it were any return date already set and then dispense with a further with notice hearing making the injunction (whether or not varied) continue to trial or further order. The judge will consider all the evidence and determine whether the injunction should be set aside or varied using the same approach as on any return date.

29.10   Applications with notice

The procedure will differ according to whether there is an order without notice in place and whether the same judge deals with the with notice hearing. If there was an order without notice and it is the same judge hearing the with notice application, it may be possible to introduce the evidence leading to the grant of the order without notice very briefly leaving it to the defendant to explain why the order should not be continued until trial or further order. If you have a different judge, or if there was no without notice hearing or order, it will be necessary for the claimant to deal with the case more fully.

The hearing of the with notice application will have been fixed when the application was issued.

Once counsel for the claimant has introduced counsel for the other parties, the nature of the application should be explained briefly. The statements of case should be explained to show the causes of action relied upon. Unless the judge indicates that it is unnecessary, the next stage is to explain the evidence before the court. Counsel for the claimant should take the judge through the evidence in support without comment (which may mean reading it out to the judge), the evidence in opposition should be gone through by counsel for the defendant(s) without comment, and finally any evidence in reply should be gone through by counsel for the claimant. When the evidence stage has been completed counsel should make their submissions. Counsel for the claimant should address the court in support of the orders sought, going through the proposed order in detail. Counsel for the defendant(s) will then answer (if called upon to do so). Finally (if called upon to do so), counsel for the claimant can reply. The reply should not be merely a repetition of the opening submission but should address the points made by counsel for the defendant(s).

It may be possible for counsel to agree before the hearing what test should be applied by the court. It should not be necessary to explain to the judge the test to be applied if you are relying upon *American Cynamid v Ethicon* [1975] AC 396. You should be familiar with the decision of *Series 5 Software Ltd v Philip Clarke* [1996] FSR 273, which reconsiders or explains the factors to be taken into account in granting an injunction, as well as any other up-to-date authorities on the factors to be considered in granting an interim injunction. If your case falls within an exception to the test in those cases, you may have to explain why it is exceptional and the test that is then to be applied.

In many cases there will be discussion between counsel over the possibility of the application being disposed of by the parties giving undertakings (see **29.12**). Such discussions will be very practical but still require tactical consideration. If undertakings are offered in lieu of an injunction it should be made clear whether the offer is an open one (ie one that can be mentioned to the judge) or is made 'without prejudice' (ie may only be used on any questions of costs).

In many cases that strict sequence of events for a with notice hearing will be varied at the request of the judge who will have particular questions or issues that he or she wishes counsel to deal with as they arise. The result may be that the evidence stage becomes muddled with the submissions stage. If the judge announces that he or she is going to grant an injunction, there may be further discussion about the wording at that stage, even though it may already have been dealt with in submissions. In a complex case counsel may be asked to prepare a form of wording that reflects what the judge ordered.

Finally, the judge will need to deal with the costs of the injunction. See **Chapter 34**. If costs were reserved to this hearing, it is important that they are mentioned to the court.

29.11   The order

It is extremely important that the order is clearly worded so that the defendant will know exactly what he or she can or cannot do. In the county court the word 'forbidden' is now used instead of 'restrained' and 'servants or agents' has disappeared when the defendant is an individual rather than a firm or company.

The order should also contain a penal notice. The penal notice is the warning that tells the defendant that he or she must obey the order or be guilty of contempt of court for which he or she may be sent to prison. In the county court the wording now appears in bold immediately after the name and address of the defendant to whom the order is addressed. In the event of breach, the new CPR, Part 81 sets out the comprehensive procedure to be followed for committal applications. Specialist family law practitioner texts should be consulted with regard to the enforcement of injunctions made under the Family Law Act 1996 which may involve powers of arrest and direct police involvement.

29.12   Undertakings

At any hearing attended by the party against whom the injunction is sought, an offer may be made of an undertaking in lieu of an injunction. Such an offer is almost invariably given without any admission of liability. An undertaking is a promise to the court to do or refrain from doing some stated act or acts. It is enforceable in the same way as an injunction.

When undertakings are given in lieu of an injunction there is sometimes a dispute as to whether the party seeking the order has to give the undertaking as to damages. The practice in the Chancery Division is that a cross-undertaking as to damages will be given unless the contrary is expressly agreed at the time. No similar presumption applies in the Queen's Bench Division or the county court so any cross-undertaking must be recorded in any order.

Just as a party may apply to vary or discharge an injunction, application may be made to be released from an undertaking given. The application should be made in the usual way, with evidence in support, explaining the basis for the application (eg that there has been a change in circumstances or that there has been unnecessary delay by the claimant in prosecuting the action).

30

Applications in the Chancery Division

30.1 Chancery Division proceedings

Claims involving Chancery business may be dealt with either in the High Court or in a county court. CPR, PD 7A, para 2.5, defines 'Chancery business' as including any of the matters specified in the Senior Courts Act 1981, Sch 1, para 1. The classes of claim specified in Sch 1, para 1 are those relating to:

(a) the sale, exchange or partition of land, or the raising of charges on land;

(b) the redemption or foreclosure of mortgages;

(c) the execution of trusts;

(d) the administration of the estates of deceased persons;

(e) bankruptcy;

(f) the dissolution of partnerships and the taking of partnership or other accounts;

(g) the rectification, setting aside or cancellation of deeds or other instruments in writing;

(h) probate business, other than non-contentious or common form business;

(i) patents, trade marks, registered designs, copyright and design right;

(j) the appointment of a guardian of a child's estate; and

(k) the exercise of the High Court's jurisdiction under the companies legislation.

The Civil Procedure Rules and Practice Directions supplementing them contain information on Chancery Practice. Additional practical information may be found in the *Chancery Guide*.

30.1.1 Applications

Any procedural application (eg for directions) should be made to a Master unless there is some special reason for making it to a judge. Otherwise the application may be dismissed with costs. Some applications, particularly for interim injunctions, have to be made to a judge. CPR, Parts 23 and 25, contain rules as to how applications may be made and it is worth noting that some applications can be dealt with without a hearing, or by a telephone hearing. Further details can be found in *A Practical Approach to Civil Procedure*, chapter 20. An application is usually for interim relief although orders may be made that finally dispose of a question or an issue in a proceeding (eg the vacation of a caution on a register of title, or the grant of a declaration).

30.2 Procedural aspects

Unless an application is to be made without notice, or the court gives permission to the contrary, the documents that must be filed with the listing office are the application notice (minimum four copies where the proceedings involve one defendant and additional copies for further defendants), two copies of the claim form and two copies of the judges' application information form (containing details of solicitors, counsel and parties, etc). The application notice must be served a minimum of three clear working days before the hearing (not including Saturday, Sunday or recognised holidays) and must not include either the day of service or the day of the hearing. The normal CPR rules on service apply; see *A Practical Approach to Civil Procedure*, chapter 6.

Applications are generally heard in open court. Where it may be unjust for the application to be heard in public, the judge has a discretion to conduct the hearing in private.

30.2.1 Skeleton arguments

The general rule is that for the purpose of all hearings before a judge skeleton arguments should be prepared. The exceptions are where the application does not warrant one, for example, because it is likely to be short, or where the application is so urgent that preparation of a skeleton argument is impracticable, or where the application is ineffective (see **30.3.4**) and the order is agreed by all the parties.

On judges' applications without notice, the skeleton argument should be filed with the papers that the judge is asked to read on the application. In more substantial matters, such as applications by order (see **30.3.1**), they should be filed not less than two clear days before the hearing. In all other applications to a judge, including interim applications, they must be filed no later than 10.00 am on the day before the hearing. Skeleton arguments of up to 25 pages should be filed by email to the email addresses set out in the *Chancery Guide* at para 14.8. Any skeleton argument of more than 25 pages should be provided in hard copy to the Chancery judges' listing office (para 14.8(2)).

Skeleton arguments must begin with an estimate of the time required for pre-reading and a time estimate for the hearing (*Chancery Guide*, para 5.13), and must comply with the guidelines in Appendix 7 of the *Guide*. Failure to lodge this document in accordance with the *Guide* may result in the matter not being heard on the scheduled date and/or disallowance of the costs of preparation and/or an adverse costs order (see the *Chancery Guide*, para 7.31).

30.2.2 Bundles, time estimates and reading lists

Bundles of documents for use in court will generally be required for all hearings if more than 25 pages are involved (and may be appropriate even if fewer pages are involved). The efficient preparation of bundles of documents is very important. Where bundles have been properly prepared, the case will be easier to understand and present, and time and costs are likely to be saved. The representatives for all parties involved must cooperate in agreeing bundles for use in court. Documents in agreed bundles are admissible as evidence at the hearing unless the court orders otherwise or a party gives written notice objecting to the admissibility of particular documents (PD 32, para 27.2). The court and the advocates should all have exactly the same bundles (*Chancery Guide*, para 7.12). Detailed guidelines on the preparation of bundles are set out in the *Chancery Guide*, Appendix 6. These should always be followed unless there is good reason not to do so.

The general rule is that the claimant/applicant must ensure that one copy of a properly prepared bundle is delivered at the listing office not less than three and not more than seven clear days before the hearing of an application by order or trial. However, the court may direct the delivery of bundles earlier than this. Where oral evidence is to be given, a second copy of the bundle must be available in court for the use of the witnesses. In the case of bundles to be used on judge's applications (other than applications by order), the bundles must be delivered to the clerk to the interim applications judge by 10 am on the morning preceding the day of the hearing unless the court directs otherwise (para 7.15).

Bundles lodged at court must be in their final form, and parties must not request alterations without good reasons. Where documents are copied unnecessarily or bundled incompetently, costs of preparation may be disallowed. Where the provisions of the *Chancery Guide* as to the preparation or delivery of bundles are not followed, the bundle may be rejected by the court or be made the subject of a special costs order (para 7.10).

When lodging the agreed bundles there should also be lodged an agreed time estimate, together with an agreed reading list and an agreed time estimate in respect of that reading list. The time estimates and reading list must be signed by the advocates for the parties. Failing agreement as to the time estimates or reading list, then separate reading lists and time estimates must be submitted signed by the appropriate advocate (para 7.30).

If the case is one that does not require the preparation of a bundle, the advocate should check before the hearing starts that all the documents to which he or she wishes to refer and that ought to have been filed have been filed, and, if possible, indicate to the associate which they are (para 7.16).

30.3 Conduct of applications before the judge

30.3.1 General

The interim applications judge is available to hear applications each day in term and an application notice can be served for any day in term except the last (*Chancery Guide*, para 5.9). If the volume of applications requires it, any other judge who is available to assist with interim applications will hear such applications as the interim applications judge may direct. Special arrangements are made for hearing applications out of hours and in vacation.

Where the circumstances of a case require a 'short notice' period (less than three clear days' notice to the other side), permission to abridge time may be obtained on an application without notice, usually made after the midday adjournment.

Counsel wear business suits and do not robe on interim applications (Chairman of the Bar Council's letter, 2 June 2009), although the judge will wear the judicial gown. The traditional practice is that the judge will ascertain at the sitting of the court which of the listed applications will be 'effective', that is disputed, and, if so, what counsel's time estimate is, or 'ineffective', that is disposed of by agreement or that the parties wish to be adjourned. The current practice is to concentrate on the time estimate for the application, with the judge not particularly insisting on counsel stating whether their application is 'effective' or 'ineffective'. It is a matter of courtesy both to the court and to other counsel and litigants:

(a) to be present in court when the judge takes his or her seat;

(b) to be ready to say whether the application is 'effective' or 'ineffective' (if required);

(c) to have carefully considered the estimate of length and to have agreed that estimate with one's opponent;

(d) not to waste the time of the court when the judge is going through the list 'first time round' by explaining the substance of the application instead of simply indicating whether it is effective or ineffective/the time estimate.

Although the judge has a discretion as to the order of hearing applications, he or she will normally deal with ineffective applications first, for example, applications that are to be adjourned or have been settled, or, under the current practice, by taking any urgent applications first and the others in order of their time estimates. Counsel are often 'released' until stated times of the day based on the time estimates of the applications that will be dealt with at earlier stages of the day.

Applications likely to take two hours or more (para 5.12) will usually be given an order that they are given a subsequent fixed date for hearing (they are then called 'interim applications by order'). In these cases the judge will, at the first hearing, hear argument for any application for a court order to last until the application is heard fully. The hearing where the main application will be fully argued is fixed through the solicitors or the clerks to counsel for all parties with the Chancery judges' listing office (para 5.15). All other listed, unlisted and applications without notice will be heard in the order determined by the judge. Those affecting the liberty of a subject (eg for release from committal to prison for contempt, or for *habeas corpus*) are always accorded priority.

Counsel with effective applications may be asked to wait, in case another judge becomes free to hear the matter. The judge may transfer any application as deemed appropriate, irrespective of priority. Counsel should not leave the precincts of the court unless released by the judge until a particular time. Counsel should also ensure that the court staff can easily locate them if a judge becomes free. Any application that at the end of the day is part heard (ie unfinished) will normally head the list for the next court day.

30.3.2 Time estimates

Time estimates are critical. The applications judge will determine only applications that are estimated to last less than two hours. Counsel will be required to lodge with the Chancery listing officer a written time estimate signed by the advocates for all the parties as soon as possible after the application notice has been lodged. An indication may be given that an application by order is to be treated as urgent. If it is apparent that it will be likely to last more than two hours, the only proper course is to inform the court that it is ineffective, and 'second time round' to inform the judge to the effect, 'This application is likely to occupy the court for two days, and I therefore ask your Lordship to stand it over as an interim application by order. Subject to your Lordship's approval, the defendant is to give certain undertakings in the meantime.'

30.3.3 Unlisted and emergency applications

Frequently, counsel is instructed to apply to the court urgently without notice, which means there will not have been time for the application to appear on the court's list. It also happens that instructing solicitors sometimes forget to lodge the papers for applications on notice in accordance with the directions mentioned above. Counsel may in these circumstances ask the judge to hear the matter although unlisted. The judge's clerk should be notified (usually through counsel's clerk) as early in the day as possible, that an application is to be made, and two copies of the proceedings (showing the title of the claim), and the draft of the order to be sought should be made available. If the proceedings have not yet been issued, every effort should be made to issue the claim form before the application is made. If this is not practical, the party making the application gives an undertaking to the court to issue the claim form forthwith. The usual practice is to rise in counsel's place after the judge has worked through the list for the first time, and to say words to the effect, 'I have an unlisted application in the claim of Smith and Jones [giving the claim number]'. Such an application will only rarely be ineffective, and counsel should go on to indicate the time estimate. Unless the application affects the liberty of the subject or is of exceptional urgency and importance, listed applications will be given priority.

30.3.4 Ineffective applications

An application can only genuinely be described as 'ineffective' if there is no point of disagreement between the parties that requires the decision of the judge. Counsel must ensure that all such points have been dealt with, and not attempt to be heard early in the list under the guise of an ineffective application. The degree of information that the judge will require to have on the substance of an application depends on the nature of the order that the court is to be asked to make. It is usual to indicate in very general terms the nature of the claim (eg 'This is an application for an injunction to restrain the defendant from dealing with certain land which is alleged to be subject to an option agreement'). Counsel will then usually inform the judge orally of the terms of the order that the judge is invited to make. If the order involves undertakings to the court or submission to an order (other than a purely procedural order) by one of the parties, the judge is likely to wish to know the exact terms of the undertakings. It is therefore not merely a formality to say, 'The parties have agreed *subject to your Lordship's approval* that the application should stand over for 14 days on the defendant's undertaking not to dispose of the land known as [describing it]': the terms of the undertaking or an order in the same terms are subject to the approval of the judge.

30.3.5 Effective applications

The sequence in which effective, ie disputed, listed applications are dealt with is at the discretion of the judge. Normally the judge will direct that the shorter applications be heard first. Naturally, this must not be abused by underestimating the time that the matter will take. The procedure will then follow this outline:

(a) Counsel presenting the application will open by giving a short account of the facts giving rise to the application.

(b) Counsel for the applicant then makes his or her submissions on the evidence as presented.

(c) Counsel for the respondent makes his or her submissions.

(d) Counsel for the applicant is entitled to reply to the submissions of the opposing party.

30.3.6 Agreed adjournments

If all parties to an application agree to do so, an application can be adjourned for not more than 14 days by attending the Chancery judges' listing officer on the ground floor, Rolls Building with signed consents from all parties before 4.00 pm on the day before the listed hearing (*Chancery Guide*, para 5.19). A litigant in person who is a party must attend before the Chancery judges' listing officer as well as sign a consent. Not more than three successive adjournments may be made and no adjournments are to be made to the last two days of any term. Undertakings previously given to the court may be continued unchanged over the duration of any adjournment. If an existing undertaking is to be varied or a new undertaking given, the adjournment must be dealt with by the judge.

An application may be adjourned to be heard as an application by order without attendance before the judge where the parties are agreed that the application will take two hours or more (*Chancery Guide*, para 5.20). The consents signed by all parties should also contain an agreed timetable for the filing of evidence or confirmation that no further evidence is to be filed. Any application arising from the failure of a party to abide by the timetable and any application to extend the timetable must be made to the judge.

30.3.7   Drafting of orders

It may often be possible for the court to prepare and seal an order more quickly if a draft of the order is handed in. Speed may be particularly important where the order involves the grant of an interim injunction or the appointment of a receiver without notice. In all but the most simple cases a draft order should be prepared and brought to the hearing (*Chancery Guide*, para 9.5).

The court may in any case direct the parties to agree and sign a draft order. Where a draft or an agreed statement of the terms of an order exists in electronic form, it is often helpful if the draft or agreed statement is provided to the court by email or on a digital storage device as well as in hard copy, particularly if the order needs to be drawn up quickly. Any digital storage device supplied for this purpose must be new and newly formatted before writing the material on it so as to minimise the risk of transferring a computer virus. The current word-processing system used by the Chancery Associates is Word for Windows 2003.

Orders will be drawn up by the court, unless the judge or Master directs that no order be drawn. Unless a contrary order is made, or the party concerned has asked to serve the order, a sealed order will be sent to each party.

30.3.8   Use of information technology

The Civil Procedure Rules 1998 have various provisions about the use of information technology in the conduct of cases. Various documents may be filed at court by email (PD 5B and *Chancery Guide*, para 14.7). This is not available for any step where a fee is payable (PD 5B, para 3.2). In the Chancery Division the court prefers documents to be filed in Word 2003 in .doc format, although it can cope with documents in the newer .docx format or PDF format. Documents are treated as filed on the date they are received by the court (PD 5B, para 8.2), unless they are received after 4.00 pm, in which case they are treated as being filed on the next day that the court is open (para 8.4). Signatures, for example on statements of truth, are made by typing the name on an electronic version of the document, or by applying a facsimile of the signature. The document with the original signature must be retained (para 9). Most documents are filed without hard copies. A document that is required by a rule or Practice Direction to be filed at court is not filed when it is sent to a judge by email (para 8.9).

In any case where the solicitors for one or more parties take the view that some form of IT will assist the presentation of a case, the solicitor should obtain, at an early stage, directions from the judge who is to try the case. Where no nomination of a specific judge has yet been made, solicitors who wish to use any form of IT should invite the Chancellor (by request to his or her clerk) to nominate a judge to hear the case including all interim applications. The solicitors for all parties should try to agree a common protocol for the electronic exchange and management of information.

The *Chancery Guide* contains specific provisions relating to transcripts, the use of fax, and evidence by video link. See the *Chancery Guide,* paras 14.1–14.17.

The Companies Court

31.1 Insolvency proceedings: winding-up petitions

31.1.1 Introduction

A petition for the compulsory winding up of a company incorporated by registration under the Companies Acts may be presented by the company, or its directors, or by any creditor or creditors (including any contingent or prospective creditor or creditors), or by a contributory (ie shareholder) or contributories, various officials (eg Secretary of State for Business, Innovation and Skills and the Attorney General), administrators and administrative receivers, or by all or any of those parties, separately or together (Insolvency Act 1986, s 124(1)). A great many junior barristers will find that they are briefed to appear on creditors' winding-up petitions in the Companies Court (see the *Company Law in Practice* manual, **chapter 9**). An inexperienced advocate should beware of believing that such petitions present no difficulties simply because they are very numerous and usually undisputed. Before appearing on the hearing of such a petition, the advocate should study carefully the relevant provisions of the Insolvency Act 1986 and the Insolvency Rules 1986 (SI 1986/1925), which will be referred to in this chapter as 'the Act' and 'IR 1986'. Substantial modernisation of the IR 1986 is planned for implementation in the future, but as implementation remains uncertain, this chapter will deal with the law as it stands in February 2014. References to forms, by number, are references to the forms prescribed by the IR 1986. The IR 1986 prescribe the form that a petition should take (see Sch 4, Form 4.2). Where written evidence is required, it is generally given in witness statements verified by statements of truth. Generally the High Court and county courts have concurrent jurisdiction and a petitioner may choose in which court to proceed.

31.1.2 Evidence verifying petition

The petitioner or someone with knowledge of the matters giving rise to the petition must sign a statement of truth verifying the petition (see IR 1986, rr 4.7 and 4.12(4)) stating a belief that the allegations in the petition are true. This may be endorsed on the petition or in a separate document (typically a witness statement). If a witness statement is used, it must state various facts about the company and the petition in order to comply with IR 1986, r 4.12.

31.2 The court

High Court winding-up petitions are listed for hearing before the Registrar of the Companies Court sitting in open court on Wednesdays at 10.30 am. Petitions are listed in 30-minute batches, so that a number of matters will be found in the list marked 'not before 11.00' and so on. Counsel must be robed, and the Registrar is addressed as 'Sir'.

31.3 Petitions by creditors

While petitions may be presented by a variety of parties mentioned earlier, the most common category of petitioners are creditors. To qualify as a creditor within the meaning of the Insolvency Act 1986, the petitioner must establish that a debt is due from the company to him or her that is not bona fide disputed on substantial grounds. Some creditors may be described as 'trade' creditors (meaning that their debts have been incurred in the course of the company's business). Others may be 'judgment' creditors where the company has failed to satisfy a court judgment made against it.

31.3.1 Restraining presentation of the petition

If the company disputes the *locus standi* of the petitioner as a creditor, on the ground that the debt upon which a petition is to be or has been presented is disputed, the company may make an application for an injunction to restrain the presentation or advertisement of the petition (which occurs after the petition has been served on the company). Such application must be made to the judge by the issue of an originating application (Form 7.1). See *Company Law in Practice* manual, **9.6.**

If the company fails to take such preventive steps, it may still dispute the petitioner's entitlement to a winding-up order on the ground that the debt is disputed by filing a witness statement setting out the dispute at least five business days before the hearing (IR 1986, r. 4.18). Because of the danger of spurious disputes being used to defeat creditors, the Companies Court judges have introduced a practice of requiring the company in doubtful cases to make a payment into court of (or otherwise securing the amount of) the debt, pending an application for summary judgment by the petitioner.

31.4 Before the hearing

The following is a checklist of the matters that must have been attended to by the instructing solicitors before the hearing. Counsel should ensure that he or she has copies of these documents in preparing the case for the hearing and that any defects that are found in them, for example, inconsistent dates or sums owed, erroneous title of company in the advertisement, etc are discussed with the solicitor before the hearing. If there has been non-compliance with the rules, remedial action will be required, as indicated after each point.

31.4.1 Petition and verifying evidence

Counsel should have a copy of the petition and, if it is verified in a separate document, the verifying witness statement. Problems with the petition, such as insufficient particulars of the debt, or incorrect details dealing with the EC Regulation on the jurisdiction of insolvency proceedings, have to be dealt with by standing the petition over for amendment.

31.4.2   Evidence of service

Service must be proved by a certificate of service (IR 1986, r 4.9A), which must be verified by a statement of truth (r 13.13(16)). The certificate of service should give various details about the company and the petition, and state the date on which the petition was served. It is a strict requirement that it must also specify the manner in which service was effected (r 4.9A(2)(h)). Service of the petition and verifying written evidence must generally be effected at the company's registered office: IR 1986, r 4.8(2). Permissible methods of service are set out in r 4.8(3), which provides:

> *Service of the petition at the registered office may be effected in any of the following ways—*
>
> (a) *it may be handed to a person who there and then acknowledges himself to be, or to the best of the server's knowledge, information and belief is, a director or other officer, or employee, of the company; or*
>
> (b) *it may be handed to a person who there and then acknowledges himself to be authorised to accept service of documents on the company's behalf; or*
>
> (c) *in the absence of any such person as is mentioned in sub-paragraph (a) or (b), it may be deposited at or about the registered office in such a way that it is likely to come to the notice of a person attending at the office.*

If service by any of the above methods is not practicable, the petitioner may instead either:

(a) effect service at the company's last known principal place of business, under r 4.8(4); or

(b) apply by an application without notice, supported by a witness statement, for an order for substituted service under r 4.8(6), (7).

The Court Manager of the Companies Court is authorised to deal with applications for substituted service.

Any order for substituted service must be attached to the certificate of service (r 4.9(3)).

31.4.2.1   Remedies

If the certificate of service is defective, the court will have to be asked for an adjournment of the petition either:

(a) to file a fresh certificate if the petition was properly served but the certificate does not correctly state the facts or fails to specify the manner of service; or

(b) to effect reservice, if the petition has not been properly served.

If the company appears at the hearing, it may seek dismissal of the petition on the ground that it has been advertised after defective service. If the company has been properly served and appears at the hearing, a defect in the certificate of service will cease to be relevant.

31.4.3   Advertisement

Unless the court directs otherwise, each petition must be advertised once in the *Gazette*. There is a prescribed form of advertisement (Form 4.6):

> *The details that must be included in the advertisement of the petition are partly set out in IR 1986, rr 12A.33 and 12A.34 (which set out requirements that must be included in all gazetted notices) and r 4.11, which sets out additional information to be included in advertisements of winding-up petitions:*
>
> (a) *details of the office-holder if the petition is presented by an office-holder as set out in r 12A.33(2)(a) to (e);*

(b) *the court's name and the number allocated to the petition;*

(c) *the registered name of the company;*

(d) *the company's registered number;*

(e) *the company's registered office, or*

    (i) *in the case of an unregistered company the postal address of its principal place of business;*

    (ii) *in the case of an overseas company, the address at which service of the petition was effected;*

(f) *any principal trading address if this is different from the registered office;*

(g) *any name it was registered under in the 12 months prior to the presentation of the petition;*

(h) *any name or style under which it carried on business or which it used when incurring the relevant debt;*

(i) *that a petition has been presented for winding-up of the company;*

(j) *the name and address of the petitioner;*

(k) *the date on which the petition was presented;*

(l) *the venue fixed for the hearing of the petition;*

(m) *the name and address of the petitioner's solicitor (if any); and*

(n) *that any person intending to appear at the hearing (whether to support or oppose the petition) must give notice of that intention in accordance with r 4.16.*

A copy of the advertisement should be included in the brief for counsel for the petitioner. Unless it is the company's own petition, the advertisement must have appeared not less than seven business days after service of the petition, nor less than seven business days (which do not include Saturdays, Sundays or bank holidays) before the hearing date (see IR 1986, r 4.11(2)(b)). This is a most important requirement, as it enables the company to prevent the highly damaging consequences of advertisement by applying for an injunction if the petitioner's debt is disputed. Counsel should ensure that the advertisement complied with rr 4.11, 12A.33 and 12A.34, that there are no printing errors in the advertisement, and the time requirements have been met.

31.4.3.1 Remedies

If the advertisement rules have not been complied with, the court may dismiss the petition. In the case of premature publication, if the publication is a day early, for example, because of an innocent failure to count a bank holiday, the court may waive the defect. Counsel should point out the premature advertisement, state the reason shortly, and ask that the defect be waived. There is always a serious risk that the petition will be dismissed on this ground.

If a court orders that a petition be re-served due to defective service, counsel should ask whether a second advertisement will also be required. If this is required, counsel may request that the required time periods be abated, although this is at the discretion of the court.

31.4.4 Certificate of compliance

A certificate of due compliance shows the dates of presentation, service, advertisement, and hearing (Form 4.7), together with a copy of the advertisement. The present practice is to stand petitions out for 14 days to allow time to file the certificate where this has not been done in time. The Registrar will normally mention this matter as soon as the petition is called on.

31.4.5   List of appearances

Every person including creditors or the company itself intending to appear on the hearing to support or oppose the making of a winding-up order must give notice to the solicitors for the petitioner not later than 4.00 pm on the business day before the hearing (IR 1986, r 4.16). Failure to comply means that person cannot appear without the permission of the court. If the company intends to oppose the petition, its witness statement must be filed in court not less than five business days before the hearing (IR 1986, r 4.18). It is the duty of the petitioner's solicitors to prepare a list of the persons who have given such notice (Form 4.10, known formally as the 'list of appearances', informally in court as 'the list', and colloquially from its colour as 'the blue form'). The list must be handed in before the hearing (IR 1986, r 4.17(3)). If it is not handed in, the Registrar will usually simply say when the petition is called on 'There is no list', and decline to proceed further.

31.4.5.1   Remedy

The only help for this is to make sure that the solicitors' representative is seen well before the time for which the petition is listed, and told to hand in the list when the current half-hour's petitions are over. If the list has not been handed in, ask the Registrar to 'take this matter second time round'.

31.5   Substitution

If the original petition is not proceeded with (because the petitioner withdraws), or is not advertised, or in other similar circumstances (see IR 1986, r 4.19(1)), the court may, on such terms as it thinks just, substitute as petitioner any creditor or contributory who in the court's opinion would have a right to present a petition, and who is desirous of prosecuting it. The 'new' petitioner asks for a substitution order (see **31.7**, 'The Hearing', Counsel C).

31.6   Noting the back sheet

It is helpful to compile the relevant information and the dates on which the required steps were taken for use as a quick guide during the hearing to avoid having to search through a file during the presentation. One example would be as follows:

Re: [name of company]
Trade creditors' petition based on a statutory demand in the sum of £ . . .
List: [enter any creditors, contributories, or others supporting/opposing the petition and the nature of their interest]
Co: [note whether the company will make an appearance]

Relevant dates:

Presented: [eg 24/4/14]
Verified: [24/4/14]
Served: [7/5/14]
Cert.S: [12/5/14]
Advert: [28/5/14]
Cert. Comp: [2/6/14]
UCO (Asking for the usual compulsory order)

31.7 The hearing

The following applications may be heard in unopposed petition situations:

(1) Associate:	'Petition number 546, Tyro Advisers Limited.'
Counsel A	
(for Petitioner):	'This is a trade creditor's petition based on a statutory demand for the sum of £32,459 odd. The company is not represented, and the list is clear (or "negative"). I ask for the usual compulsory order.'
Registrar:	'Usual compulsory order, main proceedings.'
(2) Associate:	'Petition number 547, D-I-Y Services Limited.'
Counsel B:	'This is a petition based on a statutory demand for unpaid solicitors' fees.'
Registrar:	'This petition was advertised only five business days after service, and r 4.11 has not been complied with.'
Counsel B:	'Sir, I am instructed that my instructing solicitors unfortunately overlooked the fact that seven business days must elapse between service and advertisement, and therefore did not omit from their calculation of the time two weekends and a bank holiday. In those circumstances, I ask that the defect be waived.'
Registrar:	'No. These errors are capable of causing severe damage to a company which may wish to dispute the debt. There has been no effort in this case by the solicitors to cure the error, or to communicate with the court office in lieu of complying with r 4.11. In the circumstances I will dismiss the petition.'
Counsel C:	'I appear for Suppliers Limited, a supporting creditor which has not given notice to the petitioner's solicitors prior to this hearing. My client has a trade debt amounting to £78,968 odd, and my application is for permission to be added to the list out of time and for an order substituting my client as petitioner.'
Registrar:	'I will give you permission to be added to the list out of time on the usual terms. I will also make an order substituting Miss C's client as the petitioner, and adjourn the petition for 28 days for amendment of the petition, re-service and re-advertisement.'

31.8 Notes on the hearing

(a) It is usual to describe the basis of the petition and to show what is alleged to prove the inability of the company to pay its debts (in case (1) it is failure to comply with a statutory demand, but other evidence may also be relied upon).

(b) The court is told whether the company is represented.

(c) The court should be informed whether there are any supporting or opposing creditors or contributories on the list of appearances and, if so, how many of each and whether any of them have in fact appeared at the hearing. If there are none, the court is told that the list is clear or 'negative'.

(d) The usual compulsory order is set out in Form 4.11. (See *Company Law in Practice* manual, **Figure 9.3**.) The reference to 'main proceedings' (see the Registrar's order in answer to counsel A) is to the EC Regulation on insolvency proceedings, and means the debtor company's main interests are in England and Wales and not in another EU state.

(e) The 'usual terms' on which a creditor is added to the list of appearances out of time are that the applicant's solicitor undertakes not to seek any costs of giving notice or of the application to be added to the list in the event of a compulsory winding up being made. (A substituted petitioner will normally obtain an order for the subsequent costs of amendment, re-service, re-advertisement and hearing.)

31.9 Opposed petitions

If it becomes apparent that the petition is opposed, the Registrar will adjourn the matter for hearing before the judge because the Registrar only has jurisdiction over unopposed petitions.

31.10 Adjournments

If an order is made, the winding up commences with the presentation of the petition (s 129(2) of the Act). Section 127 avoids dispositions of property of a company made after the commencement of the winding up, unless the court has otherwise ordered (see *Company Law in Practice* manual, **9.8**). For this reason, the court will not permit a petition to remain outstanding for protracted periods (except in the case of petitions by contributories, where a winding up is sought, the company is solvent, and the judge has made appropriate orders under s 127). Even if the petitioner and the company have agreed that the company should have time to attempt to pay the petition debt, the court will only grant an adjournment if there is a good reason, and only on condition that the petition is advertised in time for the next hearing. A second adjournment is unlikely to be granted (PD Insolvency Proceedings, para 11.5.1).

31.11 Rescission of a winding-up order

An application for the rescission of an order must be made within five business days after the date the order was made (IR 1986, r 7.47(4)). Applications can only be made by a creditor, a contributory, or by a company jointly with a creditor or with a contributory. The application must be supported by written evidence of the company's assets and liabilities. If the petition is unsuccessful, the costs will normally be ordered to be paid by the petitioner.

Possession cases

32.1 Introduction

32.1.1 Types of cases included

You may be instructed to act in a claim for the possession of land in a variety of circumstances. A landlord may seek to recover possession of residential or commercial property from persons to whom the landlord has granted a tenancy or a licence or from trespassers. A mortgagee may seek to enforce the charge on the mortgagor's property to sell it to obtain the money owed under the mortgage. Although different considerations apply to each, all are covered by CPR, Part 55 or CPR, Part 56.

This chapter considers the different circumstances. The requirements of CPR, r 55 and CPR, PD 55A (hereafter, APD), which apply to all possession cases issued after 15 October 2001, are considered first, highlighting the matters that you must check. The common matters to check in respect of cases of possession by landlords generally (residential, commercial and trespassers) are then considered. There are then three separate sections dealing in turn with specific considerations in respect of trespassers, residential occupiers and commercial occupiers. Mortgage possession cases, being based on a different relationship, that of a lender enforcing the charge on premises, are covered at the end.

32.1.2 Civil Procedure Rules

32.1.2.1 Which court

Proceedings must be issued in the county court for the district in which the land is situated unless there are exceptional circumstances that justify bringing them in the High Court (CPR, r 55.3(1) and (2)).

If the case is in the High Court, you should check that there is a certificate stating the reasons for bringing it there and that the circumstances do come within those set out in APD 55.3, para 1.3 that may justify starting a claim in the High Court. These include matters involving complicated disputes of fact or points of law of general importance. The value of the property and amount of the financial claim may be relevant circumstances but will not alone normally justify starting the claim in the High Court (APD 55.3, para 1.4).

32.1.2.2 Statements of case

(a) *Content* Check that the claim form, particulars of claim, defence and any counterclaim and defence to counterclaim are in the correct form and contain all the information required by the CPR, both generally (CPR, Part 16) and the additional requirements set out in APD 55. Thus, for example, check that the general requirements for possession proceedings set out in APD 55 and, if it is a Possession Claim Online (PCOL), BPD 55.4 are fulfilled. This includes identifying the land, stating whether it is residential property, and the ground on which possession is claimed, and giving full details of any mortgage or tenancy agreement, and of every person who, to the best of the claimant's knowledge, is in possession of the property. Note in particular the requirement in PD 16, para 7.3 to attach to the particulars of claim a copy of any agreement on which the claim is based. Any written tenancy agreement should be attached. There are additional requirements in respect of residential occupiers, trespassers and mortgage arrears claims.

(b) *Service* Check that the requirements in respect of service have been fulfilled. Note that in possession cases, the particulars of claim must be filed and served with the claim form (CPR, r 55.4; but note that there are different requirements with a PCOL). Generally the court will have served the documents and there will be no issue as to service. However, where the parties have elected to serve themselves, check there is a certificate of service. In many possession cases, the defendant occupants do not respond to the particulars of claim and do not appear. It is therefore important that the court is satisfied that they have been properly served. CPR, r 55.8(6) specifically requires the claimant to produce the certificate at the hearing. In cases against trespassers, there are special rules as to service that must be fulfilled (see **32.3**).

32.1.2.3   The fixed date hearing

Under CPR, r 55.5(1), on issue of the possession claim form, the court will fix a date for the first hearing. The defendants must be served a certain number of days before the hearing, the number of days varying according to the type of case and property (see CPR, r 55.5). Ensure they were served in time. The aim of this first hearing is to identify whether there is any defence to the claim. If so, the court will use the hearing to give case management directions to prepare for trial. If not, the court may decide the claim at this hearing.

(a) *If the defendant does not appear* If you are instructed to appear at such a first hearing, it may be that the defendant has not filed a defence. If acting for the claimant you must be ready to prove your case at the first hearing. This means having the evidence to do so. Under CPR, r 55.8(3), where a claim has not yet been allocated to a track (or where the court orders otherwise), any fact that needs to be proved may be proved by evidence in writing. Thus, you may find that you are instructed to appear on the basis of the statements of case and witness statements with any documents annexed to the statements of case or exhibited to the witness statements. Check you have all relevant documents.

(b) *Where the defendant does appear* Even if no defence has been filed, the defendant may turn up at the hearing. Failing to file a defence does not preclude him or her from taking part in the proceedings, although it may be taken into account when the court decides costs, for example, of an adjournment. If acting for the landlord, you will need to determine from the defendant or the legal representative whether the defendant does intend to defend. If he or she does, the court is unlikely to hear the case that day, partially because the defendant is unlikely to be ready to proceed and partially because the court will not have time to hear it as usually a large number of cases are listed. However, you should attempt to determine what the defence is and check whether an adjournment will be sought or case management directions can be agreed. If instructed on behalf of the defendant, you will need to take careful instructions from your client to determine whether or not there is a defence and, if so, whether you wish to seek an adjournment to have time to consider the case in more detail or whether it would be appropriate for case management directions to be given.

(c) *The risk of 'consent orders'* If the defendant does not contest the case or, although taking issue with some of the allegations, is prepared to agree to a possession order (eg on payment of money to him or her to leave), be aware of the dangers of 'consent orders' in possession cases. A tenant cannot contract out of statutory protection given by the Rent Act 1977 or the Housing Acts 1985 or 1988. The court cannot make a 'consent order' against such a tenant unless there is either an express admission that the Acts do not apply or it is established by evidence or admission that a ground under the Act is made out and, if appropriate, it is reasonable to make a possession order. An order made without such concession or establishment is a nullity and can be challenged by judicial review even where both parties were legally represented and consented to the order (see *R v Bloomsbury & Marylebone County Court, ex p Blackburne* (1985) 275 EG 1273). In addition, where you are acting for the defendant who may become homeless and apply to the local authority for housing, be aware that consenting to an order may be interpreted by the local authority as becoming homeless 'intentionally' thereby depriving him or her of any call on the local authority's duty to rehouse those in 'priority need'.

(d) *Track allocation and case management directions* Where no order is made at the first hearing, unless an adjournment is granted, the case will be allocated to either the fast track or the multi-track (cases will only be allocated to the small claims track if both parties agree—CPR, r 55.9(2)). In deciding which is the appropriate track, the court will take into account the usual factors set out in CPR, r 26.8 and those in CPR, r 55.9, which include the importance to the defendant of retaining possession and to the claimant of vacant possession. The court will also make appropriate case management directions including the usual ones in respect of disclosure, witness statements and experts (where relevant).

32.1.2.4 Preparing for a contested hearing

Where you are instructed to appear for one of the parties in a contested hearing (the most usual type of case in which counsel is instructed), you will need to check that all the case management directions have been complied with (eg disclosure completed, witness statements exchanged, directions in respect of experts fulfilled). You also need to check that you have a copy of the trial bundle, which does include all the necessary documents, for example, statements of case, witness statements, expert(s) reports where relevant and relevant documents. Ensure as well that relevant witnesses and experts have been warned to attend and, where necessary, compelled to attend by witness summons.

You need to check that the evidence covers all the necessary allegations made by your client. Thus, if acting for the landlord, ensure the evidence does cover all the matters that he or she must prove to establish the right to possession and to rebut any defence raised. If acting for the defendant, check that the evidence is focused on rebutting the landlord's allegations and proving any positive defence raised by your client. Although the matters to be checked depend on the type of case you have, there are some matters common to all possession claims, which are set out below.

32.2   Possession by landlord—common matters to check

32.2.1   Landlord's title

The landlord must prove his or her title to the land. This means proving that he or she has the interest in the land that gives him or her the right to seek possession. Well drafted statements of case should state what the landlord's title is (eg freehold or lease-hold). Frequently there is no issue between the parties as to title. However, where there is a dispute as to the landlord's title or where the defendant does not attend the hearing, s 67 Land Registration Act 2002 renders official copies of the register and documents filed at the Land Registry including charges admissible to the same extent as the originals.

The landlord must also show that he or she has the immediate right to obtain possession against the named defendant. This means that there is no interest between the landlord and the person against whom he is seeking possession. Thus, for example, a landlord has no right to obtain possession directly against a sub-tenant. If he or she wishes to get possession against the sub-tenant, he or she must seek possession from his own tenant. Generally (although not always), if the landlord does get possession against his or her own tenant and that tenancy ends, the sub-tenancy will also end and entitle the landlord to possession against both the tenant and the sub-tenant. Check that the landlord is not attempting to take action directly against a sub-tenant without seeking possession from the tenant.

32.2.2   Tenancy or licence

The occupant's status may be disputed as protection is often afforded to tenants but not to licensees. In construing the agreement between the landlord and the occupant the court will consider the substance of it and be astute to detect 'sham' terms or agreement. You therefore need to ensure that you are au fait with the current law on the factors that determine the difference between a licence and tenancy, consider carefully the written agreement (if any) and/or what was agreed orally and the circumstances in which the letting was made and have your arguments ready. Where proceedings are brought under the specialised proceedings for 'trespassers' (see **32.3**), you need to check that the occupancy is one that permits this procedural method to be used (see **32.3**).

32.2.3   Nature of premises and use by occupant

Check the type of premises that form the subject matter of the proceedings. The nature of the premises and the use by the occupant determine the type of statutory protection that might be afforded to the occupant. The form of security and requirements to be fulfilled to gain security are different for residential and business tenants. There are different provisions in respect of proceedings against trespassers in residential and non-residential premises (CPR, r 55.5(2)). Mortgagors of residential premises have more protection against possession being granted than those of commercial premises.

Where statutory protection is claimed but disputed on the basis of use by the occupant, you may need to check the agreed use under the tenancy agreement and the actual use by the occupant from the start of the tenancy to determine what, if any, statutory protection exists at the time of the proceedings. There is much case law on this and on what level of 'business' use can bring a tenant out of protection under the Acts covering residential premises.

32.2.4 Other terms of the agreement

Check the terms of the agreement between the landlord and the occupant; in particular check the provisions for ending the agreement. Statute generally adds to the protection of the occupant but does not reduce any protection afforded by the agreement. Thus, even where tenants have statutory protection, the landlord will generally have to show that he or she has complied with the terms of the agreement as well as the statutory provisions.

32.2.5 Terminating the right to occupy

Check whether the tenancy is a fixed-term or periodic tenancy as different considerations apply to terminating them.

32.2.5.1 Fixed-term tenancies

Where the landlord claims that a fixed-term tenancy has expired, check that it has. Even where the period set out in the tenancy agreement has expired, the tenancy does not terminate but is continued by statute if it is a residential tenancy that comes within the Housing Act 1985 or Housing Act 1988 (a statutory periodic tenancy will arise) or a commercial tenancy that comes within the Landlord and Tenant Act 1954 (a continuation tenancy will arise).

The landlord has the power to terminate the tenancy before the fixed term has expired only if the tenancy agreement contains a provision enabling him or her to do so. Where the landlord purports to end the tenancy during its currency, you need to check whether the landlord is exercising a right under a 'break' clause or under a 'forfeiture' clause.

(a) *Break clauses*   A break clause is one that entitles the landlord (or less commonly the tenant) to end the tenancy before the end of the fixed term in certain circumstances, usually either at a particular point in the tenancy (eg at the end of the seventh year of a 21-year agreement) or on the happening of a specified event (eg the landlord's need to redevelop). Check that the circumstances come within the clause and that any procedures required by the agreement to terminate the tenancy have been strictly followed. Thus, for example, it may require that a particular period of notice be given to end on a particular date (eg three months' notice expiring at the end of the seventh year of the tenancy).

(b) *Forfeiture*   A forfeiture clause is one that entitles the landlord to end the tenancy for breach by the tenant. Forfeiture is an ancient remedy of a landlord that is extremely complex with much relevant case and statutory law that may require some research on your part if you know nothing about it. It is too complex to deal with in any detail in this manual and the following is an outline of the basic points to check in such a case. First, check that the tenancy agreement/lease contains a forfeiture clause, that it enables the landlord to forfeit in respect of the alleged breach by the tenant, and that any procedure required by the agreement has been followed. Check that the landlord has not done anything after knowing of the breach that could be construed as waiving the breach. If the breach of covenant alleged is anything other than non-payment of rent (or a few other limited exceptions), check that a notice under the Law of Property Act 1925, s 146 has been served prior to forfeiture proceedings being commenced and that the notice fulfils the necessary requirements. If the allegation is that the tenant is in breach of repairing obligations, check that the notice fulfils the requirements of the Leasehold Property (Repairs) Act 1938. Finally, check what relief from forfeiture may be claimed by the tenant or sub-tenant and whether this is likely to be granted. At present, the court's construction of the Housing Act 1988 is that where the landlord claims possession during the fixed term, the claim is under the statute and not for forfeiture. The tenant therefore cannot apply for relief from forfeiture. The position under the Housing Act 1985 is unclear as, although the concepts are the same, the wording of some of the relevant provisions is different. There are no provisions in the Rent Act 1974 that prevent forfeiture of a protected tenancy or the tenant claiming relief.

32.2.5.2   Periodic tenancies

Many of the proceedings in which you will be involved will relate to periodic tenancies, where no fixed term was agreed by the parties. At common law such tenancies continue to renew themselves each period unless one of the parties terminates the tenancy by service of notice to quit. Statutory intervention renders any common law notice to quit ineffective and substitutes its own procedure, which the landlord must follow prior to instituting proceedings in respect of residential tenancies that come within the Housing Act 1985 and the Housing Act 1988 (see later). Statutory intervention also alters the position in respect of commercial premises under the Landlord and Tenant Act 1954, which requires certain statutory notices to be served and, until they are, generally the tenancy continues. In respect of other tenancies (eg those that have no statutory protection or that come within the Rent Act 1977), the common law rules apply and you need to check that a proper notice to quit has been served by the landlord seeking possession.

In respect of notices to quit, you need to check three things. First, check that the period of notice is sufficient. At common law this is generally a full period of the tenancy (eg a monthly tenancy requires a full month's notice). The only exception is a yearly tenancy where only a half year's notice is required. In addition to fulfilling the common law requirements, where the Protection from Eviction Act 1977 applies (ie in respect of dwellings), the notice to quit must give a minimum period of four weeks from the date of service of the notice (a notice under the Protection from Eviction Act 1977 must also contain prescribed information to be valid). Second, check that the notice expires on the anniversary of the commencement of the tenancy (eg a monthly tenancy commencing on the 10th of the month may only be terminated by a notice to quit that expires on the 9th or 10th of the month as it takes effect at the very end of the 9th/start of the 10th). Finally, check that notice has been effectively served on or before the date from which time runs on the notice.

32.2.6   Against whom is the claim brought

In addition to checking that the landlord has the immediate right to possession (see **32.2.1**), you need to check that all relevant parties have been joined. Although the general rule is that when the landlord terminates the tenancy and obtains a possession order, the possession order is effective against all occupants, this is not always the case. A subtenancy may survive if it comes within the provisions of the Rent Act 1977, s 137 or the Housing Act 1988, s 18. In addition, occupants may have claims under other provisions, for example, matrimonial rights. It is therefore usual to join all adult occupants of the premises as defendants. Special rules apply to seeking possession against squatters where the number of occupants and/or their names may not be known to the landlord (see **32.3.3**).

32.3 Trespassers

There are special procedures available where there is a clear-cut case by the landlord that either the occupants entered and remained without his or her consent or any licence granted by the landlord has been terminated. The procedures cannot be used against tenants and are not appropriate where there are genuine issues about the status of the occupant. They are most commonly used against squatters (ie those who entered and remained as trespassers). Generally such proceedings involve residential premises, although the procedure also covers commercial premises.

32.3.1 Correct court

Check that the case is in the correct court. It must be issued in the county court for the area in which the land is situated. If the case is brought in the High Court, check that there is a certificate stating the reasons for bringing it there, and that the circumstances do come within those set out in PD 55.3, para 1(3), which may justify starting a claim in the High Court. Note in particular that a claim against trespassers may be brought in the High Court where there is a substantial risk of public disturbance or of serious harm to persons or property that properly requires immediate determination.

32.3.2 Procedure appropriate?

CPR, Part 55, contains specific provisions for obtaining possession of land against trespassers, squatters and licensees whose licences have been determined. The provision enables possession to be obtained quickly and on the basis of the claim form, particulars of claim and witness statements. This procedure is intended to be used in straightforward cases. It is not appropriate to use it where there are real issues as to the status of the occupier, for example, whether he or she is a licensee or tenant. In such case, the normal procedure should be followed. The first thing you need to check is whether this procedure is appropriate.

32.3.3 Procedure followed

Frequently the owner will not know the names of some or all the occupants. In such a case, the claim must be brought against 'persons unknown' in addition to any named defendants (CPR, r 55.3(4)).

In many cases, no defendants will appear at the hearing. However, the court will be astute to ensure that the requirements of the CPR have been fulfilled. The matters you must therefore check before the hearing are:

(a) the claim form and particulars of claim contain all the relevant information. One form of particulars of claim (N121) relates specifically to trespassers. Ensure that the matters required by APD 55.5, para 2.6 are included;

(b) service has been properly effected. Although the normal rules of service apply to named defendants, 'persons unknown' must be served by the method set out in CPR, r 55.6. This involves attaching copies of the documents to the main door or some other part of the land so they are clearly visible and inserting another set through the letter slot in a sealed transparent envelope addressed to the 'occupiers'.

32.3.4 Costs

In a very large number of cases, there are no named defendants. Thus, even where possession is granted, no order can be made as to costs as there is no named defendant against whom to make it. If there are named defendants, you need to take instructions as to whether or not you should seek an order for costs against them, if a possession order is granted.

In some cases, the defendants will appear at the hearing. Where they are not named, they should be joined as named parties, if they want to contest the case. If acting for the defendants, you need to advise them that this exposes them to the risk of being ordered to pay costs.

32.3.5 Contested cases

If the defendant(s) raise a triable issue, the court may deal with it there and then, provided the issue is simple and clearly still within the ambit of the procedure for trespassers. In any other situation, for example, a point is raised as to the status of the occupier who may or may not have been a tenant, the court will adjourn the application and direct that it be dealt with as an ordinary possession case and give directions accordingly.

32.4 Residential possession cases—ordinary proceedings

Having determined that the case before you involves possession against an occupant of residential premises, you then need to determine more precisely what, if any, protection the occupant may have against possession being obtained by the landlord. There is a long history of statutory intervention into the landlord and tenant relationship in respect of residential premises. The three current principal statutes have provisions:

(a) setting out the qualifying conditions that the occupant must satisfy to gain protection of the Act and specifying categories or circumstances that exclude protection of the Act even if the occupant satisfies the qualifying conditions;

(b) specifying the basis on which possession may be granted by the courts and the procedure that must be followed to obtain possession;

(c) implying terms into the agreement that may be relevant to the possession proceedings and provisions by which the tenant may seek to control the level of rent charged (in the Rent Act 1977 and the Housing Act 1988 only).

Some of these provisions are identical across the statutes. Some are different either radically or marginally. The following sets out those matters that you must check carefully, whatever type of protection the occupant has. It also indicates where differences occur between the statutes and where more care must be taken in particular statutes than in others.

In determining which statute might apply, check who the landlord is and the date of the tenancy. The three main types of landlord are local authorities (Housing Act 1985), housing associations (may be either Housing Act 1985 or Housing Act 1988), and private landlords (may be Rent Act 1977 or Housing Act 1988). The date that determines which Act applies in respect of housing associations and private landlords is 15 January 1989. Unless caught by one of the transitional provisions, tenancies granted on or after that date are covered by the Housing Act 1988. Housing Association tenancies granted before that date are covered by the Housing Act 1985 and private tenants by the Rent Act 1977.

32.4.1 Status of occupant

The statements of case should make it clear whether or not the occupant's status is in dispute. If the landlord is claiming a status that denies statutory protection, identify the basis of the landlord's allegations. Is it that the occupant fails to fulfil the qualifying conditions of the relevant Act or that the occupant comes within one of the categories specifically excluded from protection or both (ie pleading in the alternative that the occupants fail to fulfil the qualifying condition but, even if they do, they come within one of the excluded categories)? Check the specific provisions in the statute on which the landlord relies. In considering any case that might be used to argue the construction of the provision, check whether it related to the particular provision on which this landlord relies or a similar one in a different statute. There are small but significant differences in the wording of the statutes, and a case that appears to be 'on all fours' with your case may in fact have been decided on the basis of a different provision and therefore may be distinguished.

Where the occupant does not qualify for the protection of any statute, the landlord merely needs to prove the general matters set out at **32.2**. Where, however, the occupancy does attract statutory protection, you need to go on to check the matters set out below.

32.4.2 Procedural steps followed

32.4.2.1 Housing Act 1985

Where the Housing Act 1985 applies, the landlord must serve a notice under Housing Act 1985, s 83, within a specified period before issuing proceedings, the period required depending on the grounds claimed for possession. The notice may be invalid because it is defective or the landlord may have issued prematurely. Check that the notice is in the prescribed form and contains all the relevant information, in particular the grounds on which the landlord relies, the particulars of those grounds, and the date after which proceedings may be issued. Check that the notice was served in sufficient time to give the tenant the required period of notice prior to issue and that the proceedings were not issued before the stated date. Although the courts have the power to dispense with service of the notice, many judges are reluctant to do so. There is a large body of case law on this and, if the point is taken, you need to ensure that you are up to date on the way in which the courts are dealing with this issue.

32.4.2.2 Housing Act 1988

Where possession is sought against a tenant with protection of the Housing Act 1988, you need to check whether the tenancy is assured shorthold or assured, as the procedure to be followed differs.

(a) *Assured shorthold*   If the tenancy was granted on or after 28 February 1997, it will be an assured shorthold unless it is caught by transitional provisions or it was expressly agreed or stated that it was an assured tenancy. Many Housing Associations will so expressly state, but private landlords rarely do.

If the tenancy was granted before 28 February 1997, the landlord must prove that it satisfies the requirements in s 20 of the Housing Act 1988 to be an assured shorthold, ie that it was for a fixed term of at least six months with no power for the landlord to determine earlier than that (a forfeiture clause does not count as such a power) and proper notice in the prescribed form was served on the tenant before/at the time of entering the tenancy agreement.

If the tenancy is an assured shorthold, the landlord has an automatic right to possession provided he has served the requisite notice under the Housing Act 1988, s 21 on the tenant. The court has no power to waive this notice. Although there is no prescribed form for this, the notice must be in writing. A landlord cannot rely on this ground during a fixed term unless there is a clause in the tenancy agreement allowing him to do so (see **32.2.5.1**). Notice can be served during any fixed term provided it is of at least two months' duration and expires at or after the end of the fixed term. Notice in respect of a periodic tenancy (either as granted or as a statutory periodic tenancy arising at the end of the fixed term) must expire at least two months after service and end not earlier than the date on which the tenancy could have been determined by notice to quit at common law. It must also expire on the last day of the tenancy. So check the notice to ensure it is correct and that proceedings were not issued before the date stated in the notice.

(b) *Assured* Where the landlord seeks possession on one of the grounds under the Housing Act 1988 because either the tenancy is not an assured shorthold or the landlord does not rely on that automatic right, a notice under the Housing Act 1988, s 8 must be served on the tenant. This procedure is the same as that under the Housing Act 1985, s 83 so you will need to check the matters referred to in **32.4.2.1**. Note the court has no power to waive the notice if Ground 8 is relied on by the landlord (see **32.4.3.1**).

32.4.2.3 Rent Act 1977

Common law rules about the termination of tenancies apply to tenancies within the Rent Act 1977 (there is no statutory intervention equivalent to that in the Housing Act 1985 and Housing Act 1988 regarding notices). You will therefore need to check that the contractual (protected) tenancy has been properly terminated prior to commencement of proceedings—ie fixed-term expired or periodic tenancy determined by notice to quit—see **32.2.5**. Check also whether any notice of increase of rent has been served as this may have acted as a notice to quit provided it fulfils the requirements of notice to quit. Once the contractual (protected tenancy) is terminated the tenant remains in occupation as a statutory tenant. There is no requirement for the landlord to serve a further notice before issuing proceedings.

32.4.2.4 Form N119

Check that the particulars of claim are in the form specified (N119; or as required for PCOL cases).

32.4.3 Grounds on which possession sought

There are similarities across all three Acts as to the grounds on which possession may be obtained (although they are called 'grounds' under the Housing Acts 1985 and 1988 and 'cases' under the Rent Act 1977). In addition, all three Acts differentiate between mandatory grounds (ie those where the landlord need only prove the ground) and discretionary grounds (ie where the court must also be satisfied that it is reasonable to grant possession). It is important to note whether the ground(s) relied on are mandatory or discretionary for two reasons:

(a) If a mandatory ground is proved, the court must order possession. No further test is applied and the court has no discretion not to make an order. However, where a discretionary ground is proved, the court must also be satisfied that it is reasonable to make a possession order. You will need to be prepared to bring evidence on and argue reasonableness. Although each case turns on its facts, there is much case law on the factors that can be taken into account. The court's decision on reasonableness may be difficult to disturb on appeal.

(b) Where a court grants possession on the basis of a mandatory ground, it has limited powers to delay the order—it must grant an outright order. It cannot postpone the date by which the tenant must give up possession for more than 14 days unless there is exceptional hardship, when the date may be extended to a maximum of six weeks. Where the court grants possession on the basis of a discretionary ground, it has very wide powers to suspend the order and frequently does so on conditions. The most common situation where this happens is where an order is granted on the basis of rent arrears. The order may be suspended on payment of current rent plus £X per specified period off the arrears. So long as the tenant keeps to the conditions, the tenancy continues. Breach of the conditions of the suspended order crystallises the landlord's right to request a warrant of eviction. Where discretionary grounds are relied on, you will need to be ready to argue both whether or not the order should be suspended and any conditions.

The grounds under all three Acts divide into different categories, the most common of which are covered below.

32.4.3.1 Rent arrears

This is the most common ground for possession. There is one in the Rent Act 1977 (case 1), one in the Housing Act 1985 (ground 1), and three in the Housing Act 1988 (grounds 8, 10 and 11). All are discretionary except ground 8 in the Housing Act 1988, which is mandatory. Check the precise wording of the case/ground relied on. They are all differently worded. What precisely must be proved in respect of the arrears?

Check that the rent claimed to be in arrears is due. Check that the Landlord and Tenant Act 1987, s 48, which requires the landlord to furnish the tenant with his address in England and Wales at which notices may be served on him by the tenant, has been fulfilled. Any rent or service charge is treated as not due until the landlord complies with the section, although it is a relatively easy burden for the landlord to meet. There is a developing area of case law on what is good notice. So if this is a matter in dispute, you will need to check the current position. Check that any rent increases have been in accordance with the tenancy agreement and, where dealing with a Rent Act tenant, check that any increase has been in accordance with the provisions of the Act. Check whether any of the rent claimed is, in fact, statute barred, remembering the general rules on appropriation of payments.

Where the landlord is a local authority, registered social landlord, or housing action trust, check that the pre-action protocol for possession claims based on rent arrears has been followed. Check that the claim form and particulars of claim comply with the requirements under the CPR in respect of claims for possession, which include rent arrears as a ground. Check that there is a schedule of rent as specified in the CPR. At court ensure that you are clear precisely what rent is due at that date.

Check whether there is any potential defence to the rent claim, for example, a counterclaim by the tenant for damages for disrepair that amounts to a set-off.

Even if rent arrears are proved, for all but ground 8 under the Housing Act 1988, the court must also be satisfied that it is reasonable to grant possession and this is likely to be argued. There is a wide range of factors that the court will consider when determining whether or not it is reasonable. Frequently tenants in arrears are eligible for housing benefit but are not in receipt of it. This is a factor the court will consider when deciding whether or not it is reasonable to grant the order and, if an order is granted, whether or not to grant an outright or a suspended order. Check whether the tenant is eligible for benefit, has applied, and, if so, the reasons for any delay in the processing of the claim.

Finally, be ready to argue the conditions on which a suspended order should be granted. If acting for the tenant, check that the tenant can realistically pay off the arrears in addition to the current rent. Ensure that the tenant is aware that failure to keep the payments up will mean that the landlord can execute the order by getting the bailiffs in and that there will be no further hearing at that point unless the tenant applies to suspend or set aside the possession order.

32.4.3.2 Nuisance/annoyance

This ground is a discretionary ground under all three Acts. The grounds are similar across the Acts but there are some differences in the wording used. Check the precise wording of the case/ground on which you rely. All three impute the tenant with responsibility for the acts of a limited range of other people that differs across the Acts. Where the allegation is nuisance or annoyance, check the wording of the ground/case as to who must be affected as this also differs across the Acts. Where the allegation is of a relevant conviction, check what convictions come within the ground as this also varies across the Acts.

32.4.3.3 Other tenant's default

All three Acts include a discretionary ground for possession that may be exercised when any obligation of the tenancy has been broken or not performed. You will need to check which term it is alleged has been broken, the tenancy agreement as to the wording, and what evidence there is to prove breach. Check also whether the tenant is alleging waiver of breach by the landlord (ie the landlord with knowledge of the breach acquiesces to it). You need to be clear both on the law on waiver and the facts of your case that may be used to argue it.

The court must be satisfied that it is reasonable to make an order and can suspend any order made on conditions. Be ready to argue both of these.

32.4.3.4 Condition of dwelling house/furniture has deteriorated

A discretionary ground across all three Acts, it is slightly differently worded. Check the precise wording of the ground on which you rely. Also be prepared to argue reasonableness and whether or not the order should be suspended and, if so, conditions to be attached.

32.4.3.5 Landlord requires the premises

All three Acts have several grounds under which the landlord can obtain the premises because he or she requires them for some purpose. These differ considerably across the Acts. The Housing Act 1985 relates to public sector landlords so has a broad range of grounds under which the landlord can claim possession for various purposes or types of people (eg those with special needs). The Housing Act 1988 and Rent Act 1977 have more limited numbers of uses available as grounds but include grounds to enable the landlord to gain possession to house him or herself and/or his or her family (not available under the Housing Act 1985 for obvious reasons).

In all cases where the landlord is seeking possession on the basis that the landlord requires it for some purpose, you must check the ground on which the landlord relies and ensure that all requirements can be proved. Generally these include requiring the landlord to prove that:

(a) the tenant was given notice at the start of the tenancy that possession may be required. The court may or may not have the power to dispense with this notice;

(b) the purpose for requiring possession is that specified in the ground. Check pre-cisely what must be proved on this. For example, the landlord may require the premises for his or her own occupation. Some grounds require the landlord to have lived in the premises previously, some do not. Some require the landlord to show reasonableness of requiring the premises, while some do not.

32.4.3.6   Suitable alternative accommodation

The Rent Act 1977 and Housing Act 1988 include as a separate ground that suitable alternative accommodation is or will be available. The Housing Act 1985 does not in-clude this as a separate ground but does require suitable alternative accommodation to be provided in addition to proving some of the grounds (eg where the landlord requires premises for an alternative use).

All three Acts contain some guidance on the factors the court will take into account when considering whether the accommodation offered is suitable. Although the word-ing differs, the main considerations under the Rent Act 1977 and Housing Act 1988 are:

(a) the security of the alternative accommodation is reasonably equivalent to that enjoyed by the tenant in the current premises. So you need to check the status of the occupancy being offered, for example, a licence will not suffice;

(b) the accommodation is reasonably suitable for the tenant and his or her family. There is much case law on this particular aspect and some difference between the Rent Act 1977 and the Housing Act 1988. If this is an issue, you will need to check both what is offered and the case law on factors that the court will consider in deciding what is reasonably suitable.

32.4.4   Preparation for hearing

Having checked the points above that are relevant to your case, plan both your submis-sions and questioning of witnesses so that you are focusing on the main issues that will be of concern to the judge. Remember, witness statements stand as evidence-in-chief. If you wish to add to them or amplify them you will need to get the permission of the court. Consider whether a skeleton argument would be useful. Where appropriate, be ready to argue not just the grounds, but also reasonableness and the type of order.

Generally possession hearings are held in public. However, where possession is sought on the grounds of rent arrears, the hearing is listed in private. Check the local practice as to whether you should appear robed or not but, when in doubt, come prepared to be robed.

Local authority and large housing association landlords have large numbers of posses-sion cases for rent arrears. They generally get the procedure right but may not be very precise on the rent due. As social landlords, they are also generally reasonable when it comes to discussing the possibility of a suspended order and the conditions to be imposed. Private landlords are generally less used to possession proceedings and may be less willing to discuss the possibility of settling the case on the basis of a suspended order.

32.4.5   Costs

In cases that last less than one day, the court will summarily assess costs and you must be ready to address the court on them. PD 44, para 1.1, requires a written statement of costs to be prepared in Form N260. This is the starting point for the judge's assessment of costs. You should have a copy of the schedule and understand the basis of the figures contained in it. The court can call for evidence in deciding the figure, for example looking at counsel's brief to see the brief fee. Ensure your brief is marked!

Be alert to PD 44, para 5.1, which provides that the court may consider recording whether the hearing was fit for counsel, in particular where the paying party asks for the court to express a view or where the judge thinks the hearing was not fit for counsel.

Detailed assessment of costs is a more complicated process done by a costs officer at a separate assessment some time after the hearing. Generally the paperwork and representation at such hearings is done by the solicitor.

32.5 Possession in commercial cases

The Landlord and Tenant Act 1954, Part II, gives the occupants, if they qualify, the statutory protection of the right to apply to the court for a new tenancy at the end of their old one. The landlord can oppose the grant of the new tenancy on particular grounds.

32.5.1 Tenancy without statutory protection

Tenancies of business (commercial) premises attract the statutory protection of the Landlord and Tenant Act 1954, Part II, if they fulfil the requirements of the Act and are not excluded. A landlord may seek possession in respect of business premises alleging that the occupant cannot claim statutory protection. The main reasons by which the occupancy may not come within the Act are that:

(a) it is a licence (the Act only protects tenants);

(b) the tenant does not occupy for the purposes of a business carried on by him or her (the tenancy is held by one person and the business is run by another; a typical example would be a tenancy in the name of an individual with the business run by a company of which the individual is the majority shareholder); or

(c) the tenancy is for a short term, certainly not exceeding six months unless the tenancy contains provisions for renewing the term or for extending it beyond six months from its beginning.

If any of these are alleged, you must check both the law and facts carefully to ensure that the ground on which the landlord claims lack of protection is in fact made out.

32.5.2 Tenancy with protection under Part II of the Landlord and Tenant Act 1954

Where a tenant seeks this protection, by applying for a new tenancy under Part II of the Landlord and Tenant Act 1954, CPR, Part 56 applies.

32.5.2.1 The possession claim

A tenancy with protection of the Act is automatically continued (the 'continuation tenancy') after the expiry of the contractual term until a statutory notice is served by the landlord or the tenant. On termination of the continuation tenancy, the tenant is entitled to a new tenancy under the Act unless the landlord can prove one or more of the grounds for opposing the new tenancy set out in the Act. When instructed in a case where the tenancy does come within the Act, the two main things you must check are:

(a) The notice procedure has been properly followed. The requirements of the notice and service are detailed and there is much case law on whether or not the proper procedure has been followed. If the tenant has failed to follow the procedure as set out in the Act, he or she loses the right to claim a new tenancy.

(b) If the notice procedure has been properly followed, the landlord will be required to prove one of the grounds set out in the Act for opposing the grant of a new tenancy. There is some similarity between these grounds and those in the Acts giving protection to residential tenants in that they are based on some fault of the tenant, the landlord's own need for the premises, or an offer of suitable alternative accommodation. There is no easy division between mandatory grounds and discretionary grounds as under the statutes giving protection to residential tenants. Check the precise wording of the ground relied on and the evidence required to prove it.

32.5.2.2   Additional matters

Where instructed in a case to which Part II of the 1954 Act applies, you must also be prepared to argue:

(a) the terms of any new tenancy that may be granted. If the landlord loses in his opposition to the grant of a new tenancy and the parties cannot agree the terms, the terms will be determined by the court;

(b) compensation for the tenant if the landlord is successful in opposing the grant of a new tenancy. This is only relevant to some grounds. Check whether the ground relied on is one that can attract compensation. In addition, the tenant may be making a claim for compensation for any improvements to the premises carried out by him or her.

32.6   Mortgage cases

Possession proceedings by a mortgagee may be taken against a leaseholder or freeholder of residential or commercial premises. A mortgagee's right to possession arises out of the nature of the mortgage itself, the mortgagee taking possession of the property to sell it to recoup the money secured by the charge. Despite the fact that the basis of these proceedings is very different to that of a landlord seeking to obtain possession of premises let to tenants, such claims also come with CPR, Part 55. There is also a pre-action protocol for possession claims based on mortgage arrears in respect of residential property. Thus, the matters set out under **32.1.2** apply with specific rules in respect of mortgage possession cases where appropriate, for example:

(a) the particulars of claim must contain the information specified in PD 55.4, para 2.1 plus that specified in PD 55.4, para 2.5;

(b) where the mortgagee seeks possession of land that includes residential property a notice must be served on the property within five days of the claimant receiving notification of the hearing date and a copy of it produced at the hearing (CPR, r 55.10).

32.6.1   Matters to check

The law in this area is complex and in need of reform. It is too complex to deal with in any detail in this manual and the following is an outline of the basic points to check in the most common type of case. Generally mortgage possession cases are taken by institutional lenders that have a mortgage by way of a legal charge on the property. When the borrower defaults on the mortgage, the lender has various statutory powers in respect of the property and those powers are contained in the mortgage agreement (deed). Although the mortgagee can enforce the security through various methods, for example, foreclosure or suing the mortgagor on the personal covenant to pay, the most common method is to obtain possession to sell the property with vacant posses sion to recover the money owed to them. In such cases the main things to check are as follows.

First, check that the mortgagee has a valid charge on the property and check the terms of the agreement itself. The mortgage deed should be available (usually exhibited to the witness statement made on behalf of the mortgagee). Most mortgages are legal charges that give the lender a notional lease on the property. The mortgagee is therefore entitled to take possession of the property once the deed is executed. No proof of default by the borrower is needed. Check the type of charge and that you are clear as to all the terms of the loan (including inspecting any collateral agreements between the mortgagor and mortgagee).

Second, check whether there are any other parties with a claim on the property that may interfere with the mortgagee's right to possession and have a right or wish to be joined as a defendant or notice of the proceedings. Two common examples are tenants and spouses of owners. There may be tenants in occupation who were granted tenancies before the property was mortgaged to which the mortgagee's interest is subject as an un-registered interest that may override a registered disposition under the Land Registration Act 2002. The property may be the matrimonial home of a couple where the non-owning spouse has registered a right to occupy under matrimonial legislation (Matrimonial Homes Act 1967 or 1983 or the Family Law Act 1996). Check that the requirement under CPR, r 55.10 to serve notice on the property has been fulfilled. The notice should be addressed to the occupiers notifying them of the possession proceedings, hearing date and the name and address of the claimant, the defendant and the court. Check also that relevant information required by PD 55.4, para 2.5 in respect of such occupiers has been included in the particulars of claim.

Third, what type of mortgage forms the basis of the proceedings? The two main types are capital repayment/instalment mortgages (the mortgagor paying both capital and interest by regular instalments) and interest-only endowment mortgages (the mortgagor paying the interest on the loan and investing sufficient money regularly into a fund to be able to pay off the capital at the end of the period of the mortgage). Ensure you understand the underlying concepts of the type of mortgage in question. Also, check when and how payments (capital, interest, and any other payments) are to be made and that the relevant information required by PD 55.4, para 2.5 about the mortgage is included in the particulars of claim. Check what the alleged arrears are and how they arose. This information should be set out in the schedule of arrears required by PD 55.4, para 2.5(3). Is there any dispute over the arrears?

Fourth, check whether the court's powers under the Administration of Justice Acts 1970 and 1973 or the Consumer Credit Act 1974 may be exercised. Both of these are complicated provisions and the most common one you may encounter is that under the Administration of Justice Acts.

(a) *Administration of Justice Acts 1970 and 1973*   Where the mortgagee under a mortgage of land that includes a dwelling house claims possession (but not foreclosure), the Administration of Justice Acts empower the court to adjourn the case or suspend the possession order if it appears that the mortgagor(s) are 'likely' to be able to pay any 'sums due' under the mortgage or remedy any default consisting of a breach of any obligation under the mortgage within a 'reasonable' period.

The court may impose conditions, for example, of payment, on such adjournment or suspension. In respect of claims for possession for arrears, there are two main things to check:

(i)   What are the 'sums due': this includes the capital, interest, and any other 'further amounts'. Be clear precisely what is included in your case.

(ii) Is the mortgagor 'likely' to be able to pay within a 'reasonable time'? What proposals are there? What is the mortgagor's financial position? What period of time is likely to be 'reasonable' in the circumstances?

(b) *Consumer Credit Act 1974*   The provisions of the Consumer Credit Act 1974 will apply in place of the Administration of Justice Acts where the mortgage is a 'regulated agreement' as defined by the Act. Basically this includes those agreements where an individual is given credit and the agreement is not exempt. Most loans secured on land for the purchase of land, the provision of a dwelling or business premises or repair, improvement, etc, of a dwelling or business premises where the lender has already lent for such purchase or provision, are exempt. This would not catch, for example, a loan to buy a boat secured on the property. Note that it covers both residential and business premises. The particulars of claim should make clear whether or not this Act applies (see in particular PD 55.4, para 2.5(4)). If these provisions do apply, you will need to check:

(i)   that the agreement was 'properly executed' in compliance with the formalities of the Act. These requirements are complex, as are the effects of a failure to comply rendering the agreement 'improperly executed', which include in some circumstances an inability to enforce the agreement;

(ii) that the mortgagee has followed the proper procedure to enforce the agreement by serving a default notice in the prescribed form;

(iii) whether the mortgagor has or should apply for a 'time order' whereby the court may extend the time for payment.

Finally, in dealing with costs, generally the mortgagor will be entitled to costs of the proceedings by virtue of the mortgage agreement, even without a costs order. Where the court does make an order as to costs, for example, for detailed assessment on the standard basis, this will be subject to any term in the mortgage agreement as to costs, which many mortgage deeds contain. The terms of the agreement may entitle the mortgagor to costs that are greater than would be allowed under an assessment on a standard basis and will usually also provide that the costs can be added to the security. Where costs are likely to be an issue, whether acting for the mortgagor or the mortgagee, check whether or not you should be asking the court to deal with costs (eg if acting for the mortgagee do you wish to ask the court to restrict the mortgagor's claim for costs). If so, you need to check both the terms of the agreement and the law, in particular the powers of the court to override the contractual provisions.

32.7 Practical tips on documents and dress in claims for possession from tenants

32.7.1 Documents

1. The court bundle—see **32.1.2.4**.
2. Proof of landlord's title—see **32.2.1**.
3. The tenancy agreement—see **32.2.2**.
4. If forfeiting the lease—copy of s 146 notice (if served—see **32.2.5.1(b)**).
5. If statutory tenancy protected by:

    Housing Act 1985—copy of s 83 notice—see **32.4.2.1**;

    Housing Act 1988—copy of s 20 notice if relevant—see **32.4.2.2(a)**;

    —copy of s 8 notice—see **32.4.2.2(b)**;

    Rent Act 1977—copy of notice to quit (if needed)—see **32.4.2.3**.

6. If ground is rent arrears—see **32.4.3.1**:

    Schedule of arrears;

    Notice by landlord under s 48 LTA 1987—if needed.

7. If ground is that landlord requires premises—see **32.4.3.5**:

    Copy of notice served—if needed.

8. If commercial tenancy—see **32.5**:

    Copies of relevant notices served under LTA 1954.

9. Costs—schedule in Form N260.

32.7.2 Dress

Check with the court—practice varies.

If in doubt, take your robes.

Application for a preliminary reference to the European Court of Justice

33.1 References to the European Court of Justice: Article 267 EU

When a matter of European Union (EU) law arises before any court or tribunal, it may be possible to have the proceedings stayed in order that the particular matter be referred to the European Court of Justice (ECJ) for a determination of the relevant point of European law. Article 267 (ex 234) of the EU Treaty establishes the jurisdiction of the ECJ in these matters. In particular, it provides that the ECJ has jurisdiction to give a preliminary ruling concerning the interpretation of the EU Treaties and the validity and interpretation of EU legislation.

Note that jurisdiction is limited to examining EU law and that there is no provision for the ECJ to determine the validity or interpretation of English law (or any other national law). It is common, however, for questions to be referred in which the ECJ is asked whether a particular piece of national legislation is compatible with the EU Treaties or with EU legislation. In such cases, the ECJ usually answers the question by reference to the meaning to be attributed to the relevant EU law. Technically, it is then for the referring national court to apply that meaning to its own national law. The delimitation of jurisdictions in these cases is therefore relatively clear: it is for the ECJ to determine the true meaning and effect of EU law, while it is for the national court to apply that meaning in the context of the proceedings before it. Accordingly, the ECJ is not, in this context, a court of appeal. Rather, Article 267 provides a means of cooperation between the national court and the ECJ to ensure that EU law is properly and effectively applied.

The mere fact that a question of EU law arises does not, of course, mean that the issue should be referred to the ECJ. Every national court is required to interpret and apply EU law in the normal course of events. Generally speaking, it is only where a particular difficulty arises that cannot confidently be solved by the judge that a reference should be considered.

33.2 Which courts can make a reference?

Article 267(2) provides that where a question of EU law is raised before any court or tribunal of a Member State, that court or tribunal may, if it considers that a decision on the point is necessary to enable it to give judgment, request the ECJ for a ruling thereon. The definition of court or tribunal is a question of EU law, so that the classification of the body for the purposes of English law is not directly relevant. The court or tribunal must be a public body exercising official authority and it must have a judicial function. References have been made from the House of Lords (now the Supreme Court), Court of Appeal (Criminal and Civil Divisions), High Court, Crown Court, county court, magistrates' courts, VAT tribunals, Employment Appeal Tribunal, employment tribunals, Social Security Commissioners, and the Special Commissioners for Income Tax. It is arguable that certain professional bodies exercising disciplinary powers may be considered as tribunals. Arbitration tribunals are not competent to make a reference to the ECJ since they are not public bodies and have no connection with the exercise of official authority.

Under the Brussels Convention on jurisdiction and the enforcement of judgments in civil and commercial matters, a reference could only be made from appellate courts. This was therefore limited in the UK to the House of Lords, the Court of Appeal, and the High Court sitting in an appellate capacity. Under the Lisbon Treaty, jurisdiction has expanded.

33.3   Which courts must make a reference?

Article 267(3) provides that where a question of EU law is raised in a case pending before a court or tribunal against whose decisions there is no judicial remedy under national law, that court or tribunal must refer the matter to the ECJ.

In the UK, this was generally limited to the House of Lords, and so now to the Supreme Court. Although it is necessary to obtain leave to appeal to the Supreme Court, the Divisional Court and the Court of Appeal had specifically stated (in relation to the House of Lords) that in the absence of such leave being granted, those courts may not be considered as falling within Article 267(3). Thus, even though the clear intention of Article 267 seems to be that a party has the right to seek a reference at some stage in the appeal procedure even though the relevant court may not deem it necessary to enable it to decide the matter, the appeals procedure involving the Supreme Court may frustrate that. It is not possible to go back to the Court of Appeal after the Supreme Court has refused permission and then argue that the Court of Appeal has become the court to which Article 267(3) refers. See further **33.5**.

Where the question at issue involves the validity of EU legislation (such as a regulation or directive) it is not possible for the national court to decide that the legislation is indeed invalid, no matter how strong the arguments to that effect. The court has two possibilities open to it. It may decide, having regard to the arguments, that the legislation is valid and continue the proceedings on that basis. Alternatively, if it is of the opinion that the legislation is invalid (or that there is a strong argument to that effect), it must refer the matter to the ECJ, since only the ECJ has competence to declare EU legislation invalid. See, for example, *R (International Air Transport Association and European Low Fares Airline Association) v UK Department of Transport* (C-344/04), judgment of 10 January 2006 (The Times, 16 January 2006).

33.4   In what circumstances is a reference to be made?

Generally, a reference is only to be made if an answer is necessary to enable the court to give judgment. Accordingly, it is common practice for English courts to seek to decide a claim on the basis of English law issues that do not raise questions of EU law.

The Court of Appeal has laid down guidelines for the exercise of the discretion to refer (contained now in Article 267(2)) in rather general terms. If the facts have been found and the EU law issue is critical to the court's final decision, the appropriate course is ordinarily to refer the issue to the ECJ unless the national court can with complete confidence resolve the issue itself. In considering whether it can with complete confidence resolve the issue itself the national court must be fully mindful of the differences between national and EU legislation, of the pitfalls that face a national court venturing into what may be an unfamiliar field, of the need for uniform interpretation throughout the European Union, and the great advantages enjoyed by the ECJ in construing EU legislation. Other factors that might be considered are the delay and costs involved, the difficulty of the point of law, and the presence of similar actions before the ECJ.

A lower court might also be mindful of the fact that its decision may be appealed with a reference being sought at the appeal stage. However, if the parties have made clear that they will seek a reference at each stage, it might be more sensible to impress on the judge in the lowest court that it would save time and costs if he or she were to refer the matter immediately.

33.5   Exceptions to the requirement to refer under Article 267(3)

There are three exceptions to the general requirement to make a reference under Article 267(3) for a court from whose decisions there is no judicial remedy. First, no reference is necessary if the question raised is materially identical to a previous question already referred to the ECJ. Second, a decision for interim measures that depends on a question of EU law need not be the subject of a reference even if it is final, as long as this does not bind the court that hears the substantive action and provided that either party can ensure that proceedings in the main action are actually instituted.

Third, the national court need not make a reference if the matter is *acte clair*. The extent of this exception is not wholly clear and there has been some suggestion in recent years that it should be relaxed. However, in general it means that a reference is unnecessary where the answer is so obvious as to leave no scope for any reasonable doubt as to the manner in which the question raised is to be resolved. Before it comes to that conclusion, the court must be convinced that the matter is equally obvious to the courts of the other Member States and to the ECJ. This must involve consideration of the different language versions of the particular EU legislation. Even where the different language versions are entirely in accord with one another, it must be borne in mind that EU law uses terminology that is peculiar to it and that legal concepts do not necessarily have the same meaning in EU law and in the laws of the various Member States. Finally, every provision of EU law must be placed in its context and interpreted in the light of the provisions of EU law as a whole, regard being had to the objectives of EU law and to its state of evolution at the date on which the provision in question had to be applied.

33.6   It is the court (not the parties) that makes the reference

The decision of whether or not to make a reference is solely for the court. If the parties suggest that a reference is desirable, it is likely that the judge will agree. However, it is quite common for one party to oppose the reference and for the other to be in favour. In those circumstances, the party seeking the reference must make representations to the judge seeking to convince him or her to take this action. It is, however, not unknown for a judge to decide of his or her own motion (and even against the wishes of the parties) that a reference should be made. In those circumstances, this is solely a matter for the discretion of the judge and the parties (subject to a right of appeal) cannot resist the decision to refer.

33.7 At what stage in the proceedings should the reference be made?

A party that is seeking to have a matter referred to the ECJ should make this plain to the judge at the earliest opportunity. Apart from courtesy, it means that the judge can possibly cut the time in the national court considerably.

Before the reference is made, it is necessary for the facts to be established although the relevant facts may, of course, be agreed between the parties. In most civil matters this should not pose too much of a problem. A statement of agreed facts can then be drawn up and handed to the judge.

Criminal cases pose special problems, since once the jury is sworn in it is difficult, from a practical point of view, to make a reference to the ECJ with the consequential delay of up to two years before the jury is called on to decide the factual issue. On the one hand, the defendant may wish to argue that, even if the facts alleged against him or her are proven, there will still be no offence committed since EU law precludes a prosecution in those circumstances. This may be either on the basis that the relevant English law conflicts with EU law or that, for instance, a regulation that is central to the prosecution is invalid. In that case, the facts may be deemed to be agreed solely for the purpose of the reference. It is preferable for the question of EU law to be determined at that stage, with a reference if necessary, before the issue is put to a jury. Accordingly, the issue of EU law should be raised by means of a motion to quash the indictment before the jury is chosen. This approach has the added advantage that the defendant, particularly if he or she is of previous good character, does not suffer the ignominy of being found guilty at first instance only to be vindicated on appeal. On the other hand, once the trial has started and the jury is in place, the House of Lords has previously said that it can scarcely be a proper exercise of the court's discretion to make a reference. Instead the trial must proceed, leaving the possibility of a reference for the appellate court.

There are no hard-and-fast rules about making submissions on the point of EU law in the national court prior to the reference being made. Clearly, if the parties have agreed that a reference is desirable, counsel should immediately suggest this course of action to the judge. However, since the reference is solely at the discretion of the judge (except in the case of courts of last instance) it may well be that the judge will require argument on the point before he or she is satisfied that a reference is appropriate. From the point of view of the parties, this may well also be desirable since it gives an idea to each side as to the submission that will be made before the ECJ. (Having said that, the parties are not limited to repeating in the ECJ only those arguments put to the national court.)

33.8 Procedure for making the reference

Much of the procedure for making the reference to the ECJ is carried on behind the scenes rather than in open court. References from the High Court and Court of Appeal are now governed by CPR, Part 68. Similar rules apply to criminal proceedings (see Criminal Procedure Rules 2013, Part 75). See further Article 267 TFEU as incorporated by s 2(1) of the European Communities Act 1972 (see, eg, *Stone's Justices' Manual 2013* at 1–1430).

Under CPR, Part 68, a request for a ruling by the ECJ must be set out in a schedule to the court's order. PD 68 states that the order for reference itself should 'as clearly and succinctly as possible' identify the question(s) for the ECJ. In a schedule to the order, the court should set down:

- the full name of the referring court;
- the identities of the parties;
- a summary of the nature and history of the proceedings;
- the salient facts, stating clearly whether these are proved, admitted or assumed;
- the relevant national legal rules;
- the parties' contentions on the questions;
- an explanation of why a ruling by the ECJ is sought;
- the identity of those provisions of EU law on which the ruling is sought.

33.9 Costs and public funding

Costs will usually be reserved until the reference has returned from the ECJ. Usually costs will follow the event. Public funding is generally extended to cover the cost of proceedings before the ECJ.

33.10 Proceedings before the European Court of Justice

The proceedings before the ECJ fall into separate parts, only two of which involve the lawyers for the parties. First, the parties submit their written observations. Second, the parties subsequently make an oral presentation at the ECJ in Luxembourg. Third, the Advocate General gives his or her Opinion and, finally, the ECJ gives its decision. Lawyers are directly involved only in the first two stages. There is no need for lawyers or the parties to be present at the ECJ either when the Advocate General's Opinion is given or when the judgment is handed down.

Written observations are the most important part of the proceedings. These should be clear and concise. There is, however, no prescribed format for written observations and each counsel has his or her own style. Unlike English court proceedings, it is inadvisable to recite large chunks of case law. Rather, the precise dictum relied upon should be set out, with other references to the cases being made in footnotes. It is quite permissible for reference to be made to academic articles or books in order to substantiate arguments. As a general rule, written observations should not be overly long, although this depends on the complexity of the case. Twenty pages of argument should usually be quite enough! Another unusual aspect of the written stage is that all parties submit their observations at the same time rather than one after the other. Accordingly, there is no opportunity at this stage to know precisely what is being argued by the other side. Needless to say, this may call for some ingenuity since counsel then have to put themselves in the position of second-guessing the other side. It is also possible for Member States to intervene in the proceedings; they need not show any direct interest.

Guidance notes are given by the ECJ to all counsel prior to the oral hearing. This is a short hearing with counsel for each side having a maximum of 30 minutes. It is not an opportunity to put the entire case. Instead, the essence of the argument should be quickly put, concentrating on the strongest points. It is also the only opportunity counsel has for rebutting the arguments put by the other parties. Questions may be asked by the judges, although sometimes no questions are asked.

Some months later the Opinion will be given followed some months after that by the judgment. In all, the time between reference and judgment is usually about 18 months.

Applying for costs in a civil case

34.1 The principal costs orders

This chapter deals with making an application for an order for costs. The following are the principal costs orders:

- claimant's costs;
- defendant's costs;
- costs in the case/application;
- claimant's costs in the case/application;
- defendant's costs in the case/application;
- costs management order;
- costs thrown away;
- costs of and caused by;
- 'Bullock' order;
- 'Sanderson' order;
- costs reserved;
- no order for costs, ie each party is to bear its own costs.

For an explanation of the various orders see the *Civil Litigation* manual, **chapter 36** and CPR, Part 44, PD. Costs often turn out to be the most significant part of a case. The CPR costs regime seeks to relate the level of costs payable to the value of the dispute, in an effort to avoid the position in which the parties spend many thousands of pounds on costs of the litigation with the result that the costs incurred are out of all proportion to the value of the claim. It also seeks to provide a more balanced approach to defining the 'winner' and 'loser' to avoid the situation where a party who has been largely unsuccessful recovers all of his costs on the basis that he has succeeded on something. The CPR costs regime makes provision for the summary assessment and speedy payment of costs incurred in connection with fast track trials and other hearings, whether applications or disposal hearings, listed for one day or less. What might be termed a 'pay as you go' approach was intended to bring home to the parties and their advisers that there are costs consequences in making applications to the court. The requirement for your client to write out a cheque for his opponent's costs at an early stage concentrates minds on the costs that are being incurred in the litigation as it proceeds instead of when the big bill arrives at the end of it. This is even more apparent with the new introduction of **costs budgeting** from 1 April 2013. From an adviser's point of view it concentrates the mind on dealing with the case in a way that avoids applications to the court. In practical terms, losing an application can bring about a reappraisal of a party's position and fundamental change of attitude to the litigation as a whole. For example, a party who applies for summary judgment and fails will begin to wonder whether things really are as straightforward as he had first thought and will have to pay his opponent's costs of the application at the same time.

The CPR costs regime also allows the parties to seek, and the court to order, a payment on account of costs where a detailed assessment of the costs has been ordered. A payment on account will allow a party who has obtained a favourable costs order to recoup some of the money already spent on the litigation without waiting for the detailed assessment to be concluded many months later. It also helps to set a benchmark for the amount of the costs that might be awarded in a detailed assessment. If the paying party cannot pay a payment on account that the court has ordered, the receiving party may save himself or herself further wasted costs on concluding a detailed assessment before he or she discovers that he or she is unlikely to see any of the money.

In January 2010, the Ministry of Justice published a 'Review of Civil Litigation Costs' by Sir Rupert Jackson. Many of the recommendations in the review found their way into the Legal Aid, Sentencing and Punishment of Offenders Act 2012 which received Royal Assent on 1 May 2012. Part 2 ('Litigation funding and costs') implemented some of the Jackson recommendations regarding conditional fee agreements (CFAs), damages-based agreements (DBAs), and after the event insurance, payment of an additional amount to a claimant under CPR, r 36, and rules against referral fees. The main provisions of this wide package of reforms came into effect on 1 April 2013. They constitute what are colloquially known as 'the Jackson reforms' and are far reaching in their effect on the costs landscape. They go to the very heart of civil procedure, even amending the overriding objective at CPR, r 1.1(1) with the addition of the requirement that cases are not only to be dealt with justly, but also at 'proportionate cost'. Although the Jackson reforms will be touched on as necessary in this chapter, their more detailed outworking goes beyond the remit of this advocacy manual and as such, a specialist practitioner text on costs should be consulted for any more detailed issues arising.

34.2   How does the court decide what order to make?

The court's order will be influenced by the submissions the parties make as to what order should be made in all the circumstances of the case. Those submissions should be shaped by the desired outcome that is best suited to your client's needs given the circumstances of the case. Generally speaking, your client's needs will be financial. If an order for costs is made in your client's favour, your client will want to recoup as much as he has had to spend on his own lawyers (including you) as quickly as possible. If your solicitor client has conducted the case on credit terms, he too will want to see money flowing in his direction sooner rather than later. If your client has a costs order made against him, he will usually want to pay as little as possible as slowly as possible. For the 'pay later loser', summary costs assessments are an anathema. If your opponent is a 'pay later loser', a substantial summary costs order on an interim application may help to weaken his resolve to see the litigation through to the end of the trial. It may also weaken the resolve of those who support the conduct of the litigation through funding arrangements or legal expenses insurance. It may also help to drain him of money needed to pay his lawyers to see the matter through to the end of the trial.

Your submissions on an application for costs should also be shaped by the way in which the court reaches its decision about the right order to make. You need to know how the court reaches its decision. If you understand the way in which the decision will be made, you can apply your advocacy skills to directing the way in which the court should reach the decision best suited to your client's needs.

The court exercises a discretion in awarding costs for or against a party to the litigation. The primary rule of law is that the order made must be a just one in all the circumstances of the case. There are guidelines that govern the exercise of the court's discretion. The most important guideline is that costs generally follow the event, ie the loser will ordinarily be ordered to pay the winner's costs (see CPR, r 44.2(2)(a)). In most simple applications it is clear who is the winner and who is the loser. At trial, if judgment is given in the claimant's favour, generally the claimant will be considered the winner and vice versa. Regrettably it is not always as simple as that, for the claimant may recover relief that is either a small proportion of that which he set out to recover at the beginning of the action or the trial, or a sum that is less than the defendant offered as a Part 36 offer. If the claim relates to relief that cannot be measured in money terms, 'win' or 'lose' may be measured by reference to whether the claimant has obtained some or all of the relief he sought in the claim or whether the relief obtained by the claimant is more or less advantageous that the defendant was prepared to concede.

In deciding what order to make as to costs, the court will have regard to all the circumstances of the case. It may make different orders in respect of different parts of the case, whether defined in time or in issues, to ensure that the order made is a just order in all the circumstances of the case—see CPR, r 44.2(6). The principles to be applied are set out in CPR, r 44.2(2)–(5) together with a list of the principal matters that the court will consider in the exercise of its discretion. The list is not a comprehensive list. The Court of Appeal set out the basic principles governing the exercise of the court's discretion in *Johnsey v Secretary of State for the Environment* [2001] EWCA Civ 535. The matters set out in CPR, Part 44, r 2 together with the new overriding objectives and the principle of proportionality set the agenda for the arguments that might be raised in an application for a costs order. Given that the court has a discretion to exercise, anything is possible provided the court can be persuaded that the order suggested is fair and reasonable in all the circumstances of the case in question. The range of orders that can be described as fair and reasonable in any one case can be wide depending on the circumstances of the case. No two cases are the same and no two judges are the same. The same case might produce a different order depending on the judge that hears it. The arguments that can be raised in any given case are dependent on the outcome of the case, how the case has been conducted both before and after the commencement of the proceedings, the conduct of the hearing or trial and the practical result achieved. The court will be unwilling to order costs to be paid to a party whose conduct has caused the costs to be unnecessarily incurred (within CPR, r.44.2(5)). A failure to comply with CPR will generally result in an order for costs against the defaulting party. Unreasonable conduct by a party, for example, failing to accept a reasonable settlement proposal made without prejudice save as to costs, or failing to agree an order the court was highly likely to make, will almost certainly result in an adverse costs order against that party whether in terms of an order to pay the other party's costs or an order depriving that party of costs that would otherwise have been recovered.

Where a party succeeds on some issues but fails on others the court may make an order that reflects both the success and the failure. The order may be issue based or it may simply be an award of a proportion of the party's costs. The nature of the order may be heavily influenced by the relative success or failure whether in terms of the final outcome or the way in which disputed issues of fact are resolved for or against the parties. For example, in a five-day trial, if four days were devoted to an issue on which the claimant lost and one day to an issue on which the claimant won, the court might simply order the claimant to pay the defendant's costs of issue 1 and order the defendant to pay the claimant's costs of issue 2. Where there has been partial success the court should seek to make an order for the payment of a percentage of the winner's costs rather than an issue-based order (see *English v Emery Rheinbold and Strick Ltd* [2002] 1WLR 2409 and CPR, r 44.2(6)). This can give rise to considerable difficulty. In the example considered above the claimant's success on issue 2 may result in an award of damages in the same amount as would be awarded if successful on issue 1. In real terms one might well consider the claimant had won the war in obtaining damages but lost a substantial battle along the way. One might also consider that the defendant had scored a substantial victory on the first issue given the proportion of the total costs incurred devoted to the resolution of the issue on which the defendant succeeded. A detailed assessment on an issue basis is likely to result in the costs payable to the defendant by the claimant outweighing those payable by the defendant to the claimant in a case where the claimant was obliged to argue both issues, because the defendant failed to agree to pay the claimant the sum the court awarded in damages. One must also bear in mind that a percentage apportionment should not simply reflect the fact that the claimant has succeeded in part but must also reflect the fact that the defendant too succeeded in part, with the consequence that an issue-based approach would see money in costs flowing from the claimant to the defendant to set off against money flowing from the defendant to the claimant. In the example considered above it is not possible to state definitively what the right order is. There will be a range of orders each of which will differ from the others and all of which are unappealable. An order for the defendant to pay the claimant's costs of the claim would be a harsh order from the defendant's point of view but unlikely to be altered on appeal. Equally an order for the defendant to pay as little as 60% of the claimant's costs of the claim would be harsh on the claimant but unlikely to be altered on appeal. Where the apportionment might fall within that band may be determined by the extent to which the factual issues raised in issue 1 were resolved in favour of the claimant.

Proportionality also has an important role to play. The court must ensure that the costs awarded are proportionate to the value of the claim whether in monetary terms or importance to the parties. Arguments regarding proportionality would do well to also have regard to the new overriding objective which expressly references the fact that cases need to be conducted at proportionate cost. Proportionality arguments tend to be taken by the paying party to reduce the amount of costs payable, particularly where there is a summary assessment.

Given these potential complexities, it is of crucial importance for an advocate to devote sufficient preparation time, research and thought to creating a discrete legal argument on costs when acting in cases of greater complexity. Submissions relating to costs at the end of a long trial may well take up hours (or more) of the court's time. In such cases, you would be well advised to consider preparing a skeleton argument relating to costs issues, and to research and apply relevant authorities regarding the application of the court's discretion. Endeavour to consult good practitioner texts such as *Cook on Costs* for up-to-date guidance and commentary on costs procedure. Bear in mind that it will not be an unusual situation to find that the quantum of the costs far outweighs the value of the claim itself, meaning that the client might ultimately end up being more concerned with the outcome of the costs argument than the substantive legal case. Such is the unfortunately costly nature of litigation that triggers the necessity for due preparation of costs arguments. The case of *Carver v BAA plc* [2008] EWCA Civ 412 presents a particularly stark example of this, where a claim ultimately worth £4,686.26 (inclusive of interest) generated claimant's costs alone of around £80,000 when factoring in a success fee. It is little wonder that Ward LJ noted that the litigation of such cases 'fills one with despair'.

You should also be aware that very different costs principles will apply in differing specialist jurisdictions and in particular types of claim. For example costs in family proceedings are regulated by the Family Procedure Rules 2012, whereas procedure in the Employment Tribunal dictates that costs orders are certainly the exception rather than the norm. Detailed guidance relating to costs in such proceedings falls outside the remit of this manual and as such a more specialist text should be consulted.

34.3   Part 36 offers to settle

A Part 36 offer can turn a successful party into an unsuccessful party so far as costs orders are concerned. Before 6 April 2007, there used to be a more complex provision for defendants, requiring them to make a payment into court in order for their Part 36 offer to trigger the requisite costs consequences. However, the Civil Procedure (Amendment No 3) Rules 2006 introduced a new CPR, Part 36, which significantly simplified the system to what it is today.

Rule 36.2 sets out the general form and content of a Part 36 offer, which must be made in writing, state on its face that it is intended to have the consequences of a Part 36 offer, specify a period of not less than 21 days within which the defendant will be liable for the claimant's costs, state whether it relates to the whole or part of the claim and state whether it takes into account any counterclaim. A party can obviously make an offer to settle in any other form if it so wishes, but this will preclude the offer from triggering the prescribed consequences set out in Part 36. If this is the case, you will be more likely to construct your costs argument under general r 44.2(4)(c) factors rather than the Part 36 regime.

The consequences of acceptance of a Part 36 offer (r 36.10) and costs consequences following judgment (r 36.14) largely flow automatically without the need for the application of judicial discretion or detailed legal argument from an advocate. However, there has been a great deal of legal argument around the construction and interpretation of the phrase 'more advantageous' in r 36.14(1)(a), most notably in *Carver v BAA plc* [2008] EWCA Civ 412 and *Gibbon v Manchester CC: LG Blower Specialist Bricklayer Ltd v Reeves* [2010] EWCA Civ 726, [2010] All ER (D) 218. To this end, a new r 36.14(1)(A) was introduced on 1 October 2011, clarifying that 'for the purposes of paragraph (1), in relation to any money claim or money element of a claim, "more advantageous" means better in money terms by any amount, however small, and "at least as advantageous" shall be construed accordingly.' This almost certainly now precludes any scope for arguing any interpretative points in relation to what is or is not 'more advantageous' for the advocate, at least for monetary cases.

Further, the Jackson reforms have amended Part 36 further so that there is now an additional amount to be paid by a defendant who does not accept a claimant's offer to settle where the court gives judgment for the claimant that is at least as advantageous as an offer the claimant made to settle the claim. It is applicable to offers made after 31 March 2013. This additional sanction is set out in CPR, r.36.14(3)(d) and is calculated as 10% of damages where damages are in issue, and 10% of costs for non-damages claims. In mixed (damages and non-damages) claims, the sanction will be calculated as 10% of the damages element of the claim but note that the sanction is tapered for claims over £500,000 up to £1 million so that the maximum sanction is around £75,000 (CPR, r 36.14(3)(d)).

Accordingly, where there is an effective Part 36 offer the court should make the orders that flow from those events unless it is unjust to do so. The burden of persuading the court that it is unjust to do so falls on the party making that assertion. If you are representing the party that should receive the benefit of the orders that the court should make, you should not indulge in detailed submissions about whether it is unjust to make those orders. You should not do much more than bring the court's powers to the judge's attention and make a bald assertion that there is nothing in the circumstances of the case that makes it unjust to make the order that CPR, Part 36 directs the court to make. You should leave your opponent to raise the issue in detail if he wants to and deal with it in reply to your opponent's submissions.

34.4 Summary or detailed assessment

When you receive your brief you will need to decide whether the court is likely to conduct a summary assessment of the costs at the end of the hearing. Note that for most multi-track cases issued after 31 March 2013, the assessment of costs will flow from the new 'costs budgeting' procedure pursuant to CPR, rr 3.12–3.18, the detail of which is considered further at **34.13**. In non-costs-budgeted cases, if the hearing is listed for a day or less, the court will summarily assess the costs unless there is a good reason not to do so. A good reason not to do so is where the effect of requiring an impecunious party to pay there and then may well stifle what might turn out to be a good claim at trial. Another good reason is that something in the funding arrangement between the receiving party and his solicitor breaches the indemnity principle or renders the funding arrangement unenforceable. A good reason often given by a busy district judge is that the statement of costs appears to claim too much in amount for too much work with insufficient time to go through the details of the statement of costs in order to adequately deal with the amount payable on a summary basis. If the assessment of the costs is likely to be difficult or complicated, the court should order a detailed assessment. The court will not summarily assess the costs payable if:

(a) you do not intend to apply for an order for costs against your opponent at the conclusion of the hearing. For example, case management hearings often do not give rise to an application for costs unless the hearing has been occasioned by the default of one of the parties. In those circumstances the court will, unless there is a good reason not to, order the costs of the hearing to be costs in the case; or

(b) your lay client's costs of the litigation are publicly funded by the Legal Services Commission (see CPR, Part 44, PD para 9.8); or

(c) your lay client is a child or a protected party, unless your instructing solicitor has waived any right to seek further costs from the lay client over and above that which the court might summarily assess (see CPR, Part 44, PD para 9.9).

Please note that in both instances if you lose the application the court will summarily assess the costs payable by your client if a costs order is made in favour of your opponent. As a consequence your preparation for the hearing needs to cover the arguments you will seek to advance against a summary assessment of the costs payable and on quantification of the amount payable in the event that a costs order is made against your client. CPR, r 44.4 sets out the factors the court will take into account in deciding the amount payable. The list of factors provides a framework for your submissions. You will also obtain some assistance from the *Guide to the Summary Assessment of Costs* published by the Supreme Court Costs Office, freely available on the justice.gov.uk website. Costs estimates provided in the parties' allocation questionnaires can prove to be a useful tool to reduce the costs of the action sought on a summary assessment. For some reason the final bill always seems to be more than estimated at the outset and it is often difficult to explain why it was necessary to run up more in costs than originally estimated.

If you intend to seek an order for your opponent to pay the costs of a hearing where a summary assessment is likely, your solicitors must provide a statement of costs setting out the costs incurred in connection with the hearing. There is a practice form for the statement of costs (N260). The form itself need not be used so long as the statement, in whatever form it is produced, contains the required information. The statement of costs must be served on your opponent *and* filed with the court not less than 24 hours before the hearing. In any event, you should always ensure you have sufficient copies with you to hand both to the judge and to your opponent at court, given the possibility that the form has not found its way into the court file. You need to check that the statement contains the right information, has the right certificate as to the amount the party is liable to pay his or her solicitor and has been served in time. If this has not been done, you face the risk that the court may simply decide to make no order for costs or to assess the costs summarily in the sum of £0. The court has a discretion to exercise: it follows that it must exercise its discretion judicially and that it is just in the circumstances of the case to make such an order. The court is unlikely to do so if there is a good reason for the failure to comply with the requirements or if the failure to comply has not resulted in any injustice to your opponent. If this issue is likely to arise, you need to prepare the arguments you will put forward before the hearing starts, not at the end of the hearing when you will have little or no time to think about it.

If a summary assessment is to be made, you will need to make sure you are properly briefed by your instructing solicitor about the time spent in working on the application (or the case if it is a final hearing), the grade of fee earner chosen to undertake the work and the rates at which the time has been charged. You will not help your lay client or your instructing solicitor if you cannot provide any explanation beyond what appears in the statement of costs in the event that one or more of the items listed in the statement of costs is challenged by your opponent. You may also face the ignominious position of arguing that your own brief fee is a reasonable one in all the circumstances and that your opponent's is not. You also need some instructions from your solicitor about your opponent's statement of costs: if you lose the application, the argument will be about whether your opponent's costs are reasonable. You need to be in a position to say more than 'Having regard to the matters set out in CPR, r 44.4 the costs sought are ridiculous and out of all proportion to the costs one would expect to see in an application such as this.' You need to be able to go on and say 'because' and set out a reasoned argument. For example 'the time apparently devoted to reading the documents is excessive given that the relevant documents occupy no more than 20 pages and the claimant's solicitors were able to read them in one hour rather than the three hours claimed in the defendant's statement of costs'. As to the latter point some circumspection is required. The party making an interim application will generally have a little more to do in preparation than the party responding to it.

It may be that both sides' statements of costs seem reasonable to you. That does not mean they will seem reasonable to the court. You should *always* be in a position to justify the amount you seek in costs if asked to do so.

If the case is one in which the court is not likely to make a summary assessment of the costs incurred, you will not have to deal with the nitty-gritty of how much has to be paid at the end of the hearing. You still have to deal with the costs order that the court might make.

34.5   Preparation

You will probably not have time to prepare your submissions after judgment has been given. You must therefore prepare your submissions on costs before the hearing. You will not know whether you have won or lost until judgment is given. You must therefore prepare submissions to cater for either event. In your preparation you must consider how you would argue the submissions on costs if you were acting for the other side. If you do this, it will help to concentrate your mind on the submissions you need to make to answer what the other side may have to say against you. For weightier cases, this may well entail the preparation of a skeleton argument on costs along with a separate bundle of authorities to argue from.

Make a note of exactly what wording you wish the court to use in making its order for costs. If the order is precise, ie the words used express exactly what the order is to mean, it avoids the risk of someone seeking to place a different interpretation on the order at a later date, for example, at a detailed assessment hearing. It is highly unlikely that anyone who was present when the order was made will be in attendance when the detailed assessment takes place with the consequence that the costs judge will be guided solely by the words in which the order is expressed.

34.6   Making the application

34.6.1   When should the application be made?

The application should be made after the pronouncement of the judgment or order that the court proposes to make. An application for costs should not form part of your closing submissions or final speech. Accordingly you must make sure that you remember to make your costs submissions amidst the adrenaline rush of receiving judgment. In a minor case or application, it is entirely possible that the judge will simply be in a hurry to hear the next listed matter and, as such, it is incumbent on the advocate to ensure proper time and consideration is given to any costs issues arising.

34.6.2   Who should address the court first?

As costs generally follow the event the successful party should address the court first as the party applying for a costs order. The usual order of speeches is application by successful party, response by unsuccessful party, final comments in reply by successful party. If your opponent is speaking, *do not* interject or interrupt: wait until it is your turn. Make a note of the point made that you dispute. If you draw a margin down the side of the page in your notebook, you can note your opponent's point on one side and your response to it on the other. It is very tempting to try to puncture your opponent's balloon by a well-timed and pithy interjection that may put your opponent off the train of his submissions. If the temptation becomes irresistible remember that your opponent is likely to do the same to you. If you are going to do this you should make sure that it is a 'killer' comment and not one that will simply result in a riposte from your opponent. You will simply end up with something approaching a slanging match that will be difficult for the court to follow and your point will be lost in the wash. Do not assume that the court will ask you to respond to your opponent's submissions. When your turn comes, stand up and start to make your submissions in response. If the court does not want to hear from you the court will tell you.

In many cases the court will invite counsel for the successful party to state what order for costs is sought and then turn to counsel for the unsuccessful party to ask whether there is any reason why the order sought should not be made. You may also find that in cases where there is likely to be little dispute about what order the court should make, the court may simply state what order it proposes to make and ask whether there are any objections. If the court does not ask for objections but you have some, you have the burden of explaining that the order suggested should not be made, set out the order that should be made and explain your reasons for the order you suggest should be made. In giving your reasons you must also explain why the order put forward by the court should not be made. In these situations the normal order of speeches can get somewhat muddled. If you are the unsuccessful party you might allow your opponent the opportunity to speak first but if you do not accept the suggested order is right, you should seize the initiative and make sure your submissions form the first substantial speech the court hears. You want to try to deflect the court from following the course it has suggested before your opponent has had an opportunity to buttress the court's initial view with his or her submissions. If your opponent is saying little or nothing beyond assenting to the order suggested, your submissions will be the first substantial speech with the consequence that you are likely to have the final word after your opponent has responded to your submissions—assuming of course that your submissions weigh sufficiently with the court for it to call on your opponent to respond to them.

In some cases it will not be clear which of the parties has been successful. In that event the party that goes first is the party that made the application that the court has heard. If it is a trial the claimant goes first.

You may well find that the court will ask one or other of you what order for costs should be made. In that event, the order of speeches will be determined by the court. If the court wants to hear from the unsuccessful party first the successful party will have to wait until the submissions made on behalf of the unsuccessful party have been completed. Notwithstanding the order of speeches set out above, most courts will allow the parties a full opportunity to respond to points that have been made even if it means allowing you to speak three or four times rather than once or twice. That does not mean that your submissions can be delivered in instalments.

34.6.3   Making the application

If you are counsel for the successful party you should state precisely what order for costs you want the court to make. The order requested should be the most favourable that you can *realistically* invite the court to make. You should then go on to set out the reasons why the court should make the order you have just set out. You will often be well advised to have a fall-back position in the event that the judge is not minded to grant a costs order in accordance with your primary submission. Most courts will want to know what you want and why you want it, not the other way round. If the order you want is unusual or the factual basis is complicated, it may be better to introduce the application by giving a brief résumé of the factual matters that the court should have in mind, before stating precisely what order you seek. Then explain the reasons that justify making the order you have just stated at greater length, referring again to the factual matters that support your argument. By so doing you can steer the court towards thinking about the matters you consider highly relevant from the outset, and then reiterate those matters in your reasons. If you adopt this approach, you must be careful to ensure that the court knows at an early stage what order you want the court to make, otherwise your submissions will be made in something of a vacuum and not in the context of the order you want the court to make.

In structuring your application you should bear in mind that there are four principal questions to be considered. The first is what order should be made in principle, ie which of the orders listed earlier is the right order to make. The second is whether the amount payable should be determined on a standard or an indemnity basis. The third is the means by which the amount payable should be determined, ie summary assessment or detailed assessment. The fourth is the time by which the costs must be paid by the paying party. If there is an effective Part 36 offer, it will have an impact on the first and second questions. If the case is one in which you will be inviting the court to make a summary assessment of the costs payable, it will be convenient to deal with the first and second questions first and then deal with the question of quantifying the amount payable and time by which it must be paid after the court has decided which party is to be the paying party and which party is to be the receiving party. If you are making the application, at the outset you should state that you propose to deal with matters in that way subject to any view the court may have. If you will be inviting the court to order a detailed assessment, all three questions can be canvassed in one instalment and question 4 will be irrelevant.

In a simple case your application may amount to saying little more than the following:

> On the question of costs I invite your Honour to order the defendant to pay the claimant's costs of the claim such costs to be determined, if not agreed, by a detailed assessment on the standard basis. In the light of the judgment given in the full amount of the claimant's claim the claimant's claim has clearly succeeded. In the circumstances there is no reason why the court should not make an order for the defendant to pay the claimant's costs in accordance with the general rule set out in CPR, Part 44, r 2, paragraph (2).

In the example considered earlier, with a five-day trial and two issues you may want to say a little more given that the defendant is likely to suggest that the case is one in which the court should depart from the general rule given the defendant's success on issue 1. You should not argue in full all the points that you think you can make in answer to the defendant's likely argument, because you want to hear how the defendant puts his or her submissions before you respond to them in your final speech in reply to those submissions. In that way your submissions can be tailored to meet the argument the defendant actually raises rather than the argument you think he or she might be about to raise—the two might not be the same! The most important point for your side is that the defendant forced you to argue the whole of the case by not offering to settle or compromise on the issue on which the claimant won, so you might seek to put down a marker for that along the lines of:

> The defendant has fought the claimant's claim vigorously but with no practical benefit given the judgment given by your Honour for the full amount of the claimant's claim. The claimant was obliged to pursue his claim to trial on both issues in the case when the defendant could, and should in the light of your Honour's judgment, have conceded issue 2 and settled the claimant's claim long ago.

If the claimant made a Part 36 offer to settle at less than the sum awarded by the court, you will have to introduce the making of the offer and the consequences that flow from it. One might do so as follows:

> The claimant made a Part 36 offer on 1st February 2014 in the sum of £20,000 after witness statements had been exchanged and at a time when the claimant's position in the case was fully

known to the defendant. The time for acceptance of the claimant's Part 36 offer expired on 21st February 2014. Your Honour has given judgment against the defendant in the sum of £25,000. In the circumstances your Honour has a discretion pursuant to CPR, Part 36.14(3)(a) to order the defendant to pay interest at a rate not exceeding 10% above base rate from 21st February 2014 and a discretion to order the claimant's costs to be assessed on an indemnity basis from 21st February onwards and to order the defendant to pay interest on those costs at a rate not exceeding 10% above base rate. There is further a presumption under CPR, Part 36.14(3)(d) that your Honour should make an award of an additional amount of 10% of the amount awarded, in this case amounting to £2,500. Paragraph (3) directs the court to make those orders unless it considers it unjust to do so. There is nothing in the circumstances of the case that makes it unjust to do so and, in the light of your Honour's judgment, the defendant clearly should have accepted the claimant's Part 36 offer in February 2014. Base rate is currently 0.5% pa. In the circumstances I invite your Honour to order that the defendant pay the claimant additional interest pursuant to CPR, Part 36.14(3)(a) at the rate of 10.5% pa from 21st February 2014 along with the additional sum of £2,500. Interest on the damages awarded from 21st February 2014 until today amounts to the sum of £xxx. I also invite your Honour to order that the claimant's costs be determined by a detailed assessment on the standard basis to 21st February 2014 and on an indemnity basis thereafter and to order the defendant to pay interest at the rate of 10.5% per annum from today on the claimant's costs incurred after 21st February 2014.

You can then move on to deal with any interim payment on account of the costs that will become payable after the detailed assessment as follows:

I invite your Honour to make an order for the payment of a sum on account of the costs payable to the claimant pursuant to CPR, Part 44.2, paragraph (8). In this case the claimant has incurred solicitors' costs of approximately £10,000, and disbursements including court fees, counsels' fees and expert witnesses' fees of approximately £7,500. The claimant's costs total in round figures £17,500 inclusive of VAT. The court should ordinarily make an order for payment on account in the sum that the claimant will almost certainly collect. The position is set out in the notes at CPR paragraph 44.3.15 of the *White Book*. Some allowance should be made for the fact that there is a risk that some part of the claimant's costs may be disallowed at the detailed assessment I have invited your Honour to order. Making a generous allowance in the defendant's favour I respectfully invite your Honour to order the defendant to pay £10,000 on account of the claimant's costs within 14 days.

You will note that the sample submissions set out above clearly direct the court to the relevant rules, explain the nature of the court's powers and provide a justification for the exercise of those powers in the claimant's favour. You may wish to flag the relevant rules in your civil procedure textbook with a Post-it note so that you can quickly turn to the relevant page and direct the court to the provision in question.

34.6.4 Responding to the application

When you find yourself in the position of responding to the application (remember that in the vast majority of hearings someone will be representing a losing party and at some time or other it will be you) what you can say depends on the circumstances of the case. In the simple straightforward case canvassed earlier, you may only be able to say that there is nothing you can usefully add or some other gracious submission to the inevitable order against your client and leave the judge to make the order sought. Otherwise your response should follow the same format as outlined above, ie set out the order you invite the court to make, the reasons why it should make that order, and the reasons why it should not make the order sought by your opponent. It may be that you can find something in the circumstances relating to the manner in which the claim was conducted that has resulted in the costs incurred by the claimant being unnecessarily increased. For example, lengthy witness statements served by the claimant for witnesses who were not called at the trial. In that event your response might be along the following lines:

> Accepting as one must that the claimant has succeeded in his claim, I nevertheless submit that the right order to make in this case is an order for the defendant to pay a proportion of the claimant's costs for the following reasons. In the first place, much time has been spent on dealing with matters that have not materially advanced the claimant's case as it has progressed to trial and have not advanced the case as presented to your Honour in this court at the trial. Lengthy witness statements were served for four witnesses, none of whom have been called by the claimant. Their witness statements were not thought sufficiently useful to find their way into the trial bundle [. . . *add anything else with each new reason prefaced by 'in the second place' . . . 'in the third place' and so on*].

Listing your reasons in this way will help you to focus your submissions and give the judge a list of separate identifiable reasons to consider rather than a monologue covering many unconnected points in one lump. Your response should end with something along the lines of:

> In the light of the factors I have outlined I respectfully suggest that the proper order to make is an order for the defendant to pay no more than 85% of the claimant's costs of the claim.

In these circumstances there is a lot to be said for leaving the actual figure for the proportion of the costs until the end of your submission. If you give a figure at the outset, there is a chance that the judge's instant reaction will be that there is no way he is going to deprive the claimant of that much in costs and your reasons will then be shut out as the judge's mind closes against you in an outbreak of premature adjudication. If you give your reasons first, there is a chance that the judge will have turned his mind to accepting that some reduction has to be made before he is faced with considering the figure that you put forward. You will also have a chance to assess the judge's reaction to your submission as an indicator for where to pitch the figure for the apportionment of the costs. This might help you to put forward a figure within the range in the judge's contemplation (in which case he is more likely to think your submissions are sound) rather than a figure that is outside the range in the judge's contemplation (in which case there is an increased chance that he will think your reasons are as unsound as your figure).

In the five-day, two-issue trial example set out earlier your response should pick up from the submission made by the successful party that costs follow the event pursuant to CPR, Part 44, r 2, para (2)(a). Paragraph (2)(b) goes on to state that the court may make a different order. You might say something along the following lines:

> Although CPR, Part 44.2.2(a) provides for the unsuccessful party to pay the successful party's costs, paragraph 2(b) provides that the court may make a different order in the light of the circumstances set out in paragraphs (4) and (5) and all the circumstances of the case. In this case the court should properly make an order for the claimant to pay the defendant's costs on issue 1 and an order for the defendant to pay the claimant's costs of the case save for the claimant's costs of issue 1. The defendant was clearly the successful party in relation to issue 1. Given the time devoted to dealing with this issue the defendant should clearly be considered to be the successful party so far as the trial is concerned notwithstanding the judgment given for the claimant arising out of issue 2 which occupied only one of the five days devoted to the trial. Issue 1 was an issue on which the claimant was bound to fail for the reasons set out in the court's judgment. Those reasons were as apparent to the claimant before the trial as they are after judgment. In the circumstances the claimant could not reasonably have pursued issue 1 in the way that he has. [*One might add depending on what happened before trial.*] From the outset the defendant's solicitors have made it clear to the claimant that this aspect of the claim would fail for the reasons given in the judgment. At the CMC the defendant specifically invited the claimant to

abandon issue 1 at an early stage in the action. Your Honour may be assisted by the correspondence between the parties dealing with this. [*Hand in the relevant correspondence and then take the judge through the letters to ensure the point is driven home.*] The trial of the action could and should have been devoted to resolving issue 2 alone. Had the claimant adopted that course the costs incurred by both parties would be much reduced beyond those that have in fact been incurred and valuable court time would not have been devoted to dealing with issue 1. If one turns to CPR, Part 44.2(4)(a), the court *must* have regard to the conduct of the parties. In this case the claimant has pursued a claim in respect of issue 1 that was bound, as it has done, to fail. Subparagraph (b) requires the court to have regard to whether a party has succeeded on part of his case even if he has not been wholly unsuccessful. In this case the defendant has succeeded on that part of his case relating to issue 1, that part being by far the larger part of the case. [*You can then proceed through the various matters raised in subparagraphs (4) and (5) one by one as each one gives you an opportunity to strike the same nail in different ways and build up the appearance of a welter of points that all drive the court towards making an order for the claimant to pay the defendants costs of issue 1. Given that four days have been effectively wasted from the point of view of the claimant and the court you can also draw on the overriding objective in CPR Part 1, proportionate cost, saving expense and allocation of the court's resources, before finally concluding with something along the lines of:*] In all the circumstances of the case the just order to make is an order for the claimant to pay the defendant's costs of issue 1 and for the defendant to pay the claimant's costs of the case save for the costs of issue 1.

If the claimant has made an effective Part 36 offer, your submissions in response should focus on whether it is unjust as a matter of principle to order the defendant to pay enhanced interest and costs and whether it is unjust as a matter of fact to order the additional sum or interest at 10% above base rate as opposed to some lower figure. Further guidance on relevant principles to consider in making such an argument can be found in *KR v Bryn Alyn Community (Holdings) Ltd (In Liquidation) (Permission to Amend)* [2003] EWCA Civ 838, [2003] PIQR P30, CA.

34.6.5   Replying to your opponent's submissions

If it is your application, you should have the final word. It is not an opportunity to restate all the submissions you have already made. You should deal only with matters that the unsuccessful party has raised in answer to your submissions. Before you sit down you should ask the court whether there are any other points on which the court requires assistance. It may be that there is something troubling the judge that you and your opponent have not dealt with. The court may have in mind a different order from those suggested by the parties. If you ask and something is raised, you can at least have a go at making some submissions about the order the court is contemplating before, rather than after, it is pronounced by the court. You must also be prepared to suggest a less favourable order than that which you initially asked for if your opponent's submissions have been well received. For example on an interim application for a claimant who has been partially successful you might set out to persuade the court to make an order for the defendant to pay the claimant's costs. If your opponent appears to have persuaded the court that no order for costs is the appropriate order, you might want to suggest that the order should be claimant's costs in the case, which is something of a halfway house between claimant's costs and no order for costs.

34.6.6   Word of warning

The sample speeches just given are merely brief examples for a case **not involving costs budgets** and should not be adopted as exact templates for your own submissions in court. You must find your own words to use to set out what order you want the court to make and the reasons that justify the court making that order. You also need to monitor carefully the court's response to the points that you make. In the five-day, two-issues example, sooner or later the court is likely to point out to the defendant that the effect of the order proposed is that the claimant will effectively make no recovery in money terms for his or her costs notwithstanding the fact he or she has recovered all that he or she sought from the defendant. If this point is made strongly by the court, the defendant should consider adapting his or her submission so that the final submission as to the appropriate order is one for the payment by the defendant of a stated percentage of the claimant's costs only. You should always be prepared to put forward a different order if the response from the court appears unfavourable. 'Unfavourable' means the order you seek is not going to be made as opposed to the court simply testing the argument you have advanced.

34.7 Making the order

After the parties' submissions are concluded the court will make its decision as to costs. In simple cases the court will simply pronounce its order. You must take a careful note of exactly what order is pronounced so that you can endorse it on your brief and report it accurately to your instructing solicitor afterwards. The judge should ordinarily offer at least some reasons for the judgment, particularly if it is departing from the general rule of r 44.2. Do not be tempted to say anything about absent reasons in the belief that it will help you to appeal that decision. In more complicated cases the court will deliver a mini-judgment solely on the issue of costs setting out the court's reasons for the order that it makes. This should help to give you some insight into the court's decision-making processes that you can usefully use on future occasions. Generally speaking the points that carry weight will be reflected in the court's expressed reasons. If you made points that are not reflected in the reasons or are rejected in the reasons given, you should give careful consideration to whether the point can be presented more attractively or more effectively should the occasion arise again in the future.

34.8 Costs on interim applications

34.8.1 Generally

The same procedure applies as already explained. In the vast majority of interim applications the 'event' against which success or failure is judged is the relief sought in the application and the court will proceed to make an order for costs against one or other of the parties. At this stage there is no determination as to which party is successful in the action and which is not, so there is more scope for making an order for costs in the case or reserving the costs to the trial judge. If the application relates to something the court would have to deal with sooner or later in the exercise of its case management function, the most likely order is costs in the case. If the reality is that your client will win at trial, its effect will be little different from an order for costs in any event. The only thing you will miss out on is a summary assessment and prompt payment.

You are likely to find that many, if not most, judges dealing with costs on interim applications are reticent to make a costs award other than costs in the case. In a minor interim procedural application, the judge will have had relatively little time to become fully conversant with all the facts and issues, and will prefer to err on the side of caution when making any order for costs. You will therefore do well to consider how crucial the costs application is in any given circumstance. Check with your instructing solicitor how hard they wish you to 'push' any application for costs in the light of a successful application, and prepare your costs submissions accordingly.

Almost all interim applications will give rise to a summary assessment of the amount of the costs payable if one or other party intends to seek an order for the costs of the application in any event. You need to have a list of the points to attack in your opponent's statement of costs and a list of the points to support your statement of costs. The paying party will have to pay the assessed sum within 14 days unless some other period is ordered at the time the order is made. You need to make sure your client will be able to pay within 14 days and, if not, you need to have an explanation that covers why your client cannot pay within 14 days, what period of time is required and an argument to put forward in support of the period of time you wish the court to allow for your client to pay. If you are the receiving party, you need to know whether there is any good reason why the court should not allow further time beyond 14 days for payment of the costs as that too has a part to play in the court's decision.

34.8.2   Applications for an injunction

If the application is fought and an injunction is granted or refused, there is an event against which success or failure can be gauged. If it was an obvious case for the grant or refusal of the injunction, the successful party has a good argument to put forward for an order for costs in any event against the other party. It may, however, be that there is a risk that the claim will fail at trial, in which event the interim injunction should not have been granted. That possibility will support an argument that the costs of the injunction application should be costs in the case or costs reserved to the trial judge. If the party seeking the injunction is successful and has before issuing the application sought undertakings from the unsuccessful party that have been refused, there is a powerful argument for ordering the unsuccessful party to pay the costs of the application, based on success coupled with the unsuccessful party's conduct in refusing to give undertakings that would have avoided the need to make the application.

34.8.3   Applications for permission to amend and extensions of time

In these instances the applicant is seeking the indulgence of the court and, in consequence, the applicant will usually be ordered to pay the costs of the application. For example, where the claimant applies for and obtains permission to amend his or her particulars of claim from the district judge the defendant's submission will be along the following lines:

> Sir, this application is the result of the claimant's failure to properly set out his case at the outset when the particulars of claim were drafted. There is no good reason for the claimant's failure to properly set out his case at the outset. As a consequence of the amendment the defendant will now incur further avoidable costs in the amendment of his defence to meet the new allegations now raised rather late in the progress of the action by the claimant. In the circumstances the court should order the claimant to pay the defendant's costs of the application and the costs of and occasioned by the amendment of the particulars of claim.

The submission can be fleshed out with references to CPR, Part 44, para 2(4) and (5).

The claimant might avoid such an order if he or she can show that the amendments are due to circumstances arising after the service of the particulars of claim, for example, where the defendant's own defence raises matters that provide the basis for the amendments the claimant seeks to make, for example by asserting that some other person is liable to the claimant. The claimant might also be in a position to argue that it was obvious that permission to amend would be granted. In this type of application the applicant is able to protect himself against the costs of the hearing, if not the application itself, by asking the other party to consent to the amendment or extension of time before issuing the application. It strengthens the applicant's position when it comes to arguing that the costs have been incurred by the other party's unreasonable conduct in fighting the application rather than the applicant's need to seek the court's indulgence and does not weaken the applicant's position on costs should the application fail.

Where a court order is required, even if the other party consents to the relief required by the applicant, the applicant will usually have to bear the costs of issuing the application and preparing the evidence in support of it. If the respondent contests the application and loses at the hearing, the respondent is at risk of having to pay the costs of the hearing in any event. If the respondent's arguments regarding costs are skilfully presented and heap sufficient blame on the applicant, it should be possible to secure an order that avoids the respondent having to pay the claimant's costs even if he or she does not succeed in obtaining an order that might provide for the payment of his or her costs by the applicant.

34.8.4 Applications to set aside a judgment or for relief from sanctions

The applicant will almost invariably be ordered to pay the respondent's costs unless there is a good reason to explain why the need to make the application arose. Unless the explanation involves some fault on the part of the respondent, the applicant will be ordered to pay the costs of the application. If the applicant is able to satisfy the court that a default judgment was entered in circumstances where the proceedings did not come to the applicant's attention through no fault of his or hers, it may be possible to persuade the court to order costs in the case: things do go wrong from time to time without fault on the part of either party to the claim.

34.8.5 Applications for 'unless' orders

This type of application will arise only where the respondent is in breach of a provision of the CPR or an existing court order. In the ordinary course of events the respondent will be ordered to pay the costs of the application whether the applicant is successful or not, given that the cause of the application being made is the respondent's own default. In the unlikely event that the application is dismissed it may be possible to persuade the court that the respondent's success justifies some relief in respect of costs. That relief is unlikely to extend beyond an order for the applicant's costs in the case, ie if the applicant wins at trial he or she will recover the costs of the application and if the applicant loses at trial he or she will not have to pay the respondent's costs of the application.

34.8.6 Applications for summary judgment

There are three potential outcomes on an application for summary judgment—(1) judgment for the claimant or dismissal of the claim, (2) a conditional order, or (3) dismissal of the application. In terms of success, (1) counts as success for the applicant, (3) counts as success for the respondent, and (2) is a partial success for the applicant in that an advantageous order has been obtained against the respondent and a partial success for the respondent who lives to fight another day. The court is likely to treat the applicant who obtains a conditional order against the respondent as the successful party from a costs point of view given that it must be satisfied that it is possible but improbable that the claim or defence will succeed at trial before a conditional order can be made. The general rule applies: the successful party's costs of the application should be paid by the unsuccessful party.

Where the outcome is judgment for the claimant or dismissal of the claim the action is at an end and the successful party is entitled not only to the costs of the application but also the costs of the action. If the claim is for a specified sum of money in excess of £25, the successful applicant is only entitled to fixed costs in respect of the cost of the action in the amounts set out in CPR, Part 45. If the claim relates to relief other than a specified amount of money, for example, damages or declaratory or injunctive relief, the court should summarily assess the costs of the application and the costs of the claim with the consequence that the applicant needs to provide two separate statements of costs—one dealing with the costs of the application and the second dealing with the costs of the claim—and counsel for both parties need to be ready to make submissions relating to the summary assessment of the costs in both statements at the end of the hearing.

The best order that an unsuccessful applicant might achieve is costs in the case on the basis that at trial his claim or defence may well succeed on the merits even if not established to the level required for summary judgment in the application. To succeed in this you will have to find an argument that deflects the court from the view that success or failure is to be measured by the outcome of the application or an argument that some other factor in the circumstances surrounding the application justifies 'a different order' in the words of CPR, r 44.2(2)(b). An example of something that might assist the unsuccessful applicant is where the application is dismissed because of some point that arises very late in the service of the evidence before the hearing or at the hearing. An application based on statements of case as they stood at the date the application was issued that would have succeeded but only fails because a draft amended statement of case is produced at the last minute resulting in the dismissal of the application may also suffice.

34.8.7 Applications to adjourn or amend at trial

Usually the application is made because the applicant is not ready for the trial or hearing. Unless the applicant can show that he or she is not ready because of some factor outside their control he or she will usually be ordered to pay the costs of the application to adjourn and the costs occasioned by the adjournment of the trial or hearing. If the applicant is not ready because of some default on the part of another party in the case, it can be argued that the conduct of that party is the cause of the adjournment of the trial with the consequence that the other party should pay the costs incurred by the application and adjournment.

Applications to amend or adjourn made at the trial itself can provide a significant tactical advantage in the litigation because the burden of costs that may have to be paid as the price of securing an adjournment or amendment can be very significant. If a party succeeds at trial only because the court has allowed a late application to amend the statement of case at the trial itself, there is scope for persuading the court that the successful party should pay the costs up to the date of the amendment and recover no or limited costs thereafter—see for example *Beoco v Alfa Laval* [1995] QB 137. An application to amend at trial if granted may prejudice the position of the other party to such an extent that the trial has to be adjourned in order to permit that party to deal properly with the case in the light of the amendment permitted. In that event although the application to adjourn will be made by the party prejudiced by the amendment, the costs thrown away by the adjournment will be paid by the party whose amendment has resulted in the adjournment of the trial.

34.9 Procedural default

As CPR, r 44.2(6) makes plain, different orders may be made with respect to different parts of a claim or application depending on the circumstances of the case. The CPR provides rules governing the making of applications to the court and the evidence required both in terms of content and formalities. You will quickly learn that there are no boundaries when it comes to the ingenuity of humankind to turn the simplest procedural task into something of unachievable difficulty. If you represent the paying party, that unachievable difficulty represents an opportunity to reduce the amount you may have to pay. You can always argue that, where something has not been done properly in accordance with the rules, the receiving party should not recover the costs of doing it, for example, where a witness statement does not have a signed statement of truth it ought not to be admitted in evidence and, if it is, the party preparing it ought not to recover the costs of its preparation from the paying party. A degree of circumspection is required in taking this type of point. For example, a complaint that the witness statement referred to above does not have margins of the requisite width is not likely to carry much weight but does carry a substantial risk of creating irritation on the part of the court with the wrong party, ie you.

34.10 Reserved costs

Where the court has made an order for reserved costs on a previous occasion the costs have to be dealt with by the trial judge. If you want the costs reserved to be paid by your opponent, you must bring the order reserving the costs to the attention of the trial judge and set out in your submissions the reasons that justify the court making the order you seek in respect of those costs. If nothing is said about reserved costs or no order is made by the trial judge in relation to those costs, they become costs in the case (a different rule applies in family proceedings). It follows that if the court orders the costs of the case to be paid by your opponent, you do not need to refer specifically to the reserved costs or seek a separate order in respect of them. If you represent the party ordered to pay the costs of the case, you must raise the question of what order should be made in respect of the reserved costs in the event that you wish the court to make an order that absolves your client from paying them or provides for them to be paid to your client. Whether this is achievable depends on the circumstances in which the reserved costs order came to be made and the circumstances of the case as a whole. For example, if the claimant applied for permission to amend and there was some doubt as to whether the amendment was actually required, the court might have granted permission to amend and reserved the costs to the trial judge. If the claimant won at trial and the amendment proved to be unnecessary, the defendant might then wish to argue that he should not have to pay the costs of the unnecessary amendment and the application for it at worst and, at best, that the claimant should pay his costs of the application and amendment in any event.

Most trial judges display a marked reluctance to deal with reserved costs in any way other than as costs in the case on the ground that they cannot adequately inquire into the circumstances at the time the reserved costs order was made. If you want them to be dealt with differently, you have to make sure you clearly explain why that outcome would be unjust and will have to ensure that the judge has a clear understanding of the reasons why the court reserved the costs on the occasion on which that order was made.

34.11   Small claims track costs

CPR, r 27.14 restricts the costs recoverable in claims on the small claims track to fixed costs, court fees and witness expenses, as well as a selection of other sums linked to claims falling within the scope of the Pre-action Protocol for Low Value Personal Injury Claims in Road Traffic Accidents (the RTA Protocol) or the Pre-action Protocol for Low Value Personal Injury (Employers' Liability and Public Liability) Claims (the EL/PL Protocol). Ensure that you take instructions from your lay client as to what travel expenses they have incurred in attending court, and whether they have incurred any recoverable loss of earnings (which are capped at £90 in any event). Such small sums will still be of worth to the client, and must be diligently sought with due attention to detail. The court may, pursuant to CPR, r 27.14(2)(g), order a party that has behaved unreasonably to pay further costs that have to be summarily assessed. Whether a party's behaviour is unreasonable depends on what was done and the consequences of it for the other party and the court. The following may be held to amount to unreasonable behaviour:

- pursuing a claim or defence that enjoyed no reasonable prospect of success;
- limiting the value of the claim so as to avoid the costs consequences attaching to fast track or multi-track claims;
- failing to comply with pre-action protocols;
- filing a defence solely in order to avoid a judgment;
- failing to comply with the court's orders;
- making unnecessary applications;
- causing a late adjournment of the hearing;
- failing to attend the hearing;
- failing to negotiate properly by refusing reasonable settlement offers or obstructing negotiations;
- failing to engage with mediation (*Reed Employment plc v M Gaze & Co Ltd* [2007] CL 34).

If you are seeking costs on the ground of unreasonable behaviour, your submissions should clearly set out the behaviour that is relied on and explain why that behaviour was unreasonable. You should be in a position to demonstrate that avoidable costs have been incurred on the part of your client or that the ethos of small claims track disposal (simple, speedy and cheap) has been undermined by your opponent's behaviour. If your opponent's behaviour has inconvenienced the court, your prospects of success will be increased.

34.12 Fast track costs

Cases allocated to the fast track have their own costs regime for trial costs as set out in CPR, Part 45, Section VI. Pre-trial costs and disbursements such as expert witness fees fall to be dealt with in accordance with the normal rules by summary assessment and with a greater emphasis on proportionality than in multi-track cases. Solicitors' costs of attending the trial are limited to £345 and that may only be awarded if the court considers that it was 'necessary' for the solicitor's representative to attend to assist the advocate—see CPR, r 45.39(2)(b). 'Necessary' is not the same as 'desirable' or even 'useful'. If your solicitors have sent a representative, you should do your best to make sure that the representative does as much as possible so that you can, at the end of the case, mount a convincing submission that the attendance was necessary in the light of what the representative has done in the course of the hearing. It will also be useful to find some reason for referring to notes taken by your solicitor's representative whilst you were on your feet and unable to take your own note.

The trial costs regime provides for a fixed fee for advocates at trial graduated according to the value of the claim. In this instance it is possible for the court to award a greater fee than your clerk may have agreed for your services. In so doing CPR, Part 45 ignores the indemnity principle that is the fundamental foundation of costs orders and allows your client the opportunity to earn a modest profit from your success. The fee fixed by CPR, r 45.38 may be decreased pursuant to CPR, r 45.39(7) if the receiving party has behaved unreasonably or improperly during the trial or increased pursuant to CPR, r 45.39(8) if the paying party has behaved improperly during the trial. There is no explicable reason for the inclusion of 'unreasonably' in CPR, r 45.39(7) and the failure to include it in CPR, r 45.39(8). The one thing that can be said is that improper behaviour must mean something other than unreasonable behaviour. Unreasonable behaviour is likely to flow from a failure to conduct the trial in a sensible, practical and pragmatic manner. Improper behaviour is likely to flow from conduct that undermines the effective conduct of the judicial process in a fair and just manner. Quite what behaviour is intended to attract the operation of the punishment provisions in CPR, r 45.39(7) and (8) is unclear. Equally it is a little unclear whether the 'party' refers simply to the lay client or whether it also encompasses the party's legal representatives, including you. It probably does not include your conduct of the trial, with the consequence that the obstreperous client who refuses to answer the questions put to him can be punished for his temerity, but the client whose advocate asks contentious but irrelevant questions cannot (at least in the absence of express instructions to ask the questions). It cannot be unreasonable or improper to give evidence that the court finds unreliable or unacceptable in giving judgment. It probably will be unreasonable or improper conduct if the court finds that the evidence was given deliberately with knowledge that it was untrue. It will probably not be unreasonable or improper for one party to accuse the other of lying in his evidence; it probably will be unreasonable or improper behaviour to use the witness-box as a platform for launching an unjustified diatribe against the other party that is not associated with any of the matters that fall to be decided in the claim. The references to behaviour 'during the trial' also create difficulty. The emphasis is on what happens during the trial, not what happened before the trial started, with the consequence that unjustifiable intransigence in the agreement of evidence or documents in the run-up to the trial date falls outside the scope of the punishment provisions, even though the consequence is that a witness attends trial when it is unnecessary. For example, in a personal injury claim the claimant's claim will be supported by medical evidence. If the defendant has no medical evidence but refuses before trial to agree the claimant's medical evidence, the medical expert may need to be called to give evidence with the result that he or she attends on the day of the hearing. If, when he or she is called, counsel for the defendant asks no questions of them because he or she has no instructions as a basis for challenging any part of the evidence, it is easy to conclude that the defendant has behaved unreasonably resulting in the unnecessary appearance of the witness at the trial. During the trial, however, counsel for the defendant has acted reasonably and perfectly properly: he or she has no basis for challenging the witness's evidence and has not delayed or lengthened the trial by asking irrelevant questions. Although the matter has yet to receive authoritative consideration, it may be that a substantial failure to conduct the trial in line with the trial timetable template will amount to unreasonable or improper behaviour for the purposes of the punishment provisions.

Where both parties succeed to some extent the court has power to apportion the fixed fee for the advocate between the two parties—see CPR, r 45.38(2). You then have the opportunity to argue with your opponent as to which of you should have the larger share of the cake.

34.13 Multi-track costs: costs budgeting

Arguably the biggest change stemming from the Jackson reforms is the introduction of costs budgeting and costs management orders under the new CPR, rr 3.12–3.16. CPR, r 3.12(2) states that 'The purpose of costs management is that the court should manage both the steps to be taken and the costs to be incurred by the parties to any proceedings so as to further the overriding objective'. This costs management procedure applies to all multi-track cases commenced on or after 1 April 2013, except—

(a) cases in the Admiralty and Commercial Courts;

(b) such cases in the Chancery Division as the Chancellor of the High Court may direct; and

(c) such cases in the Technology and Construction Court and the Mercantile Court as the President of the Queen's Bench Division may direct,

unless the proceedings are the subject of fixed costs or scale costs or the court otherwise orders.

The CPR glossary defines a 'budget' as an estimate of the reasonable and proportionate costs (including disbursements) which a party intends to incur in the proceedings. This is the new tool which aims to promote the management of proportionate costs in civil proceedings. There is a template for such budgets which must be followed, found in Precedent H annexed to CPR, PD 3 EPD.3. A simpler version using only the first side of the precedent can be followed for cases where a party's budgeted costs do not exceed £25,000. This is a document that you will quickly need to become familiar with in practice, so as to be able to constructively and tactically engage with legal critique of costs budgets at a case management hearing.

The new edition of the *Senior Courts Costs Office Guide* (October 2013) gives 'practical information and guidance for dealing with this area of law' and is of 'invaluable assistance to lawyers and litigants alike'. Practitioners are therefore recommended to familiarise themselves with the guide. Nonetheless, a brief and practical overview of the use of costs budgets and costs management orders is set out here for assistance with courtroom advocacy relating to such matters.

Under the new regime, all parties, except litigants in person, must file and exchange costs budgets in accordance with the rules, or as directed by the court. This must be done by the date specified in the Notice of Proposed Allocation or, if no such date is specified, seven days before the first case management conference under CPR, r 3.13. Any party which fails to file a budget when required to do so will be treated as having filed a budget comprising only the applicable court fees under CPR, r 3.14. The case of *Mitchell v News Group Newspapers Limited* [2013] EWCA Civ 1537 offers a stark illustration of how strictly this requirement is enforced. In *Mitchell*, the failure of the claimant's solicitors to file a costs budget until the afternoon before the case management hearing led to the Master applying the new rules strictly and ordering that the claimant be treated as having filed a costs budget comprising only the court fees. The budget filed the previous day had totalled £506,425.

Under CPR, r 3.15(2) the court may make a costs management order at any time. Such an order will record the extent to which budgets are agreed between the parties and, in respect of budgets which are not agreed, record the court's approval after making appropriate revisions. Once such an order has been made, the court will thereafter control the parties' budgets in respect of recoverable costs under CPR, r 3.15. This rule demonstrates how important it is for counsel to be robustly equipped to argue the detail of the budget at any relevant hearing, so as to ensure that the most suitable budget for the court's approval. Do not expect to simply turn up to such a hearing and for it to be a 'rubber-stamping' exercise by the judge. It is equivalent in many ways to a detailed assessment hearing where the fine points of detail of estimated hours of work and disbursements need to be forensically and legally justified. CPR, r 3.18 sets out that where a costs management order has been made, the court, when later assessing costs on the standard basis, will have regard to the receiving party's last approved or agreed budget for each phase of the proceedings, and will not depart from the approved or agreed budget, unless satisfied that there is good reason to do so. This obviously dovetails with CPR, rr 44.3(2)(a) and 44.3(5), concerning the proportionality of costs.

Note however that where the parties have filed budgets, but the court has **not** made a costs management order under CPR, r 3.15, PD 44, paras 3.1–3.7 apply. Paragraph 3.2 sets out that if there is a difference of 20% or more between the costs claimed by a receiving party on detailed assessment and the costs shown in a budget filed by that party, the receiving party must provide a statement of the reasons for the difference with the bill of costs. Paragraph 3.6 states that where it appears to the court that the paying party reasonably relied on the budget, the court may restrict the recoverable costs to such sum as is reasonable for the paying party to pay in the light of that reliance, notwithstanding that such sum is less than the amount of costs reasonably and proportionately incurred by the receiving party. This is further proof of the importance for an advocate to advance realistic and persuasive submissions on the costs budget at as early a stage as possible, so as to secure a client's ability to recover reasonable and proportionate costs.

34.14 Appeals

Success and failure in an appeal are measured by whether the appeal has been allowed or dismissed. An appeal allowed in part may count as a partial success. Where the appeal is allowed the appeal court will substitute its own order for the order appealed by the appellant. The court's decision as to which party should pay the costs of the appeal falls to be decided on the same principles, and your submissions should follow the same structure, as set out above. The appeal court will also deal with the costs order made at the time the order appealed against was made. If the appeal is successful, the appeal court will make the order that should have been made at the application or trial that resulted in the order appealed by the appellant. The costs order made on that occasion must also be revised to reflect the position as it should have been had the correct order been made at the end of the application or trial. That means your costs submissions on the appeal should include those that you would, in the light of the substantive order made by the appeal court, have made at the application or trial.

34.15 Publicly funded costs

The Legal Aid Sentencing and Punishment of Offenders Act 2012 abolished the old Legal Services Commission (LSC) and gave control of legal aid to the Legal Aid Agency (LAA), an executive agency of the Ministry of Justice. A publicly funded party will now receive said funding from the LAA. At the end of any case in which a party is publicly funded, counsel for the publicly funded party must obtain an order for the detailed assessment of that party's costs pursuant to CPR, r 47.18 or r 47.19 as appropriate. Without such an order the court has no power to assess the costs that should be paid to you and your solicitor for representing the lay client. It is prudent to ask for such an order at each interim application that comes before the court.

If the publicly funded party is ordered to pay any part of the costs of the action, a costs protection order *must* be sought. The Legal Aid Sentencing and Punishment of Offenders Act 2012, s 26 replaced the Access to Justice Act 1999, s 11. Section 26(1) of the Act provides that costs ordered against an individual who is a legally aided party in relevant civil proceedings must not exceed the amount (if any) which it is reasonable for that party to pay having regard to all the circumstances, including:

(i) the financial resources of all the parties to the proceedings; and

(ii) their conduct in connection with the dispute to which the proceedings relate.

The Civil Legal Aid (Costs) Regulations 2013 are Regulations made in accordance with the Act and provide a procedure to determine whether or not a costs order could and should be made against a legally aided party. Part 2 of the Regulations deals with costs protection, which only applies to costs incurred by the receiving party in relation to proceedings which are, as regards the legally aided party, relevant civil proceedings (or contemplated proceedings) before the court.

You must be familiar with the rules and regulations that apply in respect of costs protection. If you are not, you will not be able to assist the court and run the risk of failing your client in what has become a technically complicated area of law and practice. Costs protection bites on the amount of the costs that the publicly funded party should pay with the consequence that the court should make an order for costs to be paid by the publicly funded party if that is the just order to make in the absence of public funding for that party. If a costs order has been made in your client's favour against a publicly funded party, you face the choice of inviting the court to decide what amount is reasonable there and then or leaving that question for later determination by the costs judge. If the issue is left for later determination, the publicly funded client will have to provide a full appraisal of his means, which may not be available to the trial judge. If you represent the publicly funded party, you need to have some information ready about your client's means in case the court decides to deal with ascertaining a reasonable amount there and then. If your client is totally bereft of means, you might try to persuade the court to assess the reasonable amount at £0. It will probably discourage the receiving party from taking any further steps in connection with the assessment and recovery of costs after the hearing. Be prepared to marshal arguments relating both to the financial resources of the parties **and** their conduct in connection with the dispute.

Costs protection only applies during the currency of the public funding. If the party receives public funding part-way through the action or loses public funding before the end of the action, the periods in which he or she was not a publicly funded party attract the normal orders with no protection. If public funding is revoked rather than discharged, the publicly funded party is treated as if he or she were never publicly funded at all for any part of the action. If you represent the non-publicly funded party, you need to make sure you clarify whether a certificate was revoked or discharged as it has an important impact on your client's position and the submissions you may need to make.

Two specimen orders for costs made against a claimant, who is a legally aided party, are set out in the *Senior Courts Costs Office Guide* at Appendix A-6. Familiarise yourself with the form and layout of such orders, and be prepared to make submissions that relate to their detail, including arguments on set-off if applicable.

34.16   CFAs, DBAs and QOCS

The Jackson reforms instituted significant changes to the availability of various funding arrangements and the recovery of their associated costs. Like publicly funded costs, you must be familiar with the law and practice in this area. If the funding arrangement does not comply with the relevant regulations or the relevant procedure has not been followed, the unsuccessful party may escape any liability to pay anything in costs to the successful party. The detail of these issues can be found in a relevant practitioner text, but three of the basic issues relating to the reforms are outlined here.

The Senior Courts Costs Office defines conditional fee arrangements (or CFAs) as 'an agreement with a legal representative which provides for the payment of fees or part of them only in specified circumstances ... A party who wishes to recover a success fee payable under the agreement from his opponent should serve a notice of funding on the opponent at the outset of the claim.' CFAs have been used in civil litigation since the 1990s. The Courts and Legal Services Act 1990, ss 58 and 58A, which make provision for the regulation of CFAs and the recoverability of success fees, were reformed by the Legal Aid, Sentencing and the Punishment of Offenders Act 2012, as a result of which a success fee payable under a CFA may no longer be recovered from a losing party in any proceedings, but, subject to certain limits in personal injury cases, is recoverable from the legal representatives' client. The 'success fee' can be up to 100% of the basic fee, a regulation unchanged since CFAs were first introduced in the 1990s. However, success fees in personal injury cases must now not exceed 25% of the damages, excluding damages for future care and loss. Linked to this change is the fact that clients who enter into after the event (ATE) insurance on or after 1 April 2013 will no longer be able to seek to recover the premium from the opponent in the event of a win except in certain types of cases and therefore will be required to bear the premium in the event of a successful claim.

The Damages-Based Agreements Regulations 2013 made substantial changes to the law relating to damages based agreements (or DBAs) from 1 April 2013. The explanatory note to the Regulations states that 'DBAs are a type of "no win, no fee" agreement under which a representative (defined in these Regulations as a person providing the advocacy services, litigation services or claims management services to which the DBA relates) can recover an agreed percentage of a client's damages if the case is won ("the payment"), but will receive nothing if the case is lost.' The effect of the amendment is to permit and regulate the use of DBAs in all civil litigation rather than simply their use in employment matters which had formerly been the case. The new CPR, r 44.18 sets out that the fact that a party has entered into a DBA will not affect the making of any order for costs which otherwise would be made in favour of that party, and crucially that the party may not recover by way of costs more than the total amount payable by that party under the DBA for legal services provided under that agreement.

Ensure that you are prepared at court to argue the details of any issues arising out of a DBA, whether you or your opponent are the ones acting under such an agreement. The maximum payment that can be recovered from the claimant's damages is capped at 25% of the damages (excluding damages for future care and loss) in personal injury cases; at 35% of damages on employment tribunal cases; and at 50% of the damages in all other cases. It is also important to note any shortfall between the solicitors' costs paid by the losing defendant and the agreed DBA fee. The shortfall will need to be paid by the claimant from their damages; the claimant will also be required to pay any shortfall in respect of disbursements.

A new concept introduced by the Jackson reforms in respect of costs recoverability in personal injuries cases is that of 'Qualified One Way Costs Shifting' (or QOCS) as laid out in CPR, rr 44.13–44.17. CPR, r 44.14 states that 'Subject to rules 44.15 and 44.16, orders for costs made against a claimant may be enforced without the permission of the court but only to the extent that the aggregate amount in money terms of such orders does not exceed the aggregate amount in money terms of any orders for damages and interest made in favour of the claimant.' In essence this is the implementation of the principle recommended by Jackson that a successful claimant will recover their costs from a defendant in the usual way, but if unsuccessful, the claimant will **not** be liable for the defendant's costs. Conceptually it is a way to balance out the claimant's loss of the right to recover the after-the-event insurance premium (referred to earlier) from a losing defendant.

Put simply, where there is judgment for the claimant an order may still include a direction that the claimant pay the defendant's costs. However, QOCS effectively renders such an order toothless, because there is no award for 'damages and interest' against which the costs order can bite. In such cases the role of the advocate is more likely to centre around the exceptions to QOCS set out in CPR, r 44.16 (relating to a claim being 'fundamentally dishonest') and possibly the non-discretionary exceptions set out in CPR, r 44.15. Time will tell how the definition of 'fundamentally dishonest' will be determined by the courts. It will certainly encompass fraudulent cases, but an advocate must be well equipped with up-to-date authorities and lines of argument for potentially lesser cases of dishonesty in order to make persuasive and relevant costs submissions. Counsel should also be guided by the new CPR, PD 44 which sets out the procedure to follow in such cases.

From counsel's point of view, arguments relating to funding arrangements and QOCS should only become relevant at the end of the case where a summary assessment is conducted. If a detailed assessment is ordered, the enforceability of the agreement and the amount of the additional liability payable will be dealt with at the detailed assessment. If there is some doubt over the enforceability of the funding arrangement, it may deflect the court from making an order to the payment of an amount on account of the costs payable. If your opponent has a funding arrangement, you will know of its existence but will not be entitled to see the agreement until the end of the case and after the court has decided to summarily assess the costs. You will not have time to go off and research the rules and regulations at that juncture. You may be able to persuade the court that the existence of the funding arrangement is a good reason to order a detailed assessment rather than conduct a summary assessment. In principle the existence of a funding arrangement should not deflect the court from conducting a summary assessment.

34.17 Costs in respect of pro bono representation

Since 1 October 2008, the Legal Services Act 2007, s 194(3) has enabled a court to make an order, equivalent to an order for inter party costs, against the opponent of a litigant who has been represented pro bono. However, unlike a normal costs order under which the beneficiary is the successful litigant, the beneficiary of a s 194 order is the relevant 'prescribed charity' (ie the Access to Justice Foundation). Should you be acting in such a case, ensure that you follow the guidance in CPR, r 46.7 and the associated Practice Direction. The party who has pro bono representation must prepare, file and serve a written statement of the sum equivalent to the costs that the party would have claimed for that legal representation had it not been provided free of charge.

34.18 Costs against solicitors and counsel

The court has power under the Supreme Court Act 1981, s 51 and CPR, r 44.11 to order costs against a solicitor or counsel personally. The court will only do so if costs have been wasted. Wasted costs are those incurred as a result of any improper, unreasonable, or negligent conduct, or those incurred prior to such conduct as the court considers unreasonable for a party to pay. For example the claimant may fail to appear at an interim application made by the claimant as a result of some negligent oversight on the part of the solicitor or counsel, with the consequence that the defendant's costs of preparing for the application and attending the hearing are wasted. Examples of relevant conduct are a failure by the solicitors to brief counsel in sufficient time for counsel to deal with the hearing or where counsel fails to devote adequate time to preparing for the hearing. If the party in default is publicly funded, an order for costs against solicitors or counsel personally may be the only order that will in practical terms result in payment to the other party. That factor can result in the court adopting an over-protective approach to the legal adviser who acts for a publicly funded client. It will result in the court looking carefully to see whether there is a proper basis for such an application rather than an attempt to find someone solvent to pay the costs in question. Before such an order can be made the court must be persuaded that the legal adviser in question has failed to conduct the proceedings with reasonable competence and expedition or has acted improperly, unreasonably, or negligently. The procedure to be followed is set out in CPR, r 44.6. The court must first be satisfied that there is a good reason for the legal adviser to show cause why a wasted costs order should not be made. Guidance as to the applicable principles can be found in *Ridehalgh v Horsfield* [1994] 3 WLR 462, *Filmlab Systems International v Pennington* [1995] 1 WLR 673, *Horsham District Council ex p Wensum* [1995] 1 WLR 680, and *Medcalf v Mardell* [2003] 1 AC 120. Applications should be made only where there is a very good prospect of success and the default on the part of the legal adviser can be clearly established without long-drawn-out further investigation by the court. Unless the application is going to be simple, straightforward, and short the court will probably refuse to entertain it and you will have gained nothing from attempting to make it.

You must not on any account threaten an application for a wasted costs order for the purpose of intimidating the other side. It is a contempt of court and likely to attract a highly unfavourable reaction from the judge should he get to hear of it. As a matter of personal courtesy you should tell your opponent if such an application is to be made but make it clear that you are not seeking to dissuade the party's legal advisers from fulfilling their duty to their client.

CPR, r 44.11 also allows the court to disallow costs where there has been a default on the part of a legal adviser. The court is more likely to exercise this power to prevent a legal adviser recovering payment for poor or shoddy work falling below the standard reasonably expected of him.

34.19 Future developments

There remain further recommendations in the Jackson Review for which there are, as yet, no immediate plans for formal legislative implementation. However, the whole package of reforms (whether simply recommended or actually implemented) remain powerful indicators of the present and future changing shape of costs in the legal world and, as such, merit further reading and consideration by any practitioner. The shape and interpretation of this ever changing regulation of costs will continue to be a fertile ground for courtroom advocacy in the years to come.

Employment tribunals

35.1 Introduction

This chapter considers some basic points of advocacy for a hearing before an employment tribunal. This is not intended to be an exposition of the principles of employment law, for which you should use the *Employment Law in Practice* manual.

You should familiarise yourself with the rules that govern the constitution and powers of the employment tribunal in England and Wales. The current rules are to be found in the Employment Tribunal (Constitution and Rules of Procedure) Regulations 2013 (SI 2013/1237). These new rules are a radical departure from the previous 2004 rules. The rules contained in Schedule 1 apply to all proceedings before an Employment Tribunal except for National Security proceedings and equal value claims. Such cases involve Schedules 2 and 3 modifying the rules in Schedule 1. These rules will be referred to as the '2013 Rules', and any references to rules in this chapter are to the 2013 Rules, unless stated otherwise. A large number of statutes give jurisdiction to the employment tribunal to determine questions. This chapter is concerned with the most common claims, namely unfair dismissal claims, redundancy claims and contract claims.

35.2 Some expressions explained

You may encounter a number of expressions with which you may not be familiar. The main ones are:

Claimant	The individual making the claim
Respondent	The entity (commercial or individual) who is the subject of, and typically resists, the claim
ET1	The number given to the form used as the Applicant's Originating Application (cf Claim Form)
ET3	The number given to the form used as the Respondent's Notice of Appearance (cf Response or Defence)
Compromise agreement	A binding agreement settling a complaint complying with the statutory requirements of s 147 Equality Act 2010 (as amended), s 77(4A), Sex Discrimination Act 1975; s 72(4A), Race Relations Act 1976; s 288(2B)(c), Trade Union and Labour Relations (Consolidation) Act 1992; s 9(3)(a), Disability Discrimination Act 1996; or s 203(3)(c), Employment Rights Act 1996
Constructive dismissal	A resignation by the employee that amounts in law to a

	dismissal (as being the acceptance of a serious breach of contract by the employer)
COT3	An ACAS settlement form, which is signed by the parties and has binding effect
ACAS	The Advisory, Conciliation and Arbitration Service, which receives a copy of every claim for unfair dismissal and has a statutory responsibility to attempt to achieve a settlement of the claim
Preliminary hearing	An initial jurisdictional hearing
Pre-hearing review	The sifting process designed to eliminate weak cases
Recoupment	The system by which certain state benefits may be reclaimed from part of the compensatory award in an unfair dismissal claim.

35.3 Steps prior to any hearing

As stated previously, the current rules are the 2013 Rules, meaning a new procedural code. Readers should familiarise themselves with the 2013 Rules. Guidance on tribunal procedure under the 2013 Rules can be found in the ***Employment Law in Practice*** manual, **chapter 4**. These should be read alongside President David J Latham's Presidential Guidance—General Case Management, issued on 13 March 2014 ('the President's Guidance'). The overriding objective of the tribunal is (as in CPR) to deal with cases fairly and justly, under reg 2 of the Regulations. There is an express obligation on the parties and their representatives to assist the tribunal to further the overriding objective. Time is to be calculated for steps to be taken in the case in accordance with reg 4 of the Regulations.

It is envisaged that cases will be subject to active case management in much the same way as civil proceedings in the courts under the Civil Procedure Rules (CPR). Rule 29 gives the tribunal power to make case management orders. Preliminary hearings will consider issues like qualification/entitlement to claim, compliance with time limits and case management. There is an agenda form required for case management which is attached to the President's Guidance.

The tribunal will set down the timetable for steps in the case such as disclosure, exchange of witness statements and agreement of a trial bundle to be carried out. The President's Guidance states 'Orders are important. Non compliance with them may lead to sanctions. Therefore if a party is having difficulty in complying with an order they should discuss it with the other parties and then apply to the Tribunal to vary the order.'

If representing a claimant, a very important step is the timely payment of the hearing fee required by r 40. A notice to pay the fee is issued when the hearing is listed. Failure to pay, unless an application for remission is made, will lead to the claim being dismissed.

A danger which exists for all parties is the tribunal's power to make an unless order under r 38.

It would appear that the previous powers to order a party to provide further information (analogous to CPR, r 18) and disclosure, and require written questions to be answered which had existed under the old r 10 have been preserved and slightly extended by r 31 of the 2013 Rules: 'The Tribunal may order any person in Great Britain to disclose documents or information to a party (by providing copies or otherwise) or to allow a party to inspect such material as might be ordered by a county court or, in

Scotland, by a sheriff.' A corresponding power to order a person to attend a hearing exists in r 32.

If you are instructed before any proceedings are issued, you should consider whether a binding compromise agreement can be negotiated that avoids the need for a claim to be made. The criteria for such an agreement are set out in the statutory provisions listed under the explanation of the term 'Compromise Agreement' (see **35.2**). In addition, a certificate must be obtained from ACAS to show early conciliation has been considered before a claim can be made.

The tribunal will direct for bundles of documents required for the hearing to be agreed and prepared in advance. Guidance on bundles is given at **35.10**.

35.4 Listing of hearings

Every party shall receive at least 14 days' notice of the date fixed for the final hearing, as a result of r 58.

The notice of hearing is accompanied by information about the documents required for the hearing (unless this is already in the tribunal's directions), the facilities available at the particular employment tribunal, and a map showing the location of the tribunal.

Please note that as a result of the President's Guidance, timetabling within the hearing, where the hearing lasts one day or more, is likely.

35.5 Arriving at the employment tribunal

Whoever you are briefed to appear for, arriving at the tribunal at least an hour early is a must. To keep costs down (which generally are irrecoverable) counsel is generally instructed very late in the life of a tribunal claim, often just for the hearing itself. As a result, counsel will need to take instructions in advance of the hearing either in relation to any gaps in the papers or new matters occurring since the documents were prepared.

The employment tribunal has separate waiting rooms for claimants and respondents, so it is important that you go to seek your client in the correct room.

Another important reason for arriving early is that it is good practice to explore the possibility of reaching a settlement with your opponent. Even 'at the door of the court' it is possible to reach a settlement. This is recorded in either a 'Tomlin' or consent order, which is 'rubber stamped' by the tribunal. For guidance on drawing up such settlement agreements, you are referred to **chapter 11** of the ***Employment Law in Practice*** manual.

35.6 Addressing the employment tribunal

The employment tribunal usually consists of an employment judge sitting alone. Unfair dismissal claims are now decided by an employment judge sitting alone. Less common is a full panel consisting of an employment judge and two wing members. Tribunals will occasionally sit with two persons (provided one is a chairperson) if the parties consent, in which case the judge has the casting vote. The judge (who is legally qualified) tends to deal with most points that arise during the hearing (after consulting the other members where necessary). The members of the panel are generally lay people, but are chosen to represent both employers' groups and employee associations, unions etc to achieve a balanced tribunal.

The parties normally sit at tables facing the tribunal, with the witnesses using a smaller table nearer the tribunal or in the centre between the representatives. In most tribunals the applicant will sit on the right (looking towards the employment tribunal) and the respondent will sit on the left.

In London, the members of the employment tribunal are normally present in the room used for the hearing when the parties are brought in by the clerk. In some tribunals outside London the parties and public are shown in first, in which case you should stand when the tribunal members arrive.

Although witnesses stand to take the oath or to affirm at the beginning of their evidence, all other steps take place with everyone seated, including counsel addressing the tribunal. When your witnesses have finished their evidence, at the point at which you would normally ask the judge whether he or she has any questions, you should ask either 'Do you, Sir/Madam, or your colleagues have any questions for this witness?' (when you have a full panel) or 'Do you, Sir/Madam, have any questions for this witness?' (if appearing before the employment judge alone). The employment judge will normally ask each member in turn whether they have any questions (often they do have questions) and will then ask any questions of his or her own.

There are some subtle differences in how you present your advocacy depending on whether you are appearing before a panel or the employment judge sitting alone. The employment judge and members if addressed individually are 'Sir' or 'Madam'; they can conveniently be referred to collectively as 'the tribunal' or 'this tribunal' or through the chair as 'you and your colleagues'. When appearing before the full panel, you need to take a thorough approach and must deal with all the issues in the case, both legal and factual. Because the panel members other than the employment judge will not be lawyers, you will need to take care in explaining points of legal principle clearly and simply.

However, when appearing before the employment judge sitting alone, you must remember you are appearing before a legally qualified person of many years' experience. Generally the hearing will be dealt with at a quicker pace, as the employment judge will be familiar with the law. Employment judges also tend to be more interventionist; they will ask many questions and move you along where considered necessary. It is also highly likely the employment judge will limit witness handling and exercise control over how the hearing is carried out.

35.7 Adjournments

The employment tribunal has a general power to adjourn any hearing. The power must be exercised in the interests of justice in the individual case in accordance with the overriding objective that is part of the procedure of the employment tribunals. There is no power to impose conditions upon an adjournment (such as one party paying costs) although an order for costs may be made in the normal way; see **35.10.9**.

One commonly occurring situation where an adjournment may be needed is when one of the parties or a witness is unable to attend the hearing due to illness. Such applications will be decided in accordance with the overriding objective. However, as a result of *Terluk v Berezovsky* [2010] EWCA Civ 1345, the main issue is whether it was fair to adjourn the hearing since, if the refusal is appealed, the appellate tribunal will look into both that question and whether in consequence of the refusal of an adjournment the hearing was fair. Medical evidence of the illness will assist in demonstrating the illness is genuine and so ought to be obtained where possible.

Two particular situations involving adjournments require special mention: first, where there are also other proceedings between the same parties (eg a wrongful dismissal claim); and, second, where there are criminal proceedings pending.

35.7.1   Interaction with other contractual claims

In unfair dismissal cases the compensation powers of the employment tribunals are severely limited by statute. In situations where the contract of employment grants significant compensation for the employer's breach of contract, an employee may wish to bring a wrongful dismissal claim as well as a claim for compensation for unfair dismissal. Where the compensation exceeds £25,000, which is the tribunal's limit for breach of contract claims, the claim would be made in the High Court. A very long line of cases exists that considers when the employment tribunal claim should be adjourned pending the determination of the wrongful dismissal claim; see, for example, *O'Laire v Jackal* [1991] ICR 718 and *Bowater plc v Charlwood* [1991] ICR 798, which identify some of the factors that ought to be considered.

Since 1994, employment tribunals have had power to determine contractual claims under the Employment Tribunals Extension of Jurisdiction (England and Wales) Order 1994. You should look at the text of the order for its full terms. The most important qualifications are that the claim must be made within three months of the effective date of termination or the last day worked (although there is a limited power to extend time) and there is a limit on damages of £25,000.

One reason why employment tribunal claims are adjourned pending the resolution of other contractual claims is that employment tribunals are not bound by the strict rules of evidence. Since a decision reached by an employment tribunal will give rise to an estoppel *per rem judicata* in a subsequent court hearing, the preference was to have the court hearing first. In *O'Laire v Jackal* a decision by the employment tribunal was described by Browne-Wilkinson LJ, a former President of the Employment Appeal Tribunal, as 'plainly wrong', yet the High Court and Court of Appeal were bound by it.

35.7.2   Criminal proceedings

Employment tribunals often have to decide whether to adjourn proceedings for compensation for unfair dismissal pending criminal proceedings against the employee. The fact that the employee has been charged with a criminal offence certainly does not mean that his or her dismissal will always be fair (even if the offence arises out of or at his or her work). However, a conviction will often affect an award of compensation for unfair dismissal. Employment tribunals have a wide discretion to adjourn pending criminal proceedings and frequently do so despite the decision in *Bastick v James Lane (Turf Accountants) Ltd* [1979] ICR 778 in which the decision not to adjourn was upheld on appeal. Perhaps the crucial words in the decision of the Employment Appeal Tribunal in that case are (at p 784) that:

> we are bound to conclude that, although it would have been perfectly reasonable to come to the opposite conclusion, nevertheless the conclusion which this chairman reached is not so unreasonable a conclusion as to lead us to a finding of perversity.

The common decision to adjourn also avoids the difficulty highlighted in *Ladup Ltd v Barnes* [1982] ICR 107. In that case the employment tribunal found a dismissal unfair when the employer dismissed on learning that the employee had been arrested and charged with growing and possession of cannabis plants. The employment tribunal awarded compensation. Later the employee was convicted of possession of cannabis. The employment tribunal refused to review its decision (see **35.12.1** for an explanation of review). The Employment Appeal Tribunal allowed the appeal against the refusal to review the decision and found that the employee had contributed towards his dismissal 100%, thus extinguishing his compensation.

35.8   Preliminary hearing

A preliminary hearing is normally ordered where there is a legal or jurisdictional issue to be determined before any consideration of the merits of the claims. Under r S3, a preliminary hearing can deal with the following:

- preliminary consideration of the claim;

- making a case management order;

- determining a preliminary issue;

- considering whether a claim or response or any part of a party's case should be struck out;

- considering if a deposit order should be made under r 39;

- exploring the possibility of settlement or alternative dispute resolution (including judicial mediation).

Therefore the previous procedure of holding pre-hearing reviews to filter out cases which are weak has been superseded.

A preliminary hearing can be ordered at any stage prior to the hearing of the claim (at the request of one or more parties or by a judge). It is imperative that the legal or jurisdictional issue is carefully defined so that all relevant evidence is given and submissions are made. So, for example, if the jurisdictional issue is whether a claim for compensation for unfair dismissal is made within time, it should be decided if the subsidiary question, ie to grant an extension of time, if necessary, is to be heard at the same time (as would be normal), or only after a decision has been made as to whether the claim was in fact in time.

The most common examples of preliminary hearings are:

(a) a hearing to determine whether the claim has been brought within the relevant statutory time limit and, if not, whether time should be extended under the relevant power;

(b) a hearing to determine whether the claimant is an employee within the meaning of the Employment Rights 1996, s 230(1) (unfair dismissal and redundancy claims). Alternatively, a hearing to determine whether the claimant is a 'worker' for claims involving the Working Time Regulations 1998 (as amended) in relation to working time, rest breaks, and annual leave issues;

(c) a hearing to determine whether the claimant has the necessary length of service to qualify to bring the claim.

If the disputes of fact that have to be resolved at the preliminary hearing are inextricably linked to the merits of the case, an employment tribunal may refuse a separate preliminary hearing. A common example would be where there is confusion as to the fact of and exact date of dismissal that is relevant to determine whether the claim is brought within time and whether any extension of time should be given. In such a case it is easier to hear all the evidence and determine all the issues together.

A preliminary hearing will usually be heard by an employment judge sitting alone. See **35.6** for guidance on how to address the employment judge sitting alone.

The Rules suggest that written representations and oral argument can be used but make no express reference to oral evidence being heard. In practice oral evidence is required at most preliminary hearings before the legal or jurisdictional issue can be properly decided and a number of decisions have criticised attempts to short-circuit the need to make proper findings of fact; see, for example, *BL Cars Ltd v Brown* [1983] ICR 143. An unusual example of a case where oral evidence was not taken can be found in *Janstorp International (UK) Ltd v Allen* [1990] IRLR 417, where the employment tribunal decided whether wages in lieu of notice fell within the statutory definition of 'wages' without hearing evidence and the Employment Appeal Tribunal gave guidance on situations where a case might be decided without hearing evidence. It is occasionally possible to agree facts for the purposes of a preliminary issue but the employment tribunals are not strictly bound by that agreement. Mummery J (as he then was) has warned of the dangers that exist if the facts are agreed hurriedly at the door of the hearing or during the hearing, and that errors can have most unfortunate consequences: *Waters v Metropolitan Police Commissioner* [1995] IRLR 531.

If the employment tribunal decides that a party's contentions have 'little reasonable prospect of success' (the standard required under r 39), then a party may be ordered to pay a deposit of up to £1,000 as a condition of the case proceeding to a full-hearing. This is on top of any payable issue fee or hearing fee. Account must be taken of the means of the party being ordered to pay the deposit (r 39(2)). If the deposit condition is not complied with, the claim or response (or certain specified parts of it) may be struck out.

If the person against whom the order is made pays the deposit, it will then be returned if the claim is withdrawn before the main hearing, in the unlikely event of the claim succeeding, or if the claim continues but an award of costs is not made against the party paying the deposit.

At such a preliminary hearing the employment tribunal considers the pleadings and the contentions of the parties, but does not make detailed findings of fact and rarely hears any oral evidence. If you represent the party against whom the hearing has been convened, you should be prepared to explain the basis of your case clearly and succinctly. Since the employment tribunal does not make a detailed inquiry into disputed facts at this stage, it should be asked to accept the facts asserted as correct at that stage. It is recommended that in preparation for such a hearing you have identified the relevant statutory provisions, tribunal rules and authorities that apply. Submissions will need to be carefully prepared given the tribunal's wide powers and their possible consequences.

35.8.1 Procedure at a preliminary hearing

The procedure at a preliminary hearing is similar to that at a main hearing. The party upon whom the burden of proof lies will normally go first. The burden is usually upon the claimant employee to show that the employment tribunal has jurisdiction to hear and determine the claim. The claimant's representative will briefly outline the basic facts indicating the extent of the preliminary issue. The claimant's evidence will then be given, cross-examination will take place, and, if necessary, any re-examination or questions from the employment tribunal. Any witnesses for the claimant will then be heard. Thereafter any witnesses for the respondent will be heard. The respondent's counsel will address the employment tribunal and, finally, the claimant's counsel will have the last word.

The employment tribunal will often give a brief decision very quickly to be followed by written reasons in short or extended form (see **35.10.6**).

35.9 Directions hearings/case management hearings

Employment tribunals can make use of directions hearing and case management hearings held under r 29 (which are similar to case management conferences in the courts), which can be held at the tribunal or by telephone. The case management discussion is not a pre-hearing review, since it deals with how the case will progress rather than whether it should progress at all. These hearings are normally before an employment judge sitting alone.

The old practice of asking for directions and obtaining orders by letter, without notice to the other side, has been abandoned. When asking for any order by letter, the tribunal will want to know whether the other party has been given notice of the application and will not make an order unless the other party has had an opportunity to make representations.

As with case management conferences in a court, the case management hearings are intended to increase judicial control over the proceedings. At a case management discussion you should be familiar with the facts and the issues that have to be determined in the case, as well as each of the orders or directions that may be required. The tribunal will record the result of the discussion including any admissions made as to the issues to be determined. The tribunal will often wish to fix the hearing date or dates during the discussion so that the directions and timetable can be given in the light of the time available before that hearing. It is therefore important to attend with dates to avoid for the advocate, the party, and any witnesses.

35.10 The substantive hearing

The preparation for the hearing should include attempting to agree a bundle of documents for the hearing. Unless it is required by the tribunal's order, it is recommended that parties should agree a bundle, if only to the extent that they agree these are the documents to be put before the tribunal, rather than their relevance, significance or authenticity. If agreement cannot be reached, each side should prepare its own bundle. However, the tribunal is likely to take a very dim view of such practice as an agreed bundle is a standard direction in tribunal claims. Bundles should be indexed at the front, paginated, and ideally presented in a ring binder.

If appearing before a full panel, it will be necessary to produce six copies of it (three for the tribunal members, a witness copy and one for each party). If appearing before the employment judge sitting alone, four copies are required.

Tribunals frequently request the representatives of the parties to agree what is known as a 'list of issues', which attempts to identify the legal and factual issues to be considered by the tribunal. This needs to be done with care as the tribunal often restricts itself to consideration of these issues alone. However, tribunals have been alerted to the fact they must not accept a list uncritically, since the tribunal has 'their own duty to ensure that the case is clearly and efficiently presented' as a result of *Price v (1) Surrey County Council (2) Governing Body of Wood Street School* UKEAT/0450/10/SM.

If there is a claim for reinstatement or re-engagement, the respondent should be in a position to give any evidence opposing the making of such an order at the main hearing.

It is usual for directions to require the parties to prepare written witness statements for each witness. The directions will usually require they are exchanged in advance of the hearing. The practice of the tribunal during the hearing is that the witness statement is 'taken as read' after the witness swears or affirms. The witness statement constitutes the evidence-in-chief. The employment tribunal generally limits supplementary questions to matters arising on exchange of witness statements and more recent events. Cross-examination and questions from the tribunal will follow.

There is a power for the employment tribunal to receive written representations or submissions provided that they are given not less than seven days before the hearing (r 42). This is not the same as admitting written evidence.

The hearings are held in public. There is a limited power to hear part or all of the claim in private under r 50. There is also a very limited power to impose reporting restrictions and to prevent the identification of a person affected by a sexual harassment allegation. In England and Wales the witnesses normally remain in the tribunal room throughout the case and hear the evidence of earlier and later witnesses.

35.10.1   Non-attendance

If one party does not attend, the clerk normally tries to contact the party to see if there is any reason for the non-attendance (such as not receiving the notice of hearing). You should also ask if any written submissions have been submitted by the absent party. (Please also see **35.7** for guidance on seeking adjournments in the event of a party being unwell.)

If the party absent is the one with the burden of proof, then the other party may ask for a finding in its favour without hearing evidence. If the employment tribunal adopts the approach and the finding is in favour of the employee, the employment tribunal will still have to calculate the redundancy payment or determine the remedy for an unfair dismissal. If, for example, the employer admits dismissal but does not attend to establish an acceptable reason for dismissal, the applicant may seek a finding of unfair dismissal. The statutory presumption that a dismissal was for redundancy in the Employment Rights Act 1996, s 163(2) applies only to a claim for a redundancy payment and not to claims for unfair dismissal and so would not assist the absent employer.

35.10.2   Opening

At the substantive hearing the first issue is which side opens the case. Generally, the party with the burden of proof will go first. Hence, in wage claims, contract claims, and discrimination claims (where uniquely the burden later shifts), the claimant will go first. In unfair dismissal or redundancy claims, if dismissal is admitted, the respondent employer will go first, because the respondent must still establish the reason for dismissal. If dismissal is not admitted, then the claimant employee will go first and must show that there was an actual or constructive dismissal.

It is important that it is established whether the entire case is to be heard at once or whether the question of liability is to be separated from the question of remedy. Many employment tribunals prefer to consider remedy separately after deciding liability, even if both aspects are dealt with on the same day. If the remedy of reinstatement or re-engagement is sought by the claimant, separate subsequent consideration of remedy is usually directed as detailed evidence may have to be heard on the availability of other jobs. If no indication is given by the employment tribunal on this point, representatives of the respondent are advised that a ruling should be sought well before the claimant begins giving evidence about his or her losses resulting from dismissal if they wish to limit the claimant's entitlement to a remedy. When this aspect is being considered you should ensure that it is clear whether or not liability includes any finding of contribution towards dismissal and/or any deduction for the risks of a fair dismissal, or a finding that at a specified date the claimant was likely to have been dismissed in any event. These findings can be used to reduce any compensation.

The opening can be extremely brief. Employment tribunals are regularly critical of overlong openings by counsel. It is useful to indicate the correct basic facts or the extent of the dispute about those basic facts—such as dates of employment, rates of pay, job description, place of work. Any amendments to the ET1 (the originating application) or the ET3 (the respondent's notice of appearance) should be made at this stage. If the respondent's business is not obvious, a brief explanation of the business may assist the tribunal. It is often helpful to give some indication of the size and administrative resources of the respondent in opening, mentioning the size of the business, and/or the number of staff employed at the claimant's place of work and generally. Finally, it is often much quicker to take the employment tribunal through the bundles of documents in opening rather than ask each witness to 'produce' documents that it has been agreed should be placed before them.

35.10.3   The taking of evidence

Evidence is usually taken on oath or affirmation. Before the hearing the clerk will normally check who is giving evidence and how they wish to take the oath so that the necessary form of oath and appropriate holy book will be ready. As in court, a separate oath will be taken by any interpreter. As in court the oath should be taken standing and whilst everyone else is silent (never use this time to take last-minute, spoken instructions).

Witnesses are normally released once their evidence has been taken. However, you should ask the employment tribunal to release a witness before allowing a witness to leave.

Once all of the witnesses for a particular party have been heard, the advocate 'closes' the case for that party by saying 'That is the case for the claimant/respondent' (as appropriate). This does not affect the right to make a closing speech. If more than one claim is being heard at the same time, the evidence that is relevant and admissible on each claim may require careful consideration. The most common problem is where claims for wrongful dismissal and claims for unfair dismissal are heard together.

(a) At the liability stage of a claim for unfair dismissal, the employment tribunal is focusing on the knowledge and actions of the employer up to and at the time of dismissal. No account should be taken of subsequently discovered facts (until remedy is considered): *Devis (W) & Sons v Atkins* [1977] AC 931. Thus, for example, evidence coming to light after dismissal supporting an allegation of misconduct is not admissible in the unfair dismissal claim.

(b) In a wrongful dismissal claim, as in most contract claims, the tribunal is concerned to determine whether the employee was justifiably dismissed summarily. Subsequently discovered misconduct and subsequently discovered evidence can be relied upon by the employer to justify the dismissal: *Boston Deep Sea Fishing & Ice Co v Ansell* (1888) 39 Ch D 399.

35.10.4 Submissions of no case to answer

Although it is possible to make a submission of no case to answer at the end of the evidence from the party with the burden of proof, such a practice should only be used in exceptionally plain and obvious cases. Before making a submission, take care to determine whether the employment tribunal will regard you as having elected to call no evidence if you make a submission (as would be the case in a civil trial but not in a criminal trial).

35.10.5 Closing submissions

Employment tribunals often criticise lengthy closing speeches and excessive reference to authority. The party with the burden of proof should have the final say. You can usually assume that the employment tribunal will be familiar with the leading cases. If the law in your case is more complex, then you may need to cite authority, in which case you may find a written skeleton argument extremely useful. If you are citing authorities, you should bring copies for the tribunal (three copies if appearing before a full panel) and your opponent. If this is not possible, let the clerk to the tribunal know in the morning so that copies can be obtained for the employment tribunal.

35.10.6 The liability decision

If time permits, the employment tribunal will give a decision on liability very shortly after hearing closing submissions. A written decision will then be sent to the parties at a later date signed by the chair. If not, the decision will be made later and notified to the parties in writing. The mandatory requirements for orders, judgments, and reasons are now to be found in rr 60–62.

35.10.7 The remedies issue

If the claim is for a redundancy payment, the calculation of the correct payment should be a matter of simple mathematics, applying the formula in the Employment Rights Act 1996, s 162.

If the claim is for unfair dismissal, employment tribunals are obliged to consider an order for reinstatement or re-engagement and only thereafter to award compensation. In practice orders for reinstatement or re-engagement are extremely rarely sought and even more rarely made by a tribunal. If re-engagement or reinstatement is sought, employment tribunals will normally hear evidence from both parties. If only compensation is sought, the tribunal will normally only hear evidence from the applicant about efforts to find a new job and any temporary or permanent position found.

If the employment tribunal announces that a dismissal is unfair, it is quite common for the parties to be recommended to attempt to reach a settlement because the financial benefits of settlement can be considerable (see **35.11**).

35.10.8 Interest

In awards of a redundancy payment or compensation for unfair dismissal no interest is included in the award. However, interest will run in respect of an unpaid award from 42 days after the date of the decision—the period allowed for lodging an appeal (see **35.12.2**).

35.10.9 Costs

In the past, costs were rarely awarded by an employment tribunal. As a result, the parties usually bore their own costs. The 2013 Rules are likely to cause great changes in practice. There are three types of costs orders that can be made: a costs order; a preparation time order; and a wasted cost order. The rules for the making of costs orders can be found in the Tribunal Rules, rr 74–84. The power to award costs in practice is now similar to that in ordinary civil proceedings.

Costs orders can be made under r 76 in respect of either:

(a) costs incurred in preparing or presenting a party's case where represented by either legal representation or lay representation (r 75(1)(a));

(b) tribunal fees paid by a party (r 75(1)(b));

(c) expenses incurred by either a party or a witness either connected to or for the purpose of attending a hearing (r 75(1)(c)).

Preparation costs orders can be made under r 76 in respect of time spent by an unrepresented party on working on the case, except for time spent at any final hearing (r 75(2)).

It is important to note that a costs order and a preparation time order cannot be made in favour of the same party in the same proceedings (r 75(3)). The procedural requirements can be found for such orders at r 77.

Such orders can only be granted—

(a) where a party has acted vexatiously, abusively, disruptively or otherwise unreasonably in either the bringing of the proceedings (or part) or the way that the proceedings (or part) have been conducted (r 76(1)(a));

(b) when any claim or response had no reasonable prospect of success (r 76(1)(b));

(c) where a party has been in breach of any order or Practice Direction or where a hearing has been postponed or adjourned on the application of a party (r 76(2)).

Please note that a respondent shall be made to pay costs if a final hearing in an unfair dismissal case is postponed or adjourned if the claimant expressed a wish to be reinstated or re-engaged no less than seven days before the hearing, and the postponement or adjournment has been caused by the failure to obtain reasonable evidence as to the availability of the job from which the claimant was dismissed or of comparable or suitable employment (r 76(3)).

The costs order made can be summarily assessed by the tribunal up to the value of £20,000 (r 78(1)(a)), or assessed by detailed assessment (r 78(1)(b)), unless the costs relate to attendance at court by a party or a witness or a tribunal fee. If parties agree the amount of costs payable, the tribunal may order that agreed amount (r 78(1)(e)).

Rules 79–82 should be consulted in relation to preparation time orders and wasted costs orders.

The application for costs is normally made at the end of the hearing. If no decision is announced at the end of the hearing, the question of costs would have to be considered at a further hearing (involving additional expense) or by written representations. The Employment Appeal Tribunal has suggested that to avoid a further hearing a party could indicate that, if successful, he or she wished to apply for an order for costs. In practice that is rarely a sensible approach as: (a) it is not until the basis of the decision is known that the application for costs can properly be formulated by labelling the conduct frivolous, vexatious, or merely unreasonable; and (b) the employment tribunal could not be informed of the decision at any pre-hearing review before they have arrived at their own decision.

35.11 **Settlement**

Employment tribunals frequently encourage parties to settle claims 'at the door of the court'. If a liability decision is announced, a further opportunity is often given for settlement before the employment tribunal rules on the remedy. In addition to the usual benefits of settlement, there is one factor peculiar to claims before employment tribunals that you should bear in mind. The factor is the effect of recoupment of state benefits received by the employee after termination.

The position is governed by the Employment Protection (Recoupment of Jobseekers' Allowance and Income Support) Regulations 1996. In short, if a claimant is awarded compensation for unfair dismissal, an employment tribunal has to calculate the period covered by past loss and the net award made for that period (known as the prescribed element). The Secretary of State is then informed of the decision and will reclaim any benefits paid in that period up to the amount awarded. Thus the claimant actually receives less than the sum awarded to him but the respondent pays out the amount awarded, diverting some part to the government, to repay the public purse for benefits paid to the claimant.

If a settlement is reached, there is no recoupment of benefit, provided the prescribed element cannot be identified. In this respect the approach in employment tribunals is quite different from the approach in personal injury actions. In many unfair dismissal cases the sum that will be recouped will be a substantial part of the compensatory element of the award.

If the employee has been unemployed for, say, six months prior to the hearing and has received £4,000 in recoupable benefit, the position is as follows:

(a) If the employment tribunal awards compensation of £5,000 for the six-month period of loss, and further compensation (including a basic award) of, say, £5,000, the respondent will have to pay out £10,000, but the claimant will only receive £6,000 of that sum.

(b) If the case is settled, there is no recoupment of the benefits of £4,000 received. Thus, an agreed settlement of £8,000 payable to the claimant will mean that both parties are better off by £2,000.

If you reach a settlement at the hearing, you should ensure that it is binding and enforceable. There are a number of ways of making the settlement binding. Many chairs have their own preferred way and some will seek to impose their preferred approach on the parties. The most common methods are a 'consent order' or a type of 'Tomlin' order.

(a) A simple consent order for payment can be made by an employment tribunal. There will be no recoupment because there is no prescribed element to which a recoupment notice can be applied.

(b) Employment tribunals do not favour the normal 'Tomlin' form—where the proceedings are stayed indefinitely—as they are anxious to close their files. A common practice is therefore to order that the claim is dismissed on withdrawal by the claimant at some future date, unless either party notifies the employment tribunal that the claim should be released. If, for example, the settlement payment is to be paid in 21 days, it might be convenient for the case to be dismissed on withdrawal by the claimant in 42 days' time if a request for a further hearing has not been made within 35 days. If the payment is received, no request is made and the claim ends in 56 days. If the payment is not made in 21 days (or even shortly thereafter), the claimant would request a further hearing well within the 35 days allowed.

Advice on how to draft orders is given in **Chapter 11** of the *Employment Law in Practice* manual.

35.12 Further steps

There are two ways of challenging a decision of an employment tribunal: by review and by appeal.

35.12.1 Reconsideration of judgments

The tribunal has limited powers under rr 70–73 to reconsider a decision made by the employment tribunal. It was rarely exercised under the old Rules. An application by a party for a review must be in writing made within 14 days of the date the decision was sent to the parties. The employment tribunal has power to review its own decision of its own motion without time limit. The party seeking the reconsideration must show that it is necessary in the interests of justice for the matter to be reconsidered. On reconsideration, the decision may be confirmed, varied or revoked. If revoked, it may be taken again. See r 70.

35.12.2 Appeal

An appeal against the decision of an employment tribunal lies on a point of law to the Employment Appeal Tribunal: Part II, Employment Tribunals Act 1996. The procedure is governed by the Employment Appeals Tribunal Rules 1993 (SI 1993/2854) as amended. The notice of appeal normally has to be lodged within 42 days of the date on which the written decision of the employment tribunal was sent to the parties. There is a detailed and extremely useful EAT Practice Direction that you should study, which is beyond the scope of this chapter. It can be found at: <http://www.justice.gov.uk/downloads/tribunals/employment-appeals/forms-and-how-to-appeal/EAT_PDF.pdf>.

36

Remands/adjournments

Among the first court appearances you are likely to undertake during your second six months' pupillage are an application for a remand in the magistrates' court, an application to stand a case out of the list in the Crown Court, or an application to adjourn a hearing in the county court/High Court or in a tribunal. Often the case will not actually be your case but that of a member of chambers. As you progress in practice, however, you will continue to find that there are many occasions when it is necessary to apply for a remand or adjournment in cases of your own and often you will consider such an application appropriate even where your instructing solicitor has not briefed you specifically for that purpose. Sometimes, unforeseen circumstances arise at a court or tribunal hearing that make it necessary to make or respond to such an application with little notice.

36.1 Preparation

Before you make an application for a remand or adjournment, investigate the reasons for the case not being ready to proceed. The most common grounds for applying for a remand/adjournment are insufficient time to prepare the case (eg investigations incomplete; client only recently instructed solicitors; public funding just granted; late service of affidavit or witness statement; late disclosure of documents); or the court or tribunal or one of the parties is not in a position to proceed (eg witness unavailable; pre-sentence report required; lack of court time).

Consider the history of the case; if it is not your case, try to speak to counsel whose case it is. Have there been any previous adjournments in the case? For what reason? Has there been any delay on your client's/solicitor's part? Can you explain the delay? Always ensure you have clear instructions on these matters and have advised your solicitors where it may be necessary to lay the blame for undue delay at their door. Ensure you have a chronology of the progress of the case clear in your mind.

Advise your client of the reasons for an application to adjourn being appropriate and the consequences this may have for him or her, for example, on the question of costs. In some cases, the client may instruct you to proceed even if you are not fully prepared, for example, he or she may prefer to proceed with the witnesses that have attended rather than risk the costs of an adjournment or the agony of further delay simply to secure the attendance of another witness. (It is sensible to invite your client to endorse this instruction on your brief.)

Consider the steps, if any, that have been taken to notify the other party and the court or tribunal of the application to adjourn the case. Be in a position to explain the absence of any notice. Inform your opponent at the earliest opportunity of your intention to apply for an adjournment. Discover whether your application is likely to be/will be opposed.

Look at the merits of your application. Will your opponent be prejudiced by an adjournment or can any prejudice be compensated, for example, by an order for costs? Will you be prejudiced by a refusal to adjourn? How vital is it to your case? If you have time, make a note of the main points of your argument.

Consider how long you realistically need to be ready to proceed with the case.

Apply your mind to any orders or directions you want the court or tribunal to make pending the adjourned hearing (whether you are making or responding to the application), for example, permission to amend a statement of case; permission to file further witness statement(s); specific disclosure of documents; an interim injunction to maintain the status quo or to protect your client; continuation of any existing order(s) such as an interim injunction; an interim order to provide for your client, for example, order for maintenance or contact with his or her children; the grant of bail or the continuation of an existing surety. Where appropriate, try to agree any orders/directions with your opponent.

Ask yourself what order for costs you want the court or tribunal to impose in the event of your/your opponent's application for an adjournment being successful, for example, an order for the costs thrown away; costs reserved. Advise your client of any risk that he or she will be ordered to pay the costs (or your solicitors if the fault lies with them).

Never assume that the court or tribunal will accede to your request for an adjournment. Be prepared to proceed if your application is refused **but** never assume an obligation to do a case in such circumstances when you do not feel professionally qualified to do so. If you face such a possibility when the brief is one delivered to another member of the Bar and you are simply making the application because he or she cannot be at the hearing, you must discuss the matter with them beforehand and make your position clear to them. If the brief is one that has been delivered to you, then you should not hesitate to discuss your position with your former pupil supervisor or a senior member of chambers. It may be necessary later to speak directly to your instructing solicitor. Always remember, the interests of the client come first.

36.2 Making the application

When your case is called on for hearing, inform the court or tribunal at the outset that you have an application to make for a remand/adjournment/the case to be stood out of the list (as appropriate) and indicate if your application is opposed/unopposed.

Set out the reasons for your application in a succinct manner. If appropriate, refer the court or tribunal to any affidavit or document that is relevant to the application for an adjournment. Explain any delays—be honest. Deal with the merits of your application and the manner in which any possible prejudice to the other party can be met, for example, an order for interim relief, an order for costs.

Be as brief as possible and do not repeat your arguments! Do not try to argue the merits of your substantive case. Remember that at this stage you are applying for an adjournment.

Tell the court or tribunal how long you will need before you are in a position to proceed with the hearing of the case.

It will then be your opponent's turn to address the court or tribunal. If resisting such an application, he or she will emphasise any delay on the part of the applicant and the inconvenience and/or prejudice his or her client will suffer as a result of the delay, which cannot be met in any other way, for example, by an interim order or an order for costs.

You may then have a further opportunity to address the court or tribunal in response to your opponent's submissions. Do not use this as an opportunity to repeat your arguments.

If the application to adjourn is either unopposed or succeeds, indicate to the court or tribunal the orders or directions that you seek in the interim and whether any or all of them are agreed subject to the court's or tribunal's approval.

Make or respond to the application for costs (see **Chapter 34**).

Bail application

The following is a checklist for the preparation and conduct of a bail application. Reference should be made to the *Criminal Litigation and Sentencing* manual (**chapter 3**) for the procedure.

37.1 Preparation

The first and most important step is to discover what the objections are to bail. These may be fairly obvious, for example, your client may have allegedly committed the offence while on bail for another offence; or may have a history of absconding; he or she may be charged with a serious offence such as supplying drugs or a series of offences such as burglary.

If not apparent, then ask the prosecuting advocate what are the objections to bail. Get to court early enough to have the opportunity to speak to him or her; in the magistrates' court, he or she is likely to be dealing with a considerable caseload.

Ensure you have an up-to-date copy of the defendant's antecedents (especially their convictions, if any); if you don't have it, ask the prosecution for a copy. Never rely solely on a client's description (or recollection) of his or her past record.

Consider with your client whether he or she wants you to make a bail application and advise on the prospects of success. Some clients are realistic and appreciate when their prospects of obtaining bail are hopeless; others anticipate a custodial sentence and prefer to serve part of their eventual sentence on remand (see Criminal Justice Act 2003, s 240(3)). Consider whether it is the right time to make a bail application or whether it is appropriate to wait, for example, until you have been served with advance disclosure of the prosecution case, have fuller instructions, or there is a surety at court.

Consider the strength of the prosecution evidence. If advance information has not yet been served on the defence, consider the nature and extent of the charge(s), the amount of any money involved, the gravity of any alleged injury; ask the prosecutor for basic information such as whether there are any eyewitness accounts, whether the evidence is circumstantial, whether the defendant is alleged to have confessed.

Take the fullest instructions from the client that time permits upon the circumstances of the alleged offence(s), and his or her tentative plea.

Go through the client's previous record in detail, establishing the circumstances of any serious or similar offences to the present charge(s), whether he or she pleaded guilty in respect of any past offences, the reasons for any previous failure to appear, whether he or she has ever been convicted of committing an offence while on bail.

Find out the client's present circumstances: job, home ties, responsibilities, the potential/probable effects of a continued loss of liberty.

Look at whether there has been any change in the client's circumstances since the time of the alleged offence, for example, has he or she moved from the area, changed his or her group of friends? Is any change likely in the future?

Discuss any possible conditions that can be put forward to meet the objections to bail and whether your client is prepared to abide by them. Consider practical solutions to the objections, for example, if the defendant has no fixed abode, is a place in a bail hostel or other accommodation a possibility? Speak to the probation officer at court about this; if necessary, ask for your case to be put back on the list for this purpose. Note that bail hostels will not normally consider a defendant with a drug habit or convictions for violence. If possible, discuss any proposed conditions with the prosecutor in advance to determine whether such conditions would meet the objections. (If so, the bail application will become effectively 'unopposed' and offering the 'agreed' conditions to the court will be likely to succeed.)

Consider whether any surety is (or is likely to be) available, the amount any proposed surety is/would be prepared to offer; if the proposed surety is at court, ensure he or she understands the meaning of standing as a surety and the likely consequences in the event of the defendant absconding. Consider whether a proposal to lodge security at court is a practical option (normally more appropriate in the case of a foreign defendant or where a risk of leaving the country is involved).

37.2 Making the application

In making your application for bail, keep it as brief as possible and to the point. Do not repeat yourself, do not wander off on a tangent or lecture the court on the law or upon your client's rights to bail. Deal with your points in a logical sequence, making your strongest points first and last. Do not make weak points that will detract from the strength of your other submissions.

Deal with the objections in two ways. *Step 1*: undermine/cast doubt on their validity. Show the court that there are no 'substantial grounds' for the objection(s). *Step 2*: propose how such objections (if still of concern, in that there may be a 'real risk') could sensibly be met.

Example 1. If the objection is that the defendant is likely to commit offences while on bail, draw the court's attention to such matters as the weaknesses in the prosecution case, your client's intention to plead 'not guilty'; the fact that he or she has always pleaded guilty in the past, or has no history of committing offences while on bail; the dissimilarity between the present charge(s) and his or her previous offences; the amount of time that has elapsed since his or her last conviction; the fact that he or she has an address to stay at away from previous associates or has moved since the time of the alleged offence(s). Suggest possible conditions such as: a condition of residence, a curfew, restriction to/from a particular location.

Example 2. If the objection is that he or she is likely to interfere with witnesses: draw the court's attention to the fact that there is no suggestion the defendant has ever done so before; and/or that no threats or pressure are alleged to have been made/applied in this case; point to the lack of any close connection between the defendant and the witness (eg family relationship, neighbour) that would enable him or her to influence the alleged victim/witness if he or she were released on bail. Suggest possible conditions such as: prohibiting the defendant from contacting or interfering with any witness; restricting his or her entry into the areas where the alleged victim/witness lives.

Example 3. If the objection is that the defendant is likely to abscond: highlight such matters as the fact that the defendant has never done so before; or explain the circumstances of any failure to appear in the past (eg dates mixed up; went to the police/court as soon as he or she realised); and/or point to the fact that he or she has in the past attended court even where he or she has pleaded guilty or anticipated a custodial sentence; address the court upon the weaknesses in the prosecution case and/or the unlikelihood of a custodial sentence even if the defendant were to plead guilty/be convicted; emphasise the defendant's community ties, employment, secure home, family responsibilities as indicators of the unlikelihood of his or her absconding. Suggest possible conditions such as: (daily) reporting to the nearest police station; condition of residence; residence at a bail hostel; surrendering his or her passport; providing a surety; lodging security.

There are some cases where it is simply not possible to undermine the objections. If the defendant has a history of absconding, it is useless to argue that 'she has learned her lesson and has asked me to assure the court that she will not abscond again'. That will get you nowhere! If you cannot deal with the objection(s) in this way, be realistic about it. Concentrate your efforts upon persuading the court that there are (stringent) conditions that could be imposed to ensure the defendant's good behaviour and attendance at court.

Having dealt with the objections to bail, it may assist to point out the likely consequences of a continuing loss of liberty upon the defendant, for example, losing his or her job; mortgagee possession proceedings in respect of his or her home; children will be taken into care.

If you call any proposed surety, establish his or her relationship to the defendant; then ask questions designed to elicit that he or she understands the meaning of what he or she is proposing and the consequences if the defendant fails to attend the trial (eg 'Do you understand that you will be liable to forfeit such a sum if the defendant absconds?'); establish the amount of money he or she is proposing to pledge and the manner in which he or she would raise that sum in the event of the defendant absconding (it should be otherwise than by selling/mortgaging his or her home, such as from savings in the building society), for example, 'Are you worth £x after all your debts are paid?'; 'How would you raise that sum if ordered to do so?'; confirm that he or she is still prepared to stand as a surety to ensure the defendant's surrender to bail (eg, 'Are you still prepared to stand surety in the sum of £xxx?').

If bail is granted, ensure your client understands the nature and extent of any conditions imposed and the likely consequences if he or she breaches them.

If bail is refused by the magistrates, obtain a copy of the magistrates' certificate recording their reasons for the refusal (see the Bail Act 1976, s 5(6A)). Consider with your client whether he or she wishes you to renew the application before the magistrates on the next or a subsequent court appearance or whether he or she wishes to appeal to a Crown Court judge for bail. You must know the procedure on the application itself and also that relating to appeal. Advise your client realistically of the prospects of such an appeal.

37.3 Procedure

37.3.1 Bail applications

Figure 37.1 charts the procedure in a magistrates' court when the magistrates, having asked the defence whether there is an application for bail, receive an answer in the affirmative.

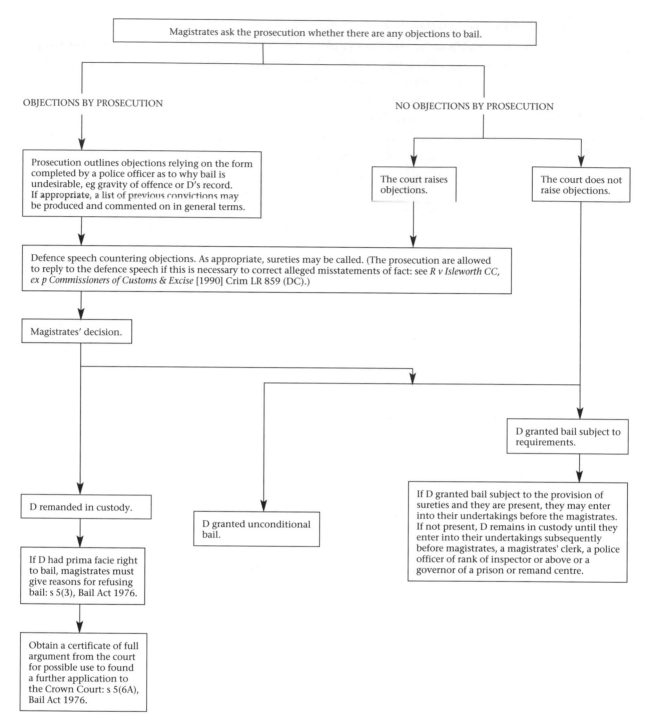

Figure 37.1   Bail application in a magistrates' court—flow chart

38

Conducting a *voir dire* or 'trial within a trial'

Whenever you are instructed in a trial, one of the most important things to consider as you prepare the case is the admissibility of the evidence. Whatever your initial view, the complexion of a case can change dramatically if evidence is excluded. Whether you are prosecuting or defending you must confirm in your own mind that the prosecution evidence can legitimately be put before the court. If you are defending in the Crown Court and in your opinion there is prosecution evidence that should be excluded, you will have to ask the judge to hold a *voir dire* or 'trial within a trial' to rule on the question of admissibility. The position in the magistrates' court is different and we will consider those differences later in the chapter.

38.1 A *voir dire* in the Crown Court

38.1.1 Defence

As you prepare your case for trial you must identify any parts of the prosecution evidence that you think should be excluded. Evidence may be excluded for many reasons. It may be unfair to admit the evidence (Police and Criminal Evidence Act 1984, s 78). It may be that your client made a confession and you say it was obtained under oppression or has been rendered unreliable as the result of something said or done (Police and Criminal Evidence Act 1984, s 76). You may just take the view that the evidence is more prejudicial than probative (*Sang* [1980] AC 402). Whatever the reason, if you decide to challenge the admissibility of the evidence there will need to be a *voir dire* so that the judge can decide whether the evidence should be admitted or not. The *voir dire* or 'trial within a trial' takes place in the absence of the jury so that they never hear evidence if it is excluded by the judge.

38.1.1.1 Should I raise the issue at all?

Sometimes there will be reasons for not holding a *voir dire*. Remember that a *voir dire* is a trial on the issue of admissibility and so witnesses will be called to give their oral testimony. The witnesses will be examined by the prosecutor and by you. The testimony they give will form the basis for your argument about why the evidence should be excluded. If you think that the chances of persuading the judge to exclude the evidence are slim, but that the jury will find your arguments persuasive, you may not want to give the witnesses a chance to practise their evidence. If the judge does not exclude the evidence you will have to cross-examine the witnesses again in front of the jury, but this time they will know what you are trying to achieve and may be better able to resist you.

38.1.1.2   When should I raise the issue?

As you read the prosecution evidence and your instructions you should make sure that you are aware of any potential admissibility issues quickly. You may not be able to decide whether to challenge the evidence immediately, but by being aware of a possible challenge you can take instructions from your client and make a final decision in advance of trial. At the plea and case management hearing (PCMH) you will have to complete a standard form that will ask you to indicate whether there are any admissibility issues to be resolved. Some of the questions that the form asks are set out below and demonstrate that you must have a very clear idea about how the trial will proceed from an early stage.

---

22 Defendant's interview(s)

21.1 Specify any issue relating to the admissibility of all or any part of the defendant's interview(s). Can the issue be resolved now? If not, when? Are skeleton arguments needed and, if so, when?

22.2 By how much can the interview(s) be shortened by editing/summary for trial? Give a timetable for the service of any proposed summary by the prosecution and agreement/counter-proposal by the defence.

22.3 Specify any other issues concerning the defendant's interview(s).

29 Hearsay

Are any directions necessary in relation to hearsay application?

30 Admissibility and legal issues

What points on admissibility/other legal issues are to be taken? Is it necessary for any to be resolved before trial?

The complete PCMH advocates' questionnaire is available at <http://www.justice.gov.uk>.

Having identified in the PCMH form that you wish to challenge the admissibility of evidence, the judge will decide when the *voir dire* should be held. There are three possibilities: first, in advance of the trial; second, at the beginning of the trial before any other evidence is called; and, third, during the trial immediately before the challenged evidence is called. Which option is chosen will depend on a number of factors, such as how important the evidence is, whether the prosecution will still have a case if the evidence is excluded, the ease with which the prosecution can open the case without reference to the disputed evidence, the ease with which the witnesses can attend to give their evidence.

Sometimes, despite excellent preparation, things will arise during the trial that you could not have anticipated. Evidence that previously seemed incontrovertible may suddenly be open to challenge. If this happens, then you must raise the matter with the judge as soon as you reasonably can. 'As soon as you reasonably can' may be in the middle of a witness's oral testimony. As with any matter of law, you will indicate to the judge that you need the jury to leave court, using a form of words like, 'Your Honour, a matter of law has arisen that you may wish to consider in the absence of the jury'.

Depending on the complexity of the issue, the judge may require you to provide a skeleton argument and authorities in advance of the *voir dire*. There is no requirement for the judge to do this and in ordinary cases the issues will be sufficiently discrete and straightforward that it will not be necessary.

38.1.1.3   How do I prepare?

A *voir dire* is a trial on a particular and discrete issue, the admissibility of the evidence that you are challenging. Successful preparation will identify precisely what you are challenging, why you are challenging it, and where the judge's power to exclude it comes from. Witnesses who give evidence during the *voir dire* often have a great deal to say about other topics and, if your preparation is not sufficiently focused, it is easy to stray into matters that are not relevant to the question of admissibility. If this happens there is a real risk that you will confuse the court about what your point is, or that you will cause the judge to lose patience, or that you will damage the rest of your case by revealing too much information to the witness or the prosecutor. Remember that you may not succeed in having the evidence excluded so you should try to keep some questions in reserve to ask in front of the jury. If the evidence is not excluded you may want to plan a completely different line of cross-examination for the witness so that you retain some element of surprise.

Begin by clearly identifying the evidence that you say should be excluded. The easiest way to do this is to mark the relevant sections physically, by putting them in brackets or striking them through. Sometimes this will be easy because you are challenging all of the evidence of a particular witness. But often you will only be challenging part of the evidence. For example, you may choose to challenge the admissibility of a whole interview, perhaps because your client was refused access to a solicitor. But you may only want to challenge some of the interview, for example, only those parts that amount to a confession.

Next, identify the law on which you need to rely. Flag in your copy of *Archbold* or *Blackstone's* where the judge's power to exclude the evidence comes from (Police and Criminal Evidence Act 1984, s 76 or s 78, *Sang* [1980] AC 402) and familiarise yourself with the tests set out there. Identify and flag any cases on which you wish to rely and make sure you have copies for the judge and the prosecutor.

Draft the submissions that you would like to make to the judge if the evidence comes out as you expect. This may seem like the final stage, but it isn't. If you have a clear idea about what you need to say to the judge at the end, you will also have a clear idea about what (and what not) to establish from each witness during their oral testimony. This draft will act as a guide for the preparation of your witness handling and the standard against which you will judge its success.

Draw from the plan each point that you need to establish from each witness. This will form the basis for your witness handling. Be prepared for the evidence to be different from what you expected. This is not unusual, nor is it necessarily a disaster. As you progress through your witness handling you will need to decide whether the evidence is coming out in a way that strengthens or undermines your application and manipulate your final submissions accordingly.

Having said all of that, never make an unnecessary application. You may find that the prosecutor agrees with some or all of your points and is prepared to edit documents or control witnesses to ensure that certain evidence is not put before the court. Proper organisation of your thoughts will make it more likely that you can persuade the prosecutor of your view, so before you speak to the prosecutor, be as clear about your arguments as you would be if you were going before the judge.

38.1.1.4   Checklist

(1)   Start to consider questions of admissibility the first time you read the papers.

(2)   Be ready to identify areas of challenge as early as the PCMH.

(3)   Identify precisely which parts of the evidence you say should be excluded.

(4)   Identify the law on which you will rely, in particular identify the tests for exclusion and any authorities that support your argument. Make copies where necessary.

(5)   Draft your closing submissions on admissibility.

(6)   Use your draft submissions to prepare tightly focused witness handling.

(7)   Discuss the issues with the prosecution to see if any agreement can be reached that would remove the need for argument, or at least reduce its scope.

38.1.2   Prosecution

When you are prosecuting you need to take care that the evidence on which you propose to rely is properly admissible. Partly this is so that you are prepared to respond to any challenges made by the defence, but it is also to do with your particular responsibilities as the prosecution advocate.

The Code for Crown Prosecutors makes it clear that prosecutors have a duty to make decisions about the admissibility of evidence when deciding whether to prosecute at all, and so you need to consider the admissibility of your evidence irrespective of whether the defence choose to challenge it.

4.6   When deciding whether there is sufficient evidence to prosecute, prosecutors should ask themselves the following:

Can the evidence be used in court?

Prosecutors should consider whether there is any questions over the admissibility of certain evidence. In doing so, prosecutors should assess:
(a) the likelihood of that evidence being held as inadmissible by the court; and
(b) the importance of that evidence in relation to the evidence as a whole.

Is the evidence reliable?

Prosecutors should consider whether there are any reasons to questions the reliability of the evidence, including its accuracy or integrity.

Is the evidence credible?

Prosecutors should consider whether there are any reasons to doubt the credibility of the evidence . . .

3.6   . . . Review is a continuing process and prosecutors must take account of any change in circumstances that occurs as the case develops . . .

The full code is available at <http://www.cps.gov.uk>.

If you have decided that your evidence is admissible, or is not likely to be excluded, then you should already have an idea of how you would respond to a challenge from the defence.

You should know in advance whether any of your evidence is going to be challenged because you will have been told at the PCMH or, if you weren't at that hearing, you will have read the PCMH form. Even so, it is sensible to ask the defence advocate before trial whether there is any evidence they now propose to challenge. It is important that you know this because, if the defence are successful, the jury will never hear the evidence, and so you should not refer to it in your opening speech.

If the defence are proposing to challenge any of your evidence, you should decide whether you agree that it (or any of it) should not be admitted. If you do not agree, attempt to get a clear view of precisely what evidence the defence are proposing to challenge.

If the defence are proposing to make a challenge to the admissibility of evidence that was not disclosed at the PCMH, the matter should be raised with the judge before you open the case. This will allow the judge to make a decision about when the *voir dire* should take place. You may want the *voir dire* to take place before you open your case so that you can make the fullest possible opening, but witness arrangements may mean that that is impossible.

Prepare to deal with a challenge to the admissibility of your evidence in a similar way to the way you would if you were making the challenge.

38.1.2.1 Checklist

(1) During your preparation, check that you are satisfied about the admissibility of the prosecution evidence.

(2) Speak to the defence to confirm their position before you open your case.

(3) If evidence is to be challenged, check that the judge is aware and ensure that a decision has been reached about when the challenge will take place.

(4) Identify precisely the evidence that the defence say should be excluded.

(5) Identify the law on which you will rely, including the relevant test(s) for exclusion and any authorities. Make copies where necessary.

(6) Draft your submission.

(7) Prepare your witness handling with close reference to your draft submission.

38.2 The *voir dire* or 'trial within a trial'

As the name suggests the *voir dire* is a discrete trial on a point and will take the same form as the trial of the offence itself. The precise form it takes will be determined by the type of evidence that is being challenged and the power to exclude that the judge is being asked to employ. Generally the form of the *voir dire* will be as follows.

(1) The defence open by setting out the evidence they say should be excluded and on what basis.

(2) The witnesses are called and examined.

(3) The defence make full submissions in favour of exclusion.

(4) The prosecution make full submissions against exclusion.

(5) The judge rules on admissibility.

A common example of when a *voir dire* or 'trial within a trial' will be required is when the defence challenges, or the judge questions, the admissibility of a confession upon which the prosecution seeks to rely. An example of the procedure in such cases follows in **38.3**.

38.3 Example of a 'trial within a trial' in *R v Lewis and others*

IN THE CROWN COURT SITTING AT LEWES

R v Lewis and others

Instructions to counsel for the prosecution

Counsel has herewith:

1. Bundle of witness statements

2. Antecedent history of the accused

Counsel is instructed:

    (i)   to prosecute in this matter and

    (ii) to settle the appropriate indictment.

Case Summary

On 16.4.XX a branch of the South Downs Building Society was held up at gunpoint by two masked men. One kept watch by the door, observing both the people inside the branch and passers-by. The other demanded money from a cashier. On obtaining a hold-all containing £15,967, the two men fled on foot. They were pursued by a passer-by and one of the men stopped and shot the pursuer, a Mr Goodbody. They then made good their escape, using a car parked nearby.

The prosecution case theory is that three of the accused, namely Lewis, Duke and Ella, were involved in the actual robbery with Ella as the driver of the escape vehicle, a stolen Audi motor vehicle. The fourth accused, Peterson, stored the vehicle in his garage for several days prior to the robbery.

Original charge

Against Finlay LEWIS, Arthur DUKE, Gerald ELLA and Leonard PETERSON.

You are charged that, on the 16th day of April 20XX, you did rob Mary Penny of £15,967, contrary to the Theft Act 1968, s 8(1).

STATEMENT OF WITNESS

<u>Statement of</u>:	Mary Penny
<u>Age</u>:	Over 18
<u>Occupation</u>:	Building society cashier

[Usual declaration omitted]

I am a cashier for the South Downs Building Society. I work in the Churchill Square Branch. I have been there for about 4 years.

I remember the 16th of April 20XX. I was at work that morning. At about 10 am two men entered the branch. Both were wearing dark-coloured donkey jackets which had orange fluorescent material on the top half. They had on dark balaclava helmets with 'Porky Pig' masks. They were both carrying what looked like sawn-off shotguns.

One of the men shouted for everyone to get on the floor. There was some screaming and the same man shouted to shut up.

He came to my window and said 'fill this with money and nobody will get hurt'.

He produced a nylon holdall and passed it through the window. I looked at the manager who indicated that I should do as the man asked.

I emptied the contents of the tills into the bag. This was both cash and cheques. Then I gave it back to the man at the counter.

All this time the other man had just stood by the entrance door, pointing his gun at the staff and customers.

The man with the holdall joined the other one by the door. One of them shouted 'Nobody move and you won't get hurt' and they both ran out. I think it was the man with the holdall who shouted.

I had pressed the silent alarm as the man approached my window and about two minutes after the men left, several police officers arrived.

I would describe the man with the holdall as about 6 feet tall and medium build. His voice was unusual. He had an accent. Irish is how I would describe it.

I saw his hands when he gave me the bag—they were white.

On the 26th of April I attended an identification parade at Brighton Police Station where I saw a number of men. They all looked about the same height and build as the man with the holdall.

They each said the words 'fill this with money and nobody will get hurt'. I picked out the 5th man. I am sure he was the man with the holdall.

I did not get a good look at the second man. I think he was about 2 inches shorter than the other one, again medium build. I would not recognise him again.

The whole incident lasted for about 5 minutes.

I did not see the face of either man. I did not see their hair, they were both wearing balaclava helmets. Their jackets were not tight on them. They could have been slimmer than medium build.

I saw no distinctive features on either man. The voice was distinctive.

I would call it Irish. I have no Irish relations or friends. I have not been to Ireland on holiday. I have never been to Scotland.

I can recall the voice of the man with the holdall. I am sure that the man I picked out at the identification parade had the same voice. I am not mistaken. I am not an expert on voices or regional accents.

<u>Signed</u>: *M. Penny* (witness)   Date: 16th April 20XX

STATEMENT OF WITNESS

Statement of: Reginald Goodbody

Age: Over 18

Occupation: Retired grocer

[Usual declaration omitted]

On 16.4.XX I was in Brighton, to do some shopping, my wife was with me.

We started looking around the shops in Churchill Square. Just after 10 o'clock we were going past a small parade of shops when two men ran out of the South Downs Building Society premises there. I was about 20 yards away from them. They ran towards me and my wife. They had a bag and guns. They were wearing balaclava helmets. They had workmen's jackets on—black I think, with orange patches.

I realised they had robbed the Building Society and I put up my arms to try and stop them. One got past me but I caught hold of the bag that the other one was carrying.

We got into a bit of a struggle over the bag. I think people were coming out of the Building Society by now.

The other man ran back and shouted at me to let go. When I said No, he deliberately took aim and fired. He shot me in the leg with his gun. I fell over and let go of the bag. Both of them ran off.

The one I was struggling with was about my height and build. I am 6 feet tall and weigh about 13 stone. The other one was about the same. I can't recall him clearly. I would not recognise either of them again. Their features were quite obscured by their helmets.

I went to hospital in an ambulance with my wife. It was the Royal Sussex Hospital in Brighton. I was there for 8 days. My leg was badly damaged by the shot from the gun. I lost some blood and quite a bit of muscle and flesh in my calf.

I now have to walk with a stick. I find my mobility is very restricted. I attend the hospital physiotherapy department every week to build my leg up.

The one with the bag shot me. The gun did not go off in the struggle—I am quite sure.

Signed: *R. Goodbody* (witness)   Date: 16th April 20XX

STATEMENT OF WITNESS

Statement of: Brenda BROWSE

Age: Over 18

Occupation: Housekeeper

[Usual declaration omitted]

On the 16th of April 20XX I left my home to meet a friend in Brighton. We had arranged to meet by the Oxfam shop, just along the road from Churchill Square. I got there early, at about 9.30 am. There were several cars parked around the area but I did not take any notice of them. I went to a cafe over the road for a cup of tea.

While I was in the cafe, I could see the road ahead—Mountfort Road. There was a dark blue Audi parked there with a man sitting behind the wheel. The car was there the whole time I was in the cafe. At about 10 o'clock, as I was about to leave, two men came running along the road, shouting something. The man in the car started the engine and the two men leaped into the car. It tore off down the road, towards the junction by the cafe and straight over without waiting to see if anyone was crossing the road.

I was astonished by this behaviour and made a note of the car registration number. It was EF02 JPO.

I would not recognise the two men who jumped into the car again but both were wearing workmen's jackets with orange fluorescent patches like Council workmen wear. I think they both had dark hair.

The man in the car was quite slim with dark wavy hair, fair-skinned and in his early twenties. I would recognise him again.

I am willing to attend court to give evidence.

Signed: *B. Browse* (witness)   Date: 17th April 20XX

STATEMENT OF WITNESS

Statement of: Brenda BROWSE

Age: Over 18

Occupation: Housekeeper

[Usual declaration omitted]

Further to my statement of 17th April 20XX, on the 15th of May 20XX I was asked to attend Brighton Police Station. I was met by Inspector Charger who explained that there was going to be a parade where the man I saw in the Audi might be. He explained that the man might not be there and I was to look at all of the men very carefully. He said only if I was sure I saw the same man, I should stop and point him out and if I wasn't sure, I should say so.

I was escorted into a waiting room by a WPC and eventually taken to a larger room with several men lined up against one wall. I went to one end of the line and walked along it. The seventh man was the one I had seen driving the Audi on the 16th of April. I was quite sure and I pointed him out. He did not do anything. The Inspector asked me to leave the room as the parade was now over.

I was then brought to a room where I wrote this statement.

Signed: *B. Browse* (witness)   Date: 15th May 20XX

STATEMENT OF WITNESS

Statement of: David LAW

Age: Over 18

Occupation: Detective Sergeant 494P, Brighton CID

[Usual declaration omitted]

On 16th April 20XX at 12.10 pm, as a result of information received, I went to 33 Dials Lane in Brighton where I found a navy blue Audi which appeared to have been abandoned in a hurry. The doors were wide open. Under the driver's seat were some shotgun cartridges. The registration number of the vehicle was EF02 JPO.

I had reason to believe that this vehicle had been used in an armed robbery which had occurred earlier that day in Brighton and I requested that a Scenes of Crime Officer attend the location in Dials Lane.

On 11th May 20XX, I went to a private house at 72 Power Station Row, Southwick. The door was opened by a woman who identified herself as Sharon Ella. I asked her if I could speak to Gerald Ella—she replied that he was not in. Subsequently, I attended the rear of the house where colleagues had apprehended Gerald ELLA, while he was climbing over a fence in the garden of number 72.

I said to him, 'Are you Gerald Ella?' He replied, 'What if I am?' I said to him, 'I have reason to believe you were involved in an armed robbery on the South Downs Building Society in Brighton on the 16th of April, specifically as the driver of the getaway vehicle.' He replied, 'You've got a very good imagination for a copper'.

I then told him that his fingerprints had been identified on the getaway vehicle, the navy blue Audi. He seemed to be about to fall down so I grabbed him and said, 'I am arresting you for your part in the South Downs robbery on the 16th of April 20XX. You do not have to say anything. But it may harm your defence if you do not mention when questioned something which you later rely on in court. Anything you do say may be given in evidence.' He made no reply and was taken to Brighton Central Police Station under escort.

He was later seen by myself and DC Libby in an interview room at Brighton Central at 10.25 pm on the 11th. He was reminded of the caution and I then asked him if he was prepared to talk to us about the robbery. He indicated that he did not wish to talk to us and he was returned to his cell at 10.28 pm.

I was present at 7.35 am on the 12th of May 20XX when ELLA was charged with robbery, the charge was read over to him, he was cautioned and made no reply.

At 2.40 pm on the 12th of May I interviewed Arthur DUKE at Brighton Central Police Station where he was in custody. The interview was tape-recorded and concluded at 3.02 pm.

At 6.00 am on the 13th of May 20XX I went to 22 Bramber Street, Brighton. There I saw a man I now know to be Finlay LEWIS. I said to him, 'Are you Finlay Lewis?' He said, 'Yes, why?' I told him that he had been implicated in the robbery of the South Downs Building Society in Brighton and he replied, 'Someone's a grass. I'm saying nothing till I see my solicitor.'

After a brief search of the premises, I told LEWIS that he was under arrest for robbery and cautioned him. He replied 'I'll be wanting a word with my solicitor.' He was then taken to Brighton Central Police Station and booked into a cell.

I saw LEWIS again at 2.10 pm that day in the interview room, together with DC Libby. The interview was tape-recorded and ended at 2.25 pm.

At 4.45 pm on the 13th of May 20XX LEWIS was charged with robbery, the charge was read over to him, he was cautioned and made no reply.

<u>Signed</u>: *D. Law* (witness)   Date: 18th May 20XX

<u>STATEMENT OF WITNESS</u>

Statement of: Alan LIBBY

Age: Over 18

Occupation: Detective Constable 675P, Brighton CID

[Usual declaration omitted]

At 6.00 am on the 12th of May 20XX, I went to a private flat at 344 Lewes Road, Brighton, together with several other officers. The door was answered by a man I now know as Arthur DUKE. I said to DUKE, 'I have reason to believe that you were involved in an armed robbery last month on a Brighton building society. Have you got anything to say?' He replied, 'You've got the wrong man this time.' I asked if we could look round his flat and he said 'Yes'.

On the floor of a wardrobe in the bedroom I found a balaclava helmet. A shoebox in the same wardrobe contained six shotgun cartridges. Hanging in the wardrobe was a navy-blue donkey jacket with an orange fluorescent upper half. I said to DUKE, 'Where did you get this jacket?' He said, 'I've had it for a while now. I wear it if I get any building-site work.' I then showed him the balaclava and cartridges and said, 'How do you explain these then?' He did not reply.

I said, 'I am arresting you for robbing the South Downs Building Society in Brighton on the 16th of April this year.' I cautioned him and he made no reply. He was taken to Brighton Central Police Station.

At 2.40 pm on the same day, I was present when DS Law interviewed DUKE at Brighton Central Police Station. The interview was tape-recorded. I produce the master tape as exhibit AL/1 and the record of the taped interview (ROTI) as AL/2.

At 5.25 pm on the 12th May 20XX DUKE was charged with robbery, the charge was read over, he was cautioned and made no reply.

On the 12th of May at 10.50 pm, I went to 65 Brighthelmstone Street where I saw a man I now know to be Leonard PETERSON. I said to him, 'Are you Lennie Peterson?' He said, 'That's right. Who are you?' I showed him my warrant card and explained that I was investigating the robbery of the South Downs Building Society.

I said, 'I have reason to believe that you garaged the car for the gang before the robbery. What have you got to say?' He said, 'I know nothing about it.' I said, 'It's right that you've got a lock-up garage at the back of the house, isn't it. That's where the car was kept.' He replied, 'Who's been talking out of turn?'

I said, 'The car was stolen on the 9th of April—that's a week before the robbery. It had to be kept somewhere, out of sight. I think you warehoused it for the gang. For all I know, you stole it, too.' He said, 'Look, I'm no car thief. Gerry ELLA asked me to keep it safe for him until he needed it. He brought it round on the 9th and took it away on the 16th. That's all I know.'

I told him he was being arrested for the robbery and cautioned him. He made no reply and was then taken to Brighton Central Police Station.

At 7.30 pm on the 13th of May 20XX at Brighton Central Police Station PETERSON was charged with robbery, the charge was read over to him, he was cautioned and replied, 'I've been very silly and it's all for nothing. What can I say?'

On the 13th of May at 2.10 pm, I attended an interview of Finlay LEWIS by DS Law in an interrogation room at Brighton Central Police Station. The interview was tape-recorded and I produce the master tape as exhibit AL/3 and the record of the taped interview (ROT I) as AL/4

<u>Signed</u>: *A. Libby* (witness)   Date: 18th May 20XX

Extracts from record of taped interview of Arthur Duke by DS LAW, produced by DC Libby (AL/2): —

Q.   Do you want us to wait for your lawyer?

A.   No, let's get it over.

Q.   As I mentioned on the way here, we've found some fingerprints on the Audi and it looks like they are yours.

A.   Oh yeah?

Q.   I'm serious. Those prints place you in the car. Take them together with what we found in your home . . .

A.   All right. It was never meant to end up the way it did.

Q.   What do you mean?

A.   The old man. Finlay's always been stupid but that tops the lot.

Q.   So it was Finlay that shot Mr Goodbody?

A.   Yes.

Q.   Is that Finlay LEWIS?

A.   Yes. I should never have agreed to take part in it. Finlay had it all set up before I got invited. His original partner had to drop out—he's on remand in Brixton at the moment.

. . .

A.   Finlay had Gerry ELLA and Len PETERSON lined up. He knew Gerry from Wandsworth and Len was a friend of Gerry's.

. . .

A.   I kept watch while Finlay played the hard man with the cashier. Everything went smooth as silk until the old man grabbed Finlay's bag. I couldn't believe what they were doing. Just as I went back to help, Finlay's gun went off and the old boy went down. I don't know whether it was an accident or not.

Extracts from record of taped interview of Finlay LEWIS by DS Law, produced by DC Libby (AL/4):—

Q.   I am refusing to delay this interview so that you can have your solicitor present because I believe that delay may prevent recovery of the stolen money.

A.   No reply.

...

Q.   . . . First, I must remind you that you are under caution . . .

Q.   This was a very serious offence. I tell you now—I'm more worried about the guy that got shot than the money. Have you got anything you want to say?

A.   No reply.

Q.   Look I'll be straight with you. We've got a confession from Arthur and he's dropped you right in it.

A.   I don't believe you.

Q.   Listen to this. (Plays part of Duke's interview.)

A.   Well, it seems like you know it all. Why bother talking to me?

Q.   We need to get your side of things, to see how everything fits together.

A.   There's no point in holding back now—so much for honour among thieves. It was Arthur's idea—he's planned it for weeks before he spoke to me. We decided that we needed a driver and I knew Gerry from our time in Wandsworth.

Q.   You mean Gerry ELLA and HMP Wandsworth in South London?

A.   That's right.

. . .

Q.   Who got the car?

A.   That's down to Gerry. I don't know where it came from—he just got it for the day. The first time I saw it was when I got in it after the job.

Q.   Who did what in the shop?

A.   I asked for the cash while Arthur kept everyone calm.

Q.   With a sawn-off?

A.   You don't want heroes in a situation like that.

Q.   Like Reg Goodbody?

A.   Is he the old boy? He never should have interfered. He got what was coming to him.

Q.   From you?

A.   No way. That was Arthur. I could have got the bag away from the old man but Arthur got impatient with him.

. . .

Q.   So where's the money now?

A.   Money? That's rich. Lots of it was cheques. The rest, well, I'll need a nest egg for when I get out, eh?

Q.   So you won't tell me where it is?

A.   No reply;

. . .

Summaries of the antecedent histories of the accused men:

Finlay LEWIS (Age 40) Born Stornoway, Outer Hebrides.

18 previous convictions including 2 for wounding (s 18 OAPA) and 3 for armed robbery. Last conviction was at Portsmouth Crown Court for robbery in May 20YY. Sentenced to 10 years' imprisonment. Released June 20XY.

Arthur DUKE (Age 43) Born Catford, London.

8 previous convictions, mainly for offences of dishonesty, 1 recorded for robbery. Last conviction was at Winchester Crown Court in February 20YY for a fraud on the Department of Social Security. Sentenced to 6 years' imprisonment. Released April 20XY.

Gerald ELLA (Age 26) Born Worthing, West Sussex.

6 previous convictions, all for theft of cars, except the last one. In 20YY a 3-year term of imprisonment was imposed by Inner London Crown Court. In September last year, Brighton Magistrates' Court fined him £250 and banned him from driving for 1 year for driving while unfit through drink or drugs.

Leonard PETERSON (Age 55) Born Brighton.

16 previous convictions, all for petty offences of dishonesty. Imprisonment has been ordered in the past, but the last conviction was 10 years ago and resulted in a conditional discharge.

At the trial of Lewis and Duke on charges of robbery and wounding with intent, Miss Vaughan, counsel for the prosecution, addresses the judge:

Miss Vaughan: Your Honour, at this stage there has arisen a matter of law that need not trouble the jury.

His Honour: Members of the jury, counsel and I will be spending some time discussing matters of law and I would therefore ask you to retire to your room while these discussions take place.

The jury retire.

Trial within a trial (on Duke's interview):

Defence submissions

Challenged evidence clearly identified and the nature of the challenge is summarised.

XIC of DS Law

DS Law is called and gives evidence that he interviewed Duke and that a record was made.

Miss Vaughan: What did you actually say to Mr Duke regarding the fingerprints?

DS Law: I told Duke that we had his fingerprints from the Audi.

Miss Vaughan: What reason did you have for telling him this?

DS Law: At that time I thought that there was a strong possibility that some of the prints we found might belong to Duke.

Miss Vaughan: Can you assist by stating at what stage you became aware of the result of any checks made regarding the fingerprints?

DS Law: Some time after that interview occurred, I was informed by our forensic laboratory that none of the prints taken from the car matched Duke's fingerprints.

Miss Vaughan: Please wait there, officer, there may be some questions from Counsel for the defence.

Cross-examination of DS Law by defence

Mr Good: At the time you told Duke you had his fingerprints, you knew very well that that was not true, didn't you?

DS Law: When I told Duke we had his prints, I genuinely thought that was the case.

Mr Good: You had no basis for that belief, did you?

DS Law: I knew that fingerprints had been found.

Mr Good: You didn't know whose prints they were though, did you?

DS Law: I thought they belonged to Duke.

Mr Good: You only thought they belonged to Duke because you had decided he was guilty of the offence?

DS Law: No, that's not true.

Mr Good: It was in fact a deliberate lie which you had told, wasn't it?

DS Law: It was not a deliberate lie.

Mr Good: You needed to lie because you had no evidence against Mr Duke, had you?

DS Law: I didn't need to lie, he knew what we'd found at his place.

Mr Good: Your conduct was a deliberate deceit of Mr Duke, wasn't it?

DS Law: I would describe it as unfortunate, that's all.

Mr Good: If we are to believe it wasn't a deceit, then you made this assertion about Duke's fingerprints without any basis for doing so?

DS Law: It was unfortunate.

Defence submissions (summary)

Duke's confession immediately followed the assertion by DS Law that Duke's finger-prints had been found. The assertion made by DS Law must have been a deceit as he had no basis for making the assertion. If it was not a deceit, then it was a wholly unfounded assertion made accidentally. Either way, the assertion has rendered the confession likely to be unreliable. The confession is likely to be unreliable because, whatever the truth about DS Law's state of mind when he made it, the consequence of it was (or may have been) to convince Duke that his position was hopeless. In this position Duke's wish to have matters resolved as quickly and painlessly as possible rendered (or may have rendered) the confession unreliable. The evidence should be excluded under the Police and Criminal Evidence Act 1984, s 76(2)(b) as the prosecution has not proved, beyond reasonable doubt, that it was not obtained in consequence of anything said or done that was likely to render it unreliable. Alternatively, the confession should be excluded under the Police and Criminal Evidence Act 1984, s 78 as the admission of the evidence would have such an adverse effect on the fairness of the proceedings, bearing in mind the circumstances in which it was obtained, that the court ought not to admit it.

Prosecution submissions (summary)

DS Law did not lie to the defendant, he genuinely, albeit mistakenly, believed that the fingerprints were Duke's. The prosecution has proved beyond reasonable doubt that the confession was not obtained in consequence of DS Law's assertion and, if it were, the assertion was not likely to render it unreliable. There being no link between DS Law's assertion and the obtaining of the confession, and there being no reason to believe the confession was unreliable, the confession should not be excluded under the Police and Criminal Evidence Act 1984, s 76. The fact that what DS Law said later turned out not to be true does not mean that the admission of the evidence would have an adverse effect on the fairness of the proceedings so the confession should not be excluded under the Police and Criminal Evidence Act 1984, s 78.

The judge delivers a reasoned ruling.

38.4 The *voir dire* or 'trial within a trial' in the magistrates' court

In the Crown Court the purpose of the *voir dire* is for the discrete issue of admissibility to be determined by the judge in the absence of the jury. The rationale is clear; if the evidence is excluded, the jury do not hear it. This allows the finder of fact to focus on the admissible evidence without the risk that they will be influenced by the excluded evidence. In the magistrates' court, the magistrate is the finder of law *and* the finder of fact, so often there is no way of applying to exclude evidence without the finder of fact hearing about it (although there might be a pre-trial ruling under the Magistrates' Courts Act 1980, s 8A). So, what happens in the magistrates' court when the defence want to exclude evidence?

38.4.1 What evidence is being challenged?

The procedure that applies in the magistrates' court is determined by the type of evidence that is being challenged and on what basis. According to the Police and Criminal Evidence Act 1984, s 76(2) any application to exclude confession evidence under that provision must be determined before the court hears the evidence of the confession. As a result it was decided in *R v Liverpool Juvenile Court, ex p R* [1988] QB 1, 86 Cr App R 1 DC, that the magistrates **must** hold a *voir dire* where evidence is challenged under s 76(2), even though the finders of fact would necessarily hear the evidence whether it was excluded or not. Nowhere else is there a similar requirement. As a result, in the magistrates' court, where the admissibility of a confession is being challenged under the Police and Criminal Evidence Act 1984, s 76(2), there must be a *voir dire*. If the confession is being challenged in any other way, in addition to the s 76(2) challenge, each challenge will be determined on the *voir dire*. However, if there is confession evidence that is not being challenged under s 76(2), or if there is any other type of evidence being challenged, there is no requirement to hold a *voir dire*.

Where there is a *voir dire* in the magistrates' court, the process followed will be exactly as in the Crown Court (see Figure 38.1). Where evidence is excluded, the magistrates will simply put the evidence 'out of their minds' when considering their verdict. The magistrates could recuse themselves having heard the inadmissible evidence, but their decision on admissibility could not bind another bench (other than where made pursuant to s 8A MCA 1980), so there would be no value to the defendant in making such an application.

Where the admissibility of evidence is challenged in the magistrates' court and the magistrates are not required to hold a *voir dire*, they could *choose* to hold one, but will very rarely do so. In the course of the trial, the advocate will have to do all of the things that would otherwise have been done on the *voir dire*. Where, for example, a police officer gives evidence about the facts generally and about the admissibility issue particularly, the defence cross-examination must deal with both of these matters in a way that provides evidence to support an application to exclude, as well as a closing speech. The application to exclude will be heard by the magistrates before the defence closing speech. The defence will then present its closing speech in a way that reflects the finding on the admissibility issue.

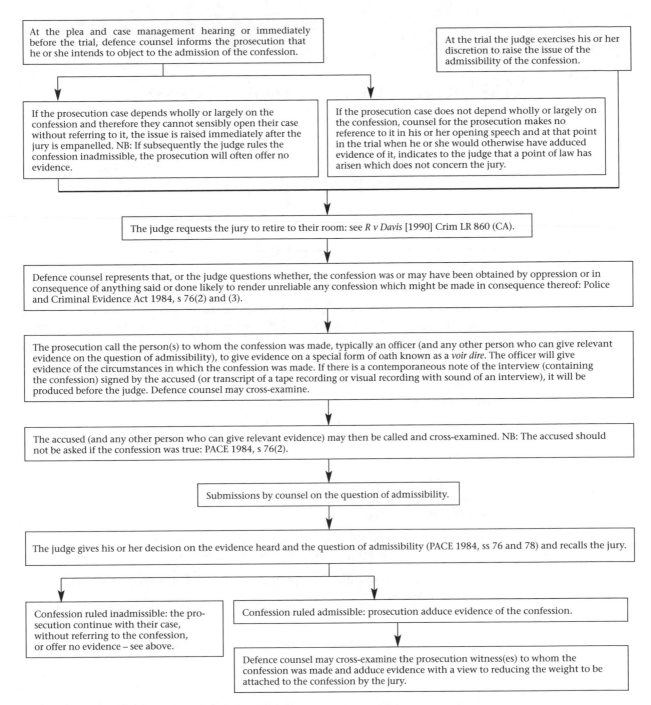

Figure 38.1 Procedure for conducting a *voir dire*

Making a submission of no case to answer

39.1 Introduction

Before you begin to prepare a case you must be fully conversant with the powers of the court to acquit a defendant at the close of the prosecution case on the basis that there is no case to answer. If you are not, whether you are acting for the prosecution or the defence, you will not be competently representing your client and run the risk that you will lose your case when you should not have done.

The rules that govern the courts' powers to acquit the defendant at the close of the prosecution case, or 'half time', are found in different places depending on whether the proceedings are summary or on indictment. In the magistrates' court the power is contained in the Criminal Procedure Rules. Rule 37.3(c) states:

> (c) at the conclusion of the prosecution case, on the defendant's application or on its own initiative, the court—
>
> (i) may acquit on the ground that the prosecution evidence is insufficient for any reasonable court properly to convict, but
>
> (ii) must not do so unless the prosecutor has had an opportunity to make representations

In the Crown Court the leading authority is *Galbraith* [1981] 1 WLR 1039. The test in *Galbraith* was set out by Lord Lane CJ:

> (1) If there is no evidence that the crime alleged has been committed by the defendant, there is no difficulty. The judge will of course stop the case. (2) The difficulty arises where there is some evidence but it is of a tenuous character, for example because of inherent weakness or vagueness or because it is inconsistent with other evidence. (a) Where the judge comes to the conclusion that the prosecution evidence, taken at its highest, is such that a jury properly directed could not properly convict upon it, it is his duty, upon a submission being made, to stop the case.

Although the authorities are different, the language in them is almost identical and, consequently, the questions the judge will ask in the magistrates' court and the Crown Court are almost identical too. If there is no evidence that the crime has been committed the defence should not have to present a case and the defendant should be acquitted at the end of the prosecution case. This is limb 1 of *Galbraith*. 'No evidence that the crime has been committed' could mean that there is no evidence of any sort, but this is unlikely ever to occur. Generally, a submission under this limb will be based on an assertion by the defence that there is no evidence in relation to one or more specific elements of the offence. That the evidence is of a 'tenuous character' covers a situation where, although there is evidence in relation to each and every element, the evidence has weaknesses that mean it is not sufficient to support a conviction. This is limb 2 of *Galbraith*. Lord Lane CJ made it clear, however, that a Crown Court judge should not acquit a defendant at 'half time' just because he didn't believe particular evidence. The question of who to believe on the facts is a matter for the jury, and the jury may take a different view to the judge. This is not the same in the magistrates' court, of course, as the judge determining whether there is a case to answer is also the finder of fact who has the last word about who is believed. As a result, where a submission based on limb 2 is made in the magistrates' court, the submission could be successful if the magistrate didn't believe the evidence. Consequently, although the tests are very similar in the Crown Court and magistrates' court, submissions in the magistrates' court can be broader in their scope.

Whether you are prosecuting or defending, you are under a duty to identify whether the evidence creates a case to answer. From the moment you begin to prepare the case, therefore, you must reflect on whether there is some evidence that relates to each and every element of the offence, and whether that evidence is sufficient in nature to support a conviction.

39.2 Defence

As a result of your preparation, you should have some idea in advance whether or not you will be making a submission of no case to answer. This will be based on the judgements you have made about the evidence on the papers. However, one of the first lessons an advocate learns is that witnesses often give evidence that is different to what was in their statement. Sometimes the differences amount to different ways of saying the same thing, but sometimes the differences change the nature of the case completely. You must prepare your case and conduct the trial in a way that allows you to see exactly how the evidence that is given orally compares to the evidence on the papers and the elements of the offence that the prosecution seek to prove. The following guide is written on the premise that you have some time to prepare the submission; but even if you don't, you will have to go through the same processes in your head if your submission is to stand any chance of success. If the way that the evidence has come out takes you by surprise, then you may want to ask for a little time to consider your position and organise your thoughts before you make a submission, but there is no guarantee you will get it. Many judges will just expect you to proceed without extra time.

Begin by making sure that your case analysis clearly sets out each element of the offence and identifies which evidence can be used by the Crown to help prove that element. Don't assume that the prosecutor is correct when they say they have a prima facie case. Holes in the prosecution case can arise as the result of gaps in the witness testimony, failures to obtain all of the specific evidence they need, or as the result of problems with technical requirements, for example continuity of possession of exhibits. How these problems arise as a matter of fact can be extremely varied, but there are some common examples. It is common, for example, for loser's statements not to be provided in cases where the loser is not a witness to the facts of the offence, like in cases of handling stolen goods or stolen vehicle offences; where this happens the prosecution may be unable to establish by evidence that the items specified in the charge were actually stolen at all. Similarly, in every case identification is an element and where the prosecution are relying on scientific evidence, like fingerprints or DNA, they must be able to show an unbroken chain of continuity of possession that proves that the sample taken from the defendant was actually that which was compared to the sample taken from the scene. These things may have nothing to do with your client's positive defence, but you must have considered them carefully; your client should only have to rely on their defence if the prosecution have raised sufficient evidence as part of their case to call for an answer. Remember also that the court will consider whether the evidence called is so tenuous that it is not sufficient to support a conviction. Look out for significant internal contradictions between the prosecution witnesses and identify whether significant weight is placed by the Crown on particularly unreliable types of evidence. Visual identification evidence is an example of a type of evidence whose nature may support a submission of no case, even though the prosecution has established evidence on each separate element of the offence. The case of *Turnbull* [1977] QB 224 provides guidance on how judges should deal with this type of evidence on a submission of no case to answer.

> When, in the judgment of the trial judge, the quality of the identifying evidence is poor, as for example when it depends solely on a fleeting glance or on a longer observation made in difficult conditions, the situation is very different. The judge should then withdraw the case from the jury and direct an acquittal unless there is other evidence which goes to support the correctness of the identification.

Having said all of that, make sure that your point is a real one. If your submission is based on a purely technical failure or on an error that relates to evidence that was not properly in dispute, the prosecutor will almost certainly be allowed to re-open their case to resolve the problem: *R v Francis* (1990) 91 Cr App R 271, CA.

If you have identified a potential submission, draft the submission that you would make to the judge if the evidence comes out as it appears on the papers, or as you would like it to appear if your witness handling is successful. This may seem like the last thing you should be preparing, but it isn't. It is only if you have a clear idea of where you want to be after your witness handling has concluded that you will be able to plan it properly and judge its success.

Plan your witness handling with careful reference to your draft submission of no case. Your draft submission should show you two key things: first, what you must cover, and, second, what you must leave alone. If you want to take advantage of a failure of the prosecution to obtain evidence in relation to a particular element (limb 1 of *Galbraith*), then avoid asking any questions that might cause the hole to be filled. This can happen by a witness giving some evidence to you that they have never mentioned before, or by evidence being sought because you have made the prosecutor aware of the problem. Remember, if the evidence isn't there, it isn't there; you don't need a witness to admit that it isn't there. If you are making a submission on the basis that there is evidence but it is of unsatisfactory quality (limb 2), your witness handling should demonstrate the particular tenuousness on which you intend to ask the judge to act. For example, in a visual identification case, your cross-examination should identify all the matters of fact that you say make the quality of the evidence 'poor'. *Turnbull* sets out clear examples of what those things might be, for example lighting conditions, time under observation, impediments to view, etc. Of course, you will have to do all of this at the same time as you cross-examine about your client's particular defence too because, if your submission fails, the defence will have to answer the prosecution case.

As you listen to the examination-in-chief and undertake your cross-examination of the prosecution witnesses, you must keep a full note of the answers that were actually given. This is not easy, as you cannot guarantee you will be supported by a solicitor and, even if you are, their note may not be reliable, so you will have to take the note yourself. But it is necessary, as no judge will take a submission seriously if it is not based on the precise evidence that was put before the court.

Finally, compare your draft submission to the evidence as it actually stands at the close of the prosecution case, consider whether any other grounds for a submission have arisen, and make a decision about whether to make your submission of no case, or not.

If you decide to make a submission, in the Crown Court it will take place in the absence of the jury. So, when the prosecution closes its case, be ready to indicate to the judge that the jury need to leave the courtroom. Generally, a form of words like, 'Your Honour, there is a matter of law that you may wish to deal with in the absence of the jury', will be appropriate. The judge may want a time estimate. An accurate estimate is notoriously difficult to give. What the judge really wants to know is whether you expect to be a few minutes, a few hours or the rest of the day, so that proper arrangements can be made for the jury and witnesses.

Elsewhere in this manual you will find general guidance on the components of a strong submission. The suggested structure, set out here, is designed to work in combination with those general considerations. If you decide to make a submission of no case, your submission will generally follow a similar pattern:

1. Set out the basis of your submission generally and specifically; whether your application is limb 1 or 2 and which part of the case you say is deficient (eg the visual identification or a failure to adduce evidence on a particular element).
2. Identify the power that allows the judge to do what you ask (eg the CPR, *Galbraith*). (How detailed your coverage of the law is will depend on the knowledge and experience of your judge.)
3. Identify any case law that assists the judge to apply the test (eg *Turnbull*).
4. Apply the particular evidence that has been put before the court to the test and case law you have identified.
5. Summarise your general submission and ask that the judge find there is no case to answer.

39.2.1 Checklist

Before trial

1. Familiarise yourself with the powers of the court in relation to a submission of no case to answer.
2. Flag up the general authorities in your *Blackstone's* or *Archbold* so that they are easily and quickly accessible.

During preparation

1. Identify the elements of the offence and the evidence that relates to each element.
2. Consider the nature of the evidence and begin to form a view about whether it may be 'tenuous'.

3. Decide whether the evidence on the papers provides a basis for a submission of no case.
4. Draft a submission on the basis that the evidence comes out as expected.
5. Prepare your witness handling to provide the evidential support required by your draft submission.

At trial

1. Keep a full note of the witnesses' oral testimony to use during your submission.
2. Identify whether the evidence is as you expected it to be, or whether there are no longer grounds for a submission, or whether there are more grounds than you had planned for.
3. Make your submission, tailoring your draft to reflect the evidence actually given and recorded in your notes.

39.3 Prosecution

As the prosecutor, you have a responsibility to ensure that the evidence you put before the court does raise a case to answer. As part of your preparation, therefore, you should have identified that there is evidence that relates to each of the elements that you seek to prove and that this evidence is sufficient in nature to support a conviction. If this is not the case, the defendant should not be prosecuted at all. The Code for Crown Prosecutors sets out this responsibility.

In preparing your case, you should have identified any potential weaknesses and have taken whatever steps are available to you to remove them. This process should have started to make you aware of what parts of your case the defence may challenge and how such a challenge can be responded to. It is important that you have considered these points because it is unlikely that a defence advocate will give you advance notice of their intention to make a submission of no case to answer, unless they are confident that the weakness cannot be repaired. The first you are likely to hear about a submission, therefore, is when the defence announce to the judge their intention to make one. It will generally not be open to you to ask for time to consider your position, because it would not be reasonable to say that you have been taken by surprise; you have a clear responsibility to assess your own case continually irrespective of the actions of the defence and so you should be in a position to justify the continued prosecution of the defendant at any time. Equally, if the evidence develops in a way that means that there really is no case to answer, your role is not to argue for a continued prosecution. Your role is to put the evidence before the court fairly and objectively and not to seek a conviction at all costs.

Your approach to preparing your case in a way that protects you from a submission of no case is almost identical to the approach you would adopt if you were making the submission.

Begin by identifying the elements of the offence and the evidence that you say proves each element. Judge the quality of the evidence against the 'tenuous' test and consider any specific guidance like that set out in *Turnbull*.

Take whatever steps you can before trial to fill any gaps in the evidence. The options open to you will depend on when you are instructed; if you are instructed on the evening before trial your options will be very limited, but if you are instructed in advance you should consider these matters in your advice to the CPS. At trial, ensure that your witness handling protects the evidence as far as possible by highlighting its strengths.

Maintain a full record of the oral testimony of the witnesses, in examination-in-chief and cross-examination, so that you can comment on the accuracy of the defence record of the evidence.

Be prepared to think on your feet if an unexpected submission arises. Make a careful note of the specific challenge that is being made and deal only with the specific challenge in your response.

Ensure that the legal propositions put forward by the defence are correct. As prosecutor, you have a duty to draw the court's attention to any misleading or erroneous assertions about the law. This requires you to be familiar with the general tests for stopping a case at 'half time' as well as the specific authorities to do with particular types of evidence. You will be failing in your duty if you simply assume that the defence's assertions about the law are correct.

39.3.1 Checklist

Before trial

1. Familiarise yourself with the powers of the court in relation to a submission of no case to answer.
2. Flag up the general authorities in your *Blackstone's* or *Archbold* so that they are easily and quickly accessible.

During preparation

1. Satisfy yourself that the evidence on which you rely covers each element and is of a sufficient nature to support a conviction.
2. If there are gaps or weaknesses in the evidence, take whatever action you can to deal with the problems. (If you are instructed early enough, write an advice to the CPS identifying what needs to be done.)

At trial

1. Conduct your witness handling in a way that protects your case, as far as possible, from a submission of no case.
2. Make a full note of the testimony of the witnesses so that you can respond accurately to a submission based on the evidence.
3. Make a full note of the defence submission so that you can tailor a properly focused response.
4. Be prepared to assist the judge in relation to assertions made by the defence about the evidence or the law that you believe to be incorrect.

39.4   Form of a submission of no case to answer in the Crown Court

1. Defence advocate indicates that there is a legal submission to be made (but not its nature).
2. Judge removes the jury from court.
3. Defence advocate makes the submission of no case to answer.

4. Prosecution responds.
5. Judge rules.

    (a) If there is no case to answer, the jury return to court and, on the judge's direction, they acquit the defendant on the relevant counts.

    (b) If there is a case to answer, the jury simply return to court, the defence presents its case and the verdict is left to the jury.

39.5   Form of a submission of no case to answer in the magistrates' court

1. Defence advocate indicates to the magistrates or district judge that they intend to make a submission of no case to answer.
2. Defence advocate makes the submission of no case to answer.
3. Prosecution responds.
4. Magistrates or district judge rules. (Where a submission is rejected reasons need not be given.)

    (a) If there is no case to answer, the magistrates or district judge will acquit the defendant on the relevant charges.

    (b) If there is a case to answer, the defence presents its case and the magistrates or district judge will be left to come to their verdict in the ordinary way.

Prosecuting a plea of guilty in the Crown Court

40.1 Preparatory steps

(a) Ensure you have a copy of the indictment. This is often settled after the brief has been sent to counsel and can therefore be missing from the brief.

(b) Make sure that the defendant is pleading guilty to the charge(s) on the facts **as disclosed** by the prosecution witness statements. If not, you will need to ensure that a 'basis of plea' document is prepared by the defence and its contents are acceptable to you and to the CPS. This ought to be an agreed document in order for the judge to accept it as the basis for determining sentence. If it cannot be agreed on, then a 'Newton' hearing is likely to be needed to resolve the dispute. See the *Attorney General's guidelines for acceptance of pleas* (eg in *Blackstone's Criminal Practice* at Appendix 2) for further details.

(c) If the defendant is in breach of any sentence previously imposed by a court, such as a suspended prison sentence, a conditional discharge, or community order imposed on an earlier occasion, ensure that you have details of the original offence(s) in respect of which such sentence was imposed.

(d) If there are other offences to be taken into consideration (TICs), ensure that the appropriate form has been prepared (this is normally done by the officer in charge of the case) and signed by the defendant. A copy of this form should be handed to the clerk of the court before the case is called on for hearing.

(e) Ensure you have an up-to-date copy of the defendant's antecedents. The court and defence counsel should also have copies in advance of the trial/listed plea. You will be required to give the antecedent information to the court (see later).

(f) Obtain instructions from the CPS representative at court as to the amount of any costs order you should seek.

(g) Be familiar with the current Code for Crown Prosecutors and the Farquharson guidelines (both available on the CPS website).

40.2 The hearing

(a) This may be a plea and case management hearing (PCMH) or the case may have been listed for a trial, following not guilty pleas entered at a PCMH. According to your brief from the CPS, the defendant will be arraigned and plead guilty to some or all of the counts on the indictment. If you are instructed to proceed with the other counts, it will be necessary to empanel a jury to try those matters. If the plea of guilty to some of the counts is acceptable, introduce yourself and your opponent to the court and inform the judge either that you are instructed to offer no evidence on the other matters or invite the judge to leave such matters 'on the court file'. Then proceed to stage (b) below. If the defendant pleads guilty to all the counts on the indictment, start by introducing yourself and your opponent.

(b) Briefly outline the facts of the offence(s) (this can be based on your CPS case summary or an agreed 'basis of plea' document). The judge is likely to have read the committal papers in any event. There is no need to go into great detail, simply deal with the salient facts either in a chronological or the most convenient order. This usually involves a summary of the way in which each offence was committed, any aggravating or mitigating features, the amount of any money, monetary value or the nature of any injury involved, brief details of the arrest, the defendant's response to the arrest/charge, any important replies during an interview, and acknowledging, where appropriate, that the defendant frankly admitted his or her guilt or cooperated with the police.

(c) If there are any TICs (offences that the defendant asks the court to 'take into consideration' when passing sentence), it is normal to mention this to the judge either before or when dealing with the brief facts. The judge will have or be given a copy of a schedule of the TICs by the clerk. Either the judge or the clerk (at his or her direction) will read out the offences and ask the defendant if he or she admits each of the offences and wants them to be taken into consideration when sentence is passed. As soon as the defendant confirms that this is the case, deal **briefly** with these other offences. It is usual to deal with them together, for example by mentioning the fact that they are all similar offences committed over X period and involving £Y.

(d) You will then have to take the judge through the defendant's antecedents (see 'Jane Forrester' below, for an example). Check that the judge has a copy.

Q: 'Does Your Honour have the antecedents of Jane Forrester dated 10 June 2014?'

In dealing with the antecedents, it is usual to read out each part of the relevant information. The order in which you deal with the defendant's history is as follows:

(i) Date of birth/birthplace, etc.

Example

'The defendant was born on 21 December 1990 in London and is now aged 23 years.'

(ii) Previous convictions.

Example

'There are a number of matters recorded against the defendant including offences of dishonesty.'

Q: 'Where would Your Honour like me to start?' (This is to enable the judge to determine which of the previous convictions are relevant.)

A: 'Deal with the last three matters—from June 2010.'

'On 2 June 2010, at the West London Magistrates' Court, for an offence of theft, the defendant was fined £400 and ordered to pay costs of £75.'

'On 9 September 2011, at the same court, for two offences of obtaining property by deception, the defendant was also fined £300 in respect of each matter and ordered to pay costs of £80.'

'Finally, on 5 January 2014, at this court, for three offences of theft, the defendant was sentenced to a period of one month's imprisonment on each count concurrent, such sentence being suspended for a period of one year.'

At this point, ask for the breach of the suspended sentence to be put to the defendant. Upon the judge's direction, the clerk will then put the fact of the conviction and sentence to the defendant and ask the defendant whether they agree with it. If the defendant does not (this is rare), it will be necessary to put the case back in the list in order to produce strict proof of the conviction, ie a certificate of the conviction (see the Police and Criminal Evidence Act 1984, s 73). If the defendant admits the details, the clerk will inform the defendant that, as the current offences were committed during the period of the suspension, the defendant may now be dealt with again in respect of the original offences.

    (iii) Give the court brief details of the facts of the original offences. If your information is sparse, and an officer is present, he or she may be able to assist the court with more detail.

    (iv) Proceed with the rest of the antecedents, ie education, employment, home circumstances.

  (e) Make any application for costs that you are instructed to make and any application for a compensation or destruction order (usual in a drugs case).

Example

'Your Honour, there is an application for a destruction order in respect of the drugs that form the subject of the charge and a further application for costs in the sum of £120.'

  (f) Finish by informing the court that you have closed your case.

'That is the case for the prosecution.'

  (g) It is now the turn of defence counsel to mitigate on his or her client's behalf.

  (h) The judge will then proceed to sentence. See *Criminal Litigation and Sentencing* manual, **chapter 13**. Be ready to assist the judge on his or her powers of sentence and be prepared to remind him or her tactfully if he or she exceeds those powers.

Antecedents of: **Jane FORRESTER**   Dated: 10.6.2014

Charged with: Possession of controlled drugs, intent to supply (x 2)

Date and place of birth: 21.12.90 (aged 23); London

Nationality: British

Date of arrest: 1.6.14/On bail

Summary of convictions: 2 findings of guilt as a juvenile

                          8 previous convictions recorded

Education: Attended Bishop's Rock Comprehensive School; left aged 16 with no formal qualifications.

Employment since leaving school: Many occasional jobs of short duration.

Presently unemployed, not claiming benefit.

Address, home conditions: 264 Bath Street, Streatham, London

Lives with parents and receives £100 p.w. from them.

No financial commitments.

Convictions recorded against: Jane FORRESTER CRD No 40457/01

Charged in name of   Jane FORRESTER

Date	Court	Offences	Sentence	Release Date
1.4.07	West London M.C.	Soliciting	Fine £20	
2.6.10	West London M.C.	Theft	Fine £400; Costs £75	
9.9.11	West London M.C.	Obtain prop by deception (x 2)	(1) and (2) Fine £300; Costs £80	
5.1.14	Inner London Crown Court	Theft (x 3)	(1)—(3) 1 month's imprisonment concurrent. Suspended 1 year	

40.3   Procedure before sentencing—a flow chart

The procedure before sentencing, once an accused, D, has either pleaded guilty or, having pleaded not guilty, is found guilty, is shown in Figure 40.1:

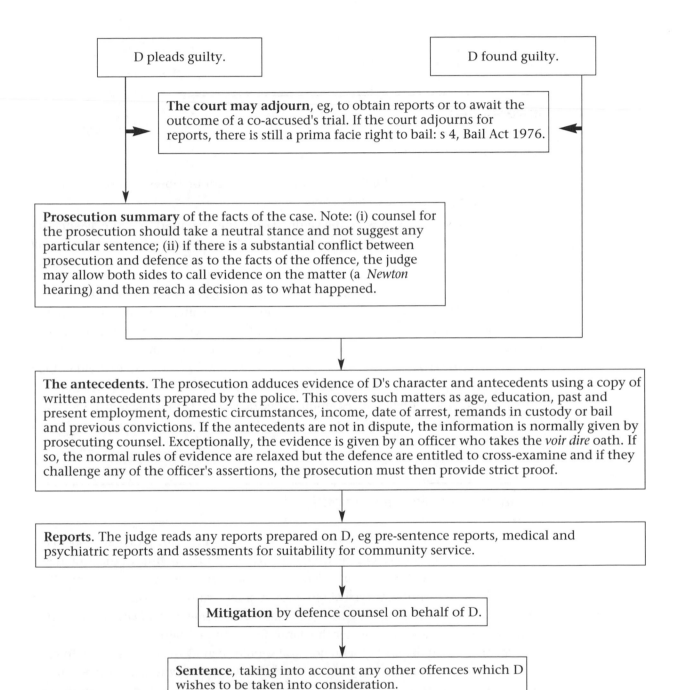

Figure 40.1   Procedure before sentencing—a flow chart

The plea in mitigation

41.1 Introduction

A plea in mitigation can be made:

(a) either after a plea of guilty, following the prosecution's presentation of the case and defendant's antecedents; or

(b) after conviction, following the verdict(s) and the presentation of the defendant's antecedents. You may find it helpful to read **Chapter 40** as well, to see the overall picture.

The objective of a plea in mitigation is to ensure that the sentence passed by the court is one that is appropriate both in the circumstances of the offence(s) and to the circumstances of the defendant. The aim is to obtain the most lenient punishment that can reasonably be imposed. It should be remembered that very few crimes carry with them a sentence fixed by law and so in most cases there is discretion in the court to decide which of a number of possible sentences is appropriate (eg whether to imprison or fine) and, within a particular sentence, a discretion to decide where, within the upper and lower limits, the particular sentence should be fixed.

41.2 Preparing to make a plea in mitigation

Always begin your preparation by checking on the sentencing principles that apply to the particular crime. You should use the Guidelines section on the website of the Sentencing Council (at <http://sentencingcouncil.judiciary.gov.uk/sentencing-guidelines.htm>. Your aim should be to identify the type of sentence or order that would normally be imposed (see *Criminal Litigation and Sentencing* manual and *Blackstone's Criminal Practice,* Section B, which sets out guidance on sentencing tariffs for specific crimes).

Having identified the type of sentence, you should then identify any aggravating features that would normally encourage a court to take the view that a sentence at the higher end of the scale would be appropriate and then see whether you can dissociate the defendant from those features. The following list of features will often be seen as aggravating: ringleader, planned or premeditated act; serious injury caused; use of weapon; unprovoked; large sum of money involved; breach of trust; reoffending soon after a court order is made; elderly/young victim; poor response to supervision; lack of concern for injured victim; lack of remorse; and offence committed while on bail.

Your next task is to identify whether there are any mitigating factors that should be brought to the attention of the court. The following list of features will often be seen as mitigating: minor role; spontaneous; provoked; minor injuries; property recovered; severe domestic or emotional stress; little or no damage to the victim; dependent children; has the care of an ill or disabled spouse; exceptional help to others; previous good character; offence out of character; long time since previous offence; out of trouble since offence; pleaded guilty; good response to supervision; full confession; gave himself or herself up; recently married; secure job; cured of addiction to drugs or alcohol; paid compensation prior to hearing; compensation offered; other restitution made or offered to victim; expression of remorse; suffered loss or injury due to the offence; mental disorder; good work record; consequences unintended; low intelligence; signs of reform; in financial problems not of own making; offence committed out of loyalty; parity with co-defendants needed; in some sex offences—willing victim; offender forgiven by the victim; and that it is a long time since the offence was committed.

41.2.1   Holding a conference with the client

You should aim to arrive at court in plenty of time to obtain the information that you need to present the plea in mitigation. You may only get the papers in the case a short while before you are due to appear in court but you should always see your client in conference before starting to mitigate in court. If, for whatever reason, you have not had enough time to get full information, you should ask the court to put the case back in the list to be dealt with later that day. If you try to make a plea in mitigation with inadequate or incomplete preparation, this may raise professional conduct issues for you; it is also likely to jeopardise your client's human rights. Where the court is told that your preparation time has been inadequate, it should consider seriously whether to adjourn the hearing (see European Convention on Human Rights, Articles 6(1) and (3)(b) and (c); *Goddi v Italy* (1984) 6 EHRR 457, *T and V v UK*, unreported, 16 December 1999, and *cf. F v UK* (1992) 15 EHRR CD 32).

During the conference with your client you should seek to establish the following facts and/or make the following assessments of your client:

(a) *Your client's age* (if relevant).

(b) *Whether your client's actual age should be ignored because he or she appears to be immature or is mentally disabled.* You should also consider whether to apply to have the case adjourned for reports to be prepared.

(c) *Your client's background*: whether there are any circumstances that might excuse or explain the offence; your client's past character (you should get a form listing any previous convictions (usually on form MG16) from the Crown Prosecution Service and take your client through it); whether this offence is similar to or different from previous offences; whether there are any underlying problems, for example drug or alcohol addiction; past instances of generosity or kindness.

(d) *Your client's involvement in the crime*: was your client a principal actor in the offence or did he or she take a minor role in it; was the offence premeditated or did it happen on the spur of the moment; what, if any, pressure was your client subject to; was it an isolated incident or does your client's criminal conduct extend over a long period; was your client influenced by another offender; if so, was he or she unable to resist that influence because of age or experience; quantify how much damage was done, or money taken and establish whether any offences are being taken into consideration.

(e) *Your client's present situation*: here you are looking for evidence of your client's stability, a regular home, job and people who will be supportive to the defendant; compare the situation as it is now with the time when the offence was committed; ask what your client has done to help himself or herself—acts showing contrition are more important than words, so establish whether your client has made any attempt at restitution. When a fine is a possibility you need to obtain considerable detail about your client's financial situation in order to help the court fix the fine at a proper level. So, you need to know your client's income after tax etc, your client's outgoings out of income and his or her capital. You also need to take your client's instructions on how much time he or she will need to pay any fine imposed and the level of weekly instalments he or she could meet.

You may want to call one or two character witnesses to speak on behalf of your client. This can be useful sometimes. You should only call people who know your client well and who can say something about him or her that is relevant in either dissociating your client from the aggravating features of the offence or enhancing the mitigating factors in the case.

Prepare your client for what will happen by giving him or her realistic advice as to the likely sentence that will be imposed and by describing the procedure in court.

41.2.2 Reading and understanding the pre-sentence report

Make sure that you have got any reports (usually from the court probation service), have read them, and that you have noted the comments made about the defendant's background, the background to the offence, and any recommendation on sentence. Note that you should comply with a request not to show a report (eg a medical report or one relating to the defendant's mental health) to the defendant and that you should always ensure that material that is given to you in confidence is dealt with on that basis.

41.3 Presenting the plea in mitigation

41.3.1 The length of the plea

It is very important to keep your plea in mitigation short. In an ordinary case, aim to keep your submission to no more than ten minutes.

41.3.2 Witnesses

After a guilty plea the defendant's instructions may be that his or her view of the circumstances of the offence are different from the case put by the prosecution; in these circumstances the court may decide to hear evidence to determine which version of the facts to accept (*R v Newton* (1982) 77 Cr App R 13; ***Criminal Litigation and Sentencing*** manual, **13.3.2**). However, in most circumstances, the need for this ought to be removed by the use of a written 'basis of plea' document—the content of this should be agreed by counsel for the prosecution and defence before the guilty plea is entered. See further the Attorney General's guidelines on the acceptance of pleas (eg in *Blackstone's Criminal Practice* at Appendix 2).

Any witnesses as to character may be called before making the substance of (or during) your plea. You can call your witness in the following way:

'Your Honour, before I address you in mitigation on behalf of Ms Smith, I should like to call Mr Jones. Mr Jones please.'

You should ask witnesses to identify themselves and explain their relationship to the defendant. Then ask any questions that will provide relevant information to be used later on in your plea. For example, if you are seeking to establish that Ms Smith's criminal act is completely out of character, you will want to call a witness who can say, based on the witness's long and detailed knowledge of her, that this act was completely out of character. You could try to elicit this kind of information from the witness with one or more of the following questions:

'Do you know Ms Smith?'
'When did you first meet her?'
'How did you come to know her?'
'As her (employer, etc) . . . have you had the opportunity of assessing her character?'
'How would you describe her character?'
'What are her responsibilities at work?'
'From what you know of Ms Smith, do you regard her involvement in this offence as in or out of character?'

41.3.3 Introducing the pre-sentence report

Usually the pre-sentence report will have been handed to the judge or magistrates before the plea in mitigation starts and it is sometimes necessary for the court to adjourn while the report is read. However, before you can refer to the contents of the pre-sentence report you will want to be sure that the judge or magistrate has a copy of it and has had a chance to read it. You can introduce the report in the following way:

'Your Honour, a pre-sentence report has been prepared, dated . . . which I shall refer to in the course of my plea in mitigation. Has Your Honour had an opportunity to read the report?'

41.4 The content of the plea in mitigation

41.4.1 Summary

You should start your plea with a summary of the main points you intend to make. You could say:

'The substance of my plea in mitigation is . . .' or
'I shall seek to persuade Your Honour that . . .' or
'Your Honour, the defendant accepts that this was a serious offence and has fully admitted his part in it. I do not propose to address Your Honour on the circumstances of the offence but will seek to persuade Your Honour that . . .'

41.4.2 Sentencing policy

You may then want to bring in the matters of sentencing policy that will bear upon the case. For example, you could say:

'In my submission, as Your Honour will appreciate, the guidelines state that sentences at the higher end of the scale are reserved for offences where . . .' (state briefly the aggravating features).

Be careful not to read out simply a long list of hypothetical aggravating features and say 'this doesn't apply here . . . that is not relevant on our facts', and so on. The judge will want you to focus on what is relevant to this case. Next you will want to explain (if you can) to the court why the defendant can be dissociated from these aggravating features, and how the evidence (what the prosecution have said, and what any witnesses have said) supports your contention. For example,

'I hope that Your Honour will accept that on the prosecution's case, the defendant can be dissociated from any aggravating features and that as a matter of principle, a sentence at the lower end of the scale is appropriate.'

In the early days, however, you may be concerned more with the appropriate type of sentence, rather than the scale.

41.4.3 Mitigating factors

You should then make specific, albeit brief reference to the mitigating factors that are relevant, for example that the defendant pleaded guilty, confessed immediately, or was previously of good character. Where relevant you should tie in your submissions on these issues with any evidence that has been given to the court, for example the testimony of the antecedents officer, any witnesses as to the defendant's character and any statements in the pre-sentence report. The pre-sentence report should be referred to by page number and where on the page the paragraph appears, so that the court is able to follow the points you are making. You should then round off this part of your submission with a plea for a sentence at the lower end of the scale if that is appropriate. For example,

'It is my submission that when all these factors are borne in mind, a sentence at the lower end of the scale is justified.'

If your client has indicated genuine remorse to you, you should refer to what the client has said to you in conference. For example,

'Your Honour, in conference Ms Smith told me how terribly sorry she is for what she has done and she has asked me to repeat this to the court.'

If you can also point to concrete signs of remorse—for example, helping the police, wherewithal to pay compensation—that will carry much more weight with the court.

41.5 Conclusion

You will then be in a position to conclude your plea. For example,

'In conclusion, Your Honour, my submission is that, both as a matter of principle and on account of the particular facts of this case, a financial penalty would be appropriate that can justifiably be put at the lower end of the scale.'

or:

'Your Honour, the defendant appreciates that a custodial sentence is justified in this case and I do not propose to seek to persuade Your Honour otherwise. However, this is a case where, I submit, there are some mitigating features that could enable Your Honour to take a lenient view and (impose a short period of imprisonment) or (suspend any sentence of imprisonment) . . .'.

41.6   Warning

Always make sure that you have properly prepared your submissions in a plea in mitigation and that they are realistic. There is no point in suggesting to the court that a case is not appropriate for a sentence of imprisonment if the sentencing guidelines make it clear that a sentence of imprisonment should be imposed. Equally there is no point in dwelling on aspects of the defendant's background that are no longer relevant to mitigating the defendant's conduct, for example when the defendant is 45 years old, revealing that his or her parents divorced when he or she was eight years old! You will also be in some difficulty if you try to tell the court that the defendant is really sorry for what he or she did, when the plea in mitigation follows conviction after a not guilty plea.

The Court of Appeal has emphasised on several occasions that it is the duty of both prosecuting and defence counsel to know what sentences may in any particular case be lawfully passed, so as to correct the judge if need be and avoid unnecessary appeals on the basis that the sentence was not one that the judge had power to impose.

41.7   Further reading

Hyam, M. *Advocacy Skills*, 4th edn, Blackstone Press (OUP), 1999.

APPENDIX
A CRIMINAL CASE: *R v HEATH*

<u>BRIEF FOR THE PROSECUTION</u>

R

v

KEVIN HEATH

Counsel has herewith:

(1) Indictment
(2) Committal statements
(3) Defendant's antecedents and previous convictions
(4) Witnesses' previous convictions
(5) Statement of Defence in accordance with the Criminal Procedure and Investigations Act 1996.

Counsel is instructed in the prosecution of the above-named Defendant who faces the two counts shown on the indictment.

The facts emerge clearly from the statements. The reviewing lawyer takes the view that a plea to s 20 GBH would not be acceptable.

Counsel will note that two of the prosecution witnesses have previous convictions. The defence must be told of these, whether or not they ask for them, in accordance with the decision in *R v Collister and Warhurst* (1955) 39 Cr App R 100 and the Attorney General's Guidelines on Disclosure, although of course their use in the trial will be dependent on getting permission from the judge under CJA 2003, s 100.

<u>IN THE CROWN COURT AT CROYDON</u>

THE QUEEN

V

KEVIN HEATH

_____

INDICTMENT

_____

Kevin HEATH is charged as follows:

COUNT 1   <u>STATEMENT OF OFFENCE</u>

Causing grievous bodily harm with intent contrary to section 18 of the Offences Against the Person Act 1861.

<u>PARICULARS OF OFFENCE</u>

Kevin Heath on the 24th day of December 2013 unlawfully caused grievous bodily harm to Jason Ball with intent to do him grievous bodily harm.

COUNT 2   <u>STATEMENT OF OFFENCE</u>

Inflicting grievous bodily harm contrary to section 20 of the Offences Against the Person Act 1861.

<u>PARTICULARS OF OFFENCE</u>

Kevin Heath on the 24th day of December 2013 unlawfully and maliciously inflicted grievous bodily harm on Jason Ball.

Date: 17 March 2014   John Collison
                                                                  Officer of the Crown Court

<u>STATEMENT OF WITNESS</u>

<u>Statement of:</u> JASON BALL

<u>Age of witness:</u> Over 18

<u>Occupation of witness:</u> Publican

This statement consisting of one page, signed by me, is true to the best of my knowledge and belief and I make it knowing that, if it is tendered in evidence, I shall be liable to prosecution if I have wilfully stated in it anything which I know to be false or do not believe to be true.

<u>Signed :</u> *J. Ball*

<u>*Signature witnessed by:*</u> *R. Maybury*   *Statement dated*: 28th December 2013.

I am the landlord of The Cutpurse public house and have been so for 5 years.

On Tuesday, 24th December 2013 I was serving behind the bar throughout the evening together with Tracey CROFT, my permanent barmaid, and a number of part-time staff.

Being Christmas Eve the pub was very busy and in general the atmosphere was noisy but pleasant.

At about 9.00 pm I had reason to speak to a youth who I know as 'Ferret'. He is in his early twenties, about 5'7" with dark hair and a pointy face. He had been in the pub since opening time and at this time he was being difficult and abusive towards Tracey who was serving at the part of the bar near the pool table. He was waving a pool cue around. I told him to pack it in or go home. I have had trouble with him in the past and banned him from my pub in June last year following a fight in my garden. I know he has been in trouble with the police plenty of times and is always playing 'Jack the Lad'.

All was well until about 10.30 when a group of carol singers arrived to sing in the public bar. This was by invitation and is something of which I am particularly fond.

The carol singers were grouped around the door. They had just begun to sing when they were interrupted by foul chanting from near the pool table. Although I could not at this stage actually see who was doing it, I had no doubt who was responsible. I felt very angry and upset and decided to take swift action as I am entitled to do by law. I went along the bar to the pool table where I could see Ferret and his friends chanting and yelling and once again Ferret was waving his pool cue about. I could see other people were getting upset. I called to him 'Alright you foul mouthed lout, shut it, and out'. I then left the bar by the hatch and went to eject him. At this Ferret came over to me and said, brandishing the cue, 'I'm going to stuff this . . .' I said 'Don't mess with me Ferret' and fearing an attack took the cue from him and threw it behind the bar, turning away from Ferret as I did so. As I turned back I heard the words 'You've had this coming, fat man'. After that, everything went blank, although I dimly remember hearing screaming.

I woke up in hospital and found out that I had been hit in my face with a glass beer mug. I have cuts to the left side of my face from my eye to my chin which needed 50 stitches. I am in considerable pain.

At no stage did I provoke this attack. I am 61 and weigh 16 stones.

I made a sketch of the layout of the Public Bar which I produce as JB/1.

I am willing to attend court and give evidence, if required.

<u>Signed</u> by: *J. Ball*   <u>Signature witnessed by:</u> *R. Maybury*

JB/1

SERVING AREA

BAR

FRUIT MACHINE

HATCH ↑

POOL TABLE

ENTRANCE

MENS' W.C. →

STATEMENT OF WITNESS

Statement of: TRACEY CROFT

Age of witness: Over 18

Occupation: Barmaid

This statement consisting of three pages, signed by me, is true to the best of my knowledge and belief and I make it knowing that, if it is tendered in evidence, I shall be liable to prosecution if I have wilfully stated in it anything which I know to be false or do not believe to be true.

Signed: *T. Croft*

Signature witnessed by: *R. Maybury*   Statement dated: 25th December 2013.

I am 19 years old and am a member of the bar staff at The Cutpurse public house. I have worked there since about December 2011.

I was working in the evening on Christmas Eve 2013 together with Jason Ball, the proprietor and my boss, and several part-time staff. It was very crowded and busy. Lots of people were buying drinks for me and Jason Ball. Jason had a Happy Hour promotion during the early evening to get people in, and everyone had a bit of a laugh when we did the karaoke competition. It was a really good atmosphere.

Among the regulars is a young man who is usually called Ferret, although I think his real name is Kevin. I do not know his last name. He has been a regular in the pub since I have worked there except for a period earlier this year when Jason Ball banned him. Jason does not like him. He has told me he thinks Ferret is mouthy and a show-off. I am not sure how long he was banned but he has certainly been coming to the pub regularly since early autumn.

Ferret was in the pub on Christmas Eve. I cannot remember when I first saw him but I think it was fairly near opening time at 6 o'clock. I served him a number of drinks. I can't remember exactly how many times I served him but I think it was about five times.

Each time I served him a pint of Tennent's, which is his normal drink. Over the course of the evening he seemed to me to get louder and more noticeable among the general crowd in the pub, making loud comments which were slightly rude and using swear words.

Before the fight, the only time I heard Jason Ball speaking to Ferret that evening was a couple of hours earlier. Ferret had been over with his mates by the pool table. However at that point he was playing the fruit machine and I was serving near it. I do not remember whether or not he had a pool cue in his hand at this point. He came over and asked for some change which I gave him. While he was waiting, he made some comments about my dress. I can't remember exactly what he said. The comments were a bit silly, about how sexy it was, why didn't I show off my legs more often, etc.

He was talking a bit loudly but I thought it was just good-humoured banter and high spirited. I didn't take offence at all and didn't really respond or say anything. Jason was serving fairly close to me at the time and seemed to take offence. He stopped serving other customers and turning to Ferret told him to 'Sod off'. He seemed quite cross when he said it but then turned away to serve someone else. Ferret seemed quite cross too. He just stopped and looked at Jason. Although Ferret had asked for change for the fruit machine, he didn't go back there. He turned and muttered something under his breath which I didn't catch. He then walked back over to the pool table area. He said something to the people he was with when he got back there and they all looked over at Jason. Ferret seemed angry still and kept looking over at Jason. Jason was just ignoring him. I did too.

The carol singers arrived a couple of hours later. I can't remember the exact time. Jason had told me he had booked them and was really looking forward to it. He also said at some point in the evening that if there was any trouble from Ferret and his lot then either they'd be out or he'd sort them out. I can't remember which one it was (they'd be out or he'd sort them out) nor exactly when he said it, although I think it was after the incident about my dress.

Shortly after the carol singers started, I could hear people singing along with them but using different words which were rude and I thought disgusting and obscene. At this point I was serving up at the end of the bar away from the pool table nearer the fruit machine. The singing was coming from over near the pool table area. Jason Ball was serving not far from me. He looked really angry. He went very red. He went round behind the bar to the part by the pool table and shouted to Ferret to get out. I can't remember the exact words he used. Jason then went out from behind the bar towards the pool table and Ferret.

It all happened very quickly. I can't remember the exact order of things. While Jason was yelling and going towards Ferret I ran around behind the bar towards the pool table area to see what was happening.

The pub was quite crowded but, once Jason yelled and went out from behind the bar towards Ferret, people moved quite quickly away from the pool table area where Jason and Ferret were. While I was running around behind the bar towards the pool table end, I couldn't see much. By the time I got up to that end, it was fairly clear. There was no one in my way and I would have been no more than 6–8 feet away.

I could see Jason and Ferret moving towards each other. Ferret had a pool cue in his hand. Jason got hold of it too and there was a bit of a struggle over it. Jason eventually got the cue away from Ferret and broke it in two and then flung it over the bar. Although I can't be sure, I think Ferret was holding the cue in one hand only until Jason Ball grabbed it and then I think both of them had both hands on it until Jason actually got it away from Ferret. Jason did break it in two before he threw it behind the bar but I can't describe it any more than that. It all happened very quickly, in a couple of minutes or less.

As Jason turned to throw the pool cue over the bar, Ferret picked up an empty beer glass which was on the pool table. It was a straight glass, not a mug. As Jason turned back towards Ferret, Ferret said something which I couldn't hear and lunged towards Jason with the glass. They were only about two or two-and-a-half feet apart. I screamed 'look out' but it was too late. Ferret just put the glass in Jason Ball's face. He was holding onto the glass and just thrust it into his face and suddenly there was a lot of blood. I think the glass broke at this point. I can't remember exactly how Ferret was holding it. I think he was holding it vertically.

Again it all happened very quickly, but I think I remember seeing the blood at the same time as Jason Ball fell to the ground. I could see that the blood was coming from his face. There was a lot of screaming and shouting after that. I heard Ferret shouting 'He had it coming, he fucking had it coming' over and over again. He sounded frightened. His girlfriend was shouting at him, calling him 'You fucking idiot'.

Ferret had tried to run off but Dave Dray and some other men were holding onto him. I waited by Jason Ball until the ambulance and police came. I could see that he had been cut very badly and I did what I could to stop the blood. I couldn't work out what had happened and I do remember saying What happened? What happened—I was confused and frightened.

Jason is a lot bigger than Ferret, who is about the same size as me. I am 5'7" tall.

I know Ferret but only as a customer of the pub. He can be quite funny at times but at other times he can be quite loud and disturb the atmosphere. Jason Ball is a good employer. I am the only permanent bar staff he has. All the others are temporary who come and go quite quickly.

I am willing to attend court and give evidence, if required.

<u>Signed:</u> *T. Croft*   <u>Signature witnessed by:</u> *R. Maybury*

STATEMENT OF WITNESS

<u>Statement of:</u> DAVID DRAY

<u>Age of witness:</u> Over 18

<u>Occupation of witness:</u> Builder

This statement consisting of one page, signed by me, is true to the best of my knowledge and belief and I make it knowing that, if it is tendered in evidence, I shall be liable to prosecution if I have wilfully stated in it anything which I know to be false or do not believe to be true.

<u>Signed:</u> *D. Dray*

<u>Signature witnessed by:</u> *R. Maybury*   <u>Statement dated:</u> 25th December 2013.

On Christmas Eve 2013 I was in The Cutpurse pub in New Addington, Croydon. I am a regular there and have been drinking there for at least 15 years. Everyone was very merry and we were all having a good drink. Jason Ball, the landlord had put on a good night— there was a Happy Hour from 6–9 pm and then there was an hour of karaoke with drinks as the prizes which began at about 7 pm, and he had also arranged carol singers to come in. The pub was decorated and was packed out. I was there with my wife and my son Joe and his girlfriend, Sanchia.

At about 11.00 pm the carol singers arrived. Shortly after they started I was in the men's having a pee. When I came out I looked over the pool table and saw some sort of scrap going on between big Jason and some little guy. I now know the little one is Kevin Heath, but I didn't know his name on that night. I recognised him from the pub but no more than that.

I saw Kevin Heath get a clout round the ear and Jason took his pool cue away from him. Kevin had been waving it around and it looked dangerous to me. I think Jason got it off him to stop trouble. I had stepped toward the two of them as soon as I saw this as it looked as if there was going to be trouble. I was no more than 10 feet away. I had a clear view. As Jason turned round to put the pool cue behind the bar the other one picked up his beer mug and smashed it into Jason's head. Jason fell like a stone. I didn't have time to call out any warning, it all happened so fast.

Kevin tried to run past the table and toward the door, but I grabbed hold of him as what he done was out of order. A couple of other men there helped me out and we held him until the police arrived. When we were waiting some women started shouting at Kevin, one was saying something like 'You idiot, you idiot, what have you done now?', someone else was crying and it had gone very quiet. Tracey Croft who works at the Cutpurse was holding Jason Ball still and trying to stop blood coming from a cut to his face. She looked up at me and Kevin and was saying 'What happened?, What happened?' She was crying. Everyone was shocked at what had happened.

When the police came they took my details and I was asked to attend Croydon Police Station to make this statement. I am willing to attend court if required.

<u>Signed:</u> *D. Dray*   <u>Signature witnessed by:</u> *R. Maybury*

STATEMENT OF WITNESS

<u>Statement of:</u> IAN MICHAEL FIRM

<u>Age of witness:</u> Over 18

<u>Occupation of witness:</u> Police Constable 2212

This statement consisting of one page, signed by me, is true to the best of my knowledge and belief and I make it knowing that, if it is tendered in evidence, I shall be liable to prosecution if I have wilfully stated in it anything which I know to be false or do not believe to be true.

<u>Signed:</u> *I. M. Firm*

<u>Signature witnessed by:</u> *R. Maybury*　　　　　　<u>Statement dated:</u> 3rd February 2014.

On Tuesday, 24th December 2013 I was on duty in full uniform in a marked police vehicle. At 11.20 pm as a result of information received I went to The Cutpurse public house, New Addington. It was very crowded when I arrived. Lying on the floor between the pool table and the bar was a man I now know to be Jason BALL. He appeared to be unconscious and was bleeding heavily from wounds to the left side of his face and I proceeded to give Mr Ball first aid. Shortly after this the ambulance arrived and Mr Ball was taken to hospital.

As a result of enquiries I spoke to a youth who I know to be Kevin HEATH. I noticed that he had blood on his right hand and spots of blood on his jacket. He was slightly dishevelled and his breath smelt strongly of drink, although he was not drunk.

I said to HEATH 'From what I have been told you hit the landlord, is this true?' And I then cautioned him. He replied 'He went for me'. I then told HEATH I was arresting him on suspicion of causing grievous bodily harm. After caution, he was taken to Croydon Police Station by other officers.

After the pub had been cleared I briefly examined the public bar area. Behind the bar near the pool table I found 2 pieces of pool cue which I produce as Exhibit IMF/1. Between the bar and the pool table I found a broken pint beer mug with jagged edges which appeared to have blood on it. This was placed in a bag and sealed. I produce this as Exhibit IMF/2.

<u>Signed by:</u> *I. M. Firm*　　　　　　　　　<u>Signature witnessed by:</u> *R. Maybury*

<u>STATEMENT OF WITNESS</u>

<u>Statement of:</u> RONALD MAYBURY

<u>Age of witness:</u> Over 18

<u>Occupation of witness:</u> DS Croydon CID

This statement consisting of one page, signed by me, is true to the best of my knowledge and belief and I make it knowing that, if it is tendered in evidence, I shall be liable to prosecution if I have wilfully stated in it anything which I know to be false or do not believe to be true.

<u>Signed:</u> *R. Maybury*

<u>Signature witnessed by:</u> *S. Gent*   <u>Statement dated:</u> 26th December 2013.

At 9.30 am on Christmas Day 2013 I was on duty at Croydon Police Station. There I saw a man I now know to be Kevin HEATH. I reminded him that he was under caution to which he replied 'I know all that—let's get on with it'. In the company of DC Tibbs I then interviewed HEATH in the interview room at the police station between 9.32 and 10.00 am. The interview was tape-recorded using two tapes. At the conclusion of the interview I sealed one of the copies and signed over the seal. I produce this as my Exhibit RM/1. I later prepared a written summary of the interview, which I produce as my Exhibit RM/2.

Later that day at 11.30 am HEATH was charged with wounding Jason BALL with intent to do him GBH. The charge was read over to him, he was again cautioned and replied 'No I've really done it this time though haven't I?'

<u>Signed:</u> *R. Maybury*   <u>Signature witnessed by:</u> *S. Gent*

RECORD OF TAPE RECORDED INTERVIEW

Person Interviewed:	Kevin HEATH	Exhibit no: RM/2
Place of Interview:	Croydon Police Station	No of Pages: 3
Date of Interview:	25th December 2013	
Time Commenced:	9.32 am	Time Concluded: 10 am
Duration of Interview:	28 minutes	Tape Reference No: RM/1/1234
Interviewing Officer(s):	DS Maybury	
Other persons present:	DC Tibbs	

Tape Counter	Person Speaking	Text
0001	RM	(Introductions) I must remind you that you are under caution. You do not have to say anything. But it may harm your defence if you do not mention when questioned something which you later rely on in court. Anything you do say may be given in evidence. Do you understand?
0008	KH	Yeah.
0015	RM	Do you object to being interviewed without a solicitor being present?
0025	KH	Well, I ain't going to get one this morning, am I? Anyway, I've done this a few times before.
0038	RM	Well, if you change your mind at any point, stop and tell me.
0049	KH	Yeah OK.
0055	RM	Now, what do you know about the glassing in The Cutpurse last night?
0066	KH	Well, not much really. That fat bastard of a landlord went for me with a pool cue. He hit me over the shoulder with it and it broke. He looked really angry as if he was going to do me again with the thick end of the cue so I punched out at him. He dropped like a stone, the girls started screaming and the geezer I know as Wally grabbed me and said that's out of order, you're staying here until Old Bill get here.
0081	RM	Were you drunk when you hit Big Jason Ball?
0089	KH	No—well merry really.
0096	RM	Are you a regular drinker?
0101	KH	Yeah.
0110	RM	What's your tipple?
0119	KH	Lager top.

0127	RM	How many do you drink on average when you go to the pub?
0131	KH	About 5/6 a night.
0144	RM	How many did you have last night before you hit Jason?
0150	KH	About 3/4.
0157	RM	Pints?
0163	KH	Yeah.
0170	RM	Any shorts?
0174	KH	No.
0181	RM	What were you doing before Jason, the publican came up to you?
0194	KH	Drinking with my mates.
0200	RM	Which ones?
0211	KH	I don't know—there were lots of them around.
0223	RM	So you must have had a pint glass in your hand?
0229	KH	Well, yeah.
0237	RM	So you must have realised when you punched out that you would hit Jason with the glass?
0242	KH	Well—no.
0250	RM	Come off it, you don't just forget you're holding a pint glass.
0265	KH	Well I did.
0273	RM	Do you know Tracey Croft?
0278	KH	Yeah.
0288	RM	Well?
0294	KH	Yeah—she's my bird—well sort of anyway.
0304	RM	Does Jason fancy her?
0310	KH	Yeah he does a bit.
0321	RM	I put it to you that you are jealous of Jason because of Tracey and . . .
0323	KH	*(interrupted)* Bollocks.
0335	RM	I'll continue, you are jealous and when Jason told you to get out of the pub in front of your mates you felt small and decided to do him.
0342	KH	Rubbish.
0351	RM	Please let me finish.
0360	KH	Sorry.

0374	RM	You had a glass in your hand and smashed it into his face quite deliberately?
		(Silence)
0380	RM	Well he didn't hit you with a pool cue did he?
0388	KH	I suppose not.
0397	RM	You got cross and did him with the glass knowing full well you had it in your hand didn't you?
0405	KH	Well yeah, I'm sorry really, it's that bloody Tracey, she's a tart.
0412	RM	But that doesn't justify you putting all those stitches in Jason's face does it?
0424	KH	No—as I've said I'm sorry, are you going to charge me?
0430	RM	I'm afraid so but you've done yourself a bit of good by being so frank.

INTERVIEW TERMINATED

Previous convictions of KEVIN HEATH

d.o.b. 1.6.89

Date of conviction	Court	Offence	Sentence
1.8.01	Croydon Youth Court	Theft	Conditional Discharge 1 year
12.11.02	Croydon Youth Court	Burglary ×3	Supervision Order 1 year
1.3.03	North London Youth Court	Threatening words and behaviour	Attendance Centre 12 hours (no order on the breach of S.O.)
6.7.07	Liverpool City Mags.	Threatening words and behaviour	80 hours' Community Service
2.2.08	Inner London Crown Court	Handling	Community Sentence 120 hours' unpaid work requirement
1.9.08	Wallington Magistrates	ABH, Criminal Damage	£200 fine/7 days £200 fine/7 days *14 days served
3.8.13	Croydon Magistrates	ABH (at Cutpurse P.H.)	28 days' imprisonment

Previous convictions of JASON BALL

d.o.b. 6.6.52

Date of conviction	Court	Offence	Sentence
12.5.88	Maidstone Crown Court	ABH	£150.00 fine
17.3.04	Inner London Crown Court	s 20 Malicious Wounding	£200 fine/£100 compensation

Previous conviction of TRACEY CROFT

d.o.b. 2.6.94

Date of conviction	Court	Offence	Sentence
1.10.12	Croydon Mags.	Theft (shoplifting)	Conditional Discharge 12 months

IN THE CROWN COURT AT CROYDON

THE QUEEN

V

KEVIN HEATH

DEFENCE
STATEMENT

Defence Statement under the provisions of Section 5 Criminal Procedure and Investigations Act 1996

1. Nature of the defence

At 6 pm on 24 December 2013, the accused went into The Cutpurse public house with his friends, including his girlfriend, Sharon Wood, and her sister Debbie. They spent a pleasant evening talking, playing pool and enjoying a social drink, aside from an incident at about 9 pm when the landlord of the pub, Jason Ball, was aggressive and intimidating towards the accused. The accused had been engaged in an informal conversation with one of the pub staff, Tracey Croft, when Jason Ball intervened and told the accused to sod off. The accused did not react and simply returned to his group of friends at the pool table. When a group of carol singers arrived around 10.30 pm, several people in the pub joined in with their singing in an irreverent and light-hearted fashion. The accused was simply one of these; he had no intention to annoy or upset anyone who was present. Those people in the vicinity of the pool table all seemed to enjoy the singing. The landlord of the pub seemed to have decided to eject the accused immediately and violently, running around the bar and shouting at the accused as he moved towards him. This instant decision was disproportionate to any need to restore order and the selection of only the accused as the recipient of the landlord's attention was quite deliberate on his part. The landlord had displayed an aggressive and hostile manner to the accused earlier that evening. The landlord clipped the accused around the head as soon as he came within reach, he then took the accused's own pool cue from him, with considerable force and violence, breaking it in two in an act of extreme aggression before recklessly flinging it away. As the landlord turned back to confront the accused once more, the accused felt that he had no alternative but to defend himself. He punched out towards the landlord, a much bigger man. The hand that he punched with had been holding his beer glass and still was, with the result that the glass smashed on impact with the landlord's face.

2. Issues taken with the prosecution case

The accused takes issue with the prosecution case that he deliberately or recklessly intended to cause grievous bodily harm to the landlord.

3. Reasons why the accused takes issue with the prosecution case

The accused takes issue with the prosecution case because he is not guilty of these offences—he acted at all times in self-defence and used only reasonable force. He was unable to retreat away from the assault on himself due to the press of people behind him and the proximity of the pool table. He admits that he struck the landlord the blow that knocked him unconscious and that he had a beer glass in his hand but had not armed himself with the glass and sought only to fend off the anticipated continuation of the assault upon him.

4.   Points of law

(i) Exclusion of police interview under s 78 Police and Criminal Evidence Act 1984, relying on breach of s 58 PACE and breach of PACE Code C

(ii) Admission of evidence of the bad character of a prosecution witness, Jason Ball, under s 100 Criminal Justice Act 2003

5.   Alibi

The accused does not deny being present at the time of the incident.

6.   Disclosure

Please disclose the following items on the Schedule of unused material which are capable of assisting the defence case or undermining the prosecution case [not included here]

7.   Declaration

I, Kevin Heath, have read and understood this defence statement. I agree with its contents and confirm that it is consistent with my instructions. I understand that if I give evidence which conflicts with it, the prosecution may apply it in evidence and use it to cross-examine me.

Signed: *Kevin Heath* (Accused)

Dated: 12 April 2014

Keymon & Keymon

147 Sutton Place

Croydon

Solicitors for the accused

<u>BRIEF FOR THE DEFENCE</u>

R

v

KEVIN HEATH

Counsel has herewith:

(1) Indictment [see prosecution brief]
(2) Prosecution Statements [see prosecution brief]
(3) Proof of Kevin Heath
(4) Previous convictions of Kevin Heath [see prosecution brief]
(5) Statement of the Defence disclosed to Prosecution [see prosecution brief]

Instructing Solicitors act for Kevin Heath who faces an indictment alleging s 18 Grievous Bodily Harm with s 20 GBH in the alternative.

Mr Heath admits his presence at The Cutpurse on Christmas Eve but says that he hit the landlord in self-defence in the form of a pre-emptive strike.

As Counsel will appreciate, there is quite a lot of background history to this matter, including the fight with Mr Ball in the summer of 2013 for which he received a sentence of 28 days' imprisonment. Mr Heath remains adamant that on the previous occasion, as on this, he was the victim and not the aggressor. Instructing Solicitors are aware of rumours concerning Miss Croft and Mr Ball. Mr Heath is an old client, though inclined to be headstrong and tends to 'want his say' in the witness box.

Instructing Solicitors have been informed of the previous convictions that some of the prosecution witnesses have. No doubt, an application should be made to put these into evidence.

If convicted, Mr Heath would be willing to undertake a community sentence. The Rev. Thanet is prepared to give character evidence on his behalf. Would Counsel please use his best endeavours on behalf of Mr Heath.

CALL KEVIN HEATH of 21 Tree Avenue, New Addington

Who will say:

On Christmas Eve I was in The Cutpurse with Sharon and her sister, Debbie Wood. I used to go there quite a lot until one day last summer when I was having a bit of a laugh with Tracey Croft in the garden (Sharon does not know this). Jason, the landlord, came over and turned nasty and smacked me in the mouth. I tried to defend myself but I got nicked and was found guilty by the Magistrates, even though I wasn't. I got a prison sentence for this and Jason banned me for 3 months. On Christmas Eve I got to the pub about seven. I was drinking pints of Tennent's. I suppose I had about 7 or 8 pints.

About 9.00 pm I was over playing the fruit machine. I asked Tracey for some change and made a couple of comments about her dress which was very low cut. Sharon was over at the pool table. Next thing Jason came over and told me to 'sod off' and leave Tracey well alone. Although I felt angry I just turned and walked back to the pool table. I never picked up a pool cue like he said. I didn't even swear at him. It's ridiculous the way he carries on—he must be almost 60 but Tracey is a young girl, not 20 yet.

When the carol singers came I was over near the pool table with Sharon and Debbie and a couple of others. When they started I suppose we were taking the mick a bit. Suddenly Jason was barging through everyone yelling at me to get out. I did have a pool cue in my hand, it's my own. Jason just came up to me, hit me round the left ear with his right hand. I tried to block him with the cue but he broke it in two and turned away and threw the bits behind the bar. As he turned back I thought he was going to attack me, so I picked up my pint mug and hit him across the head with it. I never said anything to him.

After this I panicked and tried to run off but some big geezer held onto me. The police came and I was arrested. I was then taken to the Police Station.

Since being charged I have seen Tracey Croft and she won't give evidence against me.

PERSONAL CIRCUMSTANCES

I am 25.

I have a number of previous convictions.

I live with my girlfriend, Sharon Wood, and she is expecting a baby in six months' time.

I do casual work as a roofer and take home £100 a week.

INDEX